# Letters From a Friend

JAMES M. TIFFANY

&

COLONEL DALE ACKELS, USA, RETIRED

Published by

Montezuma Publishing

Aztec Shops Ltd.

San Diego State University

San Diego, California 92182-1701

619-594-7552

www.montezumapublishing.com

ISBN: 978-1-7269-2085-8

Publishing Manager: Lia Dearborn
Cover Art: Dave Wagner, dave.wagner.art@gmail.com
Design and Layout: Angelica Lopez
Formatting: Angelica Lopez, Lia Dearborn

*for Nan and Bet*

*"One has the right to judge a man by
the effect he has over his friends."*

*Oscar Wilde*

# Table of Contents

# PREFACE

## James M. Tiffany

MARCH 8, 2021

# LETTERS FROM A FRIEND

# PREFACE

Dale Ackels and I have been friends for fifty-six years. We met at Aberdeen Proving Ground, Maryland as young Army officers assigned to the Ordnance Center and School.

What follows is an assemblage of Dale's letters written over the years. The first one I saved was in 1975. Dale and I had been friends for ten years at that point and our lives had taken very divergent paths. Subsequent letters define a life of diverse service, duty, an unrivaled commitment to country and a deep, shared friendship.

Why did I save that first letter? Probably because it was the first, fun to read and vintage Dale - keenly observant, colorful, some historical and contemporary commentary, and of course, irreverent.

Not all of the letters were written to me. Thankfully, Dale's sister, Nancy Wagner, contributed a number to this book. Over the years Nan was a more diligent and consistent correspondent with her brother than I was.

Dale's writing skills eclipse his verbal skills. He's unmatched in the written word, whether it be simple observations, recounting an event, a tale told to him worth repeating, some historically significant connection or the back-story on any topic with which he's familiar. On rare occasions, he may even speculate on the vaguely familiar. He has been a prodigious letter writer his entire adult life, to this very day. They haven't been typewritten in a number of years, Internet electronics and email have replaced the old Smith Corona. Sad for luddites. Some of his letters still have handwritten notes; he doesn't easily give ground.

I never matched Dale's letters in content or frequency. In fact, there were many times when it would be months before I responded and in one case, it was four years. You'll read about that. Somehow, it never deterred him and he would continue to write, albeit occasionally giving me a verbal swift kick to get with the program. Had I been a better correspondent there easily could have been double the number of his letters in this book.

During those ten years between 1965 and his first letter in 1975, our lives took different turns and new directions. From APG I was assigned to Bogota, Colombia in 1966 with the Inter-American Geodetic Survey, a collaborative mapping agency, the results of which were used in hemispheric defense planning. Dale was still at APG as an instructor and tactical officer but he found time to visit.

After that final assignment in South America, I went to graduate school in Arizona. Dale visited and met my new spouse on his return from Japan en route to his next assignment. I was later hired by Pan American World Airways as a Sales Manager in Detroit. A couple of years later I left that failing aviation icon and started a travel company.

During those ten years, Dale was promoted three times, saw service in Japan, Vietnam, and Detroit, and was decorated in each assignment with an award or commendation. He changed his Army career direction and became a Foreign Area Officer (Africa) after receiving an MS from Georgetown University; then travelled extensively in Africa - fourteen countries up to that point - including a stint as a Liaison Officer with the French Foreign Legion. How's that for a decade of professional activity!

My part was to put the letters in context and time - a tad more difficult because Dale usually did not include the year - letting the reader get to know a man of exceptional character, who led a life of service to his country. As you read his letters expect commentary on geo-political history, tales about memorable people, legitimate characters, family joy, the vicissitudes of everyday life, more geography than you ever knew, comments on American foreign policy, adroit and informed observations, irreverence, humor and mirth - and who on God's green earth causes mirth anymore!

Among the letters, you will find comments about enclosures. Only a few of those are included. Dale and I are inveterate savers of articles and we both are our own personal clipping service. Even today when it would be easier to send an attachment to an email, it's simply not part of how we do things. It would be contrary to our un-written rules.

Cutting articles and tid-bits out of a national magazine, or any obscure publication for that matter, or a local newspaper, then saving and sending it is the stuff of a serious friendship. We've been doing it since the beginning. If it's worthwhile, I'll file it with other "stuff" and at some point, send it off. An African world leader may be in the grave for a year when I read something in the Sunday *New York Times* that needs explanation, so I attach a sticky note to the article and add it to the file. Nothing is off-limits, even absurd comments by anyone, especially politicians, although we seem to limit those or we'd be clipping for hours and mailing costs would become prohibitive.

One additional note. I decided not to explain all the Army, government or other acronyms contained in Dale's letters. I trust the reader to understand general context, guess, or research them on Google.

And names. Same rationale. As one reads the letters, you should be able to figure out the characters and relationship to Dale or me. Some remain in our lives, some not.

This book is intended to mark a lifelong friendship. Initially, I was simply going to make copies of Dale's letters, put them in a three-ring binder and send them off to him.

I thought better of it. These letters needed to be shared with our families and close friends: Dale's wife Bet, sons Travis and Derek, sister Nancy and husband John, nephews Dave and Kurt, my life partner Patti, my daughter Heather and son Christopher and their families, close friend Christina, as well as Dale's former comrades in arms, and other friends.

We're all fortunate to have walked some paths with him and shared parts of his life.

James M. Tiffany

San Diego, California
March 8, 2021

# CHAPTER 1

## Aberdeen Proving Ground

### 1965-1966

Dale and I began our friendship at the Ordnance Center and School in the 1960's as young Army officers.

Dale received his commission from Hubert Humphrey - senior senator from Minnesota and later Vice-President of the United States - upon graduation from the University of Minnesota.

Later, an observant Pentagon Officer noticed that Lt. Ackels may have been assigned to the wrong branch of the Army, so instead of Artillery he suggested the Ordnance Corp because Dale had been a talented competitive shooter and might like to work as a junior member on a team developing the Army's new assault weapon, the M-16 at Rock Island, IL. He was assigned instead to Aberdeen Proving Ground (APG), MD.

*"It won't come as a shock to anyone who knows the Army that to this day I have never been to Rock Island Arsenal and the first M-16 I ever saw was the one I qualified on prior to deploying to Vietnam."*

When he arrived at APG in January, 1965 I was in place as the Foreign Liaison Officer, attending to foreign officers from allied nations, studying under the Military Assistance Program (MAP). They represented countries that received military aid and support - Iran, Iraq, Vietnam, Israel, Nigeria, Laos, Turkey, Colombia. They were at APG to attend the Ordnance School basic course.

My job was to introduce them to the *"non-military aspects of American life"* which was done through tours, lectures and an occasional family home stay on weekends. The proximity to Philadelphia, Washington, DC and New York made that part of the job uncomplicated, so in part, I was a military travel agent.

Dale had multiple jobs during his two-year assignment: he was first a student, and after completion of the Ordnance Basic Course the Army began to realize his leadership - his boss noted on his first Officer Efficiency Report (OER), *"Lt. Ackels was the best of the four hundred lieutenants who came through here this year"* - he was assigned as an Instructor in the Leadership Training Division of the Ordnance Center and School responsible for teaching basic military subjects: drill and ceremonies, emergency treatment of combat casualties, map reading, day and night infiltration courses and physical training. The students were freshly minted 2nd Lt.'s, some 1st Lt.'s and the occasional Captain who had finished a PhD, or law school and was fulfilling his military obligation. One such student was Captain Donald Rice who later served as Secretary of the Air Force under President George H.W. Bush.

Later in his assignment, Lt. Ackels was a Senior Tactical Officer in the OCS (Officer Candidate School) Brigade, a pre-commissioning course taking officer candidates through six months of increasingly rigorous training with the goal of graduating a 2nd Lt.

It was that one year, 1965, that Dale and I began to forge a lasting friendship. I left APG in January 1966 to an assignment in South America. Dale remained at Aberdeen for an additional year.

# CHAPTER 2

## Japan

1967–1968

Next stop for Lt. Ackels was Japan.

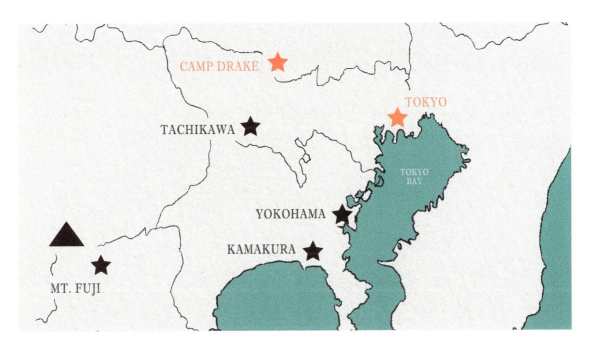

"*My initial assignment in country was as Operations Officer at the Army Ammunition Depot at Ikego, Japan, about 24 km South of Yokohama. We stored 66M pounds of missiles, artillery projectiles, mortar ammunition, small arms, grenades, fuses and miscellaneous bulk explosives in a series of tunnels that had once been an Imperial Navy torpedo factory.*"

"*Later in the tour I was stationed in Sagamihara, Japan, about 42 km North of Yokohama as Commanding Officer of the Headquarters and Headquarters Company of the US Army Depot Command. An HHC is basically a holding company for personnel about to be assigned to some organization. I had several secondary responsibilities and these provided most of the excitement in this tour. I was tasked to provide a chemical decontamination platoon, an engineer platoon, and six provisional infantry platoons to US Army Japan in support of various contingencies. We provided a water purification unit to civil authorities following a major earthquake in Misawa and I vividly recall flying to Camp Drake in a helicopter with my six platoons of sometimes infantry. It was just past sundown and we flew over several hundred thousand protesting Japanese leftist's snake dancing their way to Camp Drake. To protect the wounded at Camp Drake we were going to be authorized to use deadly force, but it never came to that. The Japanese police headed them off before they reached our gates, for which I remain eternally grateful.*"

# LETTERS FROM A FRIEND

# CHAPTER 3

---

## Vietnam

1969-1970

Dale volunteered for Vietnam while attending the Career Course for Captains and Majors at the Ordnance School. He'd tell you he would have been going anyway ... *"but it somehow seemed important to preserve the fiction that I was still master of my own destiny."* It is consistent with Dale's modus operandi to volunteer.

I was a terrible friend during that year, never writing a single letter nor did I receive a letter from him. Shame on me. This is what he later recounted to me:

*"I was the Commanding Officer of a Company in the 528th Ammunition Battalion stationed at Camp Love, a Marine Corps firebase about fifteen miles north of Da Nang."*

*"It was one of the most challenging assignments of my career. I doubt that I would have made it without having already commanded a company in Japan."*

*"This battalion was formed in Vietnam to meet a pressing need for ammunition support in the Northern I Corps Tactical Zone. We supported two Army Divisions, part of a Marine Division, a South Korean Division, a Special Forces Group, an Artillery Brigade and several aviation units with all classes of munitions."*

*"It would have been fairly routine but for the caliber of men who were assigned. Every unit in the Corp had been tasked to provide ten men to this new unit and First Sergeants being what they are provided ten of their worst offenders. Every man in one company had a court martial of some kind on his sheet, and fraggings, murders and mutiny were almost routine. I survived it but I was a proper savage when I came home."*

*"Halfway through my tour I also became Battalion Operations Officer, a slot normally filled by a Major but we didn't have one so I filled it until a Captain could be found to take the company."*

When Dale wrote to his parents or his sister, he minimized the risks and danger of being in Vietnam. This next letter was written to his younger sister, Nancy, written as if it was just another Army assignment, assiduously avoiding much commentary about the war.

Nancy and Dale enjoy a wonderful, loving sibling relationship and friendship and have always encouraged and supported each other. They also needle each other mercilessly at every possible opportunity and really don't need much provocation, but when it occurs, "Whoa Nellie" as Keith Jackson used to say. Football goes verbal.

```
                             Camp Love
                             5 Nov 69
```

Hello,

I have noted,as advancing age irresistibly crept upon you, a certain tendency toward pedantry in your various writings. I have decided that this is the inevitable result of your spending nine months out of the year talking down to your pupils. Judging by your description, a not altogether unreasonable or easily correctable failing, but faintly irritating when applied to your elder brother... A person of little learning,and even less influence in the community, but of sufficient wit that even he had figured out that his mail was probably being delayed by factors beyond his Mother's influence.

I spent the previous week taking the Grey Line tour of what is deceptively called the Northern I Corp Tactical Zone. It includes everything from the DMZ south to the Hai Van Pass just outside of Da Nang. I stopped at Phu Bai, a lovely little hamlet seldom visited by tourists but once famous for its local crafts and marketplace (bring your camera). From there I traveled north to Landing Zone Sally, again strictly for the enterprising traveller interested in local color and really getting to know the people. Try the commo bunker at happy hour for a delicious lighter fluid daquiri and snacks from the motor pool kitchen still tingling with the delicate aroma of fresh baked insulation,and topped with a light sweet made from whipped fiberglass sandbags beaten into three quarts of lukewarm delousing powder.

From there our caraven takes us to Camp Evans and Quang Tri. Camp Evans was once known for its beautiful flower festival, but this year the buds perversely grew upside down and the peasants are having a root festival. As you have probably guessed the natives of this area are also famous for their adaptability.

Which brings us to Quang Tri. Nestled in a scenic pond within easy
hiking distance of the historic old DMZ,with its bustling parkways
and lively cottage industries, Quang Tri is one place the experienced
traveller must see for himself. The usual travelogues don't do it
justice. Start your tour at the Command Post Bunker and be sure
your guide doesn't miss the rocket disassembly area in the center
of the compound. The rockets are actually assembled elsewhere, then
rapidly transported to the disassembly area where they separate themselves into their component parts right in front of your eyes. Watch
the children during the demonstrations. Don't miss the demonstration
by the three legged guard dog in the late afternoon. People who've
never been to NICTZ will find it hard to believe a three legged dog
can move that fast, or bite that hard.

While you are whiling away your life practicing talking down to people,
take quill in hand and describe in several hundred precise words what
you would like for Christmas. If you would like something native to
the area allow me to describe the possibilities. They have some
lacquer ware, but the art work is seldom anything to become excited
about. They have some gray stone carvings; the usual subjects are
angelfish, lions, old men, and vases. They also have a little bronze,
some silk smoking jackets that say VIETNAM 1969-70 in bold letters across
the back, and all the Ho Chi Minh sandels anyone could possibly desire.
You must specify Firestone, Goodyear, Michelin, or Riverside when ordering
the sandels. On special order I could get you a pair of Viet Cong pajamas,
but this will require some advance notice since the present owner will
have to be physically persuaded to divest himself of the garment.

Do not let the generally disciplinary nature of this letter's opening
paragraph prevent you from writing again soon. Even if it's only
to defend yourself against the charges I have levelled against you.
Rest assured that all your letters will be answered since I have nothing
else to do with my free time than write letters.

# LETTERS FROM A FRIEND

What follows is a letter to a retired Korean combat veteran, a friend of one of Dale's family members. It was written twenty-one years after Dale's return from Vietnam and contains amazing detail and recollection and confirms the danger to line officers not just outside the wire, but danger from within, little known to most Americans at home. Then or even now. Fragging - the murder of an officer by an enlisted soldier - was not widely reported by the American media. Body counts of NVA and Viet Cong were the measure of our supposed success and eventual victory.

# VIETNAM

MAY 3 1 1991

COLONEL A.D. ACKELS
405 FRONT STREET
BOILING SPRINGS, PA 17007

Lou:

Last autumn I recall promising you an "informal" history of the Fightin' 528th Ammunition Battalion (DS/GS) (Provisional) as it was during the middle years of the Vietnam Conflict. I've toyed with several ways of doing it, and finally settled on this approach. It may not be the best way, but it insures the regional "peculiarities" of our various companies are not overlooked.

LOCATION: As I mentioned in our various conversations, the 528th was activated in-theater. As part of the build up in the late 60's, MACV was apparently given authority to create an additional POL supply battalion in III Corps. That authority, and the TOE, lay resting quietly in somebody's safe until the Marines began pulling out of I Corps. At that point the 528th QM Bn was activated as an ammo battalion, and (on paper) sent north to be added to the newly created DaNang Support Command. DaNang Support Command subsequently grew into two general support groups, but because we had a corps-wide mission we remained under the direct control of Support Command HQ, and a superb soldier named Homer Smith. (Smith later rose to major general. He finished the war in Saigon as the last MACV commander, and later became the NATO logistics czar. More on him later).

In a physical sense, the HQ of the 528th was located 12 miles north of DaNang, burrowed into the east-facing slope of a ridge overlooking Red Beach. From the ridgeline behind us to the west was a free-fire zone. To the south were several line infantry companies and the 11th Motor Transport Battalion of the 1st Marine Division. To the east, about a mile from us, was the Force Service Regiment of III Marine Amphibious Force (III MAF), and beyond them the attack and transport helicopter units at Red Beach. National Highway 1 (QL 1) ran between us and Red Beach, and there was also a refugee center called Ap Da Phuoc on the paddy land between us and the helicopters. I don't recall what Ap Da Phuoc meant. As I remember it was some kind of "_____Happiness Center." Probably "Mandatory Happiness Center."

Straight north of us were five small Catholic villages, usually occupied by a platoon from I Company, 3-26 Marines, and a psyops team from a Marine engineer battalion. North and west of the villages was Elephant Valley, also a freefire zone and the source of innumerable rocket attacks on DaNang and Red Beach. Finally, north and east of us, at a range of 3-4 miles, was Hai Van Pass, a narrow defile connecting DaNang with the northern towns and camps at Phu Bai, Camp Evans, Dong Ha and Quang Tri.

Camp Love, where I lived throughout my tour in the RVN, was normally occupied by our Battalion HQ, the Headquarters Company, and one of our subordinate companies, the 40th Ordnance Company. The camp was owned by the 7th Engineer Battalion, Fleet Marine

Force Pacific, which had its HQ and one subordinate company there also. In addition, there was usually one Marine infantry battalion on the camp. For much of my tour it was the 3rd Battalion, 26th Marines, just back from the battles at Con Thien and the Rockpile. After they were deactivated on the runway at DaNang they were replaced by another line battalion, as I recall the 3rd Battalion, 1st Marines. That stellar group announced their arrival by mortaring Camp Love, wounding 7 men from my company and 7th Engineers. They stayed with us until 1st MARDIV pulled out, at which point we acquired B Battery, 1-44 Arty, a 40mm Duster outfit, and later, G Battery, 29th Arty, a searchlight battery from a mixed 155/8 inch howitzer battalion. (The presence of those two unusual capabilities on our camp led to some rather innovative ambushes in late 1970).

COMMANDERS: We were commanded by two rather different men during my tour. LTC Charles Hayden and LTC Leon Malouin. I respected them both greatly but they were as different in temperment and style as two men could possibly be. Hayden was deliberate and cerebral, a thinker and planner and an excellent manager. A gentleman to the core, he was inclined to believe the best of his people, and occasionally found it difficult to accept the realities of day-to-day life in the 528th and the behavior of some of the people he commanded. After leaving us he became the Spt Comd's ACofS for Security, Plans and Operations. Since his retirement (as an 06) he's settled in the Maryland suburbs of Wash, DC, where I believe he sells real estate. Malouin, on the other hand, was hot-tempered and impetuous. He once told me he was half French-Canadian and half Mohawk. Decisive to a fault, almost violent in his opinions and attitudes, he was a handsome and charismatic field soldier with enormous common sense and very few illusions about the kind of men he commanded. If he had a weakness it was his commendable belief that none of his men were so inherently evil they couldn't eventually be made into good soldiers. I once heard him tell one of my habitual offenders that if he ever did anything like that again, "I'll lock you in a CONEX container and spray it with AK-47." At the time Malouin unquestionably meant it, but within ten minutes he was sitting on an ammo box explaining for the 35th time why you couldn't call the First Sergeant a "gray, honky motherfucker," or steal the XO's jeep to go buy drugs.

I hooked up with him after the war in Alaska for a couple of weeks of fishing. I've since lost track of him, but I believe he's returned to New Hampshire and gone into farming.

ORGANIZATION: Our battalion was broken down as follows:

| | |
|---|---|
| Battalion HQ | Camp T.J. Love (north of DaNang) |
| HQ Company | Camp Love |
| 40th Ordnance Company | Camp Love |
| 571st Ordnance Co. | Phu Bai Combat Base, Quang Tri, Camp Evans, and Dong Ha Ramp |

661st Ordnance Co.     Chu Lai Combat Base and Duc Pho
                       Combat Base

In addition to these permanent sites we also operated an ASP on
LZ English (or LZ Baldy); however, it was overrun several weeks
before my arrival, with the loss of several men from our unit.
For a time we also operated a technical intelligence collection
point at Camp Love, but when the guys from APG stopped coming
around we used the equipment we'd collected as trade bait and
went out of the tech intel business.

Dong Ha Ramp was used intermittantly, but it was a particularly
thorny problem for us.  In an effort to provide better ammo
support for the troops north of Hue, particularly during Tet 69
and 70, HQ decided to open a ramp on the Qua Viet River near our
camp at Quang Tri.  The idea was to load a YFU with ammo at
DaNang and sail it up the coast to the mouth of the river,
bypassing the bottlenecks in Hai Van Pass and at Hue.  These
efforts were always preceded by shore clearing operations,
carried out by the 1st Bde, 5th Mech, or the 101st Airborne, but
the Ramp was most definitely in Indian country and almost every
trip up the River led to a firefight.  Several YFUs were holed, a
number of friendlies wounded and killed, and one of our boats
blew up and sank with the loss of everyone on it.

Each of our numbered companies supported a division size unit.
The 40th supported the 1st Marine Air Wing, 1st MARDIV, the
Special Forces and Army CSS elements in DaNang, and acted as a
corps reserve ASP.  The 571st supported the 101st Airborne, the
1st Bde of the 5th Mech, a corps artillery group (the 108th as I
recall), XXIII Corps, and those remaining elements of 3 MARDIV
still in the NICTZ.  The 661st supported the 23rd (Americal)
Division, several 1st MARDIV elements and the South Korean
Marines.

THE 661ST ORDNANCE COMPANY.  Looking back on it with the
perspective of 21 years I believe the 661st and its mis-
adventures probably set the tone for the entire battalion.  Like
our other units, it had been activated in-country by levying
existing units for individual fillers.  Most of the 661st came
from Qui Nhon and Saigon.  You can readily imagine how it was
done.  "First Sergeant.  Brigade just came down with a levy for
the battalion.  They want ten good men.  Take care of it for me,
will you?"  The resulting enema substantially improved the court
martial rates of various units in Qui Nhon and III Corps, and the
morale of their senior NCOs, but at the long-term expense of the
nascent 661st and our battalion.  When finally assembled at Chu
Lai Combat Base in Sep 69 every man in the 661st below E5 had a
summary court martial or worse on his record.

Because of the distances involved, and the lack of contact with
Chu Lai, I don't think Hayden was initially aware of the problems
developing in the company.  However, by the time Malouin took

over there was no question the 661st was a deeply troubled
organization. On his first visit to Chu Lai Malouin found drugs
being sold in the company area, the NCOs sleeping outside the
unit and completely dispirited, no formations being held, and
only 30% of the unit reporting for work in the ASP. Most of this
was the fault of the company commander. Malouin gave the
commander a couple weeks to get the mess straightened out, but it
was much too late. The commander's feeble attempts to reassert
his authority resulted in someone putting a grenade in the filler
neck of his gas tank, at which point he lost all further interest
in the unit. Shortly thereafter there was a mutiny. Twelve
black soldiers, under the leadership of a man styling himself THE
HEAD MAU MAU, barricaded themselves in their hooch with weapons,
rations, ammo and gas masks and refused to come out. By the time
Malouin reached Chu Lai the American Division MP company had
surrounded the hooch, but we were basically in a standoff.
Malouin looked the situation over, found an M48, the only tank on
the camp, and drove it up to the front door of the mutineers
hooch. I'm told he rammed the cannon thru the door, announcing
in his inimitable style that unless they put down their weapons
and surrendered he would fire the main gun. The projectile would
probably have passed harmlessly through the back wall, but the
muzzle blast in that enclosed space would have been memorable,
and after brief consultation they came out. Malouin immediately
canned the company commander and replaced him with Captain George
Tonn, who'd come down on the plane from Danang with him. George
had been in my OCS company in 1966. I remembered him as a large
shambling kid, bright as a new penny but essentially unmotivated
and just putting in time. As I recall, he was last or second to
last in his company at the end of 18 weeks, and I almost threw
him out. It would have been a serious error in judgment on my
part. Once commissioned George became a fireball. He came to
Vietnam from a successful tour as a company commander in Germany,
and as he subsequently proved, he had exactly the kind of
personality, and the grit, needed to turn that merry band of
fuck-ups into some sort of functioning unit.

But, it wasn't easy. In his first formation, held for all
practical purposes at gunpoint, he discovered there were 30-odd
men in the unit not listed on the morning report. Apparently the
reputation of the 661st had spread, and a number of AWOLs,
deserters and individuals awaiting trial on various charges had
taken up permanent residence in the company. George, and several
heavily armed NCOs, persuaded them to fall in on the company
street for a nose count, but finding the ambiance no longer to
their liking, most of the undocumented types subsequently
relocated. I heard later one of them was wanted for a pair of
murders, and I'm sure some of the others had equally intriguing
backgrounds.

The mutineers were shipped off to my company and the 571st in
chains, but the remaining members of the 661st "old guard"

immediately set out to test George's resolve. When the tactics that had worked against his predecessor failed to impress (a smoke grenade in the NCO shower, and at least one more in George's hooch) they resorted to more emphatic methods. The troops were aware George had strengthened and sandbagged his hut so they came up with the innovative notion of setting his hooch on fire and shooting him when the smoke drove him out. In the open space around his hooch, outlined against the fire, he would have made an easy target.

As the story was told to me, instead of opening the door and poking his head out, George threw open the door and came out running. Startled by the sight of a 6' 4" Ichabod Crane lookalike legging it through the sand, his killers didn't lead him enough, and he got in among the other huts before they hit him. In the dark they couldn't tell one man from another and he made good his escape.

After that incident, George formed the habit of coming back to his quarters by different routes. His hut sat on the edge of the company compound, as I recall surrounded on two sides by low, sandy ground and waist high brush. In the monsoon season it was a swamp, but in the dry season it was a kind of no-man's land, seldom traversed by soldiers or the Vietnamese laborers working in the camp. Unknown to his men, George had swamped out several paths through the brush, leading to the darkened side of his hooch. He could survey the area around his hooch from the safety of the swamp, then step quickly out of the shadows into his quarters. Several months after the fire he was sneaking up on his hut through the swamp when he almost tripped over a guy named Prince low-crawling toward his hooch with an M79 grenade launcher in his arms. George pulled his .45, stuck it up against the back of Prince's head, and relieved him of the grenade launcher. I'm certain he was tempted to pull the trigger, but he didn't and shortly thereafter Prince moved on. One by one George weeded 'em out, and with Princes' departure the 661st sort of calmed down. By the time George left it was a pretty good company, though still no place for the fainthearted.

THE 571ST ORDNANCE COMPANY. The 571st was commanded by Herman Martina, an ex-NCO, commissioned out of OCS in the same class and company as George Tonn. He'd also had a successful command tour in Europe before coming to Vietnam. Hardworking, dedicated, a bit humorless and perhaps a trifle rigid, Herman inherited several of the 661st mutineers. I don't know what his life was like before the mutiny, but after the 661st contingent arrived it became stimulating indeed.

Two men in particular come to mind. A guy named Pinkston from Delaware, and a guy named Robideaux or Robinette or something like that from New Orleans. Pinkston and the guy from New Orleans immediately set about trying to kill Herman. I don't

know how many times they fragged him.  I can recall two attempts
quite clearly, but I think there was a third.  They got his XO,
though not fatally, and several nights after his turtle arrived
they went for a twofer, trying to get Herman and his replacement
with one grenade.  Herman heard the spoon pop and rolled onto his
armored bunk, but the new kid wasn't quite so alert.  He was
chattering like a magpie when the grenade went off, shredding his
duffel bag, and his psyche, and leaving him standing there
looking like Wily Coyote.

He was a nice, sweet, pleasant boy from Seattle, looking forward
to company command with almost childish enthusiasm.  The sudden
realization that some part of his new command meant to kill him
completely unhinged him.  Two weeks after his arrival, and before
the change-of-command, he disappeared.  Several days later he was
found in DaNang, crawling around on his hands and knees outside
the White Elephant, babbling incoherent nonsense about Phu Bai
and doing a good job.  I never found out how he got down there,
but just before he left I went to see him in the psycho ward at
Charlie Med.  The doctor said it would take at least a year of
intensive psychotherapy to straighten him out and get to the
bottom of the previous two weeks.  His wife sent him off to the
wars a nice, though terribly immature, sort of a kid with a
bright future.  Three weeks later we sent her back a certifiable
wacko, unable to account for any part of his abbreviated tour in
the 571ST ORDNANCE COMPANY.

In addition to the fraggings, there was also a guy in the 571st
attacking the NCOs with a baseball bat.  There were several
assaults, but he was never caught.  I always figured the Midnight
Batsman, as he came to be called, was Robideaux/Robinette, but we
never proved it.  The attacks stopped when R/R went to prison.

Each time an attack occurred Colonel Smith would fly up from
DaNang, and each time he would say something like, "These
sonsabitches are going to kill you if I don't get you out of
here.  Let me bring in a new man?"  Each time Herman turned him
down.  Mind you, Herman wasn't doing anything wrong.  He was
simply doing his job, as he felt it had to be done.  He was a man
of great moral force and grim, unrelenting determination, and
I'll always respect him for the work he did at Phu Bai and Camp
Evans, and what he had to put up with to finish his tour on his
terms.  He simply outlasted the bastards.

THE 40TH ORDNANCE COMPANY.  The 661st and the 571st were both
over 100 miles from the HQ and DaNang, but the 40th was colocated
with us on Camp Love, just across the drainage ditch from my
company.  For the first half of my tour it was commanded by Ed
Wilson, a very large, very confident, and very tough
streetfightin' man from Akron or Dayton, or someplace in the Ohio
rust belt.  Ed had his share of malcontents, but nothing like the
rest of us, and with one exception, his weren't motivated by
racial antagonism, since Ed and his 1SG were both black.  The

exception was a card-carrying Klansman who buried three sticks of military dynamite under the orderly room with the evident intention of putting Ed and the top sergeant in low-earth orbit. Ed had also had command before Vietnam, and he also had a very strong First Sergeant, something the rest of lacked.

Each of us dealt with the collapse of the military justice system in different ways, but the 40th's response was perhaps the most innovative. The 40th's First Sergeant invented a new military job, the High Sheriff, or as he was sometimes called, the Lord High Sheriff. The Sheriff handled all disciplinary matters in the company that didn't require the red book. The first officeholder, Sheriff Bauer, was a former Golden Gloves champion. Stocky and wide, about 230 lbs. He looked like Mike Tyson with a tractor tire around his waist, and he could hit a ton. Shortly after assuming his duties Sheriff Bauer decided the 40th needed a boxing team. Not surprisingly, most of the troublemakers in the unit found themselves on it. In his capacity as coach Bauer found it necessary to spar with his charges, and in several days of "sparring" he beat the living hell out of every malcontent and potential malcontent in the unit, some of them several times.

The sheriff's only duties were to "tidy" up the men, run the unit details, and convey prisoners to the stockade. When a member of the 40th was leaving for Long Binh Jail they sometimes held a company formation to announce his departure. The Top Sergeant would summon the wrongdoer to the center of the formation, and in a bellow that would shatter Ella Fitzgerald at 400 meters, he'd read the court martial findings and say something like, "Sheriff Bauer, carry this useless sonofabitch off to prison." To my knowledge Bauer never lost a prisoner. When Bauer rotated there was widespread speculation on who would succeed to the title and perqs of the office. The matter was settled one afternoon in a company formation when Sheriff Alexander was introduced. Up to then Alexander had been working at the demil site. Nobody had mentioned him as a serious candidate, but at 6'6" and maybe 220 lbs he was undeniably qualified. After being introduced, I'm told he stepped in front of the formation and with his bare hands pulled the projectile of a 90mm antitank round out of the case. The story didn't lose anything in the telling, and he may have loosened it up before the event, but it was an impressive demonstration of something or another and it was quite clear to all the mantle had passed.

HEADQUARTERS COMPANY. Like most headquarters companys, my unit was a collection of odds and ends. I hadn't wanted a headquarters unit, but the numbered companies were all taken when I arrived and that's what I got. The nucleus of the company was a bunch of reservists left over when the 336th Ordnance Battalion went home. A reserve unit from Little Rock, they'd left 15-20 guys behind to help out until the 528th was on its feet. I was

the 4th company commander in 2 and 1/2 months.  My predecessor
was a Special Forces type who'd found a way back to Nha Trang and
had wasted little time taking leave of us.

The original HQ bunch weren't truly a problem.  The reservists
were a shaggy, ragamuffin bunch, used to being left alone and
doing things their own way.  They weren't happy about being
commanded by a regular officer, and let me know it, but none of
them had the stomach for direct confrontation and they proved to
be manageable.  Their incessant whining got on my nerves, but
they all wanted out of Vietnam as quickly as possible, and
knowing a court martial would delay their departure they more or
less toed the line.

The remainder of the unit came in with the initial levy.  There
were 5-6 fine men in the bunch, some unremarkable types, and a
few Cactus League troublemakers, but aside from drug abuse on a
colossal scale, nothing that looked impossible, given time and a
bit of continuity.

All that changed after the mutiny at Chu Lai.  Malouin radioed me
from the 661st to tell me a plane was coming in to DaNang with
five prisoners aboard.  I was to pick them up at the airbase and
hold them in my unit pending administrative action or court
martial.  Following his instructions, I gathered up two of my
bigger NCOs and drove down to base to pick up my new charges.
At that point I didn't know about the mutiny, but I figured
these guys were going to be a bit different when they led them
off in leg-irons and handcuffs.  The first one off the plane was
wearing braided black shoelaces around both wrists, purple granny
glasses, a headband, and a boony hat with I'M THE MEANEST CAT'S
ASS MOTHERFUCKER IN I CORPS tastefully embroidered on the brim.
To complete the ensemble he was carrying a copy of the Uniform
Code of Military Justice and had an opium pipe under his arm.

This individual subsequently proved to be THE HEAD MAU MAU and
the leader of the mutiny.  I confess I initially underestimated
him.  Knowing he was a junkie I figured he would stay stoned most
of the time and out of my hair.  I was wrong.  He's the only
stone junkie I ever met who seemed able to control his intake.
He was skin-popping heroin at the time, but in the various
confrontations to come there was never a moment when he wasn't
alert and on top of his game when he had to be.  He also knew the
UCMJ rather well (counting bad time he'd already stretched a 12
month tour in Vietnam into 18-19 months), and he'd figured out he
could commit offenses faster than we could write them up and
process the paperwork.  At a certain point he apparently figured
the Army would simply give up and leave him alone.  I didn't care
whether he lived or died, but decided to leave him alone unless
he disturbed me or the members of my unit.  I put him and his
four cohorts in the hooch next to mine, and saw they were kept
away from the others until the paperwork could be processed for
what I mistakenly assumed would be a quick court martial.

That worked for awhile, but I was in the process of tightening up my own unit and improving the company living area, and the presence of five belligerent slackers in the Transient Hooch quickly became a problem. Malouin leaned on them a bit, to no apparent effect, so I gave them the choice of going to work or being locked down in the hooch. They chose the hooch, but it was apparent to both of us this state of affairs couldn't last.

For some reason now lost to me, the Army decided not to court martial any of the mutineers. Several got Article 15s, one or two got shifted to other units without punitive action being taken, but the HMM remained with me while the Army tried to reconstruct his file and figure out who he actually was and where he'd been. The process dragged on longer than it should have because the HMM had, at some point in the past, gone into his file and cleaned out all records of previous confinements, court martials, and forfeitures. There wasn't anything in his jacket except a forfeiture order for one of his innumerable Article 15s. As far as the Army knew, until the mutiny he'd been a model soldier.

While we were waiting, I got a letter from his wife in Chicago demanding to know what the Army had done with her husband and why he hadn't come home at the end of his regular tour. Realizing he hadn't told her about his two special court martials, or his bad time, I wrote back explaining in excruciating detail what he'd been up to; not forgetting to mention his Cambodian wife and child in Saigon. Her response, and my continued efforts to keep him on a leash, finally led to a blowup. One evening about 2200 one of the mutineers named Ronald Patton came to see me in my hooch. He said he'd always been a friend of mine and he understood what I was trying to do with the unit, but as my friend he felt he had to tell me there was a lot of grumbling in the company. He went on to explain that I was, "bringing too much smoke on the men, and there's even talk of a fragging."

It was like the HMM to send one of his flunkies to do the dirty work, but I'd seen this coming for several weeks, and knowing it had already happened in two of our companies, I'd had a chance to think through my response and prepare myself. To understand what follows you must understand what Vietnam was like at the time. The U.S. was obviously looking for a way out. At home the antiwar movement had found its voice, and was actively trying to create disaffection within the armed forces. There were coffee shops outside most major bases and recruiting centers where young servicemembers were actively encouraged to resist the draft and assignment to Vietnam. Doubts about the War had, of course, reached the units in-country, with the result there were many young people in Southeast Asia questioning every aspect of our involvement in the region. These problems were not severe in MACV, or in the elite units like Special Forces, but in units like the 528th, and the equally snakebit 555th Maintenance

Company at Phu Bai, we had found it necessary to relearn the way we commanded and to make up special rules for our units. Each commander did it differently, but few did it entirely within the rules.

In my unit I had tried to separate those who simply wanted to survive from those who represented a real disciplinary problem. Once I had the two groups clear in my mind, I did everything humanly possible to get rid of the malcontents and improve the lives of those who were trying to do a job for me. By various informal means we'd acquired a 1-ton air conditioner from III MAF HQ for our "dayroom," then built ourselves a dayroom. We traded various things for concrete to make a basketball court, swapped a 12 and 1/2 ton all-terrain crane for sinks and pipe for the showers, built blast walls around the hooches to protect against incoming rockets and stray rounds from the perimeter, and stolen enough lobster and steak from III MAF to feed a unit three times our size. I decided to overlook the less than catastrophic misdeeds of those who seemed to be cooperating, and in every way possible tried to convince the good ones I cared about them and valued their contributions. God and motherhood stuff, the very basics of leadership, but quickly effective in a unit that had been down as long as the 528th.

The problem was what to do with those who couldn't or wouldn't reform. The jails were already full. It was impossible to get pre-trial confinement for anything but murder, and difficult to enlist any sympathy from those charged with responsibility for administering the military justice system. Westmoreland and Woolwine, indeed most of the senior commanders, were totally irrelevant to my concerns as a small unit commander. Their usual response, when they became aware of problems in a unit, was to relieve the commander and bring in some other dumb smack to pick up the pieces. Colonel Smith and Malouin were acutely aware of the problem, but because of their positions could not be seen to be actively tampering with the system. They provided unlimited psychological reinforcement, and helped when they could, but the process of fine-tuning military justice became the sole and exclusive responsibility of the company and platoon commanders, and those NCOs who still cared about their calling and were willing to support us.

I had decided that if an attempt was made on my life I would take matters into my own hands and execute those who attacked me. To that end I'd picked up a good M16, not on my property books, cleaned it, and hidden it in the walls of an abandoned bunker. I'd also cleared out and camouflaged an unused fighting hole further up the slope, with a good view of a drainage culvert in the Marine sector where I suspected my five heroes were passing thru the perimeter. If they were foolish enough to stay on Camp Love after an attempt on my life, it was my unshakeable intention shoot them all as they approached the camp or climbed out of the ditch outside the perimeter wire.

You may wonder about my mental balance and state of mind (perhaps even question my suitability for command). Frankly I could care less. You must be in that position to fully comprehend what goes thru one's mind. I had finally decided I would not be intimidated under any conceivable set of circumstances, and I would not give up control of my unit and destiny to a man like the HMM, even if I had to kill him. When Patton came to see me that night I told him, "If you try to kill me you'd better make sure you finish it. If you fail, and no one has succeeded yet in this battalion, I'm going to kill you and every man in the Transient Hooch. You've seen me shoot. You know what I can do. There's no way in hell I'll miss a 6'2" black man trying to run through a 30 inch door at eight feet."

There was a long silence, then he said, "That ain't fair. If I wasn't your friend would I have come here to warn you?" I responded that if the men in the Transient Hooch were his friends he one better throw a grenade in my company area. He thought about that ~~moment~~ then said, "That's absolute bullshit. That ain't fair and I want to see the IG!" I replied, "Patton, I want to be there when you tell the IG you came to threaten my life and I said I'd kill you if you tried. In fact, I'm so intrigued by the whole notion I'm going to drive you down there first thing tomorrow morning." I couldn't help myself and started laughing. Needless to say, we didn't go see the IG.

Tension in the unit was almost palpable for the next several days. Somehow everyone knew. I went to unusual lengths to make sure I wouldn't be an easy target, but no attempt was made, nor were the threats repeated by anyone in the Transient Hooch. The HMM eyed me speculatively whenever we met, and I took to wearing my sidearm or carrying my M16 in the company area, but nothing happened.

The impasse was finally broken when the HMM's admin discharge came through. With great glee I placed him under guard and sent him to Cam Ranh Bay, where he was to be held by the Air Police until a flight left for McChord. Unfortunately, he escaped from custody before his plane took off and worked his way back to Saigon, where he took up life with his Cambode wife and started working the black market again. You might think he would have welcomed release, but in the end he couldn't live without cheap Laotian smack. His $5 a day habit in Saigon was a $500 a day habit in Chicago, and he knew he'd never make it at home. I hope with all my heart he was still in Saigon when the City fell and he suffered a grisly and interminable death.

Over time others in the unit came to replace him in my affections. Ron Howard, a paranoid schizophrenic brought down from the 571st for medical evaluation comes to mind. When I sent him to the evac hospital they called back and told me, "This guy's crazy." I said I knew and what did they intend to do about it? The shrink said, "No I'm serious, this sumbitch is crazy. If he's using drugs leave him on them until he rotates. We can't do anything with him here. This is a hospital." From my standpoint Howard's real problem was that he allegedly had a silenced .38 which he meant to use on me. I never found his gun, but I relieved him of his ammunition, and that seemed to help.

Before it was over I also acquired Pinkston from the 571st. In civilian life he'd been a cement finisher, and I got a little use out of him building the basketball court and the showers, but he couldn't shake his determination to kill Herman Martina. I had to talk him out of stabbing my First Sergeant one night, and while awaiting trial for that relatively minor indiscretion he deserted. Never to be seen again.

One of my more interesting alumni was a guy named Wes Adams. Wes started out as my driver, primarily so I could keep an eye on him. Over time his abuse of amphetamines fried his brains and he became acutely paranoid. While in the III MAF stockade awaiting trial for assault with a deadly weapon he broke out. He worked his way back to Saigon, and hooked up with his old friend THE HEAD MAU MAU. That happened in Mar 1970. Sometime later, in June, I got a letter inquiry from some military activity in New York City asking if I had a man named Wes Adams in my unit. He'd apparently murdered an NCO in Saigon, probably while the poor bastard was celebrating his last night in Vietnam, and using his PCS orders and ID card got on a plane and went home. Wes was the only man to ever break out of the III MAF stockade. He was shot to death by an off-duty NY City Housing Authority Patrolman just a couple blocks from his home in the Bronx, carrying the murdered NCO's ID and PCS orders.

A couple of weeks after my arrival at Camp Love I discovered a portion of my company was on more or less permanent detail to an OP on the ridge behind us. The broad avenues of approach into DaNang were guarded by brigades and divisions, but there were several notches in the ridges surrounding the city, and one of these was held by a mixed force of Marines and GI's from my company. My NCOIC and the assistant commander at the OP was a Spec 4 named Ronald Parisi, soon known to me by his almost inevitable nom de guerre of Mad Dog. There's not much doubt Parisi was a sociopath of some new and particularly malevolent type, but in holding that notch against the Viet Cong he had found his calling.

There were two main force units in our area, the T89 Sapper Battalion and the R20 Rocket Battalion. R20 usually shot over us trying to reach DaNang and Red Beach, but the T89 Sapper Battalion apparently had as their sole mission in life the destruction of the ASP at Camp Love and the helicopters at Red Beach. Night after night Parisi sparred with them. Moving his wire, repositioning his weapons, putting in new holes and sensor lines, he understood better than the Viet Cong themselves how their planning cycle worked. First the initial recon, then the

mockup and rehearsal, then a final recon, and if nothing had
changed, the actual assault. Parisi would wait until they came
back for the final recon, then he'd change everything. In the
90's that's come to be called working within their decision
cycle. Parisi called it, "Fuckin' wid der fuckin' minds."

In addition to his skills as a small unit tactician, Parisi was a
superb sniper. Somewhere he'd found a starlight scope and mount
for his match grade M14, and he did deadly work with that
combination over many months. He kept a scrapbook filled with
Polaroid shots of his victims. One photo in particular sticks
with me. Parisi caught a North Vietnamese lieutenant in the
second belt of wire and shot him through the head. Several
months later he remembered he didn't have a photo of that one and
dug him up. The photograph shows Parisi in a kimchee squat, with
the lieutenant's decomposed head on a shovel, a large gaping hole
facing the camera and Parisi smiling his choirboy smile.

His last night in Vietnam he lowcrawled through the bunker line
across 200 meters of partially illuminated rice stubble, broke
into a whorehouse in the ville after curfew and got into a fight
with a Vietnamese cop trying desperately to shoot him before he
got his pants back on, and wound up in the 1st MARDIV stockade.
I got him out about 0200, whereupon he borrowed an M2 carbine
from a friend and set off to try and work his way back thru the
wire and kill the Vietnamese cop. I headed him off, and
convinced him to spend his last night in more pacific pursuits.
By the time the official report of his activities reached me, all
carefully documented, Parisi was back in the States and out of
uniform. I've often wondered what happened to him. I can't
imagine him in civilian life, unless he caught on with the N.J.
mob.

As you might have guessed, I'm decidedly ambivalent about the
528th and most of what happened while I was in it. On the
positive side we humped a lot of bullets. In spite of our
problems it came to over 1.3M tons received, stored and issued
during the time I was HQ Company Commander and Battalion S-3.
(For one month I was both).* On the negative side my
experiences in that battalion were deeply disillusioning, and
caused me to doubt my commitment to the Army and the men who led
it at that time. My experiences in the 528th also prompted me to
leave the Ordnance Corps and go into intelligence work and
special operations.

Given all that's happened, to find the 528th reactivated as a
special ops support battalion, with good men, adequate equipment
and a decidedly sexy support mission is a bit unsettling.
Everytime I think about it I start snickering and cussing, which
would probably be the reaction of most men who served in the
528th in Vietnam.

* I was HQ Company CO
for 7 months and Bn
S-3 for 7 months. For
the month of April
I held both jobs.

We seemed to do our best in a crisis, or when the T89 Sappers came around.  Until their untimely destruction one Sunday afternoon at the hands of nearly everyone in I Corps, they were just diverting enough to keep us from tearing ourselves to pieces.

If you think they'd find it entertaining (I doubt they'd find it instructive) please pass this on to the current commander of the 528th, with my regards.  If they've got a mailing list I'd like to be included in any mailing they put out; change of commands, etc.  You've aroused my curiosity, and I'd like to keep up with whatever is going on in the new battalion.

Sincerely,

Dale Ackels

1 Encl

P.S.  We never had a battalion crest.  I don't know if the 528th QM Bn did, but we used a red felt patch hung from the left pocket to further "distinguish" ourselves.  Not that anyone ever had much difficulty figuring out when we were around.

What follows next is a fictional short story about Vietnam written by Dale. I have always believed this is hardly fiction, but routed in his personal experience in Vietnam.

## Pretty Enemies

by Dale Ackels

I am called Tran. Many years ago, during the period of which I will speak, I was called Young Tran to distinguish me from my older brother, who also lived in this village during the war years. I have undertaken this task because I am now 51 years old. My health is poor, and my grandchildren and local party officials are asking me what happened in this village during the war against the *myng uy*, or the pretty enemy, as the Americans were called at that time. After much thought I have decided to make a written record of those events. What we accomplished and how we fought, and how it really was in that difficult period in our lives. I also want my grandchildren to understand the role I played. Perhaps by writing it down I can bring myself to an understanding of my own actions, and the things I did for the Party and my country.

My family were northerners, originally residents of Quang Ninh Province, which is near the Chinese border in the northern part of our country. My father died in 1961, of wounds he received fighting the French many years before, but we were Catholics and when partition came my older brother and mother moved the family south, hoping to find land and freedom from the Communists south of the demarcation line. For several years our lives were better, but when reunification talks broke down the Viet Minh returned to our area, doing political work among the farmers and rural peasants and preparing for conflict with the Saigon regime.

My older brother had a fiery temperament, quick to take offense at any slight or injustice, and when the Americans arrived in 1965 it seemed to him and my mother that the Saigon regime had simply turned the country over to another imperialist. Having lost many family members in the war with the French, my brother could not understand why the Americans had come, or what they intended to do if not take control of our country. As his anger grew the Viet Minh cadres found him increasingly sympathetic to the national cause, and in 1966 he left us and went north for political and military training.

When he returned he was different. Colder, remote somehow, but filled with anger and purpose, and hatred for the Saigon Government and the foreign governments that supported it. The Viet Minh had given his life new direction, and when he returned he was a Communist and a patriot, and a leader of the popular forces in our district. Because he had grown up in this district people listened to him, and because of his political training he was able to make the peasants understand what was wrong with our country and how our situation was part of a great global revolution. A revolution that would sweep away the imperialists and their fellow travelers in Vietnam, Cambodia and Laos. Progressive forces were on the march in Asia and my brother was able to explain to the villagers how our people would benefit from being part of the revolution, and how, under the leadership of the Ho Chi Minh and General Giap, they could assist the Party in reunifying our country.

For a boy of nine it was very exciting. I didn't really understand everything he said, but I loved my brother and when I saw how the people reacted to his ideas, how he was able to organize them and give them hope, I wanted very much to be like him and help him in his work.

My brother was also an officer in the T89 Sapper Battalion, a main force unit recruited from among the local peasants for the purpose of attacking the many foreigners on the north side of Da Nang. During those first months of intense political and military activity I seldom saw him, but because of his growing importance the National Police knew of him and when he came to see us he had to sneak into the village after curfew to see my mother and bring us money and food. When I did see him I begged him to let me come with him, but he was firm and told me I could fight when I got older. For now I was to help my mother and sister, and learn what I could of the American occupiers so that I would later be able to help the revolution.

Nevertheless, I was insistent and after many months of begging he finally decided to give me a task appropriate for my age. National Highway 1, or QL 1 as we called it, ran north out of Da Nang toward Hai Van Pass and the northern coastal cities.

Years after reunification, and after I had learned to read, I read a book by a Frenchman named Fall in which he talked about battles along the national road. He called it, "The Street Without Joy," and we endeavored, within the limits of our military strength, to insure it was. First for the Japanese and French and, in my time, for the Americans and the puppet army in the south.

To silence me, and perhaps to test my resolve, my brother gave me the task of sitting by the roadside and counting the American vehicles moving along the highway, but there were hundreds every day. My memory was not equal to the task, but to simplify the work he taught me to make a simple drawing of each type of vehicle on a piece of smooth wood: heavy cargo trucks, tankers, gun trucks, ammunition trucks and so on, and to make a mark alongside the drawing with a piece of charcoal whenever a vehicle of that type passed. At the end of the day I simply gathered up a small bundle of firewood with my plank in the middle and walked home with my bundle over my shoulder. Like any other peasant boy carrying firewood for his mother.

Whether this information was actually of any use to the Party I cannot say. Perhaps it was just a test of my loyalty and readiness to work for the revolution. Whatever its purpose, in the early summer of 1970 my brother came to me with an idea. It was a way for me to participate in the revolution, and to attack the Western aggressors from an unexpected direction. It had been noticed that every evening between the hours of four and five P.M. there was a traffic blockage around the last police checkpoint north of the city. The Government had declared a five o'clock curfew for all citizens, and for the various military forces in and around Da Nang. The proclamation said that anyone seen on the roads between the villages or walking through the fields after 5 P.M. was Viet Cong and could therefore be fired upon. The result was everyone tried to be in their village or base camps by five o'clock, but the police could not inspect everyone quickly enough and for almost an hour every day traffic along QL 1 came to a standstill.

My brother's idea was to use this period of confusion to attack special targets along the highway, and in this effort I, Young Tran of Village #5, was to play an important part in carrying out the Party's instructions. Indeed, I was the most important part of the plan. Because I was very young and thin, even for my age, I could move through the congestion without attracting notice.

At this hour the roadsides were always clogged and full of people hurrying home. Pedicabs carrying people, food, bales of used clothing, even trussed pigs; rural women with balance poles shuffling along under heavy baskets of paddy, rice, duckweed, chickens and ducks; local businessmen and government workers walking from the bus stops with their briefcases. And all of them moving on their errands through the black, choking exhaust from hundreds of busses and trucks and enemy vehicles. Particularly the big green ones with a white star on the doors, and angry young men sitting on top with their machine guns pointed down the alleys. And hundreds of children. Children everywhere. So many and so active it was as though we were invisible. Like scraps of colored paper swirling through the columns and between the people and vehicles. We were never stopped at the checkpoints, and we were permitted to approach the enemy's vehicles to ask for money and candy, or anything else the Americans cared to give us. I had done this many times myself and knew it to be a routine part of life along the national highway.

My brother's plan was to take advantage of my invisibility to enable me to ride my bicycle close to the American vehicles and shoot the passengers. I was taught to look for the little trucks with two or more antennas. This was because two or more antennas indicated a leader. Someone who needed two radios so he could talk to those above and below him. Once I had found such a vehicle I was taught, over many weeks, to peddle my bicycle alongside the open door and shoot the man in the right front seat because he was a leader and his death would frighten the other *myng uy* and thus be more valuable to our cause.

One shot in the back of his head, then peddle away. My brother believed that in the confusion the police and the enemy would assume a sniper firing from the cross streets had done it, and no one would pay attention to a nine-year old boy frantically peddling away, among hundreds of other children and ordinary citizens running in fear from the scene of the attack.

The details of how to actually do it and escape without detection occupied many hours. Approaching the target I would carry my pistol under my shirt and inside my belt, but what to do with it when I'd completed my mission? I could not get it back inside my belt while peddling my bicycle, and I could not carry it in my hand. My hand was so small I could not grip the handlebar and hold the pistol at the same time, but my brother saw this problem and solved it by adding a small wire basket to my mother's bicycle. Covered with a dirty jute cloth no one could see inside. As soon as I shot I dropped the pistol into the basket and peddled away.

I was filled with excitement and very eager to begin. Finally, after my brother was satisfied that I understood the task, he showed me the pistol I was to use. I've always assumed it came from China, but I could not read the writing on it and except for the number 54 on the sliding part I have no idea what it was called or where it came from. My brother's answer was only that it had been provided by a fraternal socialist country. We could not fire it openly without drawing attention to ourselves but at night I practiced with it until I could load and fire it with either hand, and by day I practiced hitting stationary targets by peddling by the kilometer markers and pretending to shoot them with a stick.

Even with careful preparation my first attempt was nearly a disaster. I had found a suitable vehicle parked in the northbound lane, securely caught between an American cargo truck and a Vietnamese bus. Even if the passenger saw me he could not possibly have escaped, but he was not watchful.

I was simply another boy on a Chinese bicycle, like thousands of others around the northern approaches to the city. He was talking on the radio, but I was too excited and going too fast and failed to kill him. My bullet went through his jaw, and as I passed I saw pieces of teeth and a thin film of blood smeared across the windshield. I think

I failed because I was not close enough and I was firing across my body. Indeed, I became so focused on my target I very nearly shot myself in the left elbow. He staggered out of his vehicle spitting out teeth and blood and making terrible roaring sounds, but his jaw couldn't move and the last I saw of him in my mirror he was holding his face together with one hand and pointing down the alley toward a nearby Catholic church. The eruption of noise, of shooting and yelling, that followed my shot was so disturbing I nearly ran down several people in making my escape, but no one identified me and I was able to escape without difficulty.

Clearly my brother and the other local cadre had not anticipated all the problems. Particularly the matter of how to make a killing shot on a sitting target with my weak hand. Since we always tried to kill the man in the right front seat I had to make my approach from the right side but shoot with my left hand. Something I had not practiced, but again my brother found a solution. We could not practice with real ammunition, of course, but it was common to see children my age playing with wooden guns, and my brother carved a pistol for me out of a piece of a packing crate, and I practiced with that along the village roads for several weeks until I was completely comfortable and ready to try again.

Over the next three months I killed or wounded nine of the people's enemies. Well, it was actually eight foreigners and one policeman. Many years later I found out the Americans called our policemen the "white mice." I suppose because their shirts were white and they were afraid of us. Looking back it seems an appropriate, even comical name. They were very corrupt, demanding tribute from almost everyone passing through their roadblocks and abusing ordinary citizens for no reason, and everyone, even the Government's supporters, hated them and held them in contempt. If our patrols contacted them after curfew they always ran, and in some cities we even charged them a tax on the money they took from ordinary peasants and workers.

The policeman I shot was inspecting farm produce piled on a pedicab, poking the woman's bundles with a steel rod and cursing her because she could not pay and was taking so much of his valuable time. I doubt he felt the shot that killed him. He collapsed like an empty sack. First at the knees and then progressively through his arms and chest. Like a man lying down to sleep in a public road, so quickly and softly his hat stayed on his head. Minutes later I met my brother alongside the road to tell him what I'd done and give him the pistol. This was done so that if someone actually saw me and radioed my description ahead I would not be found with a weapon. He smiled and said I had done well and the leadership would be proud of me. It was a wonderful moment, and I don't think I ever again felt so close to him.

After my sixth successful mission the atmosphere began to change along the highway. Even the *myng uy* are not completely stupid and at some point they realized this was not being done by an ordinary sniper. I think one of the radio operators sitting in the back seat saw me go by and told the authorities the QL 1 sniper was actually a small man or a boy on a bicycle. I was still successful but I began to notice that anytime a vehicle with radios was parked the men in front were sliding down in their seats with a pistol in their lap, and adjusting their side mirrors so anyone approaching from the right could be seen. It took me almost two months to kill three more *myng uy*. Several other times I almost attempted a shot, but I saw that my intended victim could see me coming and quickly pedaled away without drawing my pistol or revealing my intentions.

The end came in the dry season, several weeks before the rice harvest. After so much success I had begun to believe I could not be caught, or perhaps I had simply become careless. On this particular afternoon I had been pedaling slowly up and down QL 1 north of the checkpoint, waiting for traffic to slow down and provide a target. Shortly before curfew I found an ambulance caught in the afternoon roadblock.

I began to accelerate and reach for my pistol, but with a sudden sense of horror I realized I could see the passenger's eyes in the side mirror, which meant, of course, he could see me. I swerved to escape, but he was too quick. The door opened and he stepped out and hit me in the face with the back of his hand. I flew off my bicycle and my head hit the antenna bracket on the side of the little truck. I went down in a tangle, blood pouring from the side of my head, with the bicycle on top of me and my pistol under the truck. For a moment I was stunned by the force of the blow, and the pain in my head. The American, for I know he was one, picked up the bicycle and threw it away from me, cursing loudly and calling me the many bad names we had learned from the Americans. For a moment he even held me off the ground and stared into my face, as though expecting to find an explanation written in my eyes. Then he threw me on the ground and stepped over me. An enormous red-faced man, sweating and glaring like a temple lion. I was certain he would kill me, but he simply stood there with his legs on each side of me, panting like a dog, until the police came and arrested me.

When he first put me down I started to tremble and then cry a little. After all I was only nine years old, but some greater emotion, more pressing than the pain in my head, came over me and by the time the police arrived I was crying so strongly I could not speak. Perhaps it was fear, possibly relief, or perhaps the possibility I'd betrayed my dear brother and his comrades and the Party would hold my failure against me. Whatever the reason, I could not control my emotions. Even today I don't understand my reaction, nor how to explain it to my grandchildren. Did I feel remorse? No, of course not. It was war and we were fighting for our country and people. Regret, mixed with anger, sometimes I feel that, when I have the leisure to think of those years and the death of my mother and brother, but the tears, I never understood that and don't to this day.

In recent years Americans have started coming here to see the places where they fought us. I often ask myself how I will react if someday I see a red-haired American with a broken face and jaw. I hope it will never happen, but if the day comes I will meet him wearing my medals and apologize. And I hope he will understand why I shot him.

*With grateful thanks to the late Mrs Uyen Hegman, who explained several aspects of the culture I never understood.*

*Captain Ackels (far right)*
*with some of his Operations soldiers*

*Marble Mountain, 1969*

*Marble Mountain Today*

# CHAPTER 4

## Detroit

### 1971-1973

When Dale arrived in Detroit in December, 1970 assigned to the Army Tank Automotive Command in Warren, MI (a Detroit suburb), I had lived in Detroit for a year and was working for Pan American World Airways as the Station Sales Manager. Detroit was the newest US departure city for Pan Am with a new non-stop flight to London.

I was delighted when Dale received orders for Detroit, a sentiment not shared by him. As a returning Vietnam vet Dale was supposed to get assignment preference and had asked for *"any job in any of the eleven western states."* They sent him to Detroit.

For the better part of a year he was the Special Projects Officer *"working on things that had fallen through the cracks or did not fit into anyone else's job description."*

*"I learned how the place worked and I also learned how to prank the computer system so that my projects got processed ahead of other requisitions and projects ... a skill that would prove invaluable in the months to come."*

*"Later I had additional responsibilities ... first as Chief of the Linestopper Unit, tasked to keep twenty-eight depots all over the world in production in support of the war in Vietnam. The job came with special authority and I used it to prod contractors and make sure the supply system function as it needed to be."*

*"Then I became chief the 'Red Ball Unit' which derived its name from a WW II transportation system that carried emergency supplies directly from the Channel Ports to the front lines. Red Ball convoys ran straight through and had priority over all other traffic on European theater roads. Same today, expediting emergency items required by the soldiers in Vietnam. I had unusual latitude in how I did the job and I took advantage of it. At one point I was charged with expediting $58m in military supplies needed by ARVN (Armed Forces of Vietnam). Their acceptance of the Peace Treaty then being negotiated in Paris was conditioned on receipt of the items they said were needed to defend their country and my job was to provide it."*

*"My personal highpoint was stealing a platoon of tanks - already owned and paid for by Israelis - off a pier in Bayonne, NJ. When the sun went down they were there and when it came up they were on C5's bound for Vietnam. For some reason the Israelis took it poorly. The arrangement being negotiated in Paris specified that any equipment already en route to Vietnam or already on the Ho Chi Minh trail at the time the Peace Accord was signed could be counted as*

*delivered and we moved heaven and earth to see that everything on the South Vietnamese wish list was shipped."*

*"At one point one of my superiors told me 'Kissinger wants this stuff shipped by Friday'. I was a bit focused that day and I remember responding. 'Who the f--- is Kissinger'. His reply: 'Henry Kissinger, the Presidential Advisor, head of the negotiating team in Paris.'"*

*"Oh, that Kissinger."*

## Another letter written to Dale's sister Nancy

3 January 1971

Hi,

Thank you for the Christmas stuff. The survival gear is always nice to have-just in case I ever get trapped on Baffin Island in a blizzard, or more realistically, trapped in Hamtramck on a Sunday that Kowalewski's Sausages isn't open.

I haven't read all of the Good Earth Catalog, or Whole Earth Catalog, but then I doubt the editors have ever read all of it. I particularly liked the regional news items. The young fellow explaining his bowling handicap to the young lady at Wheeler Ranch struck a familiar chord. Estelle and Divine Right seem to share my opinion of Cincinati, prophets, bus stations, dogma, big talkers, and Volkswagon buses. Perhaps I'm reading a little into their somewhat laconic observations, but I felt we weren't more than a couple million miles apart on most issues. I'd still like to know how he manages to circumnavigate the Continent on $18 though.

I spent a quiet Christmas. Most of it with the Tiffany's, or with my next door neighbors. They are both school teachers. He teaches in a local Catholic high school, and she teaches slow learners at a Warren Elementary School. Nothing too racy about that I suppose. She's an ex-Dominican nun. She spent slightly more than ten years as "a religious." Her term, not mine. She got out before it became the thing to do, got married and settled down. It's hard to imagine her a nun. She is so exuberant and rowdy now that everybody always looks a little startled when they find out she was a detainee in a Dominican cloister for ten years. She must have loosened the place up a little from time to time. Imagine what it would be like having your first date at age 26, or explaining to a principal interviewing her for a job how she came to have 16 *14* years teaching experience at age 30.

My New Year's celebration was equally subdued. The only untoward break in my reading came about 10 when the upstairs tenant came home in the midst of a drunken disagreement with his acrimonious squaw and hurled his Christmas tree, bulbs and all, off the second floor landing. I thought it showed a certain amount of ingenuity, but his wife seemed to take offense at his relatively harmless expression of disgust, and left him. I gather from the deafening chit-chat accompanying her departure that he had earlier committed several other socially unacceptable acts, to wit: he had fallen over in a dead faint at a cocktail party, and upon being aroused had staggered somewhat recklessly across the room and into some female merrymakers lap. More or less to her discomfort. I *think* New Year's is *going* to be a mandatory health night from now *on*. I miss too much when I get into the ignorant oil. Besides, with the Brigadier General David W. Heister Memorial Drunk, and the Haiphong Bombing Memorial Drunk, I'm already just about surfeited (don't check that word too closely) with holidays.

Dale

(over)

*Heather Tiffany trailing Uncle Dale*
*Au Sable River, Michigan, Summer 1972*

*Heather and Uncle Dale*
*On her wedding day morning*
*Harbor Springs, Michigan, Fall, 1998*

This was an editorial cartoon based on a picture taken of presidential candidate Governor Michael Dukakis at the Detroit Tank Automotive Command during the 1988 election year. He was lampooned by the press because of the picture and eventually lost the election to George H.W. Bush. Fortunately, Dale avoided any tank photography during his assignment to the Tank Command eighteen years earlier, so there was not harm to his career.

Africa

# CHAPTER 5

# Change of Direction

## 1974-1976

In 1973, Dale made a decision that would dramatically change his career and his life. He applied and was accepted into the Army's Foreign Area Specialist Program (FAO), a very selective specialty. An FAO is a regionally focused expert in political-military operations with skills that are a combination of strategic focus, regional expertise, political, cultural, sociological, economic and geographic awareness as well as foreign language proficiency.

The usual path for an Army FAO is securing an advanced academic degree - Dale received his MS from Georgetown University; then the FAO Course at Ft. Bragg, NC including counter-insurgency training for six months, foreign internal defense and development, security assistance and civil affairs doctrine.

The final two requirements are studying at the Defense Language Institute (DLI) for intense training, in his case French and finishing with a year of in-country immersion stationed in Addis Ababa, Ethiopia.

That's how Dale spent the years 1974 to 1976, as a scholar soldier.

> *"The society that separates its scholars*
> *from its warriors will have its thinking*
> *done by cowards and its fighting by fools."*

> Thucydides
> History of the Peloponnesian War ( 410BC)

An Army FAO transitions from his primary career field to a full-time FAO career track. The various Army branches - Ordnance, Infantry, Artillery et al., do not like to lose talented officers. Pentagon branch assignment officers were very protective and all powerful and transfers were frowned upon. They hold the power of God, judge and jury. Dale's change of direction held the risk of a slower promotion rate and advancement. Dale may well have been on a "fast track" to flag rank had he stayed in the Ordnance Corps, but by his own admission he never would have remained on active duty. They simply couldn't have begun to tap his interests, the use of his talents or the plurality of his abilities to serve in more expansive, complicated roles.

*"I made a decision to do something more interesting. I never intended to return to the Ordnance Corps but found myself in a situation that if I did not take an assignment as an Operations Officer in the 82nd Ordnance Battalion in Korea, I would not get promoted again. My assignment officer put in succinctly*

*... 'Major Ackels if you don't take this assignment, I will stick your name in the personnel management system backwards.'"*

Roles and responsibilities of FAO's are extensive and varied. They advise senior officers on political-military operations and relations with other nations; provide cultural expertise to forward-deployed commands conducting military operations and execute security assistance programs with host nations. They typically serve tours as a Defense Attaché in a US Embassy, a political-military planner in the Pentagon and advisors to the Joint Chiefs-of-Staff and major commands, all of which Dale did in subsequent assignments at the highest level in the military.

What follows is the very first letter I saved. Dale had just arrived in Nairobi, Kenya. The second letter on Pan Am stationary was written a couple of days later to his sister, Nancy.

11 August 1975

**NEW STANLEY HOTEL**

A BLOCK HOTELS ENTERPRISE

P.O. BOX 30680 & 40075, NAIROBI, KENYA

TELEPHONE: 33233 • CABLES: SNUGGEST • TELEX: 22223

Hi,

I'm going to pour myself another mini-scotch, successfully burgled off
the incoming Pan-Am flight, and tell you about this place.

The New Stanley has proven to be most satisfactory. They have changed the
basic rate from 147 shillings/day to 164 per day, but it is a fine hotel
and ideally located for what I wanted to do. Zimmerman's and Rowland Ward,
the two "name" taxidermists are right around the corner on Standard Street,
and Bunduki Ltd, the famous suppliers of firearms and ammunition to the
safari trade, is just across the street. The big three among local hostelries
seem to be the Hilton, the Intercontinental, and the Six Eighty (named I am
told for the number of beds in the hotel). They charge the most, but in
truth offer little more than some of the older, lower rated hotels. A good
bargain hotel that seems to get short shrift from the Kenyan Government
is the Norfolk. It is owned by the same outfit that owns the New Stanley
and offers the same level of service, plus a swimming pool, for less money.
It's principal disadvantage is that it's not centrally located. The
Panafric seems to fall into the same category, though I don't know anything
about their prices. Two real bargain type hotels are the Milamani and
Brunners. Brunners is downtown, but the Milamani is quite aways out.
However, for those who intend to see Kenya on $1.16 and a pint of Gatorade,
they offer adequate accomodations at very reasonable rates.

Not the least of the attractions at the New Stanley are the celebrated Long
Bar and the sidewalk cafe called the Thorn Tree. In colonial times the
men that ran the colony used to gather here of an afternoon to have a
Pimm's Cup and decide who the District Commissioner in Nanyuki was going
to be. Aside from their caricatures on the walls there is little there
now to remind anyone of the salad days of the Empire.

The reason I'm so intrigued by the Thorn Tree is its bulletin board.
Though outdoors, the cafe is shaded by a large living thorn tree.
Around the base of the tree the management has erected a bulletin
board which most of the local young people and jet set aspirants
use as an answering service. Two recent examples will suffice:

       Giancarlo-I got bored here and went to Switzerland
       with Jean-Claude and Piero. If you want to see
       me we'll be at the Palace at Gstaad.

                     Love,
                     Puss

ASSOCIATED WITH: THE NORFOLK HOTEL • OUTSPAN HOTEL • TREETOPS • KEEKOROK LODGE • SAMBURU LODGE • NYALI BEACH HOTEL

NSH77

Or try this one:

> Dear B. George—My Dearest Love: I want to live
> our night together again.  Please call me be-
> fore you leave.  I'm still at the same ad-
> dress.
>
>                    Love,
>                    Popsie

Practically everyone who comes here is going "on safari" but what
they mean by safari and what I mean by safari are quite different.
They still offer hunting safaris but they have become almost pro-
hibitively expensive.  For one hunter and one professional they
start at $268 per day (21 day minimum), and a 21 day safari with
four clients and two professionals the figure is $13,339
Most people, out of conviction or frugality, opt for the photographic
safari, or game-viewing as its called, in the various national parks.
I've been in two of them since I arrived, Nakuru and Nairobi.  They
offer a nice, safe, sanitized experience, with a chance for the tourist
to get a little weed seed and dirt in his ears,  but any resemblance
between      these "game runs" and a real hunt is purely in the
mind of the people who have to sit through the home movies.

"Game runs" is an expression adopted by the various touring companies
to add a little sense of accomplishment to what would otherwise be
about as exciting as driving through Africa U.S.A.   The idea seems
to be to make the client think he's about to run an obstacle course.
Only divine guidance and the active intervention of Jomo Kenyatta
will bring him out the other side in one piece.  I suppose there is
a chance that an occasional elephant in Tsavo might trip over a
parked Landrover and squash the sandwiches, but the real risk is
negligible.

Among the better touring companies are Thorn Tree Safaris, Nile Star,
and Rhino.  Kerr, Selby and Downey have been in business for at least
35 years and probably do it better than anyone, but they cost an
arm and a leg.  United Touring Company is overpriced.  There is even
a touring company for Japanese.  Called Micato Tours, it even
has Japanese drivers.

This morning, while I was sitting in the Thorn Tree attacking my morning
paw paw and chortling over the latest additions to the bulletin board,
Candice Bergen came sailing by with her younger brother.  Truly I
have been blessed.

Let me know if I still owe you any money for my tickets, hotels, etc.

14 August 1975          Flight # 974
                        Date:
                        From: Nairobi

                        To: Addis Ababa

Greetings,

I have torn a page from your friend Jo-Ida's book and started
stealing paper and envelopes everywhere I go.  It ain't a bad
idea.  It's amazing how many hostelries and service companies
there are that can't resist putting their name on a piece of
paper and giving it to someone.

I have spent the last six days wandering about in Kenya, more or
less without the knowledge of the Embassy, but on the other hand,
not doing anything that would cause those good, gray souls any
heartburn either.  You may have read someplace about Nairobi
having a large game park almost within its city limits.  Called
Nairobi National Park, it harbors a fair collection of plains
game, plus the odd lion, buffalo, and black rhino.  I saw any
number of hartebeests, ostrich, Thomson's and Grant's gazelles,
impala, and rock hyrax, and I saw a few wildebeest, wart hog,
zebra, and waterbuck.  The one black rhino we saw was a big
cow.  We found her out in the middle of an open grassy hillside.
Because we had the wind on her she couldn't locate us, but she
knew we were out there somewhere and her efforts to find us and
figure out what we were made us all larf like anythin'.  I've
never had a chance to see a rhino under peacetime conditions before.
The ones I encountered in Angola were usually going by me so fast
I didn't have time to copy down their license numbers, say nothing
of sitting and ogling them for half an hour.

My second trip was somewhat more ambitious.  I drove from Nairobi
over the Rift Escarpment to Lake Nakuru.  In addition to being
the site of one of Jomo Kenyatta's residences, it is also the
home of most of the greater and lesser flamingos in East Africa.
From the road above the Lake they make a truly remarkable sight.
We eventually entered the park and walked up to within 100 yards
of several thousand birds.  Both species mingle together freely
within wading distance of the shore.  At certain times of the
year there are over 200,000 flamingos along the shoreline.  I suppose
we could see 15-30,000 birds at any one time.

There are some altogether unbelievable birds in Africa.  I don't
mean just in terms of appearance either.  The nomenclatures are
enough to stop you in your tracks.  I bought a copy of THE BIRDS OF
EAST AND CENTRAL AFRICA and carried it around with me on my
rambles.  Among those that I was able to identify we have such
taxonomist's delights as the lilac-breasted roller (suspiciously
similar in its breeding plummage to the red-headed, orange-breasted,
yellow-legged housewife), the speckled mousebird, the long-crested
hawk eagle, the laughing dove, the rufous-naped lark, the anteater
chat, the fiscal shrike, the African fire finch, and the superb
starling (which is).

Enough to titillate but hardly comparable to such flights of fancy
as the pale chanting goshawk (which actually only knows a couple

(Second page is lost and missing)

Dale was assigned to Ethiopia as a FAO trainee and Assistant Army Attaché, but his primary responsibility was to travel and apply his academic and language training to the real problems of functioning Africa.

*"I spent over one hundred days on the road and was in Ethiopia when the Emperor (Haile Selassie) was murdered ... in South Africa for the Soweto Riots and back in Ethiopia during the war between the Reds (Marxists) and the Whites (Monarchists). I traveled some thirty-three thousand miles by plane, bus, train and mammy wagon."* (Pictured below).

*Dale in central Ethiopia with tribesmen*

*"I saw what I was supposed to see within the limits imposed by my travel budget. Also, for a period of several months I was the Liaison Officer with the French Foreign Legion in what was then called the French Territory of Afars and Issas."*

Another letter from Dale to his sister Nan.

Bouaké, Ivory Coast
3 Nov 75

Greetings from the Hinterland,

If you have access to a map of
the Ivory Coast, look at the middle
of the country and you should
find Bouaké.

I've spent the last several days
prowling through markets, visiting
coffee and cocoa research centers,
eyeballing plantations, and talking
to the faculty at L'École des Cadres
du Service Civique. An institution
somewhat similar to the Red Guard,
a kibbutzim, and a cloister for
military monks. After 2 years of
training in general military subjects,
agriculture, agricultural mechaniss,
poultry husbandry, drafting, French,
masonry, metalworking, and several
other things the graduate goes to
a regional center where he trains
villagers in the various skills he
has mastered. Quite impressive, and
it apparently works.

In addition to what I'm supposed
to be doing, I have been buying

stuff practically since I got
off the plane in Dakar. To date
I have "invested" in (ahem):

1 modern painting of a slave house
1 fetish carved from a genuine
cow's leg bone by a prisoner
in the penal colony on Gorée
Island
1 Embroidered shirt
1 30"x 80" piece of Batik died cloth
(that from the Gambia)
2 Bronze Ashanti counterweights
used in weighing gold
1 Bronze mossi statue of a
horseman
2 Baoulé bronze counterweights
1 Guro mask
1 pr of ivory earrings

Tomorrow I leave for the mali-
Upper Volta border where there
should be some really excellent
Baoulé or Senuofo masks - in addition
to a sugar mill, a regional Service
Civique camp, and an interview
with the V-P of the National
Assembly. From there on to
Ghana by bush taxi or mammy
wagon, then Gabon, followed by

a brief sojourn in Zaire.
Should be back in Addis between
21-29 Nov. Sooner than I wanted,
but we are running out of
CFA francs, dalasis, cedis, zaires,
and greenbacks.

*Dale*

Addis Ababa
15 February 1976

**MAJOR A. D. ACKELS**
BOX 451
APO NEW YORK 09319

Ahem,

Say fellow linguini lovers.  It has been awhile since
I've heard from or of you.  Are you all alive and
well?  A postcard to that effect would not be
altogether out of place.

Aside from wondering what you people are doing
I have spent the last six months travelling
all over Africa.  In October and November I
started in Senegal and worked my way south
to Zaire, with intermediate stops in The Gambia,
Liberia, the Ivory Coast, Ghana, Nigeria, and
Gabon.  January and the first two weeks in February
I was similarly employed in Kenya, Tanzania, and
Malawi, the latter country a place you might investi-
gate as a future tour site.  It's scenic, cheap,
comfortable, pro-American, and English-speaking.
His Excellency the Life President Ngwazi Hastings
Kamuzu Banda has a few peculiarities that might give
one pause: no PLAYBOY magazines, no skirts above the
knee, long hair, bell-bottoms, or journalists allowed.
And no fair saying shitty things about the Life
President either, but once you get behind those few
minor hurdles it's a lovely little oasis of tranquility.
I wouldn't want to guess how long it will stay tranquil,
but at the moment it's the closest thing to a bargain-
hunter's paradise.  Short of the Seychelles.  But they
may get screwed up too after independence.

Hoping to hear from you.

# CHANGE OF DIRECTION

26 June 1976

MAJOR A. D. ACKELS
BOX 451
APO NEW YORK 09319

Greetings:

First, the matter of the savings bond.  As you may perhaps recall,
at the time of Christopher's birth I did not do the neighborly thing
and buy him one of those assinine little silver thimbles--like that
one I bought Heather.  I naively thought that given enough time
I could think of something that would satisfy my own desire to give
him something useful, and would be at the same time relatively
indestructible and usable for more than just the first couple
years of his life.  I confess myself defeated.  I'll be dipped in
messhall coffee if I'll buy him one of those engraved mugs, but
I haven't been able to think of any reasonable alternatives.  My
solution; let him buy something he wants.  By the time this bond
matures it will probably only pay for a 6-pack of Coors, but now
that I think upon the matter, that ain't a bad present for a promising
twelve year-old.  I wish I'd thought of this when Heather was born.

I was most interested in your account of the progress of Lovejoy-
Tiffany.  To my admittedly unbusinesslike mind it sounds like you
are well on the way to making a success of the thing.  I would
assume from the tenor of your note that you've made your peace
with Detroit and decided to stay.  You have my profound sympathy,
though I can readily understood how circumstances and the available
opportunities forced the decision on you.  I don't know why I was
never able to reconcile myself to Detroit.  From 8 to 5 I was happy
enough, but the rest of the time.  Gawd damn.

Since my last letter I have been in South Africa twice and taken a
backpacking trip into the Gurage Highlands of Ethiopia.  The backpacking
trip ran afoul of a gang of renegade zemetchas (the Ethiopian equivalent
of the Red Guard or Nyerere's National Service campaigners).  We outnumbered them the first time we bumped into them, which resulted in
some name-calling and waving of shifta sticks but no actual violence.
On our return trip they laid an ambush for us, which we successfully
avoided with the indispensable assistance of several highland Gurages.
By the time the zemetchas realized we had gone around them it was too
late to catch us.  Since they outnumbered us 25 to 4 and we were encumbered
by two women (one of whom couldn't have run 25 yards if a regiment of
Zulus had been chasing her) discretion seemed the best part of valor.

I also managed to be in South Africa during the recent Soweto riots.
(The source of the enclosed collection of travel stuff).  While a
most diverting place to vacation and potentially one of the most
explosive political situations on the continent (both good reasons
for my being there), South Africa is not at the moment a good place
for a well brought up young honky.  For one thing it's becoming a
THEM and US situation, and THEY have got US outnumbered.  For another
they can't tell a South African from an American.

When I left on Saturday the 19th the casualty figures stood at 100

59

dead and over 1000 wounded. By the early part of this week I
understood the death toll had reached 140. I fear it's only
the beginning. Rhodesia has at most two more years to live.
Once Smith and those other nuts in Salisbury are out of the way
it will be South Africa's turn. The two countries are vastly
different in racial and political composition; Rhodesia's
situation is less complicated than South Africa's, but the potential
for serious bloodshed and major power involvement, with all
the attendant complications that entails, is much greater in
South Africa.

Your note implied that if I wanted my letters read with full attention
by the Italian half of the Tiffany Unit I had best put more sex
and violence in them. See paragraphs 3,4, and 5 for violence. As for
sex, Ethiopia has oproven a bit of a wasteland in that regard. It's
an ideal location for medical researcher doing work in venereal diseases,
but no place for a fairly randy bachelor. I once asked an unusually
obnoxious Ethiopian why the VD rate in Ethiopia was about 85%. He
archly replied that the figure wasn't 85%, it was closer to 100%.
He went on to add that those who could afford it usually took the
cure. Too bad. Ethiopian, Somali, and Senegalese women are the
most attractive in Africa. Some of them would stop traffic anywhere.

As for the Philadelphia connection, beg pardon, my friend in Philadelphia, that seems to be in the process of coming unstuck. The last
time I saw her was in August, 1975. Distance, problems of communication,
disagreements on some fairly fundamental things and her unwillingness to
talk about them in anything other than,"Let's get married--we can work
it all out later," terms, have all contributed to the disintegration
of what was a fairly serious thing for awhile. It may still be
again. As you can tell from the preceeding paragraph I don't consider
myself committed. Neither does she. She told me before I left
she didn't intend to wait around a year or two until I made up my
mind. Reasonable enough, but since I was and am unwilling to marry
anybody without having some kind of understanding on the things that
are important to me, and since I couldn't get out of the Ethiopian
tour even if I wanted to (I was committed to it a full year before I
met Alice) our last week together was a bit tense. We shall see.

That should be enough personal stuff to whet Charlene's appetite. If
I had anything juicier I'd trot it out, but for the time being that's
all there is.

At present it looks like I will be returning to the States in August
of this year. The thing hasn't been decided yet, but since they don't
have any jobs worth doing in Ethiopia I'm pushing hard for a utilization
tour in the Lower 48 someplace. The Army wants to leave me here, mostly
to save money on the move, but I don't like Ethiopia well enough to
stay an additional 18 months. Particularly without a meaningful job.
Better to send me to South Africa, or Zaire, or even Rhodesia, than
leave me in this clap-ridden madhouse another 18 months.

I was pleased to see you've gotten involved in river riding. I always
figured you could be converted to an enthusiast for some kind of outdoor

activity if you found something you could have a goodtime at
on the first outing. The damned trout in the Au Sable River
wouldn't cooperate, and it's probably just as well you missed
the deer hunt in Utah; maybe running rivers will make a complete
convert out of you. If you do float the Middle Fork of the
Salmon I think you'll enjoy it. I've never done it but I've
seen the river. It seems to offer a little of everything; plenty
of nice scenery and plenty of white-knuckle flying.

All for now.

Dale

P.S. If you want to avoid getting another shirty letter I suggest
you not forget a Christmas card again. I don't expect to hear from
you more than once or twice a year, but if I don't get a Christmas
card I am inclined to believe disaster has struck. Death, divorce,
bankruptcy or a combination of the above.

# CHAPTER 6

## National Security Agency &
## Command and General Staff College

### 1976-1979

Dale worked for two years assigned to the Army's Special Research Unit, with his duty station at the NSA (National Security Agency). He visited me in Michigan a couple of times during that assignment but could never talk about what his job entailed. I understood. We simply caught up on personal stuff.

I know he was authoring studies for President Jimmy Carter, Zbigniew Brzezinski, the National Security Advisor, Secretary of State Cyrus Vance and General George S. Brown, Chairman of the Joint-Chiefs-of-Staff as well as the Assistant Secretary of State for African Affairs.

He wrote this:

*"I like my job. Since most of what we do is 'all source' I get to visit the CIA, NSA, DIA and several other organizations involved in intelligence production. Some of what I am finding out about their activities I already knew. Much more is new and quite intriguing. I wish I could tell you about the 'intelligence community' and perhaps debunk a few myths, but I'm afraid that simply isn't possible. If they have done nothing else, they have made me conscious of the need for keeping my mouth shut. Too bad. They'd make some interesting tales. It's not my job that is classified. That is no special mystery at all. It's the stuff we work with doing our job that's sensitive."*

17 December 1976

504F Placid Court
Odenton, MD 21113

Hi,

Merry Christmas from Maryland and environs. Upon my return from
the Socialist Worker's Paradise of Ethiopia I was assigned to
an outfit called the Special Research Detachment, Intelligence
Threat Analysis Division. We are a field agency of the Assistant
Chief of Staff for Intelligence. Though I live just a little north
of the District and east of Fort Meade, my office is near Baltimore-
Washington Airport. At the foot of the runway to be precise. I
can't go into any great detail on what I do; suffice to say that
it is interesting and related to my previous service in Africa.
One of the few cases in recent years where a FAST officer actually
wound up getting a utilization tour tied into his specialist
training. It didn't happen automatically, but after a reasonably
short and brisk engagement I wound up with a job that really
appeals to me. If I don't owe the Illustrious Tiffany for anything else I owe you a beer for demonstrating the possibilities
that existed for engineering assignments. With the exception
of my sojourn in Detroit there hasn't been one since I left Aberdeen
that I didn't arrange in advance. I'll be here until the Summer
of 1978, then on to Leavenworth for C&GSC. A couple weeks ago I
got picked up for that thing, deferred to 1978. So much for
Dale of the Desert.

I had planned to buy a house during this tour, but shortly after
my arrival in Washington I was told that Holy Mother Army is
planning to set up a new major command to incorporate all its
various intelligence activities under one roof, and the agency
I work for may be moved as part of the reorganization. Under
those conditions it seemed silly to buy a house. Even at 5%
per year it wouldn't appreciate enough to pay the realtor's fees
in 6-9 months. Once again I am living in an unfurnished 2 br
apartment. Number 213 in a seemingly unending chain of unfurnished
2 br garden apartments.

I appreciated the packet of assorted goodies you sent me in Ethiopia.
Because we were usually made to feel unwelcome, contact with the
outside in the form of letters and clippings was always most happily
received. In many respects my tour was better than most. I always
had an excuse to leave the country. Before I was done I had gone
33,270 miles inside Africa, by car, bus, plane, backpacking, and
horse. I think it finally came to 14 countries. I managed to be
in South Africa when the riots started, and in Zaire and Ethiopia
I managed with equal aplomb to get myself arrested. Other places--
particularly the Ivory Coast, Gabon, Malawi, Ghana, The Gambia,
and parts of Cape Province and the eastern Transvaal were everything
I had hoped Africa would be. The French Territory of Afars and
Issas was also a most unusual experience. No doubt it will soon be

the scene of an all-out genitalia to the bulkhead war between
Somalia and Ethiopia, but until the French leave early next year
it will remain virtually unique.

CHARLENE'S SPECIAL ITEMS OF INTEREST:  As you may remember--for
two years prior to my departure for Ethiopia I was carrying on
with a lady in Philadelphia.  Shortly before my departure she
gave me an ultimatum of sorts--something like a fish or cut bait
set of options.  I cut bait and went to Ethiopia.  We kept in
touch while I was gone, but when I got back she hunted me up to
tell me she had fallen in love with some double divorcee.  I
can't make up my mind whether I'm relieved or sorry.  I think
I'm relieved, but the margin is not too wide.  She was a great
old girl, and if we could have found some common ground on
problems of careers and lifestyles I would have married her
in a minute.  More candid than that I don't know how to be.
Anyway, I'm on the loose again and Washington isn't a half
bad place to be in that condition.

I hope all four of you are well and that everyone of consequence
in southeastern Michigan is now firmly in the camp of Lovejoy-
Tiffany and associates.

Dale of the Desert

*Major A. D. Ackels*
*504F Placid Court · Odenton, Maryland 21113*
17 September

Hi,

I've owed you a thankee note since my departure,
but one thing and another has intervened to fore-
stall sending it.  Mostly I was waiting for the State
of Maryland to make up its mind when goose season
should open.  They have finally announced it for
Friday, 21 October.  Please let me know if Jim
still plans to come out here and participate in this
grand undertaking.  If you're coming, I suggest
you fly out Thursday night.  Friday we'll pursue
the wily Canadian goose, and Saturday we might
have to go watch Maryland play Duke.

I thought you might also get/out of an article on
air travel in West Africa. I'm sending you under
separate cover.  Whoever David Lamb is, he must
have travelled a bit in the old sod.  I've benefitted
from Air Zaire's scheduling at least once myself.
Everytime Mama Mobutu goes to Belgium to spawn she
takes the DC-10 with her.  That means its been gone
at least once a year ▄▄▄ since Air Zaire bought it.
If bribery, bad language, and the occasional
grabbing of airport managers by the lapels are foreign
to the American way of doing these things, West
Africa is not for our countrymen.  There's something
clearly wrong with that last sentence, but what the
hey.  It's late and my creativity is laboring under
a light load of peach daquiris.

Thank you again for taking such good care of me over
the 4th of July weekend.  I enjoyed the whole thing
very much.  I enjoyed it so much I took another ten
days and went to California to try it again.  Shot
some doves, sat on the beach at Bodega Bay eating
oysters and drinking steam bear, even did a little
photography.

Best,

*Nan's going to have a baby in February.*

This next letter is an example of the recognition that Dale received throughout his career as his responsibilities increased and he was part of critical policy decisions at the highest level of government.

At the time this letter was written, the author, Richard Moose, headed a bureau of over fifteen hundred people, most experienced careerists with acute knowledge of the African Continent.

Remember that before this NSA assignment, Dale had just spent a year crawling all over Africa as an Army Foreign Area Officer, and, I believe had more firsthand experience than many trained civilian Foreign Service Officers working at Foggy Bottom.

I cannot imagine higher praise than the following statement:

*"No one outside the Department has had a greater resource in our understanding of the military aspects of the situation then Major Ackels .... his careful and informed judgements, based on extensive first-hand experience in the area have allowed us to work with the confidence that at least a few of the imponderables of the Horn have been eliminated."*

# LETTERS FROM A FRIEND

ASSISTANT SECRETARY OF STATE
WASHINGTON

November 9, 1977

Major General William I. Rolya
Commanding General
US Army Intelligence and
   Security Command
Arlington Hall Station, Virginia 22212

Dear General Rolya:

The Bureau of African Affairs has been particularly
fortunate over the past several months to be able to
call on the services of Major Dale Ackels of your
command.  As you know, the conflict in the Horn of Africa
and the military balance between Ethiopia and Somalia
are not only current issues, but matters of considerable
concern to the highest levels of the US Government.

We in the Bureau of African Affairs call on the intelligence community for information and analysis in our
work, not only to follow day-to-day developments, but
for authoritative background necessary for the formula-
tion of our policy recommendations.  No one outside the
Department has been a greater resource in our understanding of the military aspects of the situation than
Major Ackels.

When we need information or analysis, he has been quick
to respond, and his careful and informed judgments,
based on extensive first-hand experience in the area,
have allowed us to work with the confidence that at least
a few of the imponderables of the Horn have been eliminated.

I am therefore grateful to you and your command for the
assistance you have rendered in making his expertise so
readily available, and thus permitting him to make a major
contribution to the formation of our policy in the Horn.

Sincerely,

Richard M. Moose

*1978*

21 October

Major A. D. Ackels
Apt 122, 12210 Heady Ave
Ferrelview, Mo 64163

Greetings from wherever the Hell Ferrelview is:

It occurs to me that I'd better check and
see if my/our Thanksgiving plans are still
valid.  You were laughing so hard the last
time I talked to you I thought it might
have slipped your mind that you'd mentioned
coming to Detroit for turkey day.  I'll
give you a chance to reclama.  Where groceries
are concerned I don't usually do that, but
what the. hey....

Leavenworth is proving to be much like
every other Army school I've ever attended;
laundry lists to memorize, practical
exercises to occupy the daylight hours,
and a good juicy field manual for my evening
reading pleasure.  Too bad.  It could
be the most important educational center in
the Army if run with a little more pizzazz.

Don't know yet where I'll go when I leave here,
but it looks like an ordnance battalion in
Korea.  Other options include the African
desk at DCSOPS, and a teaching position
at the Army War College.  The latter two are
my choices, but ordnance has first claim on
me so I may have to go to Korea.   Enough
of that.

Let me know about the other thing.

*Dan*

The Command and General Staff College (CGSC) is the graduate school for officers who are going places. After eighteen years on active duty, Dale was in that strata. It's a ten-month program which includes instruction on leadership philosophy, military history, military planning, theory of war and doctrine and many other topics.

What follows is a short-story Dale wrote about a non-course experience at CGSC. Enjoy.

# The Fort Leavenworth Fox Hunt

by Dale Ackels

Fort Leavenworth is an old post by Army standards, a fixture on the eastern edge of the Great Plains since 1827 and the jumping off place for many of the expeditions that opened and explored the Far West. It was also the eastern terminus of the Santa Fe Trail, and our first regiment of heavy dragoons was activated there in 1836. At one time it was also the Cavalry School of Application, one of two places where the Cavalry commanders of the Civil War and Indian Wars learned their trade. At mid-century the Mormon Battalion passed thru enroute to California, and Doniphan's column of Missouri Volunteers also staged there on their epic cross country march to the Mexican War.

As the frontier settled, missions changed and the focus shifted to education. In the early 20th century Leavenworth became a crucial part of the Army's educational system; the home of the Army's Command and General Staff College where Eisenhower, Bradley, Gerow and many other key figures in the World Wars received their mid-career staff officer training.

But it's that historical connection with the mounted arm of service that is the linchpin of my story. In 1978 I was posted to Leavenworth to attend the Command and General Staff College. In reading about my new posting I discovered the wonderful museum, the airfield, the orienteering club, even the National Walnut Reserve, but I also found that Fort Leavenworth had, and still has, the only fox hunt in the Armed Forces. In 1970, eight years before this story takes place, there were 120 registered foxhunts in the United States, but Leavenworth is the only place in the Army I've ever heard of that still rides to hounds in the classic Anglo-French tradition.

At the time it was all done by subscription. Individuals bought and trained their own horses and purchased their own clothing and tack, but the Club maintained the kennels and owned the pack, and provided for their maintenance and welfare out of subscriptions paid by the riding members-and I suppose their guests.

It was an old and well established activity on the Post and members took justifiable pride in maintaining their connection with Army history and the traditions of fox hunting generally.

Horses and jumping were probably the most important part of it, but the dogs mattered too. There were perhaps 40 in the pack, some of them tall and clean-limbed in the classic American foxhound tradition, but some were also imported from France and England. Shorter, heavier, with big feet and heavy, strong legs, this latter group represented 400 years of careful breeding, and the membership was justifiably proud of their pack and all it represented.

They didn't do it every weekend, but by some means I heard there was a hunt scheduled and on the appointed Sunday morning I drove out to the stables and introduced myself to the Master of the Hunt. I certainly had no intention of riding with them, but I did want to see it. At the time I didn't own a horse and I certainly didn't own the necessary clothing and boots, nor did I have the faintest notion of the protocol involved, but I was doing quite a bit of photography in the 70's and I wanted to post myself at a potentially interesting spot and see if I could photograph the event as they passed over an obstacle. I'd try to capture the dogs, the horses and riders, and maybe some of the color and pageantry of the thing. The hunt master was agreeable and I drove back across the Post to the spot he suggested, which was very near the Main Gate and within a few hundred yards of the town of Leavenworth.

They weren't hunting a live fox. There were foxes on Post but not enough to sustain steady pressure over any appreciable period of time. One of the members had gone out before dawn and using a drag had laid out a scent trail that would take the dogs and riders around the Post in a more or less clockwise direction, ending up back at the stables, hopefully in three or four hours.

My position was on a knoll looking to my left at a slightly higher knoll with a fence across it.

The hunters would approach from the north at a gallop, then slow to take a jump at the brow of the hill where several rails had been removed to make it easier for the inexperienced riders. From there down into a swale, turning right at the boundary fence, followed by a longer but steep reach up the hill toward me and then out of sight to the west. If all went according to plan I might have a minute or two to take my pictures and get out of the way. In essence it was a giant 90 degree turn with the hunters well within camera range from the moment they approached the first fence 'til they rode out of sight behind me.

Within twenty minutes I could hear the hunter's horns and the hounds approaching, and by the time the leaders reached the fence I was set up and shooting. The first hounds had just cleared the fence when I glanced downhill to my right and saw a small, long-haired red dog and a somewhat larger black and white mixed breed loitering just inside the fence line. Obviously town dogs, they'd found a place to get under the fence and do a little exploring. Probably been doing it for months, but today was going to be the wrong day for a little innocent mousing on Government property. I remember thinking, "This is about to get interesting." The pack had stalled a bit at the jump and several riders had to dismount and throw some of the younger dogs over the fence, but when the first hounds saw that red dog at the bottom of the hill, the tone of the thing changed dramatically. From a leisurely, tongue-wagging romp in the countryside to something much more serious and purposeful.

All the hounds were across the fence now and in full pursuit. An avalanche of orange and white and brown, roaring and bellowing down the hill at their best speed, determined to catch that pseudo fox and tear it limb from limb. For a second the red dog didn't understand his peril but when he looked up slope and saw that tsunami of canids bearing down on him, he actually screamed. With less than a hundred yards between him and vivisection he and the black and white dog broke for the fence, slid under the wire, barely breaking stride, and fled into the town, never to be seen again.

Their disappearance had no impact on the hounds. They'd seen their prey and they'd seen the general direction it had taken and they didn't even slow down at the fence.

Some of the less experienced dogs hit the fence and bounced off like racquetballs, but most went under the wire and down the main street of the town, spreading like warm molasses and gradually fragmenting into smaller groups as they stopped to explore potential hiding places and garbage cans, and places where cats might be found on a regular basis. The Master of Hounds and his whips, which I learned is a job title not an implement, couldn't immediately reach the pack and were forced to ride a quarter mile to the Main Gate and then double back to where the dogs were last seen, which put them at an acute disadvantage in finding their dogs and bringing them back on Post.

Sunday in Leavenworth was about to get interesting. The citizens woke that morning to a sound not heard since the 10th Cavalry left. Mounted horsemen were trotting through their streets, and expressing themselves in language some hadn't heard since Basic Training. And most had never heard at all.

"Major!! Damn you to everlasting Hell, get out from under that porch!"

And then from another direction, in a deep baritone drawl, "Leave it! Leave It! Ranger come heah to me you worthless potlickin' sumbitch." Followed a few seconds later by, "Oops, sorry m'am."

His choice of language was both appropriate for the occasion and biologically correct, though from all appearances not terribly effective. As for the second comment, I suspect when a rear window flew up and he found himself looking in someone's bedroom window, and in eye contact with a decidedly skeptical housewife he felt some sort of apology was in order. The lady in question probably wasn't going to see the humor in this for several more hours, but at the moment she took strong exception to a stranger dressed like an 18th century jockey standing in her flowerbed astride an equally dumbfounded 1200 pound hunter at eight o'clock on a Sunday morning. All of it punctuated with blasts on the hunting horns and spirited conversation from both sides of the boundary fence.

It was certainly going to give the citizenry something to talk about at church that morning. Over the next 30 minutes most of the pack was gradually reassembled, some of them looking rather pleased with themselves, and herded back through the Main Gate and the hunt went on, though hounds were turning up for the next two days. Particularly from the south where most of the deserters were headed when last seen.

I knew I had several hours until the riders got back to the stables so I went to breakfast and got set up at the stables in plenty of time to pick my subjects when the riders began to trickle in. The huntmaster was the first rider in, but something was clearly wrong. One stirrup and several buttons were missing, his white breeches were torn and muddy, his horse was exhausted and several of the dogs coming in with him had wire cuts and other evidence of hard usage. Those riders that came after him also looked a bit used up, the novice riders looking particularly dazed, and all showed signs of an interesting day in the country.

I'd seen the huntmaster earlier and remarked on his appearance. He was a very senior colonel but substantially over the Army's weight limits. The garrison adjutant, if memory serves, was mounted on a massive Appaloosa. But in spite of their shared weight and girth, and the "whump" he made when his posterior extremities hit the saddle, sort of like a watermelon falling from a third floor window, he could ride like a Comanche and both of them could jump, which made his obvious fatigue and reappearance more difficult to understand. When I asked him what happened, he thought a minute and then with a heartfelt sigh he said, "Dogs jumped a coyote on the west side of the Post and we had to go with him to keep from losing the whole pack. Headed straight for Wichita when I last saw him, with some of the dogs still on him." Then with a shrug and another sigh, "Damned near killed me. You got a beer?"

Hunting means different things to different people, and there aren't many kinds of hunting I haven't tried a time or two, but riding to hounds is one I probably don't need to consider, or reconsider in this instance. I suspect the iron laws of economics have substantially diminished the number of registered hunts across the country and it is now too expensive for most. But big horses, hard riders and willing dogs, and nobody usually gets killed -- where's the downside in that? It's probably not the way they do it in Europe, or Virginia, but as practiced at Fort Leavenworth in the late 70's, it had its moments and I still smile when I think of it.

Some background on the letter that follows. A CEO client called me and wanted information "from an expert" about hunting bear and sheep in the United States. He knew full well I didn't have many big-game hunters in my travel company, but was testing us to provide accurate detail and information. Fair enough.

His company was significant in our revenue stream with hundreds of employees travelling all over the world.

He was an effective CEO, but his *modus operandi* was brusque, impatient and senior staff feared his explosiveness.

Our contract was year-to-year, but only renewable if we won it on a bid basis. We received high marks from the employee base, but I always worried about his travel arrangements. God forbid if there was ever any screw up - a limo driver caught in traffic and late for his airport pick-up or a hotel not having the correct category room available. Simply stated, we would have been toast. I was never under any illusion about that.

Who was my "expert"? None other than Dale Ackels who I asked to provide a couple of names of outfitters, guides, or companies. What follows is a classic Dale response, four pages of precise information with recommendations and detail that took hours to compile, well before the internet.

Another reflection of what it means to be a friend of Dale Ackels.

# NSA & COMMAND AND GENERAL STAFF COLLEGE

25 March 1979

. Major A. D. Ackels
Apt 122, 12210 Heady Ave
Ferrelview, Mo 64163

Jim:

After you hung up the other morning (It was morning wasn't it?) I
thought of a couple other things that will have an effect on
Herr Doktor's hunt.

1) Every state in the continental U.S. (except Alaska) that has
a sheep population has a special drawing for permits to hunt them.
Herr Doktor (hereinafter known as H.D.) will have to apply for
a permit in each state. For practical purposes that means Wyoming, *Montana*,
Idaho, and possibly Colorado. Several months after submitting the
application and fee he will be notified if he has drawn. If he
receives no response H.D. will be safe in assuming this is not going
to be his year. His fee will be refunded if he doesn't manage to
draw a permit.

2) That leaves Alaska and Canada. Apparently as a result of
Congressional inaction, President Carter has recently put several
million acres into the national park system in Alaska. Included
in that total was some of the best Dall sheep range in the state.
No one seems quite sure what that's going to do to next hunting
season, but it could mean that some of the most successful and reliable
outfitters won't be hunting in '79.

3) We need to find out more about H.D.'s physical condition. The problem won't be as acute in the bear hunt, though he will be expected to do
some brush busting, but I can't think of anyplace in the world where
you can ride a jeep into good sheep range. The function of the horses
is to save you, the hunter, part of the climb. If H.D. won't ride a
horse that means he's going to have to do it all with his own gouty
little size 13 AAA brogans. He needs to understand, in advance, that
mountain sheep live on mountains, usually sans jeep trail, Holiday
Inns, comfort stations, blinds, and beaters, and he ░░ is going to
have to go up there after them. They ain't going to come down to
meet him. If he knows that, and makes the trip anyway, he's got no
complaint coming.

Now that the admin announcements are cleared up we can get on with
it:

        BEAR HUNT

        Alaska Dept of Fish & Game
        Subport Bldg
        Juneau, Alaska
        99801
        907 465-4100
        1979 regulations will be published
        in June but write now for answers
        to specific questions and copy of
        last year's regs.

        Keith C. Koontz
        Box 87
        Savoonga, Alaska 99769

79

I doubt that Koontz
offers a brown bear
hunt, but I know he
hunts grizzlies.

Teslin Outfitters
Teslin, Yukon, Canada
Tel: Teslin 3391
Doesn't hunt brown bear,
but does hunt grizzlies.
Also guides for sheep. Might
enable you to combine the
two hunts in one area.

Brewster's Yukon Pack Train
Mile 1016, Haines Junction
Yukon Territory, Canada
Hunts grizzlies, Dall sheep,
and caribou.

Pelly Mountain Outfitters
Box 4492, Whitehorse
Yukon Territory  Y1A 2R8
403 667-6767
Hunts both kinds of bear
and Stone sheep.

Perry Linton
Mackenzie Mtn Outfitters
Box 2277
Yellowknife, Northwest Territory
Hunts grizzlies and sheep.

Paul Munsey
Box 1186
Kodiak, Alaska  99615
907 486-3040(April-Sept)
A brown bear specialist.

Jack Atcheson
3210 Ottawa Street
Butte, Montana  59701
This guy is in the same business
you are. He puts together
hunting trips, in any combination,
to anyplace you want to go. Some
people swear by him, others merely
swear in his general direction.
Be a little cautious. He was involved in some sort of skullduggery
several years ago involving illegally
taken sheep. Specify, or have H.D.
specify, that the hunt is to take place

under the rules of fair
chase.  That's more than a
moral concept, it's a body
of rules adopted by Alaskan
guides to govern and describe
what is and is not ethical
behavior in the game field.

✳ Frontiers International Travel
Box 161
Pearce Mill Road
Wexford, PA  15090
Another packager of trips, but
he does a good job and seems
concerned with his reputation.
He can take care of pulling
a bear and sheep hunt together.


Remember to ask for references from each of these guys when you
write.  They'll respond with a price list, some sort of brochure,
and sometimes a map of the area they hunt.  My listing of
Alaskan brown bear guides appears to have been carried off by
gypsies.  I'll find it by the end of the week and send along
the names of a couple more bear specialists.

SHEEP HUNT

Ask Frontiers about a Wyoming
sheep hunt.  Assuming that
H. D. draws a permit, they
might be able to help.

✳ Bob Kjos
Mile 422
Alaska Highway
Toad River, British Columbia
Highly recommended sheep guide,
but MUST ride a horse.

✳ Keith N. Johnson
2302 McKinley
Spenard, Alaska
99503
Hunts Dall sheep.

Idaho Dept of Fish & Game
600 S. Walnut
Box 25
Boise, Idaho  83707
208 384-3700
Ask them for a copy of the regs
and an application for a sheep

permit. Also ask them to
send a list of licensed big
game guides. Make a Xerox copy,
send it to me, and I'll check
off those I know anything about.

Montana Dept of Fish and Game
Helena, Montana
59601
406 449-2535

Colorado Division of Wildlife
6060 Broadway
Denver, Colorado  80216
303 825-1192

Wyoming Dept of Fish & Game
Cheyenne, Wyoming
I don't have an address for these
guys, but ask for the same things:
sheep permit and list of guides.

All things considered I believe I'd concentrate on a combination
hunt for sheep and bear in Canada or Alaska. The odds of drawing
successfully in Wyoming, Idaho, or Montana are probably about
1 in 50, and you'd still have the problem of moving him to
Alaska for the second half of the hunt. If H. D. only wants
Rocky Mountain Bighorn sheep, as opposed to the Dall, Stone,
and Desert subspecies, then you're stuck with the American west
or Alberta, Canada. One more address:

British Columbia
Dept of Recreation & Travel
Fish and Game Branch
1019 Wharf St
Victoria, B.C.
Canada  V8W 2Z1
Ask for rules and list
of guides.

I also encourage you to write Jack Atcheson. In spite of my
reservations, he will send you enough printed material to burn
the proverbial wet elephant, and give you some idea of what's available
and what it will cost.

*Indicates I've hunted with them or they've been recommended to me
by reliable men.

Jim—The remainder of the list.  All these guys specialize in brown bears.

> Branham Adventures
> Box 6184
> Anchorage, Alaska  99502
> 907 277-9403
> The founder of this organization, Bud
> Branham, was one of the best men
> in Alaska.  With a name like Branham
> Adventures they may have branched out
> into hooking rugs and primal scream
> therapy, but try 'em anyway.  They
> hunt bear and sheep so you may
> be able to kill H.D. with one stone
> here.

> Lynn M. Castle
> L&S Outfitters
> Box 1616
> Fairbanks, Alaska  99701

> Don Dehart
> Hart D Ranch
> Gakoona, Alaska  99586
> 307 632-4802

The other two guys outfit for both bear and sheep also.  The more I think about H. D.'s qualifier the more it bothers me.  Virtually none of these hunts are going to be easy.  They can be made easy, but H.D. isn't going to see any game that way.  He's got to understand that he's expected to hike and climb under adverse weather conditions, carrying his own rifle.  If his only experience with big game hunting has been in Europe or Africa he's got a small surprise coming.  Best he know about it advance.

> Your faithful Indian companion, woods person, and
> correspondent,

> Dale of the Desert*

*(Or dessert, whichever happens to be handy.)

# CHAPTER 7

## Korea

### 1979

After completion of the Command and General Staff College, Dale was sent to Korea as the Operations Officer of the 82nd Ordnance Battalion.

*"We were responsible for ammunition support for all US Forces on the Korean Peninsula, and in a crisis the Korean Army. This was a nuc and conventional munitions battalion, which made it occasionally interesting, but basically I as just checking a box."*

*"I never intended to return to the Ordnance Corp but found myself in a situation where if I didn't, I wouldn't get promoted again. As my assignment officer succinctly stated it ... 'Major Ackels, if you don't take this assignment, I will stick your name in the personnel management system backwards."*

I offer a personal observation: my hope is that the Army and DOD has learned that talent isn't just linear, ordered, or assigned by branch. Had Dale not entered the Foreign Area Officer program, our country would have been denied a significant talent in adding depth and talent to our relations with countries little studied by other than academics.

# LETTERS FROM A FRIEND

# CHAPTER 8

## Office of the Joint Chiefs, Joint Special Operations Command & Unconventional Warfare

### 1980-1985

## OFFICE OF THE JOINT CHIEFS, JOINT SPECIAL OPERATIONS COMMAND & UNCONVENTIONAL WARFARE

From August to November 1980, Dale was working in the office of the Joint Chiefs of Staff in the Pentagon, a career enhancing assignment, but not his favorite work location. According to him, he was doing *"mostly routine stuff."* He did allow that authoring *"the Joint Strategic Planning Document and Supporting Analysis for 1983-1990"* was important work, not to speak of *"participating in negotiating a base access agreement with Somalia and Kenya."*

Out of the clear blue in October 1980, just a couple of months into the job, Dale received a directive to report to Ft. Bragg. Turns out he was being vetted for a new organization and had been nominated as a candidate by the Army Chief of Staff, General Edward L. Meyers.

Some background: in May 1980, after the failure of the Iran hostage rescue, the Joint Chiefs commissioned a Special Operations Review Group to conduct a comprehensive review of the operation.

The final report as written by the Chairman, Admiral J.L. Holloway, III, USN (Ret.) provides details:

*"We were chartered by the Joint Chiefs to do an essentially forward-looking, no-holds-barred assessment of the attempted rescue operation. Our purpose was to independently appraise the rescue attempt so we could recommend improvements in planning, organizing, coordinating, directing, and controlling any such operations in the future."*

The Report, [Iran Hostage] Rescue Mission Report is "an unclassified version of a highly classified report which has been sanitized within the Organization of the Joint Chiefs of Staff."

*"As for membership, our Group consisted of six flag and general officers representing all four Services. In combination, the Group possessed wide experience in military operations, and especially clandestine or special operations. Each obviously had a unique set of credentials, and each could focus his individual efforts accordingly. None had been associated in any way with the planning, preparation, or conduct of this particular operation. Nor had we known about it before the fact.*

The report was voluminous, complex and ended with the following recommendations to the Joint Chiefs:

*"A Counterterrorist Joint Task Force (CTJTF) be established as a field agency of the Joint Chiefs of Staff with permanently assigned staff personnel and certain assigned forces."*

*"The Joint Chiefs of Staff give careful consideration to the establishment of a Special Operations Advisory Panel, comprised of a group of carefully selected high-ranking officers (active and/or retired) who have career backgrounds in special operations or who have served at the CINC or JCS levels and who have maintained a current interest in special operations or defense policy matters."*

What quickly resulted was the establishment of the Joint Special Operations Command (JSOC) under whose aegis Delta Force, Seal Team 6, the 75th Ranger Regiment and other select units operate. Past and present members of JSOC have participated in all of our nation's wars and contingency operations since it was activated.

Dale was one of the founding members of the Joint Special Operations Command (JSOC). This is how he remembered those years.

*"We stood up on 22 October 1980 and immediately began planning a mission in Central Asia. Over the next nearly five years I participated in our efforts to find BG Dozier,\* the Boma Hills Rescue, the Grenada Operation and other missions still too sensitive to discuss."*

*"The best years of my career."*

During this period of time, Dale's letters had no information about his work, his job, but he maintained his equanimity, irreverence, interest in a plurality of subjects and wonderful correspondence.

---

\*     Brigadier General James Dozier, was the senior US Officer at NATO Southern European Land Forces when kidnapped in December, 1981 by the Italian Red Brigade in Verona, Italy and held for forty-two days. Captors were killed and BG Dozier was rescued.

20 Dec 80

LTC A.D. ACKELS
P O BOX 70362
FT BRAGG, NC
28307

Greetings:

After all my self-righteous squawking about
Christmas cards I almost didn't get my own
done this year.  I plead press of business,
plus an unexpected PCS move just before
the holiday season began.

When last we talked I was on my way to Washington
to join the Joint Staff for three years of fun
and frolic at the seat of power.  I thought that
nothing could touch me for at least two of those
three years and I'd have a chance to settle down,
maybe chase around a bit, and do myself some
good in the process.  Shortly after I arrived
I got promoted and shortly after that I got
moved to Fort Bragg to join something called
the Joint Special Operations Command.  It is
precisely what it sounds like.  I suppose I could
have thrown a fit  and gotten out of the job,
but it was a nominative position (Chief of Staff)
and I didn't feel like I could turn it down.
It should be interesting.  Among other things
it requires me to report to jump school shortly
after the turn of the year.  Ah well, I can use
the money.

As for the chasing, I did do myself some good
in that department and will probably (though
not certainly) need the services of a best man
sometime this spring.  Hold yourself on runway
alert.  I'll provide the tux.  You have to figure
out how to get there. *(And how to explain to
the Bishop that you're consorting with heretics
again).*

Best,

*For the time being it's probably best
that you not mention my connection*

93

with JSOC. I don't want some goggle-eyed Iranian waiting on my doorstep ten years from now to redress some great wrong inflicted on him by American commandos. The rules for this organization are still being written, but in the unlikely event that someone asks about me, just tell them I've got a staff job at Ft Bragg.

'19 Feb 81

LTC A.D. ACKELS
0 BOX 70362
FT BRAGG, NC
28307

Greetings:

In case you've been wondering what finally became of all that idle chat about a wedding, I've decided to fill in some details. Because it will be very, very small we decided not to fool with invitations. The minimum order is 25 and we only need five. Please consider this your formal invitation/notification, In case you're a purist: LTC and Mrs Erik V. Slotkin invite you to the wedding of their daughter Maria Elena Slotkin to LTC Alden Dale Ackels on Saturday, 4 April, at the Community Church, Guerneville, California.

You may remember the church. I once drove you by it on our way to Armstrong Grove and the big redwoods. There will just be parents, Nan and John and their two boys, the best man, and the best woman. Charlene is, of course, strongly encouraged to attend, as is Heather, Chris and anybody else who can establish his or her bona fides as a Tiffany. We're not going to have a reception, but immediately after the wedding all 10-15 of us will adjourn to a nearby restaurant for dinner and a bit of celebration. There's also a rehearsal and a rehearsal dinner the night of the 3rd. Please let me know who's coming and I'll make reservations for you at one of the motels close to my folks house.

Though born at Bolling Air Force Base, she's Russian on both sides as far back as anyone cares to check. At the time of the Revolution her paternal grandfather was the Czar's military attache in Tokyo. At the same point in history her maternal grandfather was running a Czarist military academy in Tehran. The maternal grandfather was shot to death by Iranian bandits before he could leave, but the paternal grandfather emigrated to Paris, then later to Charlottesville where he finished his days teaching physics at the University of Virginia. His son, Maria Elena's dad, was a career Air Force officer. Because of his language skills he was Roosevelt's translator at the Tehran Conference, later performing the same mission for Truman at Potsdam. In between he led the team that arrested Grand Admiral Doenitz, and performed various other tasks somewhat beyond the purview of a normal blue-suiter's career pattern. A most interesting man, with a fund of stories about Stalin, Molotov, and lesser lights in the Russian Government at that time.

I met Maria Elena at the Defense Language Institute in 1974. At the time she was teaching in the Russian Department. She later came to Washington and got involved in other work related to her special area of interest, where I once again caught up with her.

I've included a couple photographs to complete
the descriptive process. We seem to suit each other
in most ways, though she's an only child
and carefully reared, and will doubtless go into
shock when she encounters some of my less reputable
associates. How does one explain Parker to someone
raised on ballet, Russian literature, and the opera?
It may not be possible, though I've tried to prepare
her. I thought she was going to become catatonic
when she got her first look at Fayettenam, North
Carolina. But then, I almost become catatonic when
I look at it, and I've already seen it twice before.
Ah well, it's an experiment of sorts. If it works
wonderful, but if it doesn't I'll go bear hunting.

Let me know how and when you arrive. If you want
to write use the address on the envelope. I don't
have a home phone, but my office number is 919
396-6232 or 9936.

Best to all,

17 March 1981

LTC A.D. ACKELS
P O BOX 70362
FT BRAGG, NC
28307

Jim:

In case you haven't bought your airline ticket
yet, don't bother. There won't be a wedding.
I called it off, more or less without a dissenting
opinion, two nights ago. The thought of leaving
Washington, a job she liked, the attractions
of living in the capital, and her first look at
Fayette Nam, NC, put her in a tailspin. Discussion
of those points led to other grievances, real and
imagined, and ultimately the whole thing came
unravelled. Too bad, but then again it isn't.

I bought a house here in Fayetteville. Since
I thought I was going to be here 3 years I
thought I might as well. Since then I've appeared
on the alternate command list, which means I
may move out sometime in FY 82 to take over a
battalion. Given the number of moves I've
made in the last 16 years (that's how long it's
been) I'd just as soon stay here, but I may not
have a choice in the matter.

I don't have a phone yet (it'll be unlisted in any
event) but my new address will be 408 Watergap Road,
Fayetteville, NC 28304. I'll probably be moved
in by mid-April. Til then I can be reached at the
address above, and the numbers in my last letter.

Sorry,

*My best to Charlene and
the kids.*

Years later Dale wrote that,

*"My relationship with Maria Elena was a difficult time in my life. She was doing the best she could, and I enjoyed her intelligence and wit, but we were not meant to be together and if we had gone through with it we would have been long-since divorced. As she once told me, 'You're not Russian enough.' To which I plead, then and now, guilty."*

10 August 81

Greetings:

I couldn't imagine what Tiffany Travel would be sending
me in a box that size, but I confess I was surprised.
I don't know who Jim Harkness is, but he makes very nice
decoys. I suspect the loon was made for an exhibition or
a decoy carving contest, but it would be perfectly suitable
for use in someone's decoy spread. I may even rig it up
and use it myself - as a confidence decoy. No one hunts loons
on purpose, but other ducks, seeing the loon among the mallards
and other desirable species, are inclined to believe everything
is on the up-and-up and come on in. Thank you very much for
sending it to me. Sometime you must tell me what I did to
deserve it.

So far the job goes well. A great deal of travel involved,
though most of it to Washington and points further east.
I was brought here as an Africa specialist, but I've spent
most of my time writing plans and operations order and doing
liaison work with the FBI and FAA. This tour is stabilized
at 3-6 years so I'm liable to be squatting on this pile of
pine needles for some time to come. Frankly, it won't hurt
my feelings any. Seventeen PCS moves in 15 plus years is
about enough. Even Fort Bragg and Cumberland County look
good - if they'll leave me here awhile.

The remainder of the Clan Ackels is doing fine. I saw them
all in June. I took one of my second cousins from Georgia,
and went backpacking with Nan, John, and nephew David. Dave
might have been a tad young for that sort of thing, but we didn't
go far and everyone had a good time. I'm meeting my Dad in
Jackson Hole, Wyoming in September for a trout fishing trip.
He's only 66 but the way he eats and smokes I fear he's not
going to be with us much longer and I want to see more of the
old gent before he goes up in a puff of sulpher dioxide
and cinder ash some fine morning. My Mom asks about you
all the time. I rummage through my vast pile of recent letters
and bring her up to speed.

All for now. Many thanks for the decoy.

A letter to my daughter at age twelve.

5 July 1981    LTC A.D. ACKELS
P. O BOX 70362
FT BRAGG, NC
28307

Dear Heather:

Sorry I've been so tardy in answering your note of
30 May, but I've been travelling a bit and got
behind in all my correspondence.

I was particularly pleased to get the photos of
you and your brother. I sent them to my Mom in
California. You may not remember it, but you once
stayed at my Mom and Dad's house in Santa Rosa.
They remember you as a small baby, and were suitably
impressed to see what a promising young lady you've
become. The photo also gave them their first look
at young Master Tiffany. They'd never seen him
before.

I enjoyed your account of camping out in the
backyard. I would imagine the possum was roughly
twice as frightened of the 10 young ladies as they
were of him. Last month my sister, brother-in-law,
a cousin, and my 3-year old nephew went camping in
the Sierra Nevada mountains of California. It was my
nephews first experience with nature, in any form,
and he was scared of nearly everything he saw. We
gave him a stick and told him to hit anything he was
afraid of. Before he finished he'd beaten up half
the trees in Sierra County. The Forest Service may
not let us take him back if he doesn't stop flogging
everything he sees bigger than 30 inches. If my
pictures of that affair turn out, I'll send some to
you. Give you an idea of what my relatives look
like. Also, what some real mountains look like.

There isn't really much to add. Life in North
Carolina is very pleasant, sort of quiet and peaceful,
and I spend most of my time working in the yard
or working on my house. Maybe next year I'll got
to Alaska or back to Africa and do something a bit
more exciting. In the meantime stay out of brawls
with possums.

Uncle Dale

1982

15 December

Greetings from the Piney Woods:

I trust this finds everyone in reasonably
good repair and ready to celebrate the
holidays.

Since last I wrote I've (1) Broken my back
in a parachuting accident (2) Gone to
Africa two more times (3) Gone elk hunting
in Montana, and (4) Helped invade
Grenada.  Aside from that, it's been
quiet.

There's a better than even chance I'll
be moving on this summer.  I was supposed
to go to Germany, but now Kenya appears
more likely.  If I get the job I'll be
the chief of the military assistance
advisory group.  Should be fun, particularly
if the country stays peaceful and they
lift the ban on hunting.  I may open a
guide service in Mombasa.

With reasonable luck I'll be in Detroit
in late December or early January.  I'll
call if I make it.

                    Best,

# LETTERS FROM A FRIEND

Fayetteville, NC
26 Jan 83

Greetings:

You are redeemed.  I hate to wait four years to find out you're alive, but once you decide to write you do catch up nicely.  Both volume and content were impressive.  I also appreciated the extra stuff about Lovejoy-Tiffany, and read it with particular care.

I suppose I already knew your marriage had collapsed.  The last time we talked I admit hoping it wouldn't (for all the usual reasons), but I figured it was probably inevitable.  Sometime after I moved to Carolina I called your house to see who the gypsies had sold you to.  Charlene was noticeably vague about your whereabouts and plans.  I think she said something about there having been, "a lot of changes."  I interpreted that in light of our last conversation, and figured the game was on.

I believe you're the last person on Earth to walk out of a marriage for frivo-lous reasons.  I know you must have agonized over it for months, and paid a substantial psychological price for deciding to make the commitment. I hope you and Tina were able to salvage something from the wreckage.  I gather from your letter that Charlene is taking no prisoners.  If you do decide to take the next step you might consider hiring a food taster and getting fitted for body armor.  I can't help with the taster, but an outfit called Second Chance makes the vests the President wears.

As for me, I've been at Fort Bragg for 26 months.  A new personal best.  Til now I've never been anywhere longer than 22 months.  I was cruising along in the Middle East/Africa Division of J5, OJCS, when I got pulled out for this job.  I'll be here for 3-6 years, barring selection for battalion command or senior service college.  Both somewhat unlikely.  My career, such as it is, has taken too many quirky turns and I'm likely to run out of interesting options in another couple years.  I'm getting comments like,"Well you've certainly proven you can do anything," and, "Yours is certainly the most unusual file I've ever read."  That usually means attache duty in Ouagadougou is right around the corner.

Since arriving at Fort Bragg I've gone thru jump school; bought a house and filled it with the accumulated debris of 18 years; gone to Africa(3 times), Egypt(1), Europe(4), ▮▮▮ travelled all over the US(save only the upper Midwest); and gotten disengaged.

I've forgotten what I told you about that business.  Up to about 4-5 weeks before the wedding everything seemed on track, but about 4 weeks out she suddenly discovered a bushel of flaws she hadn't detected previously and decided to bring them to my attention.  I was accused of everything from being insensitive to her needs (You'd need to be a fucking mindreader, but there was some truth to it), to not being Russian enough.  May it please the court.  The defendant pleads guilty to the final charge and specification, and waives a jury trial.

She had been married before, very unhappily, but even making allowances for the jitters, things got a bit too dramatic for my tastes.  When it became obvious that my insensitivity and lack of Russianness weren't going to go away, I suggested we just forget the whole thing.  During an unscheduled break in the sobbing, she agreed.  I went back to Bragg thinking the thing was finished, but within three days she showed again, wondering when the wedding was going to take place. All various vices and character defects, real and imagined, had suddenly vanished. The next couple weeks were sort of a blur, but the net outcome remained the same. When I finally accepted it was over I came rather badly unglued. For about three weeks I did a fair imitation of a middleaged man in the ████ throes of some kind of midlife crisis. I didn't suffer too much over the loss of the girl (in the end I was the one who refused to go thru with it); it was the loss of the opportunity that seemed to eat at me. I guess I'd decided that it was time to get married, and I didn't give up the notion without a certain amount of inner turmoil.

In looking at these last three paragraphs I think I've given an unnecessarily one-sided view of these events. ████ was in a number of ways quite remarkable. She was very intelligent, widely travelled, open to new ideas, sensitive, and on the visceral level, she was easy to look at and generously constructed in all the places where generous architecture is a virtue. On the negative side she was selfish, manipulative, prone to wide swings in mood from absolute euphoria to near hysteria, and found it difficult to bring up things that really bothered her about me. In short, she was a goddamn Russian. Not a Bolshevik, just a Russian. I still feel guilty about some aspects of what happened, and wish she had remained my friend.

Enough of this bullshit. I appreciated the get-well decoy very much. It's beautifully made and enjoys pride of place in my collection. One of these days I'm going to put a keel on it and use it in a real spread. A few rubs and dings (small ones) acquired in close combat with de wily duck adds to the value considerably. Tell Heather I appreciated the thought very much.

You will always be welcome at Chez Ackels. Next month I'll be gone for considerable amounts of time, but anytime after 1 March I should be close to Fayetteville. Call me at 919 396-0455 (work) or 867-2578 to make sure I'm in the area when you plan to pass by. Piedmont serves Fayetteville from both Atlanta and DCA, and there's also a little bugsmasher airline called Sunbird that serves us from the smaller cities and Charleston.

Thanks again for the letter. Please give Charlene (and Tina?) my regards. Whatever happens to you and Charlene, you remain my oldest and most valued friend.

Regards,

25 June                                                  85

                    LTC A.D. ACKELS
                    P O BOX 70362
                    FT BRAGG, NC
Jim:                     28307

One of the ladies in the office asked
for this thing when I was finished with
it.  Said she could use it to do trip
planning in Africa.

Nothing new here.  I've been back to
the old sod recently, with side trips
to Naples and Cairo.  Neither of the
latter two stops will ever be on my
must see list, but we've got guys in
the office who go ballistic at the
thought of dragging  300 beggars thru
a souk all afternoon.

It appears I will be leaving here this
Fall.  I was to have left sooner, but my
designated replacement got killed in
Namibia on Palm Sunday.  LTC Ken Crabtree.
You may have heard about him.  A SWAPO
mine attached to a gas pump got him.
I'm going to the Army Staff--more specifically
to the Directorate of Strategy, Plans, and
Policy in the Directorate for Operations.
One of those career enhancing  ballbusters
that I already know better than to take, but
it appears to be the only option I have open
that will do me any good.  All the others
are fun, but if I take them I will still be a
lieutenant colonel at the second coming.

Best to all.

# OFFICE OF THE JOINT CHIEFS, JOINT SPECIAL OPERATIONS COMMAND & UNCONVENTIONAL WARFARE

2 3 OCT 1985

**THE TAMARIND COVE HOTEL**

P.O.BOX 429 . BRIDGETOWN
BARBADOS . WEST INDIES
CABLE:"TAMCOVE"BARBADOS
PHONE:432-1332 TELEX:WB2268

Jim:

Sorry it's taken so long, but my first priority upon
returning from Ohio was to get out a couple papers
for the War College.  Once I got that done it took
me awhile to find the box that had my B of A receipts.
These two seem to be the ones you're after.  The first
one ($491x2)is for the tickets from Fayetteville to
Miami and back.  The second set of Piedmont billings
is the extra charges I incurred by changing my tickets
when we got back to Miami.  Hope this helps.  There was
also a check for $600-$700 in the same timeframe, but
I didn't send that because it was the deposit for
Petit St Vincent and didn't have anything to do with
the air travel.

I enjoyed my brief visit to Detroit.  The visit with
Pappas and the game, and the time to get caught up.
As I recall we didn't get much time for personal
conversation at the wedding.  Don't understand why.
Just seemed to work out that way.

Bet and I are working on a trip to Charleston over
the Christmas holidays.  Like most southerners, she's
never been to Savannah or Charleston.  Takes a Yankee
to get 'em to go see their own heritage sometimes.
Next summer I'm going to be taking them all out to
the Sierras.  I'll be coming to you for tickets as soon
as we get the dates worked out.

Thanks again for your hospitality.  Keep me informed.

You in some serious shit son if you don't call the
next time you come thru Washington.

DISCOVERY BAY INN, COLONY CLUB, TAMARIND COVE HOTEL, PINK BEACH CLUB (BERMUDA)

In the last few years, well after his retirement from active duty, Dale has copied me on some e-mail correspondence he has exchanged with men he served with over the years, particularly his fellow JSOC members.

There are a couple of names that appeared in almost all of the exchanges, one was a fellow by the name of Eugene Sierras, who Dale seemed to highly regard.

I called Gene, and asked if he had any correspondence from Dale that he might like to contribute to the book. He didn't have any letters, so I asked if he could write some remembrances of their service together. This is what he wrote.

Dale Ackels

September 18, 2019

I first met Dale when I reported to JSOC in late August. I had no idea what the command was other than it was located at Fort Bragg. I reported in my service dress blues at the main personnel in processing center. I began to suspect I was in for a different experience when no on knew where I was to report. Eventually a very senior Army sergeant directed me to a nondescript wooden World War Two building with a high chain link fence surrounding it. I can't remember if there was a guard at the gate or not but I was directed to a series of wooden steps leading to a door through which I entered and introduced myself to an Air Force sergeant who advised me I had found the correct office. The way he spoke seemed almost as a congratulations for passing an unannounced test to see if I really was qualified to enter the edifice. He also advised me never to wear my Navy uniform to the headquarters again. I didn't ask him what would happen if I did but I took his advice to heart.

After I checked in the sergeant directed me to another office in another wooden building within the compound where I was to pick up Army green utility/ fatigues, a US Marine hat, combat boots and other unaccustomed accouterments. Before that I was led into the Chief of Staff's office where I was introduced to a Navy Captain, Chief of Staff, affectionately referred to as "Stormin' Norman."

I reported for duty the next day in my army utilities with the sleeves rolled up as if I had never worn the uniform before. I met the Commanding General who looked every inch the All-American paratrooper I imagined he would be from my previous experience watching war movies. It was as if he was right out of Central Casting. He was tall, lean, looked fit and robust and was soft spoken in a way that was obvious to anyone in his presence that he was a combat infantryman and a combat commander.

Eventually, I made my may to the office of the Plans and Policy Directorate, the J 5. The JS himself was a full bird Air Force Colonel named Roland Guidry, a Louisiana boy who was a special operations pilot and who had flown in the failed Iran Hostage Rescue Attempt, which was the impetus for the Joint Special Operations Command. I was introduced to most of the staff, some were deployed, among who was Dale Ackels, Lieutenant Colonel, United States Army. Since the new headquarters was still in the future, we were located in what was designated a SCIF (Sensitive Compartmented Information Facility). Strewn about on the desks, including mine, and on the daily reading board, was more classified material I had seen in my entire military career to that point.

Fortunately for me, Dale assumed the task of breaking me into the world of JSOC staff duty. I'm not sure, but I believe I was one of the few officers of 05 rank who had not been to staff school. I had no idea how to function in a headquarters staff, let alone a high powered, high visibility staff like JSOC. Dale gently introduced me into the ways and means of surviving in this environment. One of Dale's jobs was to brief VIPs on certain matters. I was privileged to be in on a few of his briefings and I soon came to realize that he had a first-rate mind. As a matter of fact, I came to realize he was one of the most brilliant officers I had served with up to that time and I don't recall anyone matching his intellect since JSOC, although I was privileged to work with some pretty smart folks both in the officer and enlisted ranks.

He also ran interference for me in intersectional competition until I had enough experience to get my feet on the ground and my understanding on the norms and mores of staff duty to not be run over.

It became obvious to me that the Army had sent some of the cream of their enlisted and officer personnel to JSOC. The Air Force was similar although they sent some of their most senior individuals, I later learned, in an attempt to 'overpower by seniority' the Army guys. (I may not be entirely correct or it might be that a small bit of cynicism developed in me during my tour.) The Marines, it seemed to me, sent some pretty good folks, all of which were pretty "gung-ho."

The Navy did send some of their finest Special Warfare officers. The rest of us were Unrestricted Line Officers of various warfare specialties not necessarily related to special operations. I believe, and confided in Dale, that I was sent because I had the necessary clearance derived from my assignment as a Communications Officer on an aircraft carrier, albeit a training one and not a ship of the line. I also would like to believe that perhaps my successful passing of a psychological evaluation for aircrews with a nuclear weapons delivery system mission had something to do with it, but that is only speculation. When I was assigned to the fleet as a Naval Flight Officer, a Radar Intercept Officer, the Phantom had the nuclear delivery mission and we trained for the LABS (Low Altitude Bombing System) mission but it soon was discontinued for F 4 aircrews and we only trained in it for familiarization.

That was my background and I soon began to function as a tactical deception officer and as an OPSEC officer (first I had to learn to spell it.) I was not hesitant about asking Dale for his advice and suggestions which I found to be spot on in almost all instances. I learned a great deal about how to function in this environment by observing him. I don't think I ever saw him raise his voice or become angry. He was an officer who spoke in a low and measured voice and when he spoke, everyone listened, including those with more seniority and/or experience. I remember the J3, a full bird colonel, who carefully listened to every word he said which was not always the case with others, including myself.

Dale had a unique ability to listen to a discussion, whether it was a proposal for a mission, a tactic, and argument or a possible solution to a problem, quickly understand the core elements and provide a recommendation or solution which, based on the information, was lucid, simple and effective. I still don't know how he did it because some of the discussions were complex and sometimes our people's lives were directly affected by it. Dale has a strong personality but had no obvious need, to me at least, to make it known. There were some very good and aggressive officers both on the staff and in our units with personalities to match. It amazed me how he could talk to both sides of two or more personalities and always seemed to be listened to and deeply respected, it not always agreed with.

On a personal level Dale met my wife and kids. At the time he was single and owned a home in Fayetteville. On one of his deployments or perhaps personal time off he asked me to look after his home and I did so. He was very appreciative of it. One of the highlights of my time at JSOC was when Dale invited me to go duck hunting with him at the Outer Banks of North Carolina. What a great time I had! I had never been duck hunting before although I used to go dove hunting when I was in high school. I remember I had a single shot .410 and managed to do OK. I had previously gone dove hunting with Dale and some of the guys on the staff. Dale knew his way around that area of North Carolina. He mentioned that he had booked a guide, one who he had previously used and thought highly of. We spent some sessions at the target range shooting trap until I improved my ability to hit most of the targets. I remember him as an excellent shot.

The time came and we drove to the Outer Banks and spent the night at a hotel, I believe in Kill Devil Hills, NC. That night we feasted on soft shell crab which were in season. I had spent several years in Virginia Beach and had eaten a large variety of seafood but never the soft-shell crab. I still remember it to this day. Very early the next morning we drove out to the guide's house and boarded his boat. He took us to a blind, and sure enough, we had good opportunities to get some shots in. I remember waiting as a flock approached our decoys and began to land. As they flew away the guide told us to take a shot. I remember the silhouettes of probably sixty ducks against the rising sun over the water. What a perfect and beautiful scene. However, I believe something similar to buck fever got ahold of me because instead of carefully aiming and leading like I had done previously with doves and had practiced with clay pigeons, I aimed at the center and pulled the trigger positively convinced I would bag several. Of course, I didn't hit anything. It was a great time. Dale managed to bag several. It soon became quiet. Dale spotted a duck flying high, probably just below the cons (condensation level, about 33 thousand feet) and told me to take a shot, which I did, and again, missed. The guide was actually pissed and berated me for taking the shot and for Dale to tell me to. But it was deserved and did not affect my enjoyment of the outing. He graciously gave me two or three birds to feed my wife and kids, which we did with wild rice and an appropriate wine.

There was a Navy Commander on the staff, a Surface Warfare Officer, with little to no background in Special Warfare or special operations, who was the liaison on the staff for the Navy unit assigned to us. He was my sponsor for my reporting and I became friends with him and also watched his home when he was on vacation. However, although his job was to run interference for the Navy unit, he had an intense dislike for the Commander of the Navy Unit. This was not entirely not understandable because the personality of the Navy Commander was such that it could irritate more strait-laced types. For example, when I was first introduced to the Navy Commander by the Commanding General, the Navy Commander shook my hand and said: "Fuck you very much." Having been forewarned by Dale of the situation, I did not experience shock and surprise, which might have happened, but simply shook his hand and said: "Pleased to meet you." The General did not seem surprised but smiled and seemed, to me at least, pleased with my response. Thanks, Dale.

It wasn't too long before the Navy Commander would ask me to do certain things for his unit, or obtain items or information. It wasn't that he wasn't using the liaison officer to do so but sometimes found it more expedient to do so through me. I was happy to do it and careful not to irritate the liaison officer who, if he was aware of these small requests, did not seem to mind. In any event, as my tour was coming to an end, the Navy Commander asked the General if I could accompany him on a tour to visit some units on a recruiting mission to England, Scotland, Italy and Egypt. I was asked to accompany him for "OPSEC" purposes. There is no doubt in my mind that the General was not aware that it was a good idea for whatever reasons I am not privy to. But I enjoyed it immensely. One thing I learned from the git-go is there was no possible way I could every match the Navy Commander in drinking, so I didn't even try to my great benefit. The Navy Commander could drink into the wee hours with his men and then go on a five-mile run with them early the next morning. I was in my early forties at the time and although I was a runner could not hope to match his performance, so I didn't. I believe the Navy Commander was a year younger.

I remember being invited by the Army guys to go to a local jump school and jump with them on one of their monthly jumps. I graciously thanked them for the invitation and felt honored to be asked, but respectfully declined. After having sat on an ejection seat for 8 years and never having to use it (came close a few times), I was in no hurry to press my luck. Dale, however, although a combat experienced infantry officer and a Company Commander for 4 tours in Vietnam, was not a paratrooper and accepted the invitation to jump with them. Unfortunately, he injured his back on a jump. I went to visit him at the Fort Bragg hospital. He did not appear to have any regrets and was obviously in pain although he didn't show it. I'm not sure if that cured his desire to leave the ranks of the "legs" and become a paratrooper or not, but it certainly didn't slow his performance down.

It was not long after that, that I left JSOC and returned to the Navy.

I learned that in the Army, Combat Arms officers are expected to have a secondary specialty. A lot of those had the Soviet Union, the possible invasion of a massive army of tanks and infantry through the Fulda Gap. Dale, however, wanted Africa as his specialty. When asked to do a fourth combat tour in Vietnam as a Company Commander, he said he would if he could have Africa as his specialty. He got it and as a result toured Africa and became familiar with it and even could speak, I believe, and understand some of the languages. I remember he came to Southern Arizona to speak with an old retired lawman who had been of several safaris and had some good advice for him. He apparently got the advice he sought and had a good time. He told me some tales he had heard from this fellow and I hope he includes it in any memoirs he might write.

I didn't keep a journal of my time at JSOC because there was so much that was classified that I didn't want to chance compromising information. To this day, I'm still not certain what has been declassified. One thing I am certain of, is that my respect and admiration of Dale as an officer and a gentleman has never diminished and I am grateful for having had the opportunity to serve with him.

# OFFICE OF THE JOINT CHIEFS, JOINT SPECIAL OPERATIONS
## COMMAND & UNCONVENTIONAL WARFARE

22 Jan 86

LTC & MRS. A.D ACKELS
1608 OLD STAGE ROAD
ALEXANDRIA, VA 22308

Dear Jim:

As promised, you'll find a generous helping of propaganda on
various inns we checked in Charleston.  We arrived the evening
of the 27th and went to ground at the Meeting Street Inn.  It
was perfect.  The front part is a reconstructed saloon and
inn dating from the 1870's.  The rear portion is an add-on,
done in the same architectural style.  It's furnished in a mixture of local antiques and reproduction furniture typical of
19th century Charleston.  It's nicely situated near the market
and close to the northern edge of the historic district, and
proved to be an ideal choice in every respect.  Our thanks
again to your staff.  They done good.

The Meeting Street Inn is part of a chain.  I've sent along their
folder.  All appear to be of equal quality.  The Battery Carriage
House is the smallest and most expensive, but I don't think
you can go wrong with any of the three.  The Meeting Street Inn
has one advantage not shared with the others.  They have a small,
elegantly appointed conference room suitable for groups of
perhaps 25-30, but just across the street someone is putting
up a new convention center and hotel that will provide anything
a conventioneer might need.  You might be able to put the VIPs
in the Meeting Street Inn, and put the commoners and the working
meetings in the new facility.

Two others we checked out were the Indigo Inn and the Planter's
Inn.  Both are comfortable and nicely done, but the locations
aren't quite as good, and the ambiance lacks something--perhaps
that final little squinch of authenticity that makes the others
so appealing.  Another place you might keep in mind for families
is called 2 Meeting Street.  Bed and breakfast I would guess.  It's
an elegant wood frame restoration, right on the Battery.  The
location and view are first class.

One of our projects was a visit to Hampton Plantation.  Once the
ancestral home of the Rutledge family, it's been given to South
Carolina to be made into a state park.  Two of the original
Rutledge Clan, John and Edward, were either signers of the Declaration
or delegates to the first Constitutional Convention.  John later
became one of the first five justices of the US Supreme Court.  I
became acquainted with the place thru the writings of the 7th generation
scion of the family--a man named Archibald Rutledge.  He died near
Hampton in 1973.  He was best known for his hunting and fishing yarns,
set in the low country where he'd grown up along the Santee River.
They had a literary quality not usually found  in the typical redneck
hunting stories.  "Me and Big Ed was baling hay in the low ground
on my sister's place when this big buck up and run crost the road.
Wa'll I'll tell you, I got so excited I near baled up my lunch bucket."
I read his short stories avidly, and later in life haunted used
bookstores looking for his hardbound stuff.  Some of the 42 books
he wrote proved to be something less than masterpieces, but the

111

State Legislature thought enough of him to make him the Poet Laureate of South Carolina before he died.  I suppose it's a testament to Rutledge's powers of description that the place looked almost exactly as I expected it to look.

The historic center of Old Charleston is a museum of architecture. Most of the rice plantations along the Ashley River  (Middleton Place, Magnolia, and perhaps Drayton Hall) suffered from Sherman's passing attentions, but the City itself was spared.  I've forgotten why, but the net result is a downtown section that accurately reflects the architecture and the tastes of a 19th century coastal city.  South of Broad Street no modifications can be made to anything, even exterior painting, with out the approval of the Board of Architectural Review.  A joke we heard toward the end of a carriage tour illustrates the situation.  "Why does it take three people to change a light bulb in Charleston?"  One to make the mint juleps, one to call the Board of Architectural Review and see is it all right, and one to stand around and say how fine the old one was.

If there's anything more important than place to a Charlestonian it's family.  The people who inhabit the historic district are to a marked degree descendants of those who settled the place in the 17th and 18th  centuries.  It's a closed society, totally denied to those who lack the necessary credentials.  A local boy named Pat Conway has made a fair living writing about the Charlestonians and their institutions (CONRACK, THE GREAT SANTINI, and the LORDS OF DISCIPLINE).  As Conway says, "During the day the streets are filled with ermine-headed children with eyes like weimaraners, who are native to this land....Aristocrats in Charleston, like aristocrats the world over, have proven the danger of sipping from the genetic cup without a sense of reckless- ness or a gambler's eye for a proper stranger."  With visions of weimaraner eyes and weasel heads clouding my vision, I was particu- larly looking forward to meeting and having a drink with an old friend of Bet's Mom who came from that environment.  A Mr and Mrs T. Allen Legare (pronounced Legree).  He was the direct descendant of a French Huegonot that came to Charleston in 1743; the family has apparently lived on Tradd Street ever since.  Like so many Allen Legare left Charleston as a young man for a spot of adventure, but he later came back to assume his responsibilies, and perhaps enjoy the benefits accruing to someone of his ancestry.  He served in the OSS in WW II, in the same team with Bill Colby (later Director of the CIA).  After the War he returned to Charleston, became an attorney, and became involved in politics.  He represented Charleston in the State Legislature for many years and apparently became a prominent attorney.  The bridge over the Ashley River is named for him.  They proved to be most interesting, even a slightly raffish couple.  I enjoyed him very much, but from listening to them talk I formed the definite impression that south of Broad Street one doesn't go around knocking on doors and inviting the neighbors over for bratwurst and beer.

Speaking of consumables; there are some very good places to eat. Of those we tried, I think 82 Queen Street and Poogan's Porch stand out.  Sweet Lydia Anne's also sounded good, but we ran out of time.  All are on Queen Street.  The cuisine is seafood and creole: she crab soup, wonderful jambalaya, shrimp creole, crawfish étoufeé, blueberry nut pie, and a wonderful thing called sweet potato pecan pie.  Night life is pretty much nonexistent, but nobody with a credit card need ever starve.

I've enclosed a separate sheet outlining our travel needs this summer.  Thanks again for helping with the Charleston trip.  Hope to see you next week, if you're still coming to Washington.

Our best regards, as always.

Dale
and Bet

# LETTERS FROM A FRIEND

# CHAPTER 9

---

# Army General Staff –
# The Pentagon Again

### 1985-1987

In mid-1985, Dale received orders to return to the Pentagon. This time assigned to Strategy Plans and Policy Directorate of the Army Staff. So, he and his new bride and two children headed north from Ft. Bragg and Fayetteville, NC.

*"The assignment began as a routine staff assignment but about six months into it I inherited an action to provide support to the mujahadin in Afghanistan and UNITA in Angola. Primarily STINGER missiles, which proved to be singularly effective in driving the Soviets out of both places. Before I turned over the project, we'd shot down seventy-seven Soviet bloc aircraft, including an IL-76 with over one hundred Soviet and Cuban soldiers onboard. As soon as I turned over the project, I was assigned to assist the FANT in driving the Libyans out of northern Chad. Gaddafi had bombed a nightclub in Europe frequented by US servicemen and President Reagan was determined to make them pay. The Libyans had invaded northern Chad to gain access to raw uranium in the Aouzou Strip and Reagan was also determined to see that Libya did not become a nuclear power. Over several months of fighting, the FANT and their allies drove the Libyans out of Chad and captured over $350M in Soviet supplied equipment."*

Chapter 11 highlights more of Dale's activities regarding STINGER missiles and some additional insights into the story.

# CHAPTER 10

## Wedding Day

April 15, 1985

A momentous year for LTC Ackels. First off and most importantly, on April 14, 1985 he married Elizabeth "Bet" Miller of Fayetteville, NC. I was best man and loved every minute of the day.

Dale asked my help in finding a suitable location in the Caribbean for their honeymoon. We talked about it and dismissed the usual places as ordinary. I was determined to find something unusual, so Lovejoy-Tiffany set to work. We finally recommended Petit St. Vincent located in the chain of Caribbean Islands called the Grenadines. It's a small, one hundred thirteen acre, privately owned island with only twenty-two cottages and requires a flight from Barbados to Union Island and its small landing strip, then a twenty minute boat ride to PSV.

One of the unique features as stated in their brochure:

*Meals are served in the main pavilion, looking out on the harbor. But most guests like to take breakfast and afternoon tea in their cottage. To have any meals served in your cottage, or on the beach for that matter, you need only let room service know.*

*Not by calling them; there are no telephones in the cottages. But there are bamboo flagpoles outside them. When you want something, you simply raise your yellow flag. Our room service patrol sights it and brings whatever you want. When you want nothing so much as to be alone, you send up the red flag. Its a simple system, but one of the features guests remember most warmly.*

*Dale and Jim, on Dale's wedding day.*

*Dale, Bet and Dale's mom, Blon.*

# WEDDING DAY

9 May 1985

Jim:

I feel we owe you some kind of report on the trip.  Particularly since you
played such an important part in setting it up and insuring its success.

We made it to Pinehurst in a faintly alcoholic stupor, accompanied by a good
deal of giggling, and here and there a missed turn.  As you saw, we also
got to the airport the next morning.

By the time we left for Barbados, both of us were once again breathing regularly
and able to sustain a conversation without recourse to stimulants.  The trip
down was brightened  by the presence of a Bajan in the seat next to me.  I
noticed he was wearing a regimental tie of some kind and asked about its origin.
He said it was the Royal Air Force Nicosia, and that he'd served in the RAF
for 22 years before retiring to take a job with BWIA for 15 years.  He said
his present occupations were social historian and journalist.  He was returning
from a trip to Charleston, SC where he'd gone on behalf of the Board of Tourism.
Charleston had originally been settled by British subjects from Barbados, and
the Board of Tourism apparently felt that sending a man to the city to point
out the historical and architectural ties might do something positive for
tourism.

He said he wrote a column for THE NATION, which appeared under his byline three
times weekly.  I subsequently dug up a copy and removed one of his pieces.
See the attachment.  As you can see from the other inclosure, THE NATION is a
lively little rag.  I was particularly taken with the following ad in the
personal section: "URGENTLY REQUIRED females to attend local ape.  Write to
Kong Enterprises, Windy Cot, Sherton, St Thomas, attention Mr King.  Applications
in writing only."  I would certainly hope so.

Alleyne also sits on the Public Relations Board of the Defense Ministry, and
is something of a Grenada buff.  I'm sending him some Grenada clippings and
photos.  I would judge him to be without important friends in Government, but
he's an interesting little fellow and has a wealth of information on Barbados.
I would guess he's also not averse to turning a honest buck or two as a tour
guide or local representative.  I've enclosed his card on the off chance that
he may one day prove to be of some use.

Your choice of the Sandy Lane was superb.  It more than lived up to expectations,
and it was very kind(and thoughtful) of you to pick up the tab and have that
bottle of Korbel's all-purpose elixir waiting at the airport.  We took it to
PSV and drank it later in the week when our champagne low-level warning lights
started to wink on.

PSV proved to be all that we'd hoped.  The photos provide more detail, but
it was perfect.  Breakfast delivered to your cottage about 0900, followed by
a leisurely day of snorkelling, swimming, sunbathing, yachting, eating, and
fishing.

On two occasions we jointly rented a 38' trimaran called the PIRAGUA and sailed
off to Sandy Island, Cariacou Island, Petit St Richardson (shown as Mopion Island
on most charts), or Salt Whistle Bay on the north side of Mayreau Island.  We also
spent a pleasant half-day snorkelling at Tobago Cays, which is just north of PSV.
One other time we rode over to Palm Island on the PSV cruiser to see if we'd
missed anything.  Turned out we hadn't.  Kitchen is indifferent and the cottages
a little rundown and in need of attention.  The "Coconut Johnny" Caldwell referred to
in the Clipper article introduces himself as a hotelier, but he's more interested in

sailing and beachcombing than in running his business.  Part of his island
is in private hands, and they don't maintain their places well.  There's
also a garbage dump in the lagoon in the middle of the island.  Ten thousand
years from now it will be an important archeological find, but right now
it's a dump.  PSV is infinitely better; in terms of food, service, ambiance,
and recreational opportunities.

Late in our stay we tried the fishing, but with no success.  There are only
two charter boats in the area, both operating out of the anchorage on
Union Island.  The ROYAL CHOPPY is a 28' Bertram sportfisherman, but the
owner reportedly  couldn't find fish in the meat counter at Piggly Wiggly.
The other boat is owned by a Frenchman.  Typical frog, he broke his steering
coming out of the anchorage at PSV and we spent 1½ hours cruising in circles
while he juryrigged a fix with his gaff handle.  Probably just as well
that we didn't strike a decent fish since the gaff was already fully employed
in steering the boat.  There are gamefish there.  We caught barracuda trolling
from the trimaran, and I saw a pompano tailing on Horseshoe Reef,west of
Tobago Cays.  I also saw a Spanish mackeral in the bottom of a Jamaican's
dory on Sandy Island, and king mackerel were running somewhere around there
the whole time we were on PSV.  They served them in the restaurant every
other day.  A good charter boat captain, say one of the guys from the Bahamas
or the Keys, could show those guys something about gamefishing, and build a
useful adjunct to the tourist business in the process.

We never got around to diving with tanks, but the snorkelling was excellent.
Sandy Island and Tobago Cays offer some of the very best anywhere.  Huge staghorn
and elkhorn corals, brain coral the size of a '56 Chrysler, sea fans, tube
worms, and wonderful diversity of reef fishes.  There were wrasses, angelfish,
goatfish, trunkfish, parrotfish, grunts, grouper, and balao; all of them
represented in several varieties and color combinations.  The first day on
Sandy Island we swam for 15 minutes thru shoals of tiny iridescent blue baitfish,
other times we followed schools of small blue and yellow grunts right into
the coral.  Only one shark seen, and that by a lady who could probably have
whipped him two out of three falls the best day he ever had.

I would enthusiastically recommend PSV to your clients; at least those who
seek full retreat from reality and who can entertain themselves.  A 2-3 day
stay is much too short.  I recommend 10-14 days.  The resident managers
also asked me to remind you that it's possible to rent the whole island,
particularly in summer.  If you're working with a group that can use
all 22 cottages,and doesn't want to get drunk and see the Copa girls every night,
PSV can handle it and would welcome the opportunity.  For the right group, it
would be a memorable experience.

Within the next few days you'll be receiving a pkg from us.  During the recent
unpleasantness in Grenada I had occasion to climb up on the fortifications at
Fort Rupert-overlooking St George.  The AAA gunners had a barracks on the roof
and I noticed that one end contained an office.  I couldn't force the door
because of debris from the airstrike, but the window was open so I climbed in
and began rummaging thru the previous occupant's desk.  Turned out the office
belonged to the political officer.  Just out of training in some hotbed of
socialist realpolitik, he had a variety of different forms in a tub file beside
his desk.  I borrowed six of them, one of which is being used to induct one James
M. Tiffany into the Grenada Revolutionary Cadets.  I trust this will find a place
where discriminating travellers (and idle loafers) will be able to see it and comment

# WEDDING DAY

on the achievement in revolutionary travel planning it represents.

Upon our return to Miami we decided we were not yet ready to face reality so
we rented a car and struck out for Key West.  We saw Hemingway's house,
stuck our head(s) in the original Sloppy Joe's Bar, ate enough conch salad,
conch fritters, and cracked conch to upset the digestive workings of a fish
eagle, and launched the first ever, serious-as-a-heart-attack,effort to
sample and catalog all the key lime pies between Homestead and Key West.
I recognize this project may strike some as frivolous, but a proper appreciation
for this heroic concoction is one of the benchmarks of a truly serious
trencherperson -- the kind of person who doesn't know the meaning of saddlebag
thighs or swag belly and doesn't care how far they are going to have to run
after the honeymoon is over.  On the off chance that the information my prove
helpful to those members of your staff who take these matters seriously, we
have added a brief summary of our preliminary findings.

| | |
|---|---|
| New Horizons<br>Key West | A vegetarian restaurant that substitutes something non-fattening for nearly every ingredient that makes a key lime pie worth eating.  For this and other crimes the chef de cuisine should have been boiled in pectin and lime peels until he reached the texture and consistency of green jello.  For those who don't like lime pie anyway, drugs are available in the parking lot across the street. See the bearded geek on the bicycle, with the Coast Guard orange T-shirt hanging down to his stacking swivel. |
| Fogarty House<br>Key West | An Italian restaurant chiefly notable for the fountain in the courtyard that makes conversation virtually impossible.  In this case good pasta doesn't necessarily translate into a good key lime pie.  Chunk pie in the fountain and order spumoni. |
| Mr Deli<br>Homestead | As I recall, Bet said this one contained some kind of adulterating substance.  Topping was also made of Cool Whip.  Will do for emergency consumption, but don't plan a special stop. |
| The Halfshell<br>Key West | A presumptuous little pie, without breeding or refinement, but suitable for immediate consumption. Should be preceeded by a couple dozen oysters, boiled shrimp, conch salad, and a liter of beer. |
| Sonny's BBQ<br>Homestead | An important local pie.  Should be good well into the 90's. |
| Old Fisherman's Cafe<br>Key West | The Chateau Margaux of key lime pies.  A big, full-bodied pie that should be bought now for long-term appreciation.  Made from the juice of real Key limes, which are smaller and tarter than commercial orchard limes.  Not suitable for |

nursing infants and people with cleft palates, but the only pie for serious gourmands.

On that elevated(and elevating) note I quit. Many thanks to all who had anything to do with setting up our honeymoon.  It was flawless,  It was the best honeymoon I've ever  had, and according to my wife, it's also the only honeymoon I'll ever have.

I also appreciate your help in making the wedding work, and in taking the time to come down and officiate.  Wouldn't have counted if you hadn't been there.

My best as always.

After 1 June my new address will be:    1606 Old Stage Road
Alexandria, VA
22308

Because of the last minute decision to go to Key West, we didn't use the last leg of our ticket.  I suspect there's no value left in them, but please take a look and credit my Visa card if there's any serious money left in the tickets.  If it's just a couple bucks, put it in the Christmas party fund.

One might ask the question: what is that Grenada Revolutionary Cadets Certificate all about? And what does it have to do with Dale and Bet's wedding? Dale mentioned the certificate in his letter but here's a bit more detail.

Major Ackels and his JSOC comrades were some of the first US forces in Grenada on October 26, 1983 on orders from President Ronald Reagan who believed that six hundred United States medical students may have been in danger from the Marxist regime that overthrew and killed the elected Prime Minister just a few days earlier. The Cuban Commander, Colonel Pedro Tortolo Comas[*] had already fled his office for the safety of the Soviet Embassy when Dale entered the adjacent office of the Political Officer the morning of Day 1. He found a number of blank certificates used to recognize both Cuban and Grenadian soldiers. This is one of them, complete with Bet and Dale's own words presented to me a year and a half later after helping plan their honeymoon to a different Caribbean island.

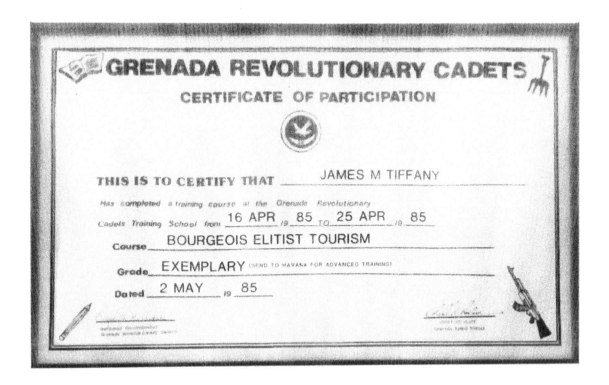

---

[*]     The Colonel is now driving a taxi in Havana, a story I thought to be apocryphal until I verified it during a visit to Cuba in 2016.

# CHAPTER 11

## Congressman Charlie Wilson

1985

Some background about Congressman Charlie Wilson (D-Texas) before Dale remembers him in a letter to a former colleague. The following quotes are from *Texas Monthly*, published in the June 2004 issue.

*"A lot of terms were used to describe seventy-one-year-old former U.S. Congressman Charlie Wilson when he represented deep East Texas on Capitol Hill from 1973 to 1996, and 'hero' was not typically among them. 'Hopeless alcoholic' was. So too was 'pussy hound.' And the occasional, less colorful term, like 'self-serving' or 'vindictive.' He was reputed to be a hard-drinking, coke-snorting, skirt-chasing, lightweight lawmaker, a water carrier for the timber industry, and worst of all, a pork barrel liberal. Though folks back home always loved him, up in D.C. there were plenty of people who considered him a joke, more notable for the good-looking women he squired around the world on the federal dime than any law he ever authored or sponsored."*

*"In a 1988 Ms. Magazine piece by Molly Ivins, he provided the following justification for the hiring practices that had earned his secretarial staff the nickname Charlie's Angels: 'You can teach 'em to type, but you can't teach 'em how to grow tits."*

*"And that easily could have been the final word on his legacy. But last May, 60 Minutes producer George Crile published a book called Charlie Wilson's War. It told a story not widely known beyond retired CIA spooks and cold war scholars, of how a lone congressman in the eighties had channeled more than $3 billion to Afghan rebels fighting the Soviet Red Army and how that aid had ended the cold war."*

*"Suddenly Charlie Wilson, Party Boy, became Charlie Wilson, Patriot."*

**Jim Tiffany**

**From:** Dale Ackels
**Sent:** Monday, January 07, 2008 8:47 AM
**To:** LJ
**Subject:** Charlie Wilson's War

Larry: OK, I've seen the film and the History Channel documentary, and I've read the Criles book, and as mentioned earlier I was involved in part of this.

As far as the movie goes, I liked it very much. It's very well done and nicely captured the feeling of that period of time and the politics of the situation. I particularly liked Tom Hanks as Charlie Wilson, except he made him smarter, funnier and more sympathetic than he actually was. But, it's still a fine movie.

Now to the grisly details. After FBNC I finagled a job on the Army Staff. I'd been operating off the books for almost five years and with a new wife and two children, I needed to get back into the mainstream of the Army. Regreening it was called, and for those who'd served at FBNC for any length of time, in that time and place it was mandatory if you ever wanted to be promoted again. And I decided I did. I was assigned to Strategy, Plans and Policy Division (or Directorate) as the Africa guy, but at that time I had absolutely nothing to do with Afghanistan, Pakistan or anything else in Central Asia. I'd been there about four months when the XO came in my office and dropped the file on my desk. Until I opened it I had no idea anything of that nature was underway. The file dealt primarily with the STINGER xfers. Until I saw the documentary I had no knowledge of the arms buys from Egypt or how we'd been supporting the Muj to that point.

Within a week, ten days at most, the first major problem appeared. We had already sold STINGER Basic to the Pakistanis and they were having trouble with it. Soviet acft were crossing into Pakistani airspace in pursuit of the Muj and the Paks couldn't hit them. Since STINGER was in the process of being fielded in our Army, and had never been tried in combat before the Paks started firing at Soviet border crossers, the credibility of the whole program was at stake and the Army had to respond to the Pak's concerns.

A friend of mine named Jerry Fry, also on the Army Staff, was the Pakistan desk officer. Jerry had been the Army Attache in Karachi, had some of the languages,
knew the organization and personalities of the Pakistani Army, and because of his assignment on the Staff was the logical guy to do it. He quickly put together what amounted to a STINGER MTT and flew to Pakistan to see what was wrong. He took with him several drones, a REDEYE, one or more STINGERs and a trained air defense gunner. A demo was arranged at their air defense school (if memory serves it was on the coast~on the Arabian Sea) and in the hands of a competent operator it was quickly shown that there was nothing wrong with the missile. Subsequent investigation showed the problem was lack of training and maintenance, and an organizational problem in that the missiles (MANPADS-Man Portable Air Defense Systems) had been taken away from the Chief of Air Defense and given to the frontline corps commanders. Without a proponent the missiles quickly deteriorated and the gunners lost proficiency. The Pakistanis had just absorbed this lesson when the first shootdown in Afghanistan occurred. Engineer Captain somebody (I remembered his name as Abdullah, but in the documentary your friend Milt Bearden says his name was Jaffer or Gaffer. I'd go with Bearden. I wasn't in theater at the time and didn't hear about it for at least two days after it happened) crept out into the airfield at Jalalabad (?) and torched at least two Hinds. The movie shows three. I'm fine with that

2/5/2008

132

too. Any whole number is fine with me, but that shootdown demonstrated to our Congressional critics the system worked and had utility in that tactical environment, and I think it showed the Muj that we had given them a good weapons system. It also embarrassed the Pakistanis in that the Afghans could shoot down a Soviet plane, but they couldn't.

Inspite of the positive jolt the first shootdowns gave all of us, there were still problems. The Muj hadn't really mastered the system yet, and were very much inclined to fire out of range. The missile only had a slant range of 5-6 miles, and could be tricked by a snowbank or brushfire. The solution to the first problem was provided by MG Donald Infante, then the boss at our Air Defense Center and School. Within a few weeks he and his staff developed a simple template affair to be worn around the neck on a cord. It had three or four holes in it, and when held at arms length each hole corresponded to one of the Soviet frontline acft. If the gunner could identify the type of acft he was looking at all he had to do was hold the template up to the sky and when the wings or the rotor blades touched both sides of the MiG-21 hole or the Hind hole it was in range.

The solution to the other problem(s) involved better training for the trainers. The facility designed to train MANPADS gunners was called a Moving Target Simulator, an instrumented dome-like affair that simulated various engagement scenarios likely to be faced by a gunner in a NATO environment. At the time I believe there were only three in the World, one in Germany, one somewhere in PACOM(?), and the one at Fort Bliss. Infante made the one at Bliss available to us to train the trainers. By day it was used by US students, but at night it was used by 5th Group and Agency guys to perfect their skills so they could train the Afghans.

I had to laugh when they introduced the Vickers character as their weapons expert. I frankly didn't know there was an Afghan Working Group at Langley. I assumed somebody was managing it, but until I saw the documentary and read the Criles book I had no idea who. The way it really worked, we didn't hear a squeak from them until they got in a jam and or didn't know what they were doing. The Oerlikon business was a prime example. They didn't know an Oerlikon from a Krupp coffee maker. All they knew about Oerlikons was what they read in the manufacturer's manual, and it was our guys who had to try and convince them, and Wilson, that the Oerlikon was not the answer to their problem. Same for how to use STINGER. Once they got over there someone figured out they really didn't know how to use them. Over a long weekend I sat down and wrote tactical manuals for the employment of STINGER in Afghanistan and Angola. I'd been to Angola during the war for independence and knew the area where they would be used rather well, but I'd never been to Afghanistan and had to rely on two officers who had, and the two relevant field manuals, to come up with an abbreviated field manual for use in the high altitude, cross-compartmented terrain typical of that environment. I guess it worked. Planes started falling out of the sky.

The other guy who should have received credit in the documentary but didn't was MG Charles W. Brown. Charlie Brown. For some reason our whole branch got transferred from DCSOPS to DCSLOG, and when it did Charlie became our boss. In the Criles book he makes the point that Wilson couldn't have gotten away with what he did without Tip O'Neill's tacit consent. Charlie was my Tip O'Neill. The Vice Chief of Staff of the Army at the time was Max Thurman. One of the Vice's primary responsibilities, over and beyond running the staff, is to husband the Army's resources and I was in the process of stealing a large number of his STINGERS for something he most emphatically did not approve of. Charlie was a barely reformed Nebraska cowboy, with a Great Plains twang and a smoker's cough, and an odd way of sort of gliding down the corridors, as though his legs hadn't quite accepted he wasn't wearing boots. But he was wonderfully personable and insightful, an honorable man, and extraordinarily shrewd and capable. And, one of the most skillful bureaucratic infighters I've ever known. Thurman wasn't too hard on lieutenant colonels and majors, but he was death on colonels and general officers and Charlie took most of the tongue-lashings and abuse meant for me. I owe him a

2/5/2008

great deal, for this and many other things, and will always think of him with respect and gratitude. In fact it was Charlie Brown who first called my attention to the Criles book.

My part in all this was to provide the missiles, train and coordinate training for the trainers, develop the tactical manuals for the Muj and UNITA, and address problems; political and military that impacted on the use of the weapons in-country. One part of that involved symplifying the Program of Instruction for STINGER gunners. I discovered that about a third of the POI was diagnostics and maintenance. I suspected neither the Muj or UNITA would waste much time on that so threw it out and rewrote the whole thing to emphasize target identification, acquisition and training. One of the 5th Group NCOs who actually trained the Muj told me they took care of their missiles like they were camels. If the weapon whistled or gurgled or lit up when they twisted this or that nob they knew the missile was feeling well and would engage. If it didn't the missile was sick and needed attention from the Americans. Which usually involved a battery swap.

Since there were no moving target simulators where the training was being done, at one point the UNITA trainees were using the South African resupply acft to practice target acquisition. I don't imagine they'd have been particularly pleased if someone had told them, but nobody got shot down who wasn't supposed to so I guess it worked out.

When I left the program the Muj and UNITA between them had shot down 77 Soviet/Cuban acft. The *piece de* resistance was an IL-76 shot down in Angola with a full load of Cubans aboard. I've forgotten the body count but it was most gratifying.

Other odds and ends:
1. The documentary makes the point that the Army was opposed to turning over STINGER to the UNITA and the Muj. This much is true.
~ We were just fielding STINGER and hadn't yet equipped the Regular Army with upgraded MANPADS. Some frontline NATO units were still using REDEYE, a first generation system of considerably less capability.
~ We'd invested millions in the technology and were probably a full generation ahead of the Soviets at that point. There was a fear the missile would fall into Soviet hands and they would reverse engineer it, to our detriment. And something like that did in fact happen.
~ We understood the potential benefits of introducing STINGER into Afghanistan as well as anyone, but by this time we'd also heard about Charlie Wilson. Legislative Liaison had told us about his alleged drug use, his drunkeness, his hit and run, and his notorious lack of discretion, and we didn't want a program we'd spent millions on held hostage by an idiot's dream of justice for the Afghan people.
~ There was also the fear some of these missiles would subsequently be used against us or our partners in Western Europe.
~ By the same token we were also aware that this represented, to a degree, payback for Vietnam. A mildly funny story related to that point. During the period of the STINGERs greatest success our DATT in Moscow was invited to the Frunze Military Academy to make a presentation to the students and faculty. During the Q and A the bright young Popovs got on him about US assistance to Afghanistan and Angola. He listened for awhile then said, "I'll make a deal with you. We'll provide exactly as much assistance to the Mujahadin as you did to the North Vietnamese. How will that be?" That pretty much ended the Afghan discussion, but it's fair and accurate to say the Army and the program manager were conflicted over the xfer of these missiles to guerrillas.
2. In the documentary Charlie Wilson, the real one, says the Chief of Staff of the Army came to see him to explain why we shouldn't give STINGER to anyone outside NATO. I doubt it. The Chief was John Wickham, and he was the last senior officer to find out about it. When I briefed Vuono, then the DCSOPS, he asked me if the Chief had been briefed and I responded, "Everybody but him."
I don't think the real Wilson would know the Chief of Staff if he tripped over him. I suspect the man

2/5/2008

he saw was Charlie Brown.   One of those times I was with him.

3.   Clarence (Doc) Long was exactly as depicted in the film and documentary.
He represented a working class district in Baltimore~Bethlehem Steel and the shipyards were in his district~and he was virtually impregnable.   Primarily because he had the largest admin support staff in Congress.   Twenty or thirty people working on nothing but constituent complaints.   Long's district got the best service he could provide and they loved him for it, but he was not the brightest light in the harbor and held his chairmanship only by reason of seniority.   I've heard him make that exact same speech he made in the film several times.   They captured it perfectly.

4.   Mike Vickers: Inspite of my comment about his bona fides as a "weapons expert" I suspect he was a good guy.   I've looked at his picture and I don't recognize him, but that doesn't mean anything.   I would imagine he spent most of his time at Langley beavering away on the project; like everyone else trying to make chicken salad out of pig's knuckles.   Hats off to  him.

5.   Same general comment on Gust.   I've looked at the pictures of him until my eyes cross and he doesn't look familiar.   If he dressed the way he looks in the still photos I've seen I probably thought he was someone's bodyguard.   I'm kind of sorry I didn't know him.

6.   As for Milt Bearden, he does look familiar.   Can't say where, but it wasn't the Embassy.   I've never been there.   Possibly in the north, but more likely in Washington DC.   I understand he's a fine man. Give him my respectful best wishes and congratulations on the recognition he's received.   Anybody who can wetnurse Charlie Wilson for that long and to that effect deserves at least the Order of Bombas y Cuerpos, with a gold liver attachment and hernia belt.

7.   Wilson did have a STINGER launcher mounted over the door in his office.   Until I saw the History Channel documentary I didn't realize it was the one used to shoot down the first Hind, but it was there.

8.   One of the other players in this melodrama was Jay Garner, later appointed by the Bush Administration to be the first political czar in Iraq.   As a colonel he was running Artillery Branch in Force Development, the guys who decide how much of something the Army needs, and the STINGERS came out of his procurements.   He was the same fine man then he is now.   And reasonably good-humored about it.

9.   And finally the matter of Chuckie himself.

~ I freely admit I wasn't around him much, but much of that was by design
From what I'd heard about him and his antics I knew we weren't going to be exchanging Christmas cards, and after the program achieved critical mass I didn't want to screw it up by some untoward remark.   Particularly if it embarrassed Charlie Brown or the Army.

~ But, having said that he was an unlikable son-of-a-bitch, arrogant in a kind of infantile way and convinced of his own rectitude.

~ The Defense Attache used his C-12 (a militarized version of the Beechcraft Super Kingair 200)  to haul Wilson around in-country.   On one of his trips to the north (probably Peshawar) Charlie had one of his chippies along and the pilot wouldn't let her on government transport for the return trip to Karachi or Islamabad or wherever he was going.   As I heard it the pilot wasn't being difficult, that was just the rules.   Congressmen's wives were no problem, Embassy staffers and wives no problem, but mistresses weren't authorized and he stuck to his guns.
In the next Federal budget Wilson struck the whole C-12 flying hour program out of the appropriations bill.   The Air Force provided some training money from other funds, but the C-12 guys were having trouble remaining proficient, and the year after he did it two C-12s crashed with some loss of life.   No one can say Wilson's actions were the direct and proximate cause of the two crashes, but the C-12 had an excellent safety record and after the training funds were restored there were no more crashes for years.   He was just being himself, but in doing so he may have added two American scalps to his belt and that is unforgivable.

~ I also have some heartburn with his abortive foray into Afghanistan.   As a soldier I hate to see anybody's life put at risk to gratify the childish impulses of
an egomaniacal jerk.   If the Soviets had known he was in Afghanistan, and God forbid they'd captured him, how would that have played?   Bearden would have had to commit everything he had in the area to

2/5/2008

save or rescue him, with what result? I wasn't anywhere close by when he did it, but I suspect Bearden was. I can't imagine anyone would let Wilson go north without adult supervision. I'd be interested in hearing what he has to say about it.

~ And finally, I'm irritated that such a slender reed should receive so much credit for the efforts of the 200-300 Americans who actually made it happen. The Mike Vickers, Gusts, Infantes, Browns, Beardens, the 5th Group trainers, and all the others who actually made Wilson's one moment of inspiration and clarity a reality.

~ I understand since his retirement from public life he's become a lobbyist. That sounds about right. Buying drinks and finding women for congressmen. He ought to be good at that.

In short, I liked the movie but I'm still comfortable with my perceptions of the real Cocaine Charlie, the man voted one of the twenty least effective legislators in the House of Representatives by House staffers; a drunken, arrogant, whorehopping blowhard and bully. Having said that, I cannot begin to explain the pivotal role he played in all this, other than to characterize him as one of Lenin's useful idiots. As I mentioned once before, I doubt Lenin would appreciate the irony. If I'm ever near the Reagan Library I plan to stop by and see if there is some kind of PDM or presidential finding authorizing all of this. I can't believe Reagan or one of his senior staffers didn't know about or authorize it.

I should also mention in fairness that some of those closest to him still think he's a prince. Tomorrow I'll send along a msg from one of his former staffers who thinks he's wonderful. Further deponent sayeth not.

2/5/2008

# CHAPTER 12

## Kenya

### 1987-1990

# LETTERS FROM A FRIEND

In the summer of 1987, the Ackels family went off to Kenya. Officially, Dale was the Chief of the Kenya-US Liaison Office at our embassy in Nairobi and the senior US military officer, reporting directly to the US Ambassador.

In an earlier day, he would have been called Chief of the Military Advisory Assistance Group (MAAG), or our Defense Attaché.

*"I ran a $211m equipment delivery and training program and assisted the government of Kenya with water projects, anti-poaching projects and anti-smuggling programs of various types."*

That's Dale's description. My belief is that his reach and effectiveness went well beyond his official duties and responsibilities due to his life-long interest in the environment, animals in danger of extinction and his influence and relationship with our US Ambassador, his boss.

Among other accomplishments, Dale organized and coordinated the construction of a 4,600-foot airfield in a remote corner of Northeast Kenya to facilitate the Government's anti-poaching efforts. He also brought potable water to a quarter of a million residents of the Coast Province of Kenya, plus qualifying Kenya for African Coastal Security funding to improve fisheries protection and narcotics interdiction capabilities.

I visited Dale, Bet and the boys with my son after Chris's graduation from high school in the summer of 1990 before he entered the Edmund A. Walsh School of Foreign Service at Georgetown University.

Upon our arrival in Nairobi, Dale said we were first going to stop at the Ambassador's residence before going home to see Bet and the boys and get settled.

*"The Ambassador would like to meet you. He's heard a lot about you".*

I knew that to be sheer nonsense. Dale wanted my son to meet the Ambassador, since Christopher aspired to be a Foreign Service Officer but, of course, Dale knew I'd enjoy the encounter as well.

I believe Dale enjoyed a relationship with the Ambassador unlike his Embassy brethren; it was evident as soon as we arrived at the Ambassador's Residence. Dale was greeted more like family than a staff member with almost an informal "Hello, Colonel" and an easy smile by the house attendant, who then only said "Library". We walked in, unaccompanied, Dale obviously knowing the floorplan.

After introductions, the Ambassador simply said, *"Dale, pour yourself and Jim a drink, you know where everything is."*

Curious? You bet. Unusual? Certainly. From my limited experience with Ambassadors, I believe that this Ambassador depended on Dale more than any other of his direct reports. Why? Because Dale, as I later concluded, probably knew more about everyday Africa than he did and the Ambassador enjoyed every official, formal discussion, but probably most ... those "over scotch" informal opportunities and discussions with Dale.

Ambassador Hempstone was appointed by President George H.W. Bush in 1989. He was not a Foreign Service Officer who ascended through the ranks of the Department of State, but he did have some qualifications required to assume the post, unlike some Republican Presidential Ambassadorial appointees later in the next century. He was a journalist and a correspondent when Kenya was fighting for independence; and editor of the Washington Star as well as a fellow who had lived and worked in Africa.

He was, indeed, a firebrand, and I think he recognized Dale in a similar light, albeit with a quieter dedication, less histrionics, more contemplative, and a knowledgeable Africa expert.

The first letter was written to his parents in Sebastopol, CA shortly after he arrived in country. The facetious Dale comes across, addressing them as Mr. & Mrs. Ackels.

The other letters need little explanation, beyond the fact that many of the referenced enclosures are not included.

2 October

# SERENA LODGES & HOTELS

| | |
|---|---|
| Post Office Box 48690 | Proprietors: |
| Telephone 339800/339801/29039 | Safari Lodge Properties of Kenya Ltd. |
| Tel. (Reservations) 338656/7 | Management Company: |
| Telex 22878 Cable Serena | Tourism Promotion Services |
| Nairobi, Kenya | (Management) Ltd. |

Dear Mr and Mrs Ackels:

You'll be surprised, perhaps even shocked, to learn that some LOL in California
is sending me notes implying I haven't met my letter-writing responsibilities
lately. To lay this vile canard to rest yet again I thought it best to
provide you with another timely update.

First, the photographs and the article. I mentioned in my last letter that
Bet and I visited the northeastern distribution center for wild horses and
donkeys just prior to our departure. These were some of the better looking
animals. Most are about the size of Welsh mountain ponies, with narrow
chests and not much power in their hindquarters, but as the photo of the
sorrel in the stall shows, they feed up into nice looking small horses. They
had one corral full of 4-7 year old stallions. That was a lively lot. They
told us people buy them anyway, presumably to have them gelded. The guy
working the corrals said a lot of those come back. They prove a bit much
for someone looking for a gentle old plug to hack around on.

Bet and the boys seem to have made the transition without unusual difficulty.
The household stuff is all here. We're in the process of swapping out some
furniture to convert one bedroom to a TV/computer room; also getting some
shelves built for the garage. Bet is signed up for the KNOW KENYA course
at the National Museum. Five or six weeks of history, culture, anthropology,
geology, religions, insects, flora, fauna, gemstones; in brief everything
anyone wants or needs to know about Kenya. She's going to know more of real
substance about Kenya than I do when she finishes. The first lectures
on early man are to be presented by Dr Richard Leakey, the son of that
Leakey and Director of the National Museum. The other lecturers are
equally distinguished, though perhaps less well known.

Bet has also tried the cuisine. At various times Nile perch and tilapia;
kongoni (Lichenstein's hartebeest), zebra, and giraffe; nyama (a meat
stew flavored with red peppers and tomatoes); ugali na sukuma (mealies
and chopped greens), kachumbari (chopped fresh tomatoes, red peppers and
onions-used to flavor meat); and matumbo (goat stomach). I confess she
didn't eat a heaping portion of matumbo, but she ate it, and she likes
roasted goat just fine.

She's also gotten into the social side of the job, though like me she seems
to enjoy the less formal outings a bit more than the formal events. The
only times I think she might have been a bit nervous were the first
reception at the Ambassador's residence, and a couple days before our
first dinner party for a mixed group of Kenyan officers and CENTCOM
staffers. Twenty minutes after she reached the Ambassador's residence
somebody walked up and said, "I thought you said your wife was new to
this business. She's working this crowd like Jesse Helms." I told him
I doubted she would appreciate the comparison, but after watching her
for a few minutes I had to agree. An outsider would have thought she had
been brought up on the cocktail and canape circuit.

A couple weeks ago she attended a tea for the newly arrived wife of the
Egyptian Defense Attache. Wives only. She got into a spirited discussion
of the difference between Sunni, Shiite, and Sufi Moslems wives, and apparently

141

had a hell of a time. She's also developed a nice touch with the Kenyan wives. We were at the Officer's Mess in Jamhuri Park a couple nights back for a Kenya Army affair. I kept seeing Bet and three of the Kenyan wives standing in front of the bar roaring with laughter. Everytime I went over there to see what I was missing everyone straightened up and went Somali on me. Still don't know what that was about, but Bet and her partners in crime had the best time of anyone there.

She's also found a couple American wives she likes, and she likes the wife of the commander of the German Military Mission, and Wing Commander Mayer's wife (UK) quite well.

The boys seem to have made the adjustment fairly well. Travis is involved in his autumnal bout with established authority, though I don't think his heart is really in it. Sort of going thru the motions because it's expected of him. Derek is probably having the most difficulty. He likes Kenya and his school just fine, but his usual method of expressing his individuality doesn't play very well here. Both his peers and his teachers are rapidly growing tired of his shrieking fits and temper tantrums, and the principal has threatened to disenroll him permanently if he doesn't stop getting into fights with the other kids. That seemed to get his attention. Since Travis had a great deal to do with teaching him these wonderful tricks, we've enrolled Travis in the program of retraining him. Can't say his heart is in it, but the thought of having Derek in the United States and his nibs still in Kenya seems to give him pause.

Their school is everything we hoped it would be. In addition to the international flavor of the faculty and student body, and in Derek's case, the much needed discipline and restraint, there are the field trips, the exposure to Swahili and French (they sometimes come home from school singing in Swahili), and the artist in residence program. Right in the middle of the campus they've built a rondavaal, which is occupied for several weeks at a time by a local artist. At the moment I think it's a local woodcarver and sculpter

We've taken the boys to Nairobi National Park twice, and two weeks ago we took them to Tsavo East for the weekend. Their reaction was a bit comical. They seemed to have trouble understanding this was really Africa and those were real animals. About the time Mike Brown parked his Toyota under a giraffe's stomach, close enough that they could see the ticks on his legs, it occurred to them there wasn't going to be station break or a fund raising telethon in the middle of this.

Bet has already told you something of Henry. His full name is Henry ODEMO Amukhaya. He's a member of the Marigoli Clan of the Baluhya, and comes from a village near Kakamega in Western Province. In case you left your African atlas at Sardine, that's near Lake Victoria in southwestern Kenya. In addition to his culinary skills (he cooks Danish, Greek, Americo-Brit, and African specialties with equal facility), he takes care of the house, organizes parties, tends bar, picks up the kids, does the shopping, and does huge abstract flower arrangements all over the house on any pretext whatever. All this for $109.09 per month.

There was supposed to be a shamba man (gardener) named Zebulon in here somewhere but he got involved in investment banking shortly before our arrival and withdrew from our service. Seems his brother was a cashier in a local bank, and embezzled 1.3M Kenya shillings (/=). 1.3M/= translates into $79,171US. Zebulon and his brother have apparently taken their overdraft and gone to Tanzania

there to buy more cows and wives and enjoy the fruits of capitalist
enterprise. Our new shamba man is named Albert NDEDA Mega. He's Henry's
first cousin. Even if he were inclined to slack off, Henry wouldn't let
him.

There is, of course, one other member of the family not yet touched upon.
Before we left we told you about Vessey and her problems with Dobermanns.
There is reason to believe she not only killed the present Israeli
ambassador's dog; she may also have killed the previous ambassador's
dog. Vessey is half Belgian shepherd and half Rhodesian ridgeback.
Ridgebacks are a breed developed in Rhodesia to course lions. As you
might expect, guard dogs are a frequent subject at cocktail parties.
Names like Tusker, Brawn, Simba, Snapper, and Tubbs gives you some
feel for what we're talking about. My personal favorite is Tubbs,
an oversize Malemute that looks like he could pull a chuckwagon.
The weekend after we arrived I took Derek down our road to
look at Tubbs--thru his front gate. Tubbs trotted down the driveway
to look us over, whuffed a couple times, and wagged his tail. Derek
took one look and vomited on my shoes, whereupon the mighty Tubbs
chuffed politely, turned on his paws and walked off. Don't know
if he was disgusted or secretely pleased with the sensation he'd
created. Even in this elite group of canine sociopaths, Vessey
enjoys an exalted reputation, though she is getting a bit long
in the tooth, if you'll pardon the pun. Fortunately, she likes
honkies just fine, even little ones. Derek is her special friend.

Our car hasn't arrived yet, but I've purchased a 1977 Audi Fox for
driving around town. Cost me $2000, which probably seems like a
great deal but compared with the $40,000 tag on a new Mercedes
or $17,000 for a four year old Landrover is quite reasonable.

One of the interesting things about Kenya is the public transportation.
You've heard of jeepnys in the Philippines and jitney busses elsewhere
in the Third World. The African equivalent is called a mammy wagon in
West Africa and a matatu in the Swahili speaking parts of East Africa.
The drivers are paid by the ton-mile or some other such arcane formula.
However it works, mileage has something to do with. In addition to gaudy
paint jobs, matatus are distinguished by their disregard for traffic
regulations, and the spectacular body counts racked up when they hit something. A good matatu crash rivals the best German alpine expeditions
for bloodshed and general mayhem. Sixteen people packed in the back
of a Toyota ½-ton have to go somewhere. If more than one matatu is
involved half the province is liable to be in mourning before they
get the parts sorted out.

Matatus are also distinguished by the slogans and good-news sayings
frequently painted on the front. It's not generally known, even in
my own family, but I am the Smithsonian's designated repository for
matatu and mammy wagon slogans. Number one on the list--FLEE FORNICATION
PLACE THY FAITH IN JESUS--was spotted in Nigeria in 1975. I was never
clear in my own mind whether I was to flee fornication in that particular
mammy wagon, or just flee in general. Since arriving in Kenya I've added
three more to the permanent collection: WHITELINE PEKEE, DELTA FORCE,
and SUCCESS IS MY LOVER. In adding these worthy selections to the master
listing I've considered and rejected the candidacy of RED HILL (redundant,
most hills in Kenya are red), MAEDELEO SUPER LINER (no imagination),
LOVE TRUCK (see also RED HILL), KAMWENA SUCCESS (ho hum), WEAVERBIRD
(good ethnics but too obvious), MATCO BUILDS--JESUS SAVES (a near thing),
and of course, BIONIC SUPER LINER. I had just finished this when the
attached WASH PCST article on matatus appeared. A trivial bit of research
but I suppose I have to include it for completeness.

In case you need to call our number is:

*overseas operator* *country code* *city code* *number*

```
011   254   2    52 08 56 (home)
                 33 82 18 (work)
                 33 41 41 (work)
                 x215
```

Your phone book won't show a city code for Nairobi, but one has recently been assigned and you need to use it to get thru.

Christmas lists will be arriving shortly. Need yours also. To reach us by 25 December packages need to be in the mail by 17 November, and cards by the end of the first week in December.

I've enclosed a couple clippings from the popular press. Press freedom is an issue here at the moment. In my next missive I'll talk more about it. That, and Kenya's human rights record, seem to occupy most of Western presses (whatever the plural is) attention.

All for now.

*Dale*

P.S. In case you get curious and want to try it, my local mailing address is Box 30137, Nairobi, Kenya. I'm sending Nan a copy of this letter, but I'm also sending her a shorter note thru the international mails to see how long it takes.

# KENYA

COL & MRS. A. D. ACKELS
BOX 71 KUSLO
APO NEW YORK 09675

12 Aug 88

Dear Jim:

Several years ago you and I talked briefly about packaging adventure
travel in Africa.  As I recall, it was sometime after you hired that guy
to run canoe trips in the upper Midwest.  Bet and I have just completed
an 11 day safari through northern Tanzania and I thought a description
might prove useful, if you ever decide to look at adventure travel again,
or you subsequently send a group to  Tanzania on a hunting or photo
safari.  I'm also going to give a copy to several friends in KUSLO, so
in several places I've also included information of interest only to
local travellers.

You may recall I visted Tanzania twice before, both times in the
mid-70's.  The first time I drove thru the northern parks in a VW combi,
the second time I landed at Dar es Salaam and drove inland to Morogoro,
then turned south to Mikumi and the northern Selous.  Tanzania was not a
particularly friendly place in those days, and it subsequently got less
friendly as their economic situation became more worrisome and the
gains they expected to realize from their particular brand of home-grown
socialism failed to materialize. Somehow it was all our fault.

In apparent recognition of the failure of his economic and social
theories, the man who took them to independence, one Julius Nyerere,
resigned his post as chief of state, and moved into semi-retirement,
though retaining his post as secretary of the single legal political
party.  He apparently wanted a younger man with newer ideas to take over
day-to-day administration of the government, but he hung on to the party
post to insure the ideological content of the regime remained more or
less intact—in the face of what he apparently expected would be an
onslaught of slavering capitalists eager to pillage fair Tanzania.
Instead of the chairman of Union Carbide and Rupert Murdoch he got
Abercrombie & Kent, plus Bet and I and two kids.  What follows then is a
reasonably factual account of our recent visit, and what touring and
tourism have become in the Socialist Worker's Paradise of Tanzania.

Our plan was to enter Tanzania at the Namanga border crossing, spend a
few days at Moshi and Arusha,( on the southern slopes of Mt Meru and
Kilimanjaro), then turn westward to Ngorongoro Crater, Olduvai Gorge,
and Serengeti, exiting thru Bolongonja Springs and the Sand River
Crossing into the Masai Mara.  When you look at a map all this looks
entirely sensible and reasonable.  We would  enter Tanzania in the
northeastern quadrant of the country, do a little sightseeing around
Kili, then turn west in a gigantic duck hook thru the northern tier of
game parks, reentering  Kenya at a seldom used but apparently  legal
border crossing in the West.  Sensible, but undoable.  To maximize use
of their hotels and tourist facilities the Tanzanian Government won't
let normal tourists out of the country at Bologonja.  They want them to
come back across the northern parks and exit again thru Namanga.
To insure they do it, TZ customarily takes away your vehicle log
book at Namanga, without which you cannot prove you own a vehicle
in Kenya.  It's fairly effective with tour operators, but a local Brit

145

told me there was a way around this particular obstacle, and with the judicious application of a little mata bicho I found he was right.  We left Nairobi on 30 July with a signed border pass allowing me to cross at Bologonja.  Assuming the functionary on the border recognized it, we should be able to follow our plan and drive back into Kenya 8 days later without difficulty.

30 July

We left Nairobi about 1230, after working thru a couple last minutes delays with an air filter, crosschecking equipment lists, and sorting out the kids stuff.  Something about whether it was better to take the laser ray gun or the GI Joe special forces machine pistol.  Best not to go into a foreign country undergunned,I suppose.  Once we got that sorted out, the three and a half hour drive to Namanga proved to be pleasant beginning.

The border crossing is chaotic on both sides, but they seemed to give the tour operators and Asians a harder time than they gave me.  We had been told we would have to pay $65 USD in cash for car insurance and road tax, but no one asked me for it and I never did pay it.  Days later at Bologonja the customs officer asked me for my insurance papers.  I told him I didn't have to pay it because my Trooper had CD plates on it. He seemed to accept that.  Still don't know for sure, but I think it's wise to plan on paying it at some point, even if you have a plausible story and can bluff your way past the border.

Once thru the border crossing the terrain  begins to change almost immediately.  The country is drier,the vegetation is different (more like the scrub country around Tsavo) and the road improves markedly.  Kenyan roads have fallen into noticeable decline lately, and the relatively smooth, hard-surfaced road on the Tanzanian side was a welcome  surprise.

The road winds around the western side of Mt Meru, into the mountain town of Arusha.  Once a German administrative HQ, the town is now the center of tourist activity in this part of TZ. ( If you ever have a chance to see the old John Wayne adventure film HATARI, the final scenes of an otherwise laughable movie were shot in downtown Arusha.)  We'd made arrangements to spend the first night in the Mt Meru Game Sanctuary, a small hostelry and private game park, recently taken over by Abercrombie and Kent at the request of the Tanzanian Government.  There are other larger hotels in the area, but they haven't yet recovered from years of mismanagement and government interference.  With the possible exception of the New Arusha, I don't recommend any of them.

The hotel itself is quite pleasant.  Our banda (cabin)  overlooked a mandmade pond visited by flamingoes and two kinds of storks.   Eland, zebra, ostrich, waterbuck, and several smaller gazelles also roam the grounds, making it a pleasant and peaceful sort of place to unwind and think about the day's travels.  About half an hour after sundown I heard a lion call about a mile to the south and east of us.  For obvious reaons it caught my attention, but I thought it too far away to represent any immediate threat, and aside from shushing the kids I did nothing about it.  Two or three

minutes later it was answered with the full-throated roar of
a hunting lion about 80 feet in front of our cabin.  Travis was
standing with us on the porch, but Derek had gone down the hill (in the
direction of the roar) to look at some of the caged animals.  Bet's
immediate reaction was that her youngest son was down there somewhere in
the dark, about to become finger food for a large and hungry lion.  The
last thunderous grunt had barely died away when I saw some sort of
dimunitive little creature dart out of the shadows, bent over at the
waist, and running like its tiny little life depended on it.  The
creature went by me so fast I was unable to confirm it was my son, but
whatever it was wore Derek's T-shirt so I decided without much further
deliberation to follow it back to the cabin.  I found Derek sitting on
the bed, his eyes the size of hardboiled eggs and his little legs
shaking uncontrollably, but otherwise unharmed.

One of the askaris ambled out from behind our banda about then.  I asked
him if by chance they had a lion caged up in the sanctuary.
He laughed and said they did.  Poor Derek had been standing
on the other side of a hedge from the brute when he
roared.  He must have thought his end had come.  I confess
I was a bit worried myself.  The situation was not beyond salvage
with a .458 Winchester, but as I started down the path I had nothing
but a tumbler of Metaxa brandy to chunk at it, and I felt more than a
bit foolish and vulnerable.

31 July

The day began with a shopping run to Arusha.  Bet and I bought souvenirs
for friends in the States, dickered with an Asian over several pieces
of particularly well-made Maasai beadwork, read the papers, and did a
bit of planning for the afternoon excursion to Moshi and Kilimanjaro.

Like Arusha, Moshi was once a German administrative HQ.  It has,
however, fallen on hard times.  The town is a dump, and the Moshi
Hotel is not fit for human habitation.  Apparently, the Tanzanian
Tourist Corporation hasn't gotten around to this one yet.

One of the reasons we wanted to see Moshi was because it's a jumping off
place for climbing expeditions going up Kilimanjaro.  I've been talking
with one of the guys in the office about climbing Kilimanjaro next year,
and I wanted to scout the lower part of the route and talk to the people
who run the expeditions.  I'd also been told there was a jeep trail up
to the 15,500 foot level, and I thought I'd try it while in the
neighborhood.

There are really only two tribes in Kilimanjaro District.  The Warusha,
nomadic stockmen, all but identical to the better known Maasai and
Samburu, and the Wachagga, a group of 100,000 odd farmers raising
coffee, bananas and maize on the south slope of Kilimanjaro.

Several years ago the Government of Tanzania made a concerted effort
to stamp out free enterprise among the Wachagga. Unlike most of
Tanzania, the Chagga had been doing rather well with their coffee, and I
suppose the Government felt they had to be reduced to the same level of
misery then being enjoyed by the rest of the country.  The Chaggas are
not fighting men, but they apparently resisted rather strongly.  At one
point I think they had to use the Army to impose socialist discipline on

147

the recalitrant coffee growers.  The Chagga responded by smuggling their
coffee across the border to Kenya.  I believe the Government has since
given up this foolishness and now lets the Chagga do pretty much as they
please without further meddling from Dar.

I never did find the jeep trail I was looking for.  We did try a 4WD
track leading to the village of Machame, but at 11,000 feet and change
we were still in Chagga coffee plantations and rapidly running out of
road  I subsequently learned the trail I was looking for was several
miles further east, at a turnout called Marangu, but that doesn't look
right on the map and I guess I'm going to have to do some additional
looking. Many Tanzanian maps are little more than negotiating positions.
Written statements of cartographic intent not meant to be binding on the
author. One should never bet the butter and egg money that anything will
be where the map says it is, unless you've already been yourself and
verified the location.

1 August

Decided to spend my birthday in Arusha National Park, just north of our
cabin at Mt Meru.  The area now encompassed within the Park,
particularly the Momella Lakes area, was originally settled by the von
Trappe family.  At least one of the grandsons, Dick von Trappe, still
lives in the area, making his living as professional hunter.

The park is 24 kilometers north of the Arusha-Moshi road, on a road that
barely qualifies as a cart track.  After touring the Momella Lakes we
came out of the Park and stopped for lunch at a new lodge called Ol'
Donyo Orok, which means something like black mountain or stone mountain
in Maasai. The place is run by a young native-born Tanzanian named
Stephanie von Menzius (as heard). Stephanie lost her husband in a plane
crash on Rubondo Island five months ago, apparently while leading a
photo safari.  They had started the lodge before his death and she's
trying to finish the building and get the necessary government permits.
The Momella Game Lodge is only 400 meters east of her place, but it's
badly run down and closed for repairs.  Lion Safaris of Nairobi has
taken it over and is doing the remodelling, but even when they get it
repaired I don't think it will be as pleasant as Stephanie's new lodge.
She's going to send us a flyer when she goes into business.  I'll send
you a copy.

Stephanie's lodge is also an excellent jumping off place for climbing Mt
Meru, and her assistant told me there is also trout fishing east of
there, on the slopes of Kilimanjaro.  When the Germans were still
farming the area they introduced trout to the western-slope streams.
The creeks are all overgrown now, and I'd have to get someone to show me
where they are, but the notion of virgin trout streams, untouched in 50
years and filled with brown trout, has a certain undeniable attraction.
My interest is based on the assumption the Chagga aren't dry fly
fishermen, or haven't got access to dynamite.

After lunch we visited Ngurdoto Crater, east of the Momella entrance but
still within Park boundaries.  It's a gorgeous little place. The walls
and rim are covered with lush tropical vegetation, and the floor is a
beautiful pale green sea of grass and water plants.  Just a few moments
after our arrival two Cape buffalo bulls charged out of cover on the
east side of the crater, followed immediately by five cows and calves.

While I was watching them cross the crater, Travis noticed three men and several fice dogs come out of the bush and look across the crater toward the departing buffalo. They weren't dressed as game scouts, and the dogs looked a bit suspicious, but I wasn't sure about them til they saw us and departed in some haste. I didn't know for sure where they were going, but I could hear their dogs coming up the side of the crater toward us and assumed they would go where their dogs went. Even if they only had bows and arrows they were still better armed than we were so we gathered up our brood and departed.

Several days later and a hundred fifty miles further west, I met a man who owned a farm in the area. He confirmed the men were poaching, and said they'd been doing it for several years--killing buffalo and giraffe for meat. The game scouts knew they were doing it, but were reluctant to push too hard for fear of retaliation by their friends and families.

I can understand the economic necessity for it, and Ngurdoto is certainly not the worst case of poaching of I've seen in the last 13 months, but on a very small scale it's still a tragedy. Ngurdoto is an astonishingly lovely spot; reason enough for visiting Arusha Park by itself, but something important will be lost when they've killed off the last buffalo and giraffe, including part of the rationale for keeping it a park.

Arusha is primarily for birdwatchers, but we did see some large mammals including Kirk's dik dik, red duiker, bushbuck, wart hog, zebra, giraffe and the previously mentioned buffalo.

2 August

In transit all day, from Arusha south to Makuyuni, then west to Karatu and a place called Gibb's Farm. Located 4 km north of the road, it's actually a working coffee plantation on the lower slopes of Loolmalassin Mountain. We couldn't see much of it that night, but when we got up next day we found it was on top of a west-facing ridge, with superb views to the south and west. The rooms are plain but clean, and the food is certainly adequate. Safari Lager isn't bad either.

Our previous day's route took us past the northern entrance to Lake Manyara NP. Manyara is the place Iain Douglas-Hamilton did most of the research for AMONG THE ELEPHANTS. I'd seen it once before many years ago, and enjoyed it, but I think Manyara is a park in serious trouble. In addition to the poaching, which I gather has been quite heavy, farmland is pressing up against the park boundaries on the east, north, and west. Even on the forested western side there are miles of coffee trees and wheat fields across the routes elephants would have to use to leave the park. I'm told the Government is trying to acquire a corridor of land to the south, linking Manyara with the much larger Tarangire Park, and giving the elephants a protected corridor out of their rather cramped quarters around the Lake. Hope so for their sake.

3 August

Gibb's Farm to Ngorongoro Crater. We reached it about two in the afternoon after a short but jarring ride. Since Arusha the roads have been abominable. We've torn the luggage rack off the roof, considerably expanded a small crack in the windshield, and cracked a weld in one of

our 5 gallon jerry cans.  By tying down the load with bunji cord,
borrowing screws from the rubber pads on the roof, scrounging several
sheet metal screws from the tractor shed at Gibb's Farm, and wrapping
one of the corner posts and crosspieces with hundred-mile-an-hour tape
we've been able to repair the luggage rack.  The rest of it we'll just
have to live with.

There are three lodges on the rim of the Crater: Ngorongoro Rhino Lodge,
Ngorongoro Crater Lodge, and Ngorongoro Wildlife Lodge.  Don't know
anything about the Rhino Lodge, but we tried the other two with somewhat
uneven results.  Our reservations were for the Crater Lodge.
Abercrombie and Kent took it over in April, at the request of the TTC,
They've made some repairs but it still doesn't amount to much
The walls are prefab concrete, bolted to steel stringers, and painted a
sort of dog's breakfast green.  A & K has slapped a lot of paint on the
outside, and done quite a bit with the Lodge and dining room, but some
of the roofs have collapsed and the interiors of the cabins are nasty.
That isn't a problem if you're paying tent camp rates, but for what
they're asking the accomodations should be better.  Our second night we
moved to the Wildlife Lodge.  Though operated by the TTC, it's far
superior.  The view is just as good, the food is better, and there's hot
water in the pipes.

The best thing about the Crater Lodge was waking up in the middle of the
night with the unmistakable feeling a large herbivore was grazing just
outside our window.  Bet got up to take a look, I suppose expecting to
find a Maasai cow or a goat,  What she found were three Cape buffalo,
the closest near enough to reach through the window and pat on the
fanny.  Almost a shame she didn't.

4 August

All day in Ngorongoro Crater.  This is the first real concentration of
game we've seen since we left Kenya.  Some 650 square miles in area, the
Crater is actually the caldera of a collapsed volcano. Somehow the
Crater has escaped the devastation visited on the other large
parks.  Probably because it's relatively easy to patrol.

In addition to 10-15 rhino, perhaps 50-100 elephants, and several
thousand zebra and topi, there are 14,000 wildebeest on the floor of the
Crater, with a generous sprinkling of the necessary predators.  The
first pride we saw had 21 lions in it, and we saw several smaller groups
and mated pairs during the day.  Our borrowed driver told us there were
4-5 prides in the Crater, though the population apparently varies as the
populations of prey animals fluctuate.  The rim isn't as steep on the
west side, and the wildebeest in particular move in and out of the Park
IAW the general patterns of migration further west.  The Crater is never
without game, but roughly 25% of the quadrupeds leave in the summer to
follow the movement of game into the Masai Mara.

One of the lion pairs we found wasn't doing anything particularly
photogenic so Bet opened her window and waved a white towel at them to
perk them up.  The lioness went from a full sprawl to red alert in some
smallish part of a second, rocking slightly from side to side to settle
her legs under her, and spreading and extending her front legs for
additional purchase.  I went clawing over the back of the seat trying to
pull in her arm, but fortunately, Bet sensed what was coming and stopped.

waving her towel. One more wave and we'd have had her in the truck with us. I don't think she's going to do that again. Aside from that, a most pleasant day and exactly the kind of thing we came to TZ to do.

That night I wandered into the A & K motor pool. For $3 their mechanic riveted the luggage rack back on. We shouldn't have anymore trouble with it but I'll play hell getting it off when it comes time to replace it with something sturdier.

5 August

The toughest days banging since we left Arusha. It's only 145 km from Ngorongoro to Seronera, but we finished demolishing our windshield, shook the newly repaired luggage rack loose, and partially unscrewed the dashboard. We spend a lot of time tacking accessories back on, but the engine, wheels, drive train and transmission are all holding up well and I can live with the rest of it if the running gear is still working.

We stopped for lunch at Olduvai Gorge, where Louis and Mary Leakey spent so many years digging up their ancestors. They've put in a small museum and there are tour guides available now to take visitors through the Gorge. It still isn't the most impressive piece of real estate in the World, but it's only 5 and 1/2 km off the road to Seronera, and for regular readers of the National Geographic, well worth the modest delay. Among other things we learned, this site has been worked by scientists of one kind or another since 1911, and its correct name is actually Oldupai Gorge. Oldupai being the Maasai word for the sanseveria robustus, a plant similar to aloe that grows widely in the area. Apparently the first Germans in the area mispronounced it. Must get off a rude letter to National Geo on this before I forget.

We picked up two stranded Italian tourists just east of the Naabi Hill entrance to Serengeti. Their driver had Land Rover parts scattered all over the road, but they didn't seem particularly worried at being out there without food or water. I don't think they even thought we'd done them a favor.

One of the reasons we wanted to come to Serengetti was to see the Seronera Lodge. It's in the process of being restored now, after many years of neglect. It was originally built by a friend of ours here in Nairobi. A man named Rob Marshall, a partner in a local firm called Dalgleish, Marshall, and a student of Frank Lloyd Wright. Though the doors don't all close, there's no hot water, the baboons sometimes help you unpack, and the food would make a spotted hyena retch, the Lodge itself is spectacular. Rob built it on a kopje, an outcropping of smooth, weathered stone typical of this part of Africa. The various public rooms are layered around natural stone buttresses, connected by concrete or stone passageways that wind through the natural outcroppings of rock. The boys immediately decided this was a place they wanted to stay forever. The swimming pool in particular, fascinated them. Though empty and dirty, it had been ingeniously attached to the side of the kopje like a swallow's nest. Two sides of it are natural rock, the third side is a free-form concrete wall anchored in rock at both corners. You enter it by walking down the sloping rock until you lose your footing and tumble into deep water. If there had been water in the pool we would have been able to swim to the manmade side, hook our arms

over the rim, and from our perch on the side of the kopje, look out over
miles of savannah and grasslands.

6 August

Our last day in Tanzania.  We are starting to catch up with the
migration.  At this time of year there are 1.5 million wildebeest,
several hundred thousand zebra, many thousands of topi and impala, and
quite significant numbers of buffalo and elephant at the north end of
the Park, all headed for the Masai Mara and better grazing.  Since
leaving Seronera we've started seeing more of them.  Some hillsides have
several thousand animals sprinkled over them, and we are seldom out of
sight of one or more herds of moving zebra or wildebeest, sometimes
mixed together in herds of many thousands.

We stopped for lunch at Lobo Lodge, another of Rob Marshall's creations,
and even more attractive than Seronera.  Lobo is the westernmost
facility in the chain of lodges spanning the northern parks; probably
also the most neglected and seldom used.  It's quite beautiful and
deserves better treatment.  I hope when the TTC gets itself properly
organized Lobo will get its fair share of the monies being devoted to
putting Tanzania back on the tourist map.

We saw klipspringers going and coming from the Lodge.  This is a new
animal for Bet and the boys, and Bet had a lot of fun watching and
photographing them.

One of the most problematical parts of the trip was the crossing back
into Kenya at Bologonja Springs.  We had a permiso signed by some fundi
in the Tanzanian High Commission, telling the immigration officer to let
us pass, but one never knows about these things and I was more than a
little curious to see how this worked out.  He gave us no trouble with
our documentation, but he refused to let us take out any Tanzanian
currency.  If I'd been thinking clearly I wouldn't have taken my
currency into the immigration building, but I had it all with me and I
didn't want to lie about it for fear he'd ask to see my wallet.

While he was reading me the appropriate parts of the customs manual a
young man sauntered in who worked for the Serengeti Research Institute,
Something about a study of quadrupeds and their relationship with the
predators.  Rather than give the money to the Government, I made an
on-the-spot donation of 6700 shillings to the SRI.  That's only about
$70, maybe enough to hang a radio collar around a topi's neck for a
month,  but the look on the immigration officer's face was ample
payment.

We crossed back into Kenya at the Sand River Crossing, without incident,
and headed for Kichwa Tembo, a luxurious tent camp on the northwest
corner of the Masai Mara where the water is always hot, the beer always
cold, and the boys would finally get to swim in a swimming pool.  Coming
into Kichwa Tembo an hour after dark I missed my turn.  Didn't realize I
was past it until we reached the ford on the Mara River.  Found the
right road on the second try, but 100 yards from camp I almost ran into
three cow elephants standing in the road.  Three maiden aunts, seen
dimly in the headlights, too engrossed in elephant affairs and perhaps
too well protected to give us a hard time.  For which I silently thanked
them.

7-9 August

For the next two days we explored the western third of the Mara.  We
have truly caught up with the migration now.  Long curling ribbons of
wildebeest are streaming into the Park from Serengeti.   Some of the
columns containing several thousand animals, each segment patrolled by a
nervous and belligerent herd bull, absolutely determined no other bull
will encroach on his section of the column.   Derek almost damaged
himself laughing when two anxious bulls heading in opposite directions
on the same side of a column crashed head-on into each other.  Both went
to their knees, though no visible damage was done to anything but their
dignity.  I have to admit wildebeest have never impressed me with their
strategic grasp.  In Angola I saw two bulls do much the same thing
trying to avoid a Land Rover, except in that case they knocked each
other out.

Plenty of lions about, we saw 17 in a single pride on the 7th and
another pair on the 8th.  A fair number of elephants, many of them said
to be refugees from the combat zone around Lake Manyara, and the
previously discussed hordes of wildebeest, topi and zebra.  Many of the
prey animals are still moving into the Park, just below the Mara Serena
Lodge.  It's been raining almost continually for three days, and the
roads are a morass, but in between sinkholes and bogs we saw the best
the Masai Mara and Serengeti (it's all one ecosystem) have to offer.
Had to trail all the way across northern Tanzania and reenter Kenya to
do it, but it was worth it.

9 August

Coming out of the Masai Mara we stopped at Cottar's Camp, some 7 km east
of the road to Narok, and just outside the northern edge of the reserve.
Bwana Charles Cottar has always been a subject of some interest to me.
He came to Kenya in 1915, as I recall, from that part of Oklahoma that
subsequently became the oil patch.  At various times a farmer and big
game hunter, he also established the first ferry service on Lake
Victoria. Fearless, abrasive, and spectacularly profane, he was killed
in 1940.  Run down and gored to death by a rhino.  For many years his
sons operated a safari camp and hunting concession in Tsavo, but when
hunting was banned, and the elephants in Tsavo began to disappear, they
moved to the Mara and bought a private home once owned by the famous
game warden, Major Lyn Temple-Boreham.  Cottar's Camp is run by the
grandson of Bwana Charles, a former PWH named Glenn Cottar.  I've heard
of him but never met him.

I liked his camp.  It's pleasantly rustic, has plenty of game around it,
and the food is the best we had on the whole trip.  No small matter in
my case, as you may recall.  Bet and I plan to go back and stay for
several days.  I'm not sure it would appeal to every tourist, but it had
the right combination of ingredients for us.

Some other details of passing interest.  First, the matter of money.
Tanzanian law requires that all services be paid for in hard currency.
You'll receive all your change in Tanzanian shillings, but at the end of
your stay you'll find there is no mechanism for changing shillings back
into any currency.  The best strategy is to take as many small bills as
you possibly can, and watch your shilling surplus carefully.  Outside
the tourist stops you can pay for meals, souvenirs, fresh food,

newspapers, gasoline, and various other necessities with shillings, but
in the hotels they accept only dollars or pounds. I don't believe
they'll even take Japanese yen. Some of the hotels claim they will take
American Express cards, but most of them don't have the necessary
forms, and in one case the machine that makes the impression was broken.
I had been forewarned that Seronera was out of American Express blanks
so I brought ten with me. When I took one out and presented it to the
desk clerk he picked it up at one corner and held it at arms length,
looking at it like something he'd found in a burn bag at the Mayo
Clinic. Finally he said, "How do I know you didn't print these
yourself?" I asked him what difference it made, so long as my card was
good I was still going to have to pay for it. He thought about that a
moment, then broke out laughing and said, "If Nairobi knows so much
about our business why don't they send us some blank forms?" I gave him
my entire supply, but it's still a good idea to bring extras. Doing it
the way we did it, figure $234.89 per day for everything: gas, oil,
food, film, rooms, parts, taxes, entrance fees, film developing and the
cost of repairing your car when you return.

Banking can also be a problem. I made my largest shilling purchase at
the Banki ya Biashara (Bank of Commerce) opposite the clock tower in
Arusha. It might better be called the Banki ya Kafka, particularly on a
Monday morning. You stand in line to pick up forms, then stand in a
another line to find out how to fill them out. Once they're properly
prepared you must go to a third window to pick up your money. Each bill
or traveller's check must have its serial number properly recorded, and
innumerable functionaries must stare meaningfully at the paperwork or
stamp it to make the thing official. I thought I'd finally put it all
behind me when I was directed to window 2 to pick up my money, but an
elderly German planter tapped me on the shoulder and told me that window
2 was actually window 1 and I was wasting my time in the line I was in.
It general it's probably easier to rob the sucker.

There's also a bit of a problem in carrying it around once you've got
it. Four hundred fifty US dollars translates into a pile of shillings
almost five inches high. I bought a massive hand-tooled belt wallet,
made out of skirting leather with a belt loop on the back. If a passing
bank messenger inadvertently stuck to  my wallet he'd have to break my
belt or pull my pants off to make off with my operational funds.

Somewhere about thirty pages back I believe I said something about the
roads. From Namanga to Arusha, and east to Moshi, they are excellent,
but from Arusha south and west to Serengeti they range from fair to
laughable. Jimmy Carter followed our route to Serengeti about a week
after we'd passed. In a later interview with President Mwinyi he
apparently told the president that Tanzania needed to do something about
its roads if it wanted to promote tourism in the northern districts. I
think that's a fair statement. On the other hand, the condition of the
roads probably acts to preserve the parks by limiting the numbers of
people who can reach them.

I had been told there was no gas west of Arusha; however, I found this
to be untrue. I left Arusha carrying 21 gallons in my tank, plus ten
gallons in jerry cans, but I found gas available at Makuyuni, Lake
Manyara, Karatu, Ngorongoro, and Seronera. I was told there was gas at
Lobo, but I didn't see it myself.

That's really about all there was to it.  Please thank Karen Jackson for
getting me on that July flight from Frankfurt.  Booking me as the
Albanian Minister of Sport, Culture and Heavy Industry was a stroke of
genius on her part.  I doubt if anyone at PanAm knows if Albania has any
sports, culture or heavy industry.   I didn't have time to buy a baggy
suit or spray my front teeth silver, but I think I carried it off fairly
well.  It wasn't as good as my Janos Kadar imitation, but it's the best
I could do on that kind of notice.

I know you're busy with your move to Birmingham.  Give my best to your
kids and Tina.

COL A. D. ACKELS
BOX 71 KUSLO
APO NEW YORK 09675

Dear Jim:

Don't quite know why this passion
for communication has come over
me, but here's another on a subject
having to do with tourism in
East Africa.  Unless the GOK
finds the will to deal with
this, tourism is certain to
take a nosedive.

I also thought you'd enjoy this
piece on Dawkins.  Don't know
what kind of press play he's
getting in Royal Oak, but
in the mid-Atlantic region
he's getting extensive coverage.
His campaign manager is the
grandson of Nick Longworth,
Speaker of the House in Teddy
Roosevelt's administration
and husband of the late Alice
Roosevelt Longworth.  Nick lived
across the street from us in
Alexandria, but we haven't seen
him since he took this job.  Be
interesting to see what Nick
thinks about Wonder Boy.

P.S. This letter was to Charlie
Askins.

# KENYA

30 Sep 88

COL A. D. ACKELS
BOX 71 KUSLO
APO NEW YORK 09675

Dear Charlie:

A month or two before my departure for Kenya I recall promising
you a letter on hunting in East Africa.  As usual, I'm a bit
tardy.  I suspect you'll find this depressing, but it may serve
to fill in some gaps in what you're hearing and reading in the
States.

One of the benefits of serving in Kenya is that I'm colocated
with two United Nations organizations whose activities bear
on the future of game and big game hunting on this continent.
I haven't yet figured out what UNDP does, but the United Nations
Environment Programme is a multi-nation agglomeration of bean
counters whose responsibilities include keeping track of how many
large game animals we've got left.

First, the rhino.  According to a UNEP study released in July 87
this is what's left.

| COUNTRY | NUMBER/TYPE | COMMENTS |
|---|---|---|
| India | 1100-1500/Indian | All in national parks |
| Nepal | 383/Indian | In two parks |
| Pakistan | 2/Indian 2/Black | Blacks are in zoos |
| Burma | Unknown | Population includes Javan, Sumatran, and Indian species |
| Indonesia | 53/Javan 200-400 Sumatran | |
| Laos | Extinct | |
| Malaysia | 57-79/Sumatran | |
| Botswana | 150/Black | All in Chobe Game Park |
| Burundi | None | See following paras. |
| Cameroon | 40-100/Black | In two game parks |
| CAR | None | |
| Chad | 6/Black | |
| Ethiopia | 4/Black | |
| Kenya | 400-415/Black 6-7/White | |
| Mozambique | 60/Unk | Located in reserves in Maputo Province |
| Rwanda | 10/Black | North end of Akagera Park |
| Somalia | 50 or less/Black | |
| RSA | 4343/Black & white | Count provided by RSA game officials |

| | | |
|---|---|---|
| Sudan | Several thousand/Both | Accurate count impossible with a war going on, but at least one of the insurgencies is probably financing their effort with the sale of horn and ivory |
| Tanzania | 200-300/Black | Government hasn't got the money or the inclination to do anything about poaching |
| Uganda | None | Wiped out by Idi Amin and Obote |
| Zaire | Unk/White | These are the northern white rhino-located in Garamba NP |
| Zambia | 100-600/Black | Probably the most threatened population on the continent |
| Zimbabwe | 1875/Black | |

By my count that comes to something like 12300 rhinos of all types left in the World, which is a catastrophic decline when you consider there were over 20,000 in Kenya alone just 20 years ago. At these rates of consumption there shouldn't be a flaccid pecker in Asia, and every Arab in Yemen should have a rhino horn handle on his toothbrush by now.

The elephants aren't much better off. I don't have data for the whole continent, but the attached readings will give you some idea of what's happened in East Africa. Kenya has lost 85% of its elephants in 15 years, Tanzania 53% in ten years, and Uganda 89% in 15 years. It's, of course, the unparalled rise in the price of ivory that's responsible. When your Dad started bringing you to Africa I'm told ivory sold for one pound sterling per pound of ivory. A recent issue of AFRICAN ECONOMIC DIGEST stated that a 5 kilo piece of ivory now brings $1000 USD in Hong Kong, and that over 1400 tons of ivory has been shipped from Africa in the last two years. That equates to approx 150,000 dead elephants. As I sit writing this the Government of Burundi is holding a single shipment of 87 tons, and Burundi doesn't have any elephants. That shipment alone is worth $15.7M USD, when and if Burundi decides what they're going to do with it.

Because the elephants have been driven into the parks most tourists don't realize what a beating they've taken. Amboseli, Masai Mara and Samburu actually have more elephants in them now than they had 15-20 years ago, but it's because they can't survive outside the parks any longer. I haven't seen a really good bull anywhere in Kenya except Amboseli. One night in April my wife photographed an old bull (one of a herd of eight) that was probably carrying 90 lbs to the side. A splendid old soak; he looked like a forklift with white tines moving off thru the gloom.

Since the 1976-77 ban on big game hunting in Kenya the plains game seems to be making a comeback. Buffalo are still plentiful, and waterbuck, impala, giraffe, zebra, wildebeest, topi, kongoni, and reedbuck are still common. In Samburu there are still gerenuk and oryx, and leopard and lion seem to be doing well enough. We also have legal hunting for upland game in Kenya, though the process of getting my shotgun registered has proven to be very complex and time-consuming. They're not so much worried about what I'd do with it as they are about what a thief might do with it.

I know you don't have much interest in fishing, but Kenya still has excellent fresh and saltwater fishing. I've been told when Teddy Roosevelt came thru here in 1909 he remarked that Kenya had everything a sportsman needed except good fishing. Stung to the quick the Brits subsequently introduced black bass to Lake Naivasha, and rainbow trout to the Aberdares and Mt Kenya. One of my friends caught 22 bass from 3-6 lbs in Naivasha last spring (in two hours), though I confess my boys and I haven't done that well yet. There are also Nile perch in Lake Victoria, to 250 lbs, but there's only one operator fishing for them and I haven't yet had time to try that.

The Kenya Coast also offers wonderful fishing for big marlin, sailfish, and yellowfin tuna. On a recent trip to Pemba Channel my friends and I caught 11 skipjack tuna, and raised and struck three marlin, the largest an estimated 300 lb black marlin that broke us off on the second jump. That's a lot of cat food, and I confess a lot of fun, too.

Not too surprising, I suppose, that these events disturb and depress me. I wanted to show my stepsons the country as I first saw it in 1975, but all I'm able to do is provide technicolor glimpses. The Rift Valley is settled now all the way to Nakuru, and the area around Narok is now all wheat farms. Tsavo is being fought over by police and poachers, and the game country north and west of the Laikipia Plains is all in farms now. Perhaps the only place left in the country where game still exists in pre-independence numbers and quality is a little pocket in the Mathews Range. I'm told the place is still paradise on earth.

Even the culture of hunting and the old way of things has almost vanished. Abdullah, the tailor that used to make safari suits overnight, now sells ready-made shirts and neckties. He can still make a safari suit, but it's made out of polyester and comes in colors that would make a self-respecting macaw throw up. No one in the shop but the old man can even remember when they did that kind of business. Rowland Ward now sells crystal decanters, wild-life prints, and wool lap robes, and the gun shop across the street from the New Stanley,where one could rent a heavy rifle or buy a box of .470 solids,is now the Elite Camera Store.

I suppose it's also possible I'm exaggerating the importance of all this. For my boys a quarter-of-a-million zebra and 1.5 million wildebeest in the Masai Mara are the good old days. Perhaps modern Kenya only pales by comparison, but I fear the trends I see and suspect Kenya lacks the political will to do anything about them before it's too late and something irreplaceable is lost.

Having said all that, I'm thinking of making another hunt in Africa before we come back. I'm in touch with a Hungarian hunter in Tanzania who seems like the right sort, but I'm looking for info on other possibilities. I can't afford another 30 day

*I suppose this paragraph seems a little contradictory. I'm not going hunting for elephants, lion, or other endangered critters. Just the common plains game and Cape buffalo. Nothing that's threatened. Wale*

swing thru Angola, but I'd be interested in any hot rumors (or hot hunters) you may ^have^ heard about.

My best as always--

P.S.  In an effort to acculturate my boys I read them books by   the early hunters and explorers as bedtime tales.  At the moment we working our way thru WANDERINGS OF AN ELEPHANT HUNTER by Karamojo Bell.  The youngest one is really into the story, but can't understand why Bell didn't use a machinegun. Child of the 21st Century.

P.P.S.  Shown below is a list of the attachments.

Encl 1 -- Dec 87 piece from THE NATION on the slaughter of the
          Mt Elgon herd.  Another case of too much publicity.
          National Geographic did a wonderful film on these
          cave-visiting elephants.  Next time anyone looked
          they had been annihilated.
Encl 2 -- Statistical summary of recent elephant survey in East
          Africa from the East Africa Wildlife Society's
          magazine.
Encl 3 -- Article from COASTWEEK ^on^ elephant population in Coast
          Province.
Encl 4 -- Aug 88 piece on solutions to the problem.
Encl 5 -- Aug 88 article on recent poaching.  This probably wouldn't
          have made the papers but some tourists heard the
          slaughter and took photos of the scene.  Government knew
          it would make the papers anyway, so.....
Encl 6 -- Richard Leakey weighs in with salvo against the Government.
          Film at eleven.
Encl 7 -- When the Government finally got concerned enough about this
          to put additional police in the field they ran into poachers.
          With these results.
Encl 8 -- More of same.
Encl 9 -- On the other hand, some of Kenya's traditional people
          are still hanging on.  This young man got quite a bit
          of play for killing a lion with a spear in his father's
          sheep pen.

JUL 1 8 1989

Dear Jim:

Just a quick note to pass on some
items of local interest, and thank
you for coming out to California
in June. I know my folks got
a big lift out of seeing you again,
and I always enjoy rambling
around the countryside and getting
caught up on your news.

In spite of the way she looked,
I fear my mother's condition
is worse. The cancer has reappeared
in her brain. She's agreed to
accept x-ray treatment & chemotherapy
but refuses to let them operate
on her again. If the first two
options don't work she's apparently
decided to die. As you might
expect, I have decidedly mixed
emotions about all this. As her
son I want her to fight it, but as
an adult I think she ought to
be able to weigh the choices and
decide her own fate. Mom and I
will get thru it however it ends,
but my Father is devastated. She's

the only person he ever cared about, and I know he thinks his smoking killed her, as indeed it probably did.

Big doings in tourism and wildlife management. Richard Leakey has taken over the wildlife department, promising to stamp out poaching. It's a shrewd move by President Moi. It takes advantage of Leakey's unquestioned skills as a fund-raiser, but if Leakey fails it's just another "cheeky white" who couldn't live up to his brag. Earlier today the GOK burned 12 metric tons of ivory—stuff confiscated from poachers over the last 3 years. ABC attended, as did most of the European press. 12 tons makes a hell of a pile of ivory, also hell of a PR gesture. Leakey was wandering around with a seй on his face—lip synching Moi's speech so the press wouldn't have any doubts who wrote it. Cheeky white.

Hope you're still planning to come out here after Thanksgiving. If you are you'll need to make plans well in advance. That's the beginning of the high tourist season. Rates go up and all the Germans in creation descend on the coast. Let me know if you want me to make arrangements at this end, or follow up on arrangements you've made.

I sent you 3 books on Japanese gardens before I left California. Let me know if they didn't arrive. I think I've still got the insurance stub around here somewhere. I also sent Tina a moderately smart-ass birthday card.

All for now — we're off to Mauritius & Seychelles.

Dale

# The Lake Manyara elephants

by Iain Douglas-Hamilton

The elephants of Lake Manyara formed one of the few populations I thought was safe. It is a small isolated park of incredible beauty, and well known in Africa for its high density of elephants and the ease with which they can be watched. Long-term elephant studies, initiated in 1966, made this one of the best-known elephant populations in Africa. It was the first where elephants were studied in the wild as individuals. Its small size makes it relatively easy to patrol, and for years it escaped the general East African elephant trend. This happy circumstance lulled me into a false sense of security.

For 20 years, I have flown periodic aerial surveys to count the elephants. From air and ground work, I knew that the population had gently increased from 1967 to 1985. In 1967 there were just over 300 elephants counted from the air and in subsequent surveys these increased to a maximum of 485 in 1981. 1984 and 1985 both gave slightly lower numbers, but well what might be expected from movements in and out of the park.

In November 1987, Professor Karim Hirji of the Serengeti Wildlife Research Institute, and I made another count. This time only 181 elephants were counted, by far the lowest number ever recorded. In just two years the population had more than halved. Dead elephants were at an all time high and numbered 94, giving a carcass ratio of 34 per cent. Just over half of the dead appeared to have died within the previous 18 months. Since dead elephants are difficult to spot from the air, it is likely that for every one we saw there was another we missed.

The Manyara elephants have now become much shyer and tend to stick in thick bush. They have almost given up the habit of walking out on the open shore in the evenings in huge herds, as used to be their custom (which is a sad loss for the tourists). The older age groups are under-represented and Patti Loesche, who studied them last year, repored that she saw one wounded elephant per day on average.

During my trip around the park for the survey, I saw one elephant with spear wounds at the Musasa river, half-way down the park. I saw none of the old matriarchs that I knew before, but I did see the three young matriarchs Tuskless, Virgo and Phoebe. One of these had no tusks, another only one. Otherwise there were no large elephants, either bulls or cows, to be seen in the park. It appears that almost every elephant over the age of 30 is missing, and must be presumed killed. It is as if a whole older generation has been wiped out.

The drop of -25 per cent year over two years is much worse than the national average. In the Selous Game Reserve, for example, elephants were decreasing at a rate of -5.5 per cent per year.

The Manyara elephant situation shows that there is nowhere that the safety of elephants can be taken for granted. If it is considered as an indicator population, the implication is that elephants are decreasing in Tanzania and possibly elsewhere faster than has been realised.

It is possible that this sudden negative trend is related to a further rise in the price of ivory. Although I have no data on the price of ivory in Tanzania, it is known that the international price of ivory showed a sharp increase in 1987. One major batch of ivory sold in Brussels at a price of about $150 per kilo, compared to $100-120 the year before. The danger is that poachers will find an incentive to come after even the small and supposedly well-protected populations like that of Manyara.

The Tanzanian national parks authorities have taken action since receiving the count report, and anti-poaching operations in Manyara have been redoubled. They still lack equipment, however, especially transport for the anti-poaching operations. It is to be hoped that international donors will step into the gap and provide a rapid response in terms of transport, equipment, fuel and whatever is needed to protect this unique population.

In addition, the ban on private trade in ivory in Tanzania needs to be reinforced, especially by consumer countries, preventing illegal Tanzanian ivory from being imported and entering their markets. It would help greatly if a TRAFFIC office were to be set up in East Africa to help monitor ivory movements abroad and, through the CITES quota system, to identify which ivory is legal and which illegal. If the illegal ivory could be eliminated, the pressure on the elephants would be greatly reduced.

# Kenya Times

### The Voice of the People

TUESDAY, AUGUST 30, 1988     PRICE 4/00     Vol. 2 No. 170

# ELEPHANTS' GRAVEYARD

## Poachers slaughter 92 animals in the last sixteen weeks

THE government has launched a full-scale operation following the killing of three rangers and 92 elephants by poachers in various national parks and reserves in the past four months, the Minister for Tourism and Wildlife, Mr George Muhoho said yesterday.

Speaking at the National Museum of Kenya yesterday, Mr Muhoho condemned the recent indiscriminate killings of elephants and the three rangers.

He said a contingent of police and administration personnel have already been deployed in the affected areas.

They have so far recovered from the poachers, 12 ivory tusks, 181 rounds of G3 automatic rifle ammunition, one empty G3 rifle magazine and a wide range of personal effects.

The minister said some bandits have been shot and wounded and other suspects are helping police with investigations.

Mr Muhoho appealed to peace-loving wananchi to come forward and help security forces by reporting to the authorities the presence of snares and suspicious characters in their areas and national parks.

The minister assured this country and visitors that the affected areas are safe and that his ministry will maintain vigilance and enforce maximum protection for humans and wildlife.

Three game rangers were on Saturday morning shot dead by armed bandits who ambushed them as they were driving through a bush off a remote market place on the Mwingi-Garissa road.

Mr Muhoho disclosed that in the last four months, 64 elephants have been killed in the Tsavo and the surrounding reserves, 11 in Kora National Reserve, 8 in the Isiolo

— *By HENRI CHUI and FRANCIS MUROKI*

National Park and in Shaba.

Meanwhile, an Assistant Minister for Planning and National Development, Mr Noor Abdi Ogle, yesterday condemned last weekend's killing of the three game rangers.

And he appealed to the government to leave no stone unturned until the perpetrators of this criminal act are flushed out and brought to book.

The assistant minister advocated for stiff punishments against the criminals saying: "It is only after ruthless actions are taken against these that we shall discourage poaching, acts of banditry and the menace of lawlessness."

Mr Ogle, who is also MP for Wajir South was reacting to an exclusive story carried by Kenya Times yesterday in which three game rangers were shot dead on Saturday morning by armed bandits who ambushed them as they were driving through a bush off a remote market place on the Mwingi-Garissa road.

Mr Ogle called on the game department in the area to mobilise all resources at its disposal to ensure that the poachers are rooted out.

'The Central African Republic's presidential Guard seized the largest haul of poached ivory in the country's history five tons from some 500 elephants. The largest tusks weighed 65 pounds and came from adult males; the smallest, weighing no more than 18 ounces, were from baby elephants and would have netted the poachers less than a dollar apiece.'

*Conde Nast Traveler*
September 1989

## AMERICAN EMBASSY
## NAIROBI
## ADMINISTRATIVE NOTICE

July 31, 1989
AN-115-89

TO:       All American Employees of the Mission

FROM:     ADM/C - Terrance M. Day

SUBJECT:  Travel Advisory - Kenya - Caution

The following travel advisory was released by the
Department of State today and is repeated here for your
information.

"The Department of State advises American citizens that
when visiting Kenya the following basic precautions should
be taken:

"There have been a few instances of attacks on tourists
along the coast south of Mombasa and in remote areas of
the country, including some national parks. Most of these
attacks, some of which resulted in deaths of tourists,
have been attributed to heavily-armed wildlife poachers.
When visiting game parks, Americans are encouraged to
travel in groups with a guide from a reputable safari firm
or a game ranger.

"Travelers should consult a knowledgeable physician about
the need to take precautions against chloroquine-resistant
malaria and other diseases prevalant in East Africa.
Occasionally, visitors to Nairobi have their purses
snatched or pockets picked. Women should take special
care with their handbags in restaurants. Valuables and
passports should be left in a hotel safe.

"The U.S. Embassy in Nairobi and the Consulate in Mombasa
are prepared to offer more specific information to U.S.
visitors, who are encouraged to register with the Embassy
upon arrival in Kenya. The Embassy is located at the
intersection of Moi and Haile Selassie Avenues in Nairobi;
the phone number is 334141. In Mombasa the Consulate is
located at Palli House on Nyerere Avenue; the phone number
is 315101.

"Expiration Date: August 15, 1990."

Colonel A. D. Ackels
Box 71 KUSLO ~ APO New York 09675

Aug 89

Jim:

I thought some of this might
be of interest to you. The
GOK has not acknowledged some
of these incidents, trying,
I suppose, to protect the
tourist industry.

Actions are being taken to
improve protection in the parks,
and the appointment of Richard
Leakey to head the new wildlife
parastatal may also do some
good. Unless and until the
Kenya Army picks up this mission
my hands are tied. I can't
provide military assistance
to police organizations. Privately
I have helped them find suitable
commercial helicopters, and
I'm trying to get Leakey in to
see several senators and congressmen with an interest in wildlife,
but at this point I've no idea
how successful I'll be.

At this point I see no reason
to scrub your planned trip in
Nov-Dec. The places we'll
go haven't been affected by
this.

# KENYA

AUG 14 1989

### INFORMATION PAPER

PURPOSE:  To update CENTCOM on the security situation in Kenya.

FACTS:    During the period March to June 1989 there have been an increasing number of attacks on Americans and other foreigners in Kenya.  These attacks have led to the publication of a traveller's advisory for Kenya.  The most serious are summarized below.

March    During the month of March three AmCit tourists visiting Kenya National Parks were robbed at gun point.  In one case, the AmCit resisted and was clubbed over the head.

April    Mombasa:  An Embassy couple vacationing at a beach hotel woke up to find thieves had entered their room and had stolen some of their belongings.

April 12  Tsavo:  Two German tourists were shot and wounded by bandits while vacationing.

April 20  Tsavo:  Three vans containing tourists were ambushed.  Two German tourists and a van driver were shot and injured.  Two AmCits and two Canadians were riding in one of the vans.

May    Mombasa-Nairobi:  British Diplomat travelling from Mombasa to Nairobi was stopped along the road by armed men who robbed him.

July 7   Meru:  Two French tourists were shot and killed after coming across a gang of armed poachers carving up a giraffe.  This park, located in north-central Kenya, has been the site of violence in the past.

July 7   Near Malindi:  A 65-year-old American nun working at the Franciscan Sisters of Mary Mission near Malindi (Eastern Coast Province of Kenya), was shot and killed by armed bandits who shot their way into a church where evening prayers were being held.  Another American nun was injured by shrapnel, and the priest was severely beaten, as were others who came to help.

July    South Coast:  Belgian tourist (with his wife) was shot and killed by robbers at roadside stand near Tiwi.  It was reported that Belgian tourist was killed after not understanding robbers request to turn over his car keys.

169

July 20    <u>South Beach</u> - One AmCit tourist was robbed on the beach
           near Tiwi Lodge/Coral Cove Cottages in a heavily used tourist
           area (south of Mombasa).  While walking along the beach, the
           AmCit was assaulted by two robbers who roughed her up and hit
           her with stones.  Robbers stole money, clothes, and pho-
           tography equipment worth approximately $450.  It appeared
           that the two assailants sought to rape her.  She said that
           the Kenyan Police had not been helpful and refused to provide
           her with a police report.

July 22    <u>Masai Mara:</u>  Two AmCits were badly beaten while camping out
           in Masai Mara Game Park.  Several burglars broke into their
           tent and hit one tourist with a club.  The other tourist, who
           was also hit in the head, remained unconscious for a short
           time. Burglars took one tourist's passport, money, and
           travellers' checks.

July 27    <u>Tsavo West:</u>  Three vans travelling near Kilanguni Lodge were
           attacked by robbers.  One AmCit was shot and killed and one
           slightly injured.  Passengers in all three vans were then
           robbed of personal belongings, money, and passports.  We have
           been informed the GSU were escorting the tour vans; however,
           due to the dust, etc., they were so far behind that the
           thieves were able to complete their mission prior to GSU
           arriving on the scene.

In addition, from March - June, 1989, 42 AmCits reported thefts to the
Consular Section; to include passports, and other personal property.
Approximately $28,000 in personal belongings and money taken in these
various crimes.

This is probably as good a place as any to comment on Dale's awards and decorations. He received recognition in every assignment throughout his career. I won't list every one,suffice it to say, some are more prestigious than others.

The Army Commendation Medal usually ends with the word ... *"brings great credit upon himself and the United States Army."* Dale received his first ARCOM at the end of his first tour of duty as a 2nd Lt. at the Ordnance School. Not many soldiers achieve that honor right out-of-the-blocks. When a soldier receives more than one, it comes with an Oak Leaf Cluster (OLC). Dale is in that select group.

In Vietnam Dale earned a Bronze Star, only awarded for service in a combat zone and the Vietnamese Cross of Gallantry with Palm, awarded to US service personnel who served in-theater during the peak years of combat.

He received three Meritorious Service Medals (MSM), number two and three with an OLC.

There are numerous others: Permanent Awards of the Defense Meritorious Medal, Superior Service Medal among them.

There are a couple of particular note: two Legion of Merit (LOM) awards, and a telex from Secretary of State James Baker in September, 1989 commending Dale for his leadership and decisive action in a difficult circumstance when he served as our senior military officer at the US Embassy in Nairobi, Kenya. To say it's rare to hear directly from a Secretary of State is an understatement. It is difficult to read. This is what the Secretary wrote to the US Ambassador:

*"Please tell Dale Ackels we were most impressed with reftel account of his conversation with general Mohamed about Somalia. A truly professional job in telling the General just how it is."*

I asked Dale about it, and in typical fashion he downplayed his importance but offered the following commentary:

*"The conversation with General Mohamed occurred when he called me in to protest the current state of the relationship with Somalia. The US had finally run out of patience and he was worried that the Somalis might spill over into the northeast quadrant of Kenya in an attempt to retake part of what they described as Greater Somalia. Since he was an ethnic Somali, he had both personal and business interests in the north, and the growing number of Somali incursions was a concern. Several years later, after Siad Barre had fallen, the*

*Kenyans solved the problem by invading southern Somalia. In effect, placing a buffer zone between their northern towns and tourist attractions, and the discord and anarchy in the southern part of that country."*

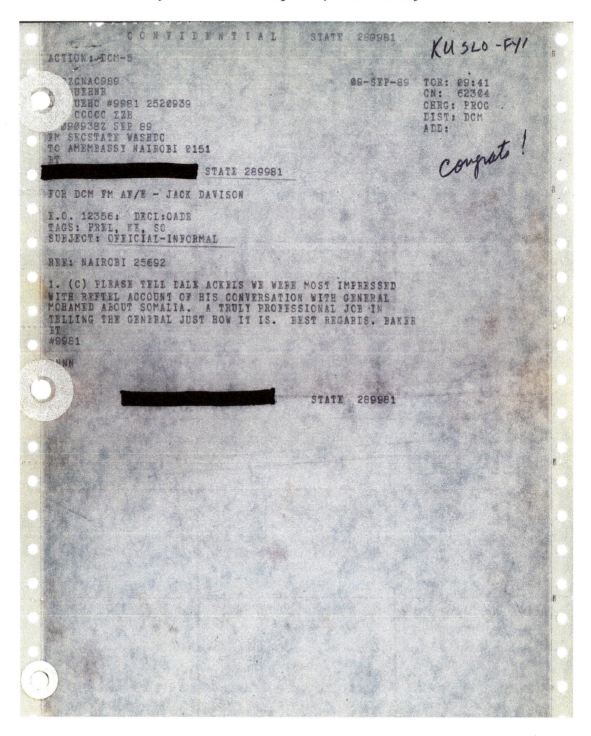

NOV 1 '89

## Colonel A. D. Ackels
### Box 71 KUSLO ~ APO New York 09675

Dear Jim:

I talked to my Dad and Nan
yesterday and they told me
about your weekend visit
to Santa Rosa.

I can't imagine anything that
would have cheered my Dad up
more.  You and one of his oldest
hunting partners are about
the only visitors he's had
that he really wanted to
see.

That was a very kind thing
to do, and I can't tell you
how much I appreciated it.
You ain't much of a correspondent
but you're a hell of a fine
person.

Best,

Dale

Col A. D. Ackels
Box 71 KUSLO ⌣ APO New York 09675
APR 2 0 1990

Dear Jim,

I'm not quite sure what happened at Christmas time. I think everyone's plans just sort of fell apart thru lack of attention. Nan was expecting you to stop by Sacramento, but I told her I hadn't heard from you about it and something else must have come up or I would have. I do appreciate your offer

to come out and be with us, but it was kind of a somber gathering and something less than a merry christmas.

Should you still be thinking about coming to Kenya take a look at mid-June. We may be in the middle of base access negotiations, which would throw a considerable monkey

wrench in our holiday plans, but that's the best time avail between now and our departure on 4 August.

I'm being reassigned to the Army War College, Carlisle Barracks, PA as the Director, of African Studies. Sort of a giant leap sideways. I tried to get a division on the west coast, but I've become so associated with Africa and our military activities on the continent that there really was no escape. It was Carlisle for the good of the Army, four different bullshit jobs in the Pentagon, or find alternative employment. Anything to stay out of the Pentagon. It's a lovely post, Bet has seen it before, when I attended, and she's looking forward to it.  That's better than half the battle.

Little else to report.  I'll be in the U.S. from 5-28 May.
5-12 May at New Cumberland, PA; 12-16 May at the Pentagon;
and 16-26 May in Tampa attending a conference at Central
Command.  Don't know where I'm staying yet.  I think it's
to be a Days Inn on the Interstate just outside Harrisburg
for the first part, and I'll be at the Wyndham Harbor Island
Hotel while in Tampa.  I'll be sure and call.

Bet sends her best,

*[signature: Dale]*

P.S. My Dad is doing very well.  He's adjusted perhaps better than
Nan and I.  He's stopped smoking, stopped drinking, lost weight
and started doing a bit of hunting and fishing.  I think he plans
to move to Nevada as soon as the probate details are ironed out.
Oddly enough I think that the intricacies of the probate process
helped pull him through.  Everybody copes in different ways,  He
did it by totally immersing himself in the details of getting Mom's
will and estate straightened out.  That wouldn't have been my
choice, but it works for him.

*P.S. I don't think I ever sent over my phone #*
*011 254 2 52 08 56 (H) and 33 41 41, X215/216 (W)*

Col A.D. Ackels
Box 71 KUSLO ～ APO New York 09675

JUL 3 1 1990

Dear Jim —
There won't be
time for much
more than a
brief note. We're
in our final
pre-departure
flail, and it's
about midnight—
three days from
departure.
As we had antici-
pated, your timing

was impeccable.
Serious rioting
broke out the
Saturday after
you left. Before
it was over 15
were dead, 60 odd
wounded, and
over 1000 were
in jail. By the
time the rioting
stopped three days
later Matiba-
Rubia and 10 other

dissidents were in detention, Paul White was in hiding, and the lawyer Gibson Kamau Kuria xx had taken refuge in the Embassy. We're still not out of it, though the quality of the debate has improved somewhat. The local pols are no longer telling KANU youth-wingers to cut the fingers off anyone giving the 2-finger (multi-party) salute, and the president has convened an election reform commission to look at changes in the voting laws, but my favorite Congressman, Howard Wolpe of Kalamazoo, is agitating for a complete suspension of military aid. If State gives in to his intimidation our program will be on its ass in 6-8 months. Ah well. New address is: Box 477 Root Hall, U.S.A.W.C., Carlisle Barracks, PA 17013-5050, after 22 August. Our best to Chris.

Dale

717 245-3022(o)

# LETTERS FROM A FRIEND

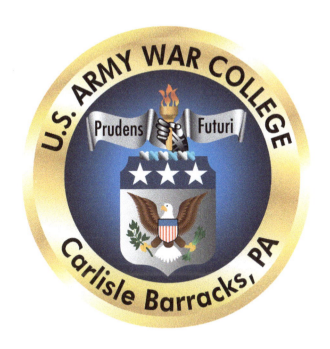

# CHAPTER 13

## Army War College & Retirement

### 1991-1994

# LETTERS FROM A FRIEND

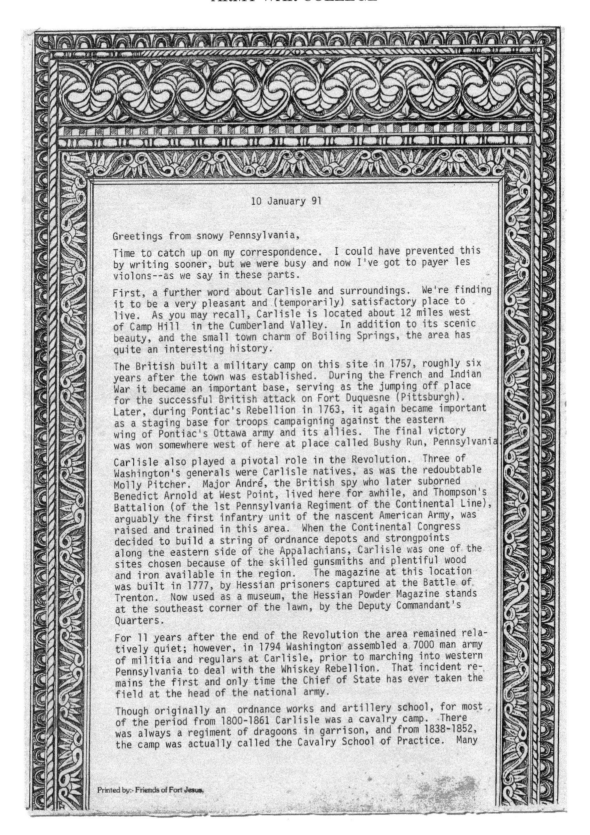

10 January 91

Greetings from snowy Pennsylvania,

Time to catch up on my correspondence. I could have prevented this by writing sooner, but we were busy and now I've got to payer les violons--as we say in these parts.

First, a further word about Carlisle and surroundings. We're finding it to be a very pleasant and (temporarily) satisfactory place to live. As you may recall, Carlisle is located about 12 miles west of Camp Hill in the Cumberland Valley. In addition to its scenic beauty, and the small town charm of Boiling Springs, the area has quite an interesting history.

The British built a military camp on this site in 1757, roughly six years after the town was established. During the French and Indian War it became an important base, serving as the jumping off place for the successful British attack on Fort Duquesne (Pittsburgh). Later, during Pontiac's Rebellion in 1763, it again became important as a staging base for troops campaigning against the eastern wing of Pontiac's Ottawa army and its allies. The final victory was won somewhere west of here at place called Bushy Run, Pennsylvania.

Carlisle also played a pivotal role in the Revolution. Three of Washington's generals were Carlisle natives, as was the redoubtable Molly Pitcher. Major André, the British spy who later suborned Benedict Arnold at West Point, lived here for awhile, and Thompson's Battalion (of the 1st Pennsylvania Regiment of the Continental Line), arguably the first infantry unit of the nascent American Army, was raised and trained in this area. When the Continental Congress decided to build a string of ordnance depots and strongpoints along the eastern side of the Appalachians, Carlisle was one of the sites chosen because of the skilled gunsmiths and plentiful wood and iron available in the region. The magazine at this location was built in 1777, by Hessian prisoners captured at the Battle of Trenton. Now used as a museum, the Hessian Powder Magazine stands at the southeast corner of the lawn, by the Deputy Commandant's Quarters.

For 11 years after the end of the Revolution the area remained relatively quiet; however, in 1794 Washington assembled a 7000 man army of militia and regulars at Carlisle, prior to marching into western Pennsylvania to deal with the Whiskey Rebellion. That incident remains the first and only time the Chief of State has ever taken the field at the head of the national army.

Though originally an ordnance works and artillery school, for most of the period from 1800-1861 Carlisle was a cavalry camp. There was always a regiment of dragoons in garrison, and from 1838-1852, the camp was actually called the Cavalry School of Practice. Many of the most important figures in the Civil War passed thru as students and faculty, including Jeb Stuart, who returned on 1 July 1863, during Lee's invasion of Pennsylvania, to shell the barracks and burn the town. Probably just as well it happened the way it did. If he hadn't been amusing himself here and hunting for shoes in York he would have been available to Lee at Gettysburg. Had Lee had him by his side throughout the battle there's no telling what mischief he might have created, or how the battle might have ended.

In 1871 the Army turned the Barracks over to the Department of Interior, who used it until 1918 as a vocational school for Indians. Pop Warner coached football here during that era, and many famous Indian athletes passed through as students. Among them Louis Tewanima, Lonestar Deitz, Bemus Pierce, Chief Bender and Jim Thorpe. During this period the Carlisle Indians were one of the major football powers in the country. Playing against Army, Pitt, Penn State, Dartmouth, and the University of Chicago (the major college teams of the era) they more than held their own. Indian Field, Armstrong Hall, Washington Hall, and many other important buildings and facilities on the Post were built during this period -- by the students.

From 1921 'til 1946 the Barracks was an Army Hospital and the home of the Medical Service School. Finally, in 1951 it became the third home of the Army War College, which had just been forced to abandon its premises at Fort McNair to make way for the newly created National War College and the Industrial College of the Armed Forces. In addition to the War College, Carlisle is also home to the Center for Strategic Wargaming, the Information Systems Command, the Military History Institute, and a couple smaller agglomerations that won't bear close scrutiny.

The War College is meant to be the final step in the professional education of a career soldier. The process that begins with the branch basic course ends here with nine months at the resident course. Selection is eagerly sought as a prerequisite to promotion to colonel and brigade command; however, the class is limited to 237 lieutenant colonels and newly minted colonels in residence, plus an equal number taking the course by correspondence. The DoD students are selected by boards meeting in Washington. Counting admin staff, there are roughly the same number of staff and faculty as students.

Most of the major military figures of the 20th Century attended the War College. Pershing, Bliss, Lejeune, Malin Craig, and Hunter Liggett came in the early years. Between wars Eisenhower, Bradley, Collins, Ridgway, Hodges, Patton, Gruenther, Lemnitzer, Wainwright, Patch, Buckner, Simpson, Krueger, Mark Clark, Jacob Devers, Bedell Smith; even Bull Halsey and Jack Fletcher the carrier admirals passed through.

In the modern era Schwarzkopf, Thurman (invasion of Panama), Westmoreland, Maxwell Taylor, Alexander Haig, Bruce Palmer, Creighton Abrams, and the current Chief of Staff of the Army and Commandant of the Marine Corps have all attended. The sense of commitment to the national interest, and the many historical tie-ins, sort of appeals to me and makes an otherwise boring job defensible. So does the notion that somewhere out in the audience are a couple guys who are going to win or lose the major wars of the 21st Century.

Where you might ask do I fit into this? I'm the Director of African Studies in the Department of National Security and Strategy. My primary responsibility is teaching. I'm responsible for 18 three hour blocks of instruction between

17 January and 19 April, and I'm a seminar leader. The seminars are the basic organizational unit and teaching vehicle of the school. There are 18 of them, each with 16 students and a 4-man teaching team assigned. One strategist, one management guy, one loggie, and one historian. A normal day might begin with a guest speaker presentation for the whole class on, for example, "Command and Control of Theater Operations." The formal presentation is followed by a Q and A period, which is followed by a 1-2 hour discussion in the seminar rooms, led by the faculty instructor from the appropriate department of the school. The relationship with the students is certainly a plus, but the time spent in seminars takes away from research and lesson preparation, and is something of a sore point with the faculty.

Speaking of the faculty, historically they've been a rather interesting lot. Roughly a third of the luminaries listed on the previous page were AWC instructors, as was George C. Marshall. At the moment Jay Luvaas, one of the preeminent military historians in the country, is on the staff. So is Colonel Art Lykke (Ret) one of the best known teachers of strategy, and Colonel Dave Jablonsky, a well-known Eisenhower scholar and student of European affairs. Colonel Harry Summers (Ret), author of the best book yet written on our failures in Vietnam, was here but he recently left to become military correspondent for a major newspaper chain and CNN. Others of less renown but equally impressive qualifications are loitering in the halls.

The faculty is not all military. There are visiting and tenured professors from SUNY, Duke, Miami, Tulane, Purdue, Harvard, Kansas, Alabama, MIT, Claremont Collge, Lebanon Valley College, and the University of Geneva. Don't quite understand how a policy freak wound up at Lebanon Valley College, but he's very good and more than holds his own with academics from some of the better known orchid gardens.

On the domestic front, we're still moving into our rental in Boiling Springs. In several of my early letters to others I described our house as a 19th Century Victorian. Since my reference books have arrived I've discovered it's actually a Gothic Revival, built sometime between 1840 and 1880. It has a rough basement, laid up with local field stone, and on the ground floor a living room, dining room, kitchen, bath and sundeck. There's also an office of sorts, made out of the old summer kitchen, with a secret passage in the walls leading to the third floor attic. The second level has three bedrooms and a bath, plus a deck that can be used in the summertime for sundowners or watching the world go by. None of the floors are level, it needs exterior paint, the outbuildings are in an advanced state of decay, and the backyard is a nature preserve, but for some reason Bet and I both like the place and expect to be quite happy here.

If a military move has five stages:

    I   Everything inside

   II  Able to touch all four walls

 III  Everything unpacked, but some of it still
       on the floor or standing in corners

 IV  Pictures hung, curtains up, but some boxes
       still in the basement

V  Claims submitted, furniture repaired, change
   of address cards accepted, children doing
   well in school, but husband has just received reassignment orders

We are somewhere between II and III.  What we're trying to do is stuff
the contents of our 5 Br house in Washington into a 3 BR.  I imagine it's
sort of like watching Dolly Parton put on a bra.  You know it's all going
in there, but it's difficult to imagine how.

Our boys seem to have made the adjustment fairly well, as has Bet.
Bet's a bit frustrated by the problems associated with the move
(lots of broken furniture, no quarters, late arrival, etc) but
she seems to like the area well enough.  In the three months we've
been in the house we've gone to four rodeos and horse shows, done
quite a bit of pheasant and deer hunting, and even hiked a short
section of the Appalachian Trail.  Might as well.  It runs thru the
town.

Travis and Derek both did well on their first report cards.  Neither
made the honor roll, but they did better than usual for their first
report in a new place.  Travis is playing basketball, and Derek is
playing drums and football, and fooling around with wrestling and skiing.
He got very excited about pony football this autumn, which I admit I
encouraged.  His Mom had doubts, but I thought that playing a contact
sport in a town where football is a viable substitute for organized
religion, would toughen him a bit and help him learn to handle pressure
and pain without whining.  His team did rather well--I think they were
5-4-1--but Derek didn't necessarily take away the things I'd hoped for.
He didn't work hard enough to play regularly, and he still tries to
get by on whining and sulking, but the players and coaches didn't show
him much mercy, and I hope his enthusiasm will carry over to next year.
I still think it will be good for him.

Many thanks for the Christmas wreath.  It was lovely, and smelled wonderful.
Sorry about the length of this, but as Pascal once said, I didn't have time
to write a short one.

P.S.  We have two Kisii stone statues you bought while in Kenya.  Want us
to ship them, or would you rather pick them up in the spring?  As you may
recall, they are long and slender and Kisii stone is soft.

P.P.S.  No indication I'm headed for the Gulf.  If it's a short war I'll
probably never go.  If it becomes a protracted conflict it becomes a distinct
possibility.

In the last two years of Dale's career, he served as Director of Africa Studies at the Army War College in Carlisle Barracks, PA. Basically he was the military equivalent of a college professor, teaching studies in national security and strategy, and leading a team teaching the Africa related curriculum at the War College.

His first letter of 10 January 1991 is vintage Dale, an historian and fervent letter writer at heart.

Col. Ackels served as the Director of the Annual National Security Seminar, an end-of-course symposium that brought together leaders from all walks of life along with members of the graduating class for a week of lectures and discussions.

Thanks to Dale, I was finessed into the 1992 group. My classmates were a judge, a senior corporate executive, two educators, an international attorney and a political activist. Remarkable interplay, debate and conversations.

The letters mention Chris, my son, who was a student at Georgetown University in Washington, DC during Dale's tenure at Carlisle and the three years he remained in Carlisle, PA after retirement. Dale looked after him during his collegiate years, particularly in 1994 when I spent a good portion of the year in London, England on business. His letters are Dad-to-Dad reports.

**U.S. ARMY WAR COLLEGE**
**NATIONAL SECURITY SEMINAR**
**1-5 JUNE 1992**
**SEMINAR GROUP #12**

(Seated, L-R) Ms. Mattie J. Amaker, Mr. Donald Halverson, Dr. Gwendolyn E. Jensen, Mr. Benicio Sanchez-Rivera, Mr. Daryl I. Skaar, Judge Harold A. Thomson, Jr., Mr. James M. Tiffany

An abstract written by Dale and approved for public release when he was a student at the Army War College.

---

**Accession Number:** ADA510917

**Title:** African .Minerals and American Policy

**Descriptive Note:** Journal article

**Corporate Author:** ARMY WAR COLL CARLISLE BARRACKS PA

**Personal Author(s):** Ackels, A.D.

**PDF Uri:** ADA510917

**Report Date:** 1978

**Pagination or Media Count:** 9

**Abstract:** Major A. D. Ackels is presently a student at the US Army Command and General Staff College. He holds a bachelor's degree in History and Political Science from the University of Minnesota and a master's degree in Comparative Politics from Georgetown University. Major Ackels entered the Army in 1965 and has since served in a variety of command and staff positions, including overseas tours in Japan and Vietnam. In 1972, he joined the Foreign Area Officer program as a specialist in Sub-Saharan Africa. Since then he has served in Ethiopia and has travelled in 14 other African nations. Field research for this article was done in Addis Ababa, at the headquarters of the United Nations Economic Commission for Africa, and in Washington, D.C., while Major Ackels was serving as an African Analyst in the Capabilities and Readiness Division of the Army's Intelligence and Security Command. In attempting to demonstrate the importance of Africa as a potential source of raw materials, this study focuses on eight metals: aluminum (bauxite), chromium, cobalt, copper, iron, manganese, platinum, and uranium. These minerals were selected because they are found in commercially exploitable quantities in Sub-Saharan Africa, because they have a variety of applications in American industry, because they represent metals for which there are at present no generally suitable substitutes, or because they represent important underused deposits of metals widely recognized to be essential to all industrialized nations.

**Descriptors:** *POLICIES, *SUBSAHARAN AFRICA, *POLITICAL SCIENCE, *MINERALS, INDUSTRIES, ECONOMICS, SECURITY, IRON, COPPER, ALUMINUM, PLATINUM, CHROMIUM, ARMY, AFRICA, UNITED NATIONS, ARMY OPERATIONS, INTERNATIONAL RELATIONS, URANIUM, COBALT, OVERSEAS, MANGANESE, NATIONS, REPRINTS, ETHIOPIA, METALS, SOURCES

**Subject Categories:** Government and Political Science Geology, Geochemistry and Mineralogy

**Distribution Statement:** APPROVED FOR PUBLIC RELEASE

MAR 05 1993

Brother Jim,

Just a note to bring you up to date on Chris' visit to central
Pennsylvania.  He worked on his sleep deficit, and we took
him to see A RIVER RUNS THROUGH IT, to the Eisenhower Farm,
on tours of Dickinson College and the Gettysburg battlefield,
and to meet and talk with Ambassador Daniel Simpson, a career
diplomat and our new Deputy Commandant for International
Affairs.

As predicted, he did want to talk about careers.  Specifically,
about how best to tailor his course of study at Georgetown to
meet his slightly altered notions of what he wants to do.
Simpson and I both worked on that.  Indeed, I decided to set
up the appointment with Simpson when I ran out of things to
say on the subject.  I don't think he will go wrong in either
the diplo and history track or the science and technology
specialization.  Simpson told him that S & T is particularly
hot now, because of the problems posed by disarmament and
nuclear proliferation, and because the environment is starting
to be seen as a diplomatic problem and receive more attention
in official Washington.  As for his interest in writing, I
told him he can do that in conjunction with a career in
diplomacy or other government service, or he can completely
reorient his course of study and become a journalism or
literature major.   Given his interest in international
relations and policy I doubt he will seriously investigate
either of these latter options, but he seems to have found
something in writing that intrigues him, and he will doubtless
continue to tinker with it in some form.

He has another thing on his agenda you may or may not hear
about.  He very much wants to stay in Washington this summer
and accept an internship at the World Bank or Wash Post, but
he's afraid to talk to you about it because he thinks it will
hurt your feelings, or you will see it as rejection.  Like
most young men his age he seems to see you in only one dimension--
as Jim Tiffany my dad.  He can't quite believe there was a
Jim Tiffany before he came along, or that there are many other
dimensions to your life and personality.  In that regard I
broadened his horizons considerably, and with a certain amount
of vehemence.  In his mind he's created an artificial Jim
Tiffany who must be somehow outmaneuvered to permit Chris'
further development.  It's bullshit, of course, but I do believe
he's ready to stop being Chris Tiffany, Jim Tiffany's boy, and
start being Chris Tiffany, reporter, bon vivant, and man about
Washington.  I told him I thought he was making a good deal
more out of this than it warranted, and that he should take
the first good opportunity presented to talk to you about
the coming summer, just as he spoke to me.  Hope he did it.
It's much on his mind.

# ARMY WAR COLLEGE

SEP 2 2 1993

Dear Jim,

Just a brief note to thank you for your hospitality, and send along some of the things I promised to provide.

I don't need either the photographs, or the magazine articles and floor plans.  These are yours to keep or pitch as the mood takes you.   One thing everyone asks when they see these houses under construction is what about the tires sticking out of the walls.  The gaps between tires are plastered over with the same adobe clay mixture used in the tires.  When complete the walls present a smooth stucco appearance, with no indication of what lies underneath.    No one will ever mistake these for English tudors, but they have their own charm, and in the Southwest they look like they've been there for centuries. (These photos were taken outside Boise.  They're not one of Taos houses.)

I saw Chris in Washington Monday night.  I paid the first half of the agreed upon bribe for getting my name changed (that boy shows potential as a sushi eater), and jawed with him for a bit more than 2½ hours.  He'd had a come-to-Jesus session with his professors in French, government and African studies earlier that day, and he felt he'd patched up his relationship with the African studies guy.  Chris felt they prof just didn't understand how serious he was about wanting to study Africa.  Once they got that hammered out Chris said they got along well.  At any rate, Chris seemed happy and focused, and ready for whatever the new year brings.  Among other things, it's going to bring another sushi dinner.

I was in Washington trying to negotiate a 3-6 month contract for a study being commissioned by the Army Staff.  They want a company named MPRI to look at how they perform their security assistance mission.   If it goes sole source I expect it will kick off about 1 Nov.  I'll have to live in Wash DC on weekdays, and the money isn't as good as some of the short projects I've done (on a daily basis), but I've committed myself to be the study leader if it goes.

Thanks again for the invitation and the hospitality.  I really got into the Michigan game, and I always enjoy having the opportunity to talk for awhile and get caught up.  I hope my parting comment to Tina didn't create problems for you.  I'd assumed from things you'd said that getting hitched again was a done deal.  As soon as I saw the look of happiness on Tina's face and the apparent irritation on yours I realized that maybe I should have made my exit some other way.  If I did jump the gun, or put you in a predicament please accept my abject apology.  I was bathed in the glow of that wonderful breakfast and can't legally be held responsible for anything I may have said.

Still haven't heard from Hart.  May have to call him and throw a little dirt on my head to patch this up.

189

6 July 94

Jim,

Enclosed you'll find a sort of buck-up card for Charley Hart. I believe he's just finished his course of radiation treatment. According to his secretary, a born again rowdy named Lacey something, he's held up rather well. No loss of weight, no serious pain, and no outward manifestations of radiation sickness. She also says his cancer cell counts are almost negligible, and his morale is good.

He also seems to be thinking about the future. She told me he's about to hire an associate, a young kid about to take the bar exam. I guess the plan is to take some of the pressure off Charley. Basically, that's the same scheme that got him to Wyoming some 25 years ago.

All of this at second hand. Charley is in Billings, where he goes to get his innards carmelized.

Haven't seen your son lately, but then I haven't done very much about hunting him down. I'll take care of that next week. Also haven't written Tina to thank her for dinner, but expect to take care of that chore this weekend.

We be in the final six week flail of Phase II of our study. Next report is due 15 August. This one will cause great heartburn. Some jobs moving, some jobs gone, and pain and aggravation almost everywhere. I can't see any way around it, but I'm going to be writing briefings and refining our conclusions pretty much full time between now and mid-August.

Incidentally, dates for my return to Wyoming have changed to week of 22-26 August, if that helps. Had to change it to accomodate customer wants. Cheeky sod. It took a quarter of a century to get Army security assistance this badly screwed up. Don't understand why he must start untangling it the week I want to go to Wyoming. When the customer sees how badly we've savaged him he may wish he'd postponed this meeting indefinitely.

The card is my hamhanded attempt to cheer Charley up. I thought you might wish to add a couple lines to other side. Either way, please drop it in envelope and mail it.

Thanks again for hospitality and usual good time.

All best wishes,

Dale

11 July 94

# durbar hotel

*INDEPENDENCE WAY PMB 2218 KADUNA TEL (062) 201100—8 TELEX 71134 CABLE DURBAR KADUNA*

Dear Christina:

This will be just a brief note to thank you for your various kindnesses during my last visit, and do a bit of personnel management and all-purpose schmoozing.

The night before we ate together Jim and I got into our usual rambling discussion about family, friends and business. When we got to you he mentioned you were still sticking it out in the inner city, and, as a matter of principle, you would probably continue to do so for the forseeable future. He also said you were still trying to find minority employees, but were having some difficulty finding people with the needed skills and work ethic.

At the time I put that information in the Tina.demich:persmgt @may94 file, but after my return to Washington it occurred to me there might be a person currently employed at MPRI who has what you're looking for. This person was hired by MPRI to develop a marketing program for the firm. Unfortunately, MPRI doesn't really need or want a marketeer. Most of our business is developed by the senior retirees who own and front the company, relying on name recognition and longstanding association with the Army to get their noses, or various other body parts, under the tent flap. Renee (Stroud) is not doing what she's paid to do, and she's looking for something more challenging.

Can't say how old she is. No more than mid-30s, but she's quite attractive, smart, in the English sense of the word, very articulate and aggressive, and she's got a kind of aura about her, almost a swagger, that I can't quite explain or define. Sort of a combina-tion of street smarts and boardroom cool she can switch on and off at will. She was in the military at one point, but has been out for several years, working here and in Europe. Lots of pr work, including a stint as the civilian press officer for operation PROVIDE COMFORT--inside Kurdistan. She's a single mom, willing to move, but not until she finishes a degree in marketing, which I believe will happen next spring. I haven't done much to energize her, other than to ask if she'd consider moving, but I'll be happy to put her in touch if you'd like to read her resumé. She's a cut or nine above the norm, and she hasn't had a chance to show what she can do here.

Jim also told me you've been getting on him about his correspon-dence, or the lack thereof. This is a laudable undertaking. I must admit he's never been noteworthy in that department, but in his defense I must also point out that he doesn't really neglect the obligations of friendship, and in my case his lack of correspondence has long since ceased to matter.

I suppose everyone who's ever met Jim has been struck by his social skills and uncanny knack for putting people at ease. I've always been fascinated by the way his affection for family and friends manifests itself in acts of _unusual_ consideration, and his special talent for turning the mundane milestones of life into something special & peculiarly memorable. The driveway painting business for Chris, and the surprise birthday party for Heather come to mind, and I'm sure you could cite several others. In my case he just sort of shows up when he suspects something of importance to me is about to happen. Two examples will illustrate the point. When I got promoted to colonel he came down to Tampa to witness the laying on of hands and socialize a bit. Somewhere during that weekend he gave me a wonderful roan-colored leather notebook, with my name, grade and the date of my promotion on the inside flap. At the time I thought it was a typically thoughtful gesture, but in the insuing years that thing has become almost part of my wardrobe. I literally take it everywhere I go, and everytime I open it I see my name and date; think of my departure for Africa and the countless other things he's done for me and my family over the years.

He showed up under similar circumstances when I retired. When I asked him what prompted him to come to Pennsylvania just then he said something like, "I was there when you came on active duty, and I thought I'd better come see you leave."

You may recall he was our best man when Bet and I got married. When he's not marrying off Texas tycoonettes to some cadet branch of the royal family he's quite possibly the best best man anybody's ever seen. He literally took charge of my half of ~~half of~~ that affair. After watching him in action for two days my Dad was moved to comment, in voice _clearly_ audible on Prince Edward Island, "That's the best damned best man I ever saw!" Somewhat later, when my Mom was dying in California, he found some kind of excuse for drifting out to California to look in on my family. He hadn't been to California since Heather was about four, but he suddenly discovered some pressing business requiring his presence there. I knew my mother was seriously ill, of course, but until he contacted me in Kenya and brought me up to date I hadn't realized how close the end must be, or what I needed to do.

The point of all this being, he is undoubtedly a lousy correspondent, but he's a wonderful human being and a priceless friend, and he's never neglected his friends in any way that counts. None of this is meant to discourage you from busting on him, as the mood takes you and the situation dictates. It'll keep him humble, and properly tuned up, and it may provoke him to send somebody an envelope full of interesting stuff. It's not generally known, but before commerce and child-rearing came to occupy so much of his time, he operated the most eclectic and wide-ranging clipping service in the Upper Midwest.

All best wishes, and thanks again for the wonderful dinner. That little Holstein did not die in vain, and that dinner will live in sainted memory for a long time.

_[signature]_

13 July 1994

Jim,

This may represent some kind of new record in communication.  Don't
know, can't recall, wouldn't matter anyway.

I saw Chris last night.  Took him to eat after he (and I) got off
work.  Overall he seems to be in good shape.  He's not eating
right, he's tired, and he's learned more about the realities of
life in the no-passing lane than he ever wanted to know, but he's
<u>cheerful</u> and sanguine about the future, and I saw nothing except
malnourishment to give a father cause for worry.  He has broken up
with his sometimes girlfriend from Hawaii, but that was not a cause
for any particular upset.  It had been a pleasant interlude while
it lasted, and he seemed to accept it was inevitable.  From his
standpoint, probably even desirable at his age.

We discussed the pluses and minuses of dating older women, the
future of the Clinton health initiative, and the proper way to
teach kids about drugs.  He's been playing some weekend soccer
and seems to be enjoying that.  He got into a pickup game with a
bunch of Uruguayans recently.  At the end of the game they broke
out a considerable quantity of coke and snorted a lunch bucket or
two.  Chris boogied, but the incident caught his attention and he
wanted to talk about that for a minute or two.

All in all, he's doing fine.  Nothing to worry about.
Probably best not to tell him I'm passing you info about his
doings.  He'd be appalled, and would probably stop yarning with
either one of us 'til he got over being mad--or reached 40,
whichever came first.

# LETTERS FROM A FRIEND

9 Nov 94

Jim,

I had dinner with Chris last night so decided to combine my
statutory reporting requirement with other business. He's fine.
Skinny and tired, but the fatigue caused by midterms. He told me
he'd aced them all so he was rather pleased with the results of
his labor. He took me on a walking tour of the campus, and I
stuffed about 400 lbs of dead fish in him--as a restorative.
Travis is coming down to spend a day with him on the 18th so I
spent most of my alloted time bringing him up to date on
my boy's activities.

Chris tells me you've bought a new house--somewhere closer to the
center of Royal Oak. I didn't realize you were going to move on
that as fast as you have. You must have found something that
really captured your imagination. Hope it works out.

Travis has finished his high school soccer career. Not perhaps
as he might have wished, but he played on three very good teams,
went to the district/state playoffs three times, and became a
rather accomplished striker. I say it ended on a down note
because he missed four of the last six games of the season due to
injury, and Boiling Springs got eliminated in the first round of
the district playoffs by a team they should have destroyed, but
all-in-all, it's been a positive experience for him and I've had
a lot of fun watching the whole process.

This valley is quite a hot bed of soccer. Cumberland Valley, the
school that John Ritchie attended, is a perennial powerhouse.
They had two high school All-Americans on last year's soccer
team, and local schools have placed several kids in Division 1-A
programs. After Travis' team bombed out, Bet and I went to see
CV play a time or two. Mercifully, Boiling Springs (an AA
school) doesn't have to play them. It's like watching UConn or
UVa play. I don't think there are enough ambulances in the
county.

Nothing new to report in our search for paradise on earth.
There's one 95 acre place outside Sheridan of interest, but the
owner won't entertain a "reasonable" offer until his listing
agreement expires, and that won't happen until the end of
December. If Sheridan doesn't pan out I guess I'll have to wait
until the end of March to go back out there. Not much point in
going back with snow on the ground. Even if I found something
that sounded right, once winter comes you can't really see what
you're buying.

I'm sorry we didn't see more wildlife in Yellowstone. I went
back thru my notes and found some totals for Bet's first visit to
the park. In three days we saw _311_ buffalo, _660_ elk, _11_
mule deer, and a fair assortment of coyotes, eagles, antelope and
assorted lesser beasties. Didn't see any bears either time, but

they're there.  It's a shame you didn't get a chance to see more
of what the park has to offer.

You seemed a little non-plussed when I discussed my Dad's
financial situation.  I wouldn't even have mentioned it to anyone
but you, but in truth it has that same impact on me.  I don't
quite know what to do or say about it.  Nan and I are, of course,
grateful for his thoughtfulness, and the sacrifice it represents,
but in a sense it's a gesture we don't quite understand.  Long
after his immediate needs were met he continued to postpone the
gratification of his own plans and desires to build this pile.
There were so many things he always meant to do and didn't do;
now he's physically unable to do most of them.  Both of us would
feel more comfortable with this if he'd take a big chunk of it
and enjoy the fruits of his labors, but he simply won't do it and
it offends him when we suggest it.  It's almost as though he
thinks no one will remember him if he doesn't make this grand
gesture.   We've both told him that even if he won't spend a
damned nickel on himself now, we consider the first claim on his
assets to be the provision of a comfortable retirement and
funding for whatever medical requirements he may have.  He agrees
with that, but in his sternest voice usually adds, "You two don't
realize how much some of these retirement programs can cost.
It takes $30,000 a year to support me in the style to which I've
become accustomed!"  At that rate he'll be dead broke near the
end of the next century.  As I said, I don't quite understand it.
I suppose it has something to do with the depression, something
to do with the way his spendthrift father ended his days, and
something to do with validating his life.  Sort of a variation on
the notion that money is the way you keep score and judge a man's
value.  I don't understand most of it, and aside from that brief
conversation in Yellowstone and this note, I've never tried to
explain it to anyone.  For the obvious reason that I can't.

I'm back in Washington again.  Started back fulltime in mid-
October, and expect to stay here until mid-November.  There's a
deliverable due on the 15th of this month.  Once the customer has
accepted that I plan to start doing most of my work at Carlisle
Barracks.  From mid-November to mid-December I'll be shifting
back and forth between Carlisle and the Washington office.  Two
days one place, three days at another.  If everything goes
according to plan we'll finish up about the 16th of December.
Can't say I'll be sorry to see it end.  I've got another customer
ready to go in Jan-Feb, and I'm tired of the commute and being
away from my family.

P.S.  I'm getting a little worried about the ski trip we spoke
about.  Should I call Judy Paxton/Payton directly?  Just tell her
what I need and what the time constraints are?  Give me a call

sometime in the next couple weeks and let me know what I should
do, please.  MPRI's Washington office is 703 684-0853, and you've
got my home phone.

P.P.S.  Ref the Boer goat; his care, feeding and location. I got
a nice letter from the Ag Attache in the embassy.  There are no
restraints on exporting live sperm or fertilized eggs, and the
only restrictions on live animals are the quarantine requirements
established by our own government.  All that crap about South
African controls was designed to protect the commercial interests
of the breeders in North Carolina.  It's still a subject of some
interest to us, but it's a speculation--like tulips in the 17th
Century, chinchillas in the '50s, European beef cattle in the
'70s and ostriches in the 90's.  Once the bubble bursts you'd
best be interested in some other aspect of the business because
the days of $18,000 bucks and $23,000 does will be over.

P.P.P.S.  Ref the basketball stuff.  Don't know anything about
the Bullock kid-never read anything about him before or seen him
play, but he sounds like a blue chip and Michigan's got him.
Iverson, on the other hand, is being touted as the next messiah.
The man who will lead Georgetown and the Big East back to center stage.

In the summer of 1994, as Dale and Bet were looking at potential retirement locations, I met Dale in Billings, Montana for three days in the Mountain West, which was as unknown to me as Mars.

We drove to Red Lodge, Montana, one of the possible places, where Dale met with a realtor ... why I kept his card is beyond me.

Next stop was Sheridan, Wyoming, another possible retirement location and ultimately their selection, in large measure because of the school system.

We stayed overnight at Charlie Hart's ranch. The three of us had been together at APG as young Amy officers and I hadn't seen Charlie in almost 30 years. He had a lucrative law practice in Sheridan and Dale had stayed in touch with Charlie, I hadn't.

The following day Dale and I then drove to Yellowstone National Park. I had an industry discount at a hotel just outside the park ... or so I thought. I got my "Y"s confused. Turned out I had a discount at Yosemite, but I didn't find that out until about 22:00 that night with no place for us to stay. To this day, Dale will almost lose consciousness, convulsing in laughter at the mere mention of that monumental display of geographic and travel ignorance. I'm certain he has shared that dozens, possibly hundreds of times at my expense. I deserve it!

It explains the note on the next page.

Dale has a penchant for collecting all sorts of information, some of which could be used to remind a good friend of a previous faux pas.

One such example is a tidbit he'd read about Yellowstone National Park:

> Sacramento, Calif -
> *You know that famous California landmark -Yellowstone National Park? An embarrassed California Assembly had to correct a geographically challenged resolution on Monday that referred to Yellowstone, which is mainly in Wyoming, as one of California's tourist attractions. The Assembly corrected the mistake, saying that "it was just a typographical error." There is a national park in California that begins with a Y - Yosemite.*

*I guess if the California state legislature doesn't know where the damned thing is, travel agents should be cut some slack!*

Eschenbach, Germany
9 Mar 95

Dear Jim,

Just before I came over here to work on this project we had Chris up to Boiling Springs for the weekend. He'd expressed an interest in learning to snowboard, and this looked like the last, best opportunity before spring. He done good. He crashed a fair amount, but everyone does when they're learning, and it certainly didn't seem to detract from his enjoyment of the day. The fact he didn't have a lot of experience skiing or surfing helped. He had no bad habits to unlearn. He certainly wasn't intimidated by the mountain, or much of anything else, and he seemed to have a good time. He also seems happy and content with everything going on in his life.

At some point in the weekend I started ragging on him about his skinnyness last summer. He acknowledged a certain lack of attention in that area, and told me that at one point he lived on peanut butter and jelly sandwiches for one week. I looked appropriately dismayed (without any difficulty at all) and he went on to say, "Don't worry Uncle Dale. I realized I was killing myself. Now I try to eat the right stuff." Peanut butter and jelly. Fuck me.

Watching Chris over the last 2 1/2 years I've come to realize that I'm going to miss some of the best and most interesting years of Travis' youth. The payoff, if you will. In my view, young Chris has become all that any parent might wish for a son. Those occasional bouts of intellectual arrogance that used to worry you seem to be gone, replaced by a penetrating curiousity and a lively and pointed sense of humor. He's really become a package, and a tribute to your parenting. Hell of a job. I'd give anything if either of my sons had his intellectual curiousity, or willingness to work hard at academic pursuits. The part that aggravates me is knowing that if they do develop a broader vision it will happen on someone else's watch, and I won't get to see it happen.

Travis has been accepted at Shippensburg and Penn State. Ship was his first choice, so he's happy and looking forward to his freshman year. I'm not sure he prefers Ship for the right reasons, but a number of his friends will be there, and that seems to matter a great deal to him. At least for the first 1-2 years.

Don't know where you're living these days so I'll send this to the old address and hope the postal service forwards it.

Dale

*Dale and his Dad at Dale's retirement in August, 1992.*

*With my daughter, Heather, Dale and Bet, September, 1993*

# CHAPTER 14

## Sheridan, Wyoming

1995-2002

Dale and Bet selected Sheridan, Wyoming as their retirement location, as I recall, because of the school system and their boys continuing education.

I know they enjoyed their initial years, as you will see from Dale's first batch of letters. He started a consulting business, Africa Research Associates, successfully using his encyclopedic knowledge of Sub-Saharan Africa to help a variety of clients and keep productive.

Three words entered their vocabulary and became the bane of their existence ... fracking and methane gas.

These three words represent the reason Dale and Bet left Sheridan, where they easily would have been content for years.

Let's start by the definition of fracking:

*"The injection of fluid into shale beds at high pressure in order to free up petroleum resources (such as oil or natural gas)."*

Merriam Webster Definition

*"Hydraulic fracturing is an oil and natural gas production technique that involves the injection of millions of gallons of water, plus chemicals and sand, underground at very high pressure in order to create fractures in the underlying geology to allow natural gas to escape. It also is called hydrofracturing, hydrofracking or more commonly known as tracking. Hundreds of different types of chemicals are used in fracturing operations, many of which can cause serious health problems-some are also known carcinogens. After hydraulic fracturing takes place, both the waste fluid that is brought back to the surface as 'flowback' as well as the fluids that remain underground can contain toxic substances that may come from the fracturing fluids."*

American Rivers Definition

Dale's letters tell the sad tale.

*23 July*

*Sheridan*

Dear Jim,

Enclosed you'll find copy of a recent
note to Christopher.  Inside my graduation
present I included a note that said I'd
soon be seeing an old friend--high up in
the State Dept heirarchy--and that I'd ask
her about the prospects for employment
in the foreign service.  This most recent
ltr to Chris contains the substance of
what she told me.  Not very encouraging,
I fear.

Travis is home for the summer.  Started
out throwing sacks in a pellet mill, but
later caught on with a fencing crew working
for the State.  Lots of overtime, and he's
making $9.14 an hour so he thinks he's
got the World by the gonads.  Best he
continue believing that for awhile longer
because he's flunked out of college.  I
don't mean he almost made it.  I mean a
total wipeout.  He's decided he's going
to stay out of school for a year or so,
make some money, buy a car and have some
fun.  Unfortunately, he's decided he's
going to do all this back in PA, with
his 16 year old girlfriend and a couple
of other also-ransx with similarly reasonable
plans for the immediate future.  We mean
to let him experience this next episode to
the fullest, without our financial support.
He says it will only be for a year, then
he's coming back and buckling down, but
my guess is we won't see much of him for
the next several years.  His counselor told
him he needed to do some growing up before
trying college again.  Now that I've been
with him for two months I have to admit she's
right.  In most meaningful respects he's
still very much a child.  Too bad for him,

but we've reluctantly conceded that we can't
live his life for him.  And we can't force
him to do something he doesn't want to do.

We're off to Cheyenne tomorrow.  100th Anniversary of Frontier Days.  For rodeo fans like us
can't miss that one.  Soon as we get home
we're off to N. Carolina for the annual
Miller Family fucking of the goats.  This
is similar to Pamplona, except it takes palce
on a beach and instead of running the bulls
through the streets they take turns running
each other through the alleys.  Each day
a new victim is selected until all have been
properly counselled on how they should actually
be leading their lives, raising their children,
and dancing in attendance on Hazel and Jerry.
Nineteen people, counting children as people,
in one beach house for 7-8 days.  As your
ex-father-in-law once said in similar circumstances,
this will be the "worst fun I've ever had."
Times like these it must be a great comfort
to have a drinking problem.  I fear I'm too
old and "sot" in my ways to learn now, but
the thought has crossed my mind.   I plan to
spend a lot of time in a beach chair, under
the house, with a stack of trivial novels
and hook and bullet magazines.  Any other
course of action, and believe me I've tried
them all, leads inevitably to madness.

Hope this finds you in better shape than
we're in.  Whether yes or no, let us hear
from you.

P.S. Someday someone is going to ask me what
was the bravest thing I've ever done.  I'm
going to ponder the matter for a brief moment,
then say, "I once took a menopausal woman to
Wyoming."  Anybody who doesn't smile knowingly
and sigh is no friend of mine.

Bat and Dale Ackels
305 Lower Prairie Dog Rd.
Sheridan, WY 82801

Chris,                                          JUL 17 1996

Got your note outlining your job plans.
Sounds interesting, though I'll have
to get out a map and find out exactly
where in China that is.  I assume
you've hired on as a contract employee
of someone, and are not going over there
on your own.  No matter.  It will certainly
be interesting.  Just the kind of thing
a young man ought to try--particularly
with a degree already in his pocket.
Be sure and send us your mailing address
when you've arrived and set up shop.

In the note I enclosed with my graduation
present I mentioned that I would soon be
seeing an old friend, an assistant secretary
of state, and I would ask her about the
career prospects with State.  She was here
a week ago, and I did have a chance to speak
to her about careers in the diplomatic
service.  Until last Saturday she was the
Assistant Secretary of State for the Oceans,
Environment, Science and Technology; she
worked all the global warming, ivory trade,
rain forest issues.  Her advice was to
try international business.  For someone
with your background and aptitudes she felt
int'l business presented real opportunities,
and a career in the foreign service did not.
Apparently the Foreign Service is in the
midst of a drawdown, and the Under Secretary
for Management, a man named Richard Moose,
who I worked for briefly in the Carter years,
is doing a particularly inept job of managing
the process.  He was the Assistant SecState
for African Affairs when I knew him, but he's
an Arky and Clinton has brought him back as
the Under Sec for Mgt.

At any rate the drawdown is not being done
well, and a number of incompetent people
are surviving at the expense of more
capable but less well connected professionals.
In that environment my friend advised
her own son to find another career. He'd
already passed his written and oral tests,
and been offered an appointment, but on
Mom's advice he's changed direction and
is now working in international business.
To summarize my friend's views, "The
Foreign Service was a wonderful career for
us (between her and her husband they held
four ambassadorships, one posting as
Deputy Inspector General of the Foreign
Service, and one assistant secretary's
job), but the old Foreign Service is disappearing
and we won't see it again for many years--
if ever. Tell your young friend to look
seriously into international business. I
think that's where the real opportunities
are." Further deponent sayeth not.

If business is of interest, your Dad is,
of course, far better qualified to tell
you about that than I. Most of what I
know about that subject I've learned since
my retirement, and most of my work has
had a defense spin to it. As I've learned
to my chagrin, the USG is no longer a
reliable employer (the government shutdown
cost me five jobs, probably six, and many
thousands in lost consulting fees). I
won't let that happen to me again.

Let us hear from you from time to time,
and say hidy to your Dad if you pss thru
Detroit enroute to China.

*Dale*

*Where the Hell is Guizhou? I
checked an atlas but didn't find it.*

## Africa Research Associates

FEB 09 1997

Dear Jim,

Good to talk to you this afternoon, and get caught up. We've been meaning to call since at least Christmas, but somehow just never got it done.

Shortly after you called we heard from Travis. He sounded pretty good. The truck washing business had picked up after a recent series of storms (truckers don't like to wash during storms because it's self-defeating, but as soon as the weather clears they come in to the truck parks to get prettied up). He'd gone hiking in the local mountains, and fooled around with his friends some and seemed to be in high spirits. Hopefully, not chemically induced, though he's promised us, and told his brother, that phase of his life is behind him. His best friend, who'd also developed a problem at the same time Travis was involved, has moved on with his life; gotten a better job and cleaned up his act. Maybe there's hope, for this and the reasons we discussed earlier.

I didn't have my exact schedule available when we talked, but this is how it looks for the next eight months.

25 Feb--7 Mar. North Carolina.

11-24 March. Southern Germany.

7-13 April. Fairfax, VA.

14-15 April. Visiting Travis in Pennsylvania.

29 Apr--21 May. Working in Louisiana.

Jun-Jul-Aug. Haying season on Prairie Dog Creek. Two maybe three cycles of irrigating, cutting, drying, baling and stacking, with several trips to local tracks and horse farms to deliver hay. Sounds busy, but there are gaps of several weeks between each cycle. Good time for you to visit. Particularly late June and July. August too dry, except in the mountains.

8-24 Sep. Sometime in this time period I'll be working somewhere for about 6-7 days.

Hope this helps your planning. Thought I'd put this missive on the "official" Africa Research Associates letterhead. The consulting business has grown beyond the cottage industry stage and I thought I'd better start acting more like a business, hence the cards

305 Lower Prairie Dog • Sheridan, WY 82801 • Phone: 307 750-2277 • Fax: 307 674-8103
e-mail: africaresearch@wyoming.com

and stationary. Looks kind of different doesn't it, and there's not much doubt what I do. Remember to send your e-mail address; better still a business card. I'm not even sure what your business address is anymore.

Dale

# SERENA LODGES & HOTELS

OCT 0 2 1997

Dear Jim,

Haven't been to either of these places in the recent past, but enjoy using paper and envelopes from earlier visits to exotic locales to liven up my correspondence. If memory serves I "borrowed" the idea from one of Nancy's friends who did a lot of travelling. I need to start writing more; my inventory is starting to overwhelm available storage.

I've been travelling a bit myself. So far this year I've taken six jobs, and rejected one or two more because they'd conflict with Derek's football or hunting season, or they'd take me out of Wyoming during haying season, when I definitely need to be at the ranch. Most of it Africa related in some fashion, but I also worked one drug suppression job in Panama, and one job in Germany and Italy that had to do with Bosnia. That's the second time I've worked in Italy in the last two years. This time I wound up at Brindisi, just across the Adriatic from our brothers in Christ, the Bosnian Serbs. I actually wasn't in Brindisi either, it's just the closest identifiable feature. We lived and worked in San Vito dei Normanii, a small town 18 km west of Brindisi. Both are in Puglia, an isolated and underpopulated region not to far from the resort community at Bari and the WW II naval base at Taranto. To my eye it looks more like the North African coast of the Med than Italy, but I enjoyed the job and locale. Not perhaps as much as Vicenza, but it was infinitely better than Zaire in the rainy season.

Not much else to report. Derek's football season is going OK. He's not starting, but he's playing in every varsity game and going both ways in the occasional JV games. (There will be one of each while you're here.) I may be expecting more of him than he has to deliver, but with his size and ability I cannot believe he isn't better than he is. I know he can do it. When he gets mad he turns into a one-man destruction derby, but he doesn't get mad very often and doesn't stay mad worth a damn. Basically, he's just a big, happy-go-lucky teddy bear--that wants everyone to like him, and desparately wants to get laid. Football for him is not about competition or winning things, it's about hanging out with his friends and being involved in something with widespread community acceptance. As you know better than most, that's not exactly my approach, but I'm coming around, and I console myself with the notion that it's far better for him to be playing and having fun than not be playing at all. And, there's always next week and next year. (As you will see from the attached article, we've suffered a bit of a team setback. Natrona County, the team that beat us in the state championship game in 1996, thumped us soundly last week. We're big and talented, but mistake prone. If the previous coach had seen one of his teams turn the ball over 11 times someone would have had to commit an *auto-de-fe* the following Monday.)

P.O. Box 48690 Nairobi. Kenya. Telephone 339800.
Telephone Reservations 339800. Telex 22878. Fax 721342. Cable 'Serena'

As for Don Travisimo, he's gone thru quite a 16 month "growth" period. Since he was thrown out of Shippensburg he's worked in a wood products plant, strung fencing, washed trucks, been a golf course attendant and a short-order cook, ushered in a theater, worked construction and been an irrigator. He's been broke a couple times, and at least once had to camp in Michaux State Forest (in PA) because he didn't have a place to live. For reasons that only recently became clear to him, blue collar work has not financed the kind of lifestyle he expected: New car, new clothes, abundant leisure time, etc. At various times he's discussed becoming a salvage diver, or taking a construction job overseas; he's even talked about the military, but until last week he was pretty much opposed to going back to school. Last week he came out here to visit, and to explain that he's decided to go back to school spring semester, if we'll help him. It'll be here at Sheridan College, unless he can convince his other "father" to finance junior college in Florida. Don't think there's much chance of that. If his biological father had wanted to stay involved in the nuts-and-bolts details of raising a boy he wouldn't have let me adopt them. If things go according to plan he'll be back here the second week in January, to begin school on the 14th. Far as I can tell, he's drug-free. He definitely seems to have turned a corner on that.

As for Dad, he's still as feisty as ever, but his eyesight is failing and he broke his back several months ago. Actually, he broke one of the spinal processes, rather than his spinal cord, but that wasn't immediately apparent. He did it turning over in bed. I thought this might be the beginning of a general decline in his health, but he more or less obeyed his doctor's instructions, and got well. He and his buddy Pat Moorehead went trap shooting last Sunday, and they plan to start pheasant hunting next Monday. I guess he's OK, but I'm not sure he'd tell me if he wasn't.

Somewhere in here is some airplane reading on Sedona too. If memory serves, once upon a time you thought you'd like to live there. I have a friend, a Japanese potter named Masako Shirai, who moved there from Studio City, California. According to her, it's still wonderful, though I know from a casual drive-thru several years ago, it's not like it once was. So much for pre-departure info. We're looking forward to your arrival.

Dale

P.S. I've been thinking about your notion of buying a Michigan parka for Derek. Please don't spend a lot of money on something like that. He'll love it, of course, and wear the Hell out of it, but we don't need house presents from you. Your presence is all we need or want. Best again.

NOV 17 1997

Jim,

As you will see from the enclosures, Sheridan lost the 4A championship game 25-20 in Evanston. Naturally we went down there for the game--438 miles one way. Coming back, in formal mourning, we ran into a blizzard and had to go 100+ miles out of our way to get home. Somber times indeed, with no ray of hope or sunshine on the immediate horizon. Several months ago, in my last ltr to Chris, I speculated that our season would end in the championship game, with seconds left on the clock and a Sheridan wideout dropping the game winner in the end zone. I wish I hadn't been so prescient. With 47 seconds left, our most reliable receiver dropped a pass on the three yard line. All he had to do was catch it and step one yard to his right to the out-of-bounds line. It hit him in the numbers and dribbled down his shirt like a plate of spaghetti. If he'd caught it and stepped out we'd have had a first down on their three, with 40 plus seconds to push over the game winner. No way they could have stopped us. We'd run on them at will most of the day--indeed dominated the stats. But, wasn't to be. I feel sorry for the poor kid who dropped the pass. He'd done wonderful things for us all year, but this will stick with him the rest of his life. Aside from that, our kids played very well.

As for Derek, he never did seem to get it together. He's lettered, and he's proud of that, but he hasn't established himself as a Sheridan quality player. They're talking about moving him to guard next year. In our offense that's a busy place to be. Lots of pulling and trap blocking. I know he can't do it this year, but maybe with a year's growth and time to reflect he'll figure it out. He's going to the University of Wyoming football camp in June. That should help. Plenty of technique and a chance to measure himself against other good players in a relatively tension-free environment. Next year's team will be loaded with talented backs and receivers, but the line will be a question mark. They're big, but ponderous, slow and of doubtful competitive zeal. Derek and a couple other young whales are going to have to find themselves or it's going to be a long, long season.

Many thanks for the jams and books. We liked the American Spoon stuff so much Bet e-mailed them and asked for the catalog. That winter compote is particularly good. We also appreciate the books. I've just about finished Hackworth's latest. Hack is his own worst enemy. He get so many things right, but he can't separate the things he knows and understands from the things he and a bunch of other hotheads believe to be true but don't understand. Now he's discovered that peacetime armies aren't as well led and trained as wartime armies!! Imagine that. Who knows what the clever bastard will ferret out next? He does serve a useful function though. Because of his wartime record he can't be ignored, and every country needs a handful of busybodies to occasionally point out that the Government doesn't have its stuff together. I don't think he's going to make Schwarzkopf's Christmas card list this year though.

212

My dance card seems to be filling up for 1998.  I'm going to Heidelberg for 15-17 days in January, then to the California desert for 13 days in March.  After that I'm going back to Washington to help write a handbook on irregular forces--my part will, of course, be Africa.  After that it's haying season, and then it's time for football again.  This ain't so bad.

Been doing a lot of hunting the last two weeks.  Shot a pronghorn just south of here on the 12th, and am working on a nice buck that's been hanging around our creek bottom. Elk season was a washout, but Bet has her buck at the locker plant already, and if I get a chance at one of the good bucks using our place for a B&B, I'll be satisfied.  Plus, there's pheasant season on the ranch, and the waterfowl on the Bighorn River.  That's just starting to get good.

Horses all well, so are we; after 30 days of official mourning things will return to normal. Good to see you again, and thanks again for all the stuff.  You know you don't have to do that, but as usual, your choices were inspired.

Go Blue--both of them.

*305 Lower Prairie Dog Road*
*Sheridan, WY 82801-9636*
*January 26, 1998*

Dearest Jim,

Had thought I'd get this written long before now. I'm not quite sure where the time goes, but it DOES go! I can't tell you how much we enjoyed your visit and truly hope you'll come again this summer and/or during football season. We're also looking forward to Heather & Scott's wedding in September. Know it'll be a lot of fun!

The Roberts book, *The Man Who Talks to Horses,* was absolutely wonderful. I devoured it and have started on it for the second read this week. It is an inspiring book. Wish I could put into practice half of the things I've learned reading it. Dale, also, perused it at his leisure and loved it! That's one that'll be re-read several times over the years! Thanks so much for your thoughtfulness.

Another thank you is in order for the beautiful cane Christmas wreath you sent. I look forward to receiving it each Christmas. Not only is it pretty and smells so good, it's a little different from your "usual" wreath. I feel a little sad when I take it off the front door and send it to the burn pile long about mid-January!

Now, back to my opening paragraph and Heather & Scott. We got a note from Heather in early Jan. We had asked for suggestions as to what she & Scott would like to have for a wedding gift. She gave some good "leads" and she also mentioned something about Chris. She didn't give any particulars, just something to the effect that some "recent happenings with Chris" and that "1998 will hold many changes in the Tiffany family". She didn't want to spill the beans, but she has succeeded in peaking my curiosity. (Her letter arrived the day after Dale left for Germany!) I trust that Chris is O.K. - perhaps marrying a young lady from China. I/we would love to hear what's happening with him.

As for "Master Travis". As far as we can tell nothing is happening with him. As we suspected, he elected not to come to Wyoming in Jan. and return to school. He came to NC for Thanksgiving and brought along Katie, his girlfriend. She seems like a nice girl, much more focused and determined than he is at this point. His/their new plan, as explained to me at Thanksgiving, is for both of them to come to WY in July/August and stay with us 'til they can find an apartment. Katie wants to transfer from Shippensburg University to Sheridan College - for 1 year (SC is a Jr. College that is designed to feed into the University of Wyoming). She, of course, will need to transfer somewhere again at the end of next year. Travis will be one full year behind her. I believe he was planning to transfer at the same time as Katie does to wherever they decide to go.

I was glad I had a week or so to go over all this with Dale before we talked to Travis. Dale had not gone to NC with me for Thanksgiving. He stayed here and fed the horses! We didn't tell him anything in particular, just tried to point out how he was limiting his options somewhat and how Katie was really the one taking a chance "in the unlikely event that their relationship crashed & burned." Still don't know what he/they will decide to do. Dale & I just try to listen when we do get to talk with him. He's still not very good about communicating. He's gotten a PO Box, so at least we can send letters periodically.

Things at the "ole homestead" are great. We've had some snow, but not an overwhelming amount like last winter and the temps have been quite a bit milder, too. I realize, of course, that winter has only just begun and that Feb. and March are still ahead of us! Dale is in Germany. He will return in the wee small hours of the morning of Feb. 2, sleep, get his clothes washed, say "Hello" to his wife & son, then re-pack and leave again on Feb. 5th. This next trip is to NC and Ft. Bragg. Relatively speaking, it's a short job. He'll be back on Feb. 13 and will be here until mid-March.

Joe & Concho are both doing well and send their regards. We do have a new addition to the household. We "saved" a kitten from being drowned by giving her a home. We had her spayed, so we won't have 200 more kittens by August! She's a really sweet, loving kitten. She's about 8 months old and a white, black and gold colored tabby. The vet said they call the color pattern "torbo". (Sounds more like a race car than a cat!) Anyway, we call her BC because she looks like a little bob cat with a long tail. (And if she gets into trouble, BC can also stand for "BET'S cat".) I nearly fell over when Dale said that we could get her if I wanted her. He's maintained for 12+ years that he's not overly fond of cats and that the only one he's ever been around that he likes is his sister, Nancy's, cat named Hershey. This kitty is such a love, that she's captured his heart, too. If the truth be known, SHE seems to favor HIM, too! Anyway, now the Ackels household count currently stands at Boys 4; Girls 2 ...we'll keep you informed of future developments!

I hope that we'll be able to get the new fence in around the house and that Dale will find a puppy as the first two projects for this spring/summer. Maybe our household will have expanded again, by the time you come. Oh yes, I also hope he can find a horse for himself by summer. Anyway, our lives are full of plans and hopes for the future. Hope yours is too. We'd love to see you again, soon. Hope your dad is doing well. Please give him our best.

Love to all,

*Bet*

MAY 1 5 1998

BEAU VALLON BEACH

P.O. BOX 400, TELEPHONE: 47036, TELEX SZ 2215, TELEFAX: 47517, CABLES: COLSTRAND

Estimado Senor:

Bet told me the good news about your granddaughter. By now I guess you've been to China and met Chris' in-laws and spouse, and seen the new baby. I've thought about you many times in the last couple months, wondering how well I'd do in similar circumstances and what the future might hold for the three of them. Nothing but the best, I hope, but Chris has certainly set himself some challenges. Somewhere in my musings it occurred to me that fatherhood has three phases. In Phase I the kid listens to what he's told, and seems to have a bright future. Good grades, good personality, happy, seemingly well-adjusted; no blips on the horizon. In Phase II the trolley runs off the tracks every now and then, but by dint of some serious parenting it gets put back on the tracks and the future still looks predictable. In Phase III you no longer have any influence over the choices your offspring makes, but you still must react to them. You don't get to vote, but you get to participate in the fun of saving junior from the predictable results of his folly. I don't know if Chris' marriage to this girl is folly or not, but at the point the baby arrives it seemed to me it no longer matters. The baby is innocent of any errors in judgment, and has no misgivings about how it got here. When Bet told me the baby had arrived I recall thinking, "Well, the game is on now, and Jim has no choice but to try and help Chris make it work." Knowing you I knew that's what you'd already decided to do anyway, but I couldn't help feeling sorry for you somehow. Wishing that somehow this had all happened differently; more predictably, I suppose.

In case you're wondering what caused this maundering outburst, I have also been doing some Phase III-ing. Travis didn't come home to start college when he said he would. He stayed in PA to be with his girlfriend. He now says he's coming back in July, to start in the Fall at USC (the University of South Coffeen, or Sheridan College as it's commonly known). His original plan was to bring his girlfriend with him, and move in with us as a couple. We've been able to convince him he should not bring Bright Eyes out here until he's had a chance to get settled in school, and get a job. We've also had to explain to him that we have no responsibility for the care, feeding, and maintenance of his live-in, and he needs to be looking at another plan. She still plans on coming out for spring semester; by that time he thinks he'll have everything set up and ready for her arrival. We shall see. I'm going to pay his tuition and costs and her parents will support her, minus their rent and groceries. He gets to do that himself. I could be wrong, but I don't think he really loves this girl. Travis is kind of a stay-at-home, and my guess is he can't confront college and growing up without bringing his last sure-thing with him. Also, can't begin to imagine why her parents are buying into their 18 year old daughter coming to Wyoming to live with a guy who has no job and no education, but they seem to think it's a fine idea. Doo da, doo da, all the doo da day.

As for Master Derek, he did win a scholarship to go to Ecuador for the summer. He'll be in Quito for most of the time, but he'll spend a week hiking in the rain forest, and a week cruising in the Galapagos Islands at the end of it. All of this after the Sheridan High football camp, and the University of Wyoming football camp. As I recall, my junior class went to the Federal Reserve Bank...on a bus. Phase II I would judge; where he's finally mastered the intricacies of being a high schooler, and started to show definite, positive signs of maturing but there's no predicting how long this golden phase will last. And only his parents realize it's not all skittles and beer from here out. I suppose I've always thought of Derek as a lovable but essentially childish ward of the A. D. Ackels Hip Pocket Foundation. He went to the junior prom this year (first big date), and when he walked out of his room in his tux I suddenly had to confront the fact that he'd finally, really changed. He looked like a man--the first time I've ever thought of him as one. What an amazing transformation, and I didn't really notice it until he put his adult rags on.

As for Bet and I, we be fine. This is the busiest time of year on the ranch. Spreading a winter's accumulation of horseshit on the hay meadows, harrowing it in, burning ditches, repairing tractors, building a new fence around the house, putting in the garden and new bookcases in my office, plus additional storage in the basement and new headgates on the supply ditch. A thousand and one things that all need to be done more or less at once, aggravated by the fact that we're having an unusually dry May and everyone in the valley has had to start irrigating already--a month before we usually begin. It was a relief to owe you a ltr and have an excuse to stop for a few hours. Fortunately, the consulting business has been good and there's enough money to pay for the improvements.

I've sent along some things for Chris. Don't know if they'll be of help in job-hunting, but guessed they might somehow prove useful. Looking forward to seeing you, and Chris' family, in September. My best to Heather...and her intended.

217

JUL 14 1998

WYNDHAM HARBOUR ISLAND
HOTEL

Jim-

Finally heard from Travis re his plans
for summer and fall. He is coming back
to Wyoming to start school. Plans on
leaving PA on or about the 10th of
August to arrive here 14th or 15th.
Months ago I repeated your offer of
a place to overnight enroute, but
that was before I found out he's bringing
his girlfriend with him* and when he
was still planning on coming in late
July. I know your house is full, and
that's close to the wedding. Please
be completely frank with me if his
(and Katie's) presence will create
problems. It was a typically thoughtful
offer, but you've got a lot on your
plate and Travis can easily make alternative
plans.

Talked to Chris several weeks back. He
called to provide details of his job,
and to ask for help in finding someone
who knew about China-related data bases.
He seemed a little subdued, but basically
positive and upbeat. Hope all is well
with him, and his family.

And now to the sports news. In my last
ltr I meant to mention that John Ritchie
got drafted by the Oakland Raiders at
the top of the third round of NFL draft.
Tampa Bay and Pittsburgh have been successful
with big backs and I guess Oakland intends
to try it too. I hope he does well. He'd
fit best at SF, but they've still got
two big, multi-purpose backs. I believe

725 South Harbour Island Blvd., Tampa, Florida 33602 (813) 229-5000

he went higher in the draft than any
Michigan player except the Heisman Trophy
winner. Could be wrong....easily, but
I never believed the Michigan offense
would make good use of him. He probably saved
his NFL career by making the move to
Stanford. They're still running the
offense Bill Walsh installed, and that
offense provides more opportunity for
a fullback to showcase his talents.

Speaking of generic football players, ours
is starting his third week in Ecuador.
Should be in the Galapagos on a sailing
ship this week. He seems to be having
a wonderful time. I think my junior class
visited the Federal Rserve Bank in San
Francisco--by bus. Oh well. Convincing
my Dad to pay, in part, for a trip to
Ecuador would probably have defeated
the diplomatic talents of Ralph Bunche,
even if I'd earned the trip. I think the
only reason he let Nan go to Germany for
a year was because someone else paid
for it. What the Hell. It could turn
this boy's life around. For that reason
alone it's worth every penny.

Let me know your druthers on the proposed
Travis visit on 10/11 August. And please
be honest.

P.S. I'm off to North Carolina (Ft Bragg)
the 16th, but Bet will be here.

* For a visit.

OCT 07 1998

Jim,

Here's some recent local sports stuff. We did beat Natrona County 34-31, but a week later lost rather badly to an excellent Laramie ballclub. Watching the kids warming up I knew we were in trouble. Sheridan was obviously listless; probably just the emotional aftermath of the previous week's victory over Natrona, but it was painful to watch. We're hoping for a revival this week in the Energy Bowl against Gillette. They're unbeaten, untied and #1 in the State among large high schools. They beat last week's opponent 62-0, but if our kids show up they won't have it that easy against us. Hard to read the personality and character of this team, but Sheridan usually wins this kind of game, and I hope they do well on Saturday. A victory against Gillette could really set us up for a run at the title. Gillette has a marquee wide receiver named Sundance Wicks. What a name for a ballplayer, particularly in a high visibility position!! Florida State or USC ought to recruit him just for the name alone.

I've also included some of the stuff available on the internet. In this case a travel advisory for France....that I hoped the French would find deeply offensive. A friend who works for a French telecommunications firm took it to Paris last week and reported that his French coworkers loved it. Oh well, back to the drawing board.

Sorry I wasn't able to hook up with Chris and find out what's going on. He has gotten a bit elusive in his old age, but I'll contact him on the net in a couple weeks and keep pecking away. I've got several things I promised to send him so I have an excuse.

Bet due back on Friday. We certainly enjoyed our weekend in Michigan, and Heather's wedding. A wonderful change of pace just before winter sets in, and in a place neither of us had ever seen before. Hope you are serious about coming out here for the championship game, if the Broncs get that far. Not that the game is that important, but it will be fun to have you on our home turf again. No great changes to see, but we've made steady progress.

All for now.

Our best, as always,

219

# LETTERS FROM A FRIEND

MAR 1 3 1999

*Dear Jim —*

Been meaning to write for several months, but haven't had
or made the opportunity 'til now.  I'm in the final stages
of a Y2K exercise in the southeastern U.S., with a little
time on my hands, so will take this chunk of time to repair
the discrepancy.

Bet and the boys are all fine.  Derek just got accepted at
the University of Wyoming yesterday, so he's in a three
foot hover, and Travis seems to be doing as well as last
semester, which is very well indeed.  Since we determined
that both boys have ADD, and got them the appropriate meds,
their academic turn-around has been nothing short of
spectacular.  Travis got a 4.0 last semester, which is
easily the best semester he's ever had, at any time in his
life, and Derek has been doing markedly better.  I think
Derek would do better still if he didn't have a girlfriend,
and wasn't involved in so many activities, but then he
wouldn't be Derek.  He seems to have a taste for smart
girls.  Only two girlfriends in his young life, but the
first one is probably in the top five in their class, and
the incumbent won a President's Scholarship, good for five
years of EE at UW.  I think girlfriend #2 will also be the
valedictorian.  Hopefully one or both of these young women
will continue to kick his ass when his Mother and I have
turned over the responsibility.

I think the application to UW signals his reluctance to
pursue footbal further.  He'd received ltrs of inquiry
from South Dakota School of Mines, University of Sioux
Falls and Rocky Mountain College, but I don't believe he'll
do it.  According to his coaches he's good enough to play
at the NCAA Div II/III or NAIA level, but I just don't
think he wants it anymore.  Can't say I blame him.  It is a
grind, and college kids hit so much harder.

We may be looking at little break in our spring schedule.
Bet is going to write you soon, but to summarize, my
mother-in-law and sister-in-law have cancelled, my cousin
and her husband went to France instead, and my mother-in-
law's college roommate and her spouse were fishing for an
invite, but in the absence of one didn't invite themselves,
as they did last year.  Travis will probably still be here;
Derek may or may not depending on time you're interested in
travelling to Wyoming, but we should have some room at the

inn.  Charlie and Ann Hart are apparently doing well.
Charlie seems very much smitten with her; almost a new man
since he got married.  He just got back from a trip to
Portugal last week, and I think they're planning to go to
Chile later this summer.  At any rate, he seemed much
intrigued with the idea of you coming out here for
branding.  Said you'd be most welcome.

John Wagner, Nan's husband, got fired two weeks ago.  His
company, The Money Store, had been bought out by First
Union Bank, and they decided to clean house and bring in
their own people.  All The Money Store's top people got
sacked, and John's separation package was most generous,
but he's never been canned before and his ego is a bit
bruised.  I expect he'll get over it, for Nan's sake I hope
so, but it's caused a bit of a stir in the Left Coast
branch of the family.

Speaking of room at the inn, I found this piece in an
airplane mag last winter and thought of you.  Sounds like a
good place to take some of your elite clients for a real
escape.  Made me a bit homesick for Japan, and I haven't
felt that way for years.

The msg I left on your voice-mail several months ago about
Hawaii was supposed to be a surprise.  Until Y2K became the
center of everyone's attention, I had a job set up in June
in Australia (or Okinawa).  On my way home I was going to
stop in Hawaii and spend 3-4 days sightseeing with Bet.  It
was supposed to be her birthday present, but the client
decided to spend his money on Y2K, the Australia business
got cancelled, and we decided to scrap the trip to Hawaii.
Bet said there were other places she'd rather go anyway.

Haven't heard a thing from Heather or Chris.  I owe Chris a
ltr, I believe.  Will probably send him an e-mail, once I
get the taxes straightened out for this year.  I've been
working my ass off this winter--I'll only be home nine days
between now and the end of April--but after that it should
be quiet at Chez Ackels.  Let us know your plans.  Letter
from Bet will probably follow, but she's not an entirely
reliable correspondent and it may take awhile.

3 Sep 99

Friend Jim,

Been saving some of this stuff for several months now, wanted to get it in the mail before leaving on my next job. The ltr includes a map for Heather and Scott. Covers the final 8 plus miles from I-90 to the house. They're expecting me to send it, but don't know I sent it thru you.

Master Derek is now a week into his college career. We dropped him off the 27th at Laramie. As predicted , he is having a spot of trouble weaning himself. Last Monday he sent three e-mails and called once. I think there have been 2-4 more since, and he's coming home tonight with his girlfriend to spend the weekend. 750 miles roundtrip. A real hairy-chested independent sort.

Travis is also back. Came home babbling about joining the Navy after college (mostly his bio father's handiwork, I suspect) but I think he's calmed down a bit, and will probably go some other way when the time comes. In the meantime, he's got to figure out where he's going to school his junior and senior years. Based on his performance his first year at Sheridan College, he can probably get in anyplace in the U.S. but with Derek also in college now, I'm kind of hoping he chooses someplace in the northern Rockies. UW is a good school, and the University of Montana is a fine school. Everything else is an also-ran, but there's a consortium of northern Rockies state universities that cut each other a break on non-res tuition so anything from the University of Idaho to South Dakota, and south to Colorado will be acceptable. We shall see.

I'm off tomorrow for 15 days in Tampa. Working on an exercise in the Middle East. I'm not an expert on the country involved, but they said they didn't care so off I go. Be home the 19th, and will stay home thru Heather and Scott's visit and the very end of elk season. Back to that for the moment. Didn't you once tell me Heather had become a vegetarian? If yes let me or Bet know so we don't serve her elk steaks or moose kabobs her first night here. Does she like chicken?

What news on Chris? I'll interrogate Heather thoroughly so tell her what you want me to know.

I couldn't resist the brief blurb about Jon Ritchie. When he showed up at Michigan Tyrone Wheatley is reported to have said, "I don't care where you've come from or what you did in high school, when you come to Michigan you have to pay your dues." Probably true and necessary, but now Ritchie starts for the Raiders and Wheatley is their backup running back. I wonder if he still feels the same way. I thought then and still think that Michigan was a terrible choice for Ritchie. The UM one-back offense reduces their fullback to a blocking back, in essence a third pulling guard. Even if he has offensive football skills he'll never get a chance to showcase them at Michigan. Stanford was a much better place for him. Though Walsh was gone, they were coached by a Walsh protege (sp) and they ran the 49er offense. Obviously the pros thought so too, though I don't think Ritchie will have a chance to run amuck until he's traded to the 49ers, which isn't impossible since Walsh is now their general manager and Walsh recruited him out of high school. Anyway, I'm looking forward to his second season and a good year for him. Sometimes I sound like I invented the kid.

Be interesting to see what Wyoming does against Tennessee tomorrow night. Over the past three seasons UW has deliberately scheduled ranked teams for their first opponent. The big name schools like it because they think it's a doable opening win, and UW likes it because it forces their kids to compete at the highest level. Over the last three years it's been Ohio State, Georgia, and Nebraska. This year it's Tennessee. They came perilously close to winning the first three, they were leading all three games at the half, and two of them at the end of three quarters, but Tennessee will be a real test.

The other stuff speaks for itself. Powder River. I'm off to Tampa.

DEC 1 7 1999

Dear Jim,

Don't know if you're still planning to come out here after Xmas, but on the off chance you won't I thought I'd send along some recent news and miscellaneous clippings I've saved. Our Xmas ltr summarizes the main stuff, but there has been some other news.

First, I found out on the 30th of September that I'm diabetic. I knew there was something wrong with me, but a routine blood screening at the local hospital also showed something wrong and subsequent tests established that sometime in the last 1-3 months I'd become a Type II diabetic. I'm not insulin dependent, nor do I have to take drugs, but I do have to lose a lot of weight and follow a much more ambitious exercise schedule than has recently been the case. Apparently I produce enough insulin for a 180 pounder, but not enough for a 233 pounder. Too bad, it was fun while it lasted. If I control my weight and exercise enough there's a 97% chance I'll never need insulin. If I don't then there will be an inevitable deterioration and I will become a Type I diabetic, with all that implies. Couldn't be simpler. Straight cause and effect. I've lost 25 lbs so far, but have another 25 to go. Most recent tests show I've got my fasting glucose back within medically safe tolerances, so this may prove to be no problem--other than some rather marked changes in lifestyle.

Second, Derek crashed coming home for Thanksgiving. They were crossing the Shirley Basin, a desolate and relatively untravelled area SW of Casper, when they hit a patch of ice and lost control. They flipped once sideways, then did a pirouette on the back wheels and spun again before slamming down into the snow on the driver's side. The driver was knocked unconscious and rather badly bruised, but Derek was able to cut him out of his safety belt and get him out of the car. Fortunately, the first car that came along was an off-duty EMT, with his bag of goodies and know-how. He stabilized Danny and kept him from going into shock, and patched up Derek's miscellaneous minor abrasions until they could be medevaced to the Wyoming Medical Center in Casper. The truck, a Toyota 1/2 ton with a lot of teenage TLC invested in it, was a complete loss. Could have been so much worse. We might have gone down to Casper to pick up two bodies. Fortunately, unbelievably, they were both wearing seatbelts and that saved their lives.

Aside from that, it's been quiet around here. I finished my last job for 1999 on the 5th of December and won't be going out again until February something. Bet has bought a couple pack llamas to play with; we've still got two horses and a vastly overindulged cat, and within the next two days the boys will be home. Until you get here that completes the ensemble. Derek has actually finished finals already and has taken a detour to go to Denver and see "Phantom of the Opera" with his ex-girlfriend, but we expect him back by Saturday.

*I object- and disagree strongly!*

Hope very much to see you out here for the Millenium Backbrief. Let us know when and where you're coming in and we'll be there. If you can't make it give us a call over the holidays.

All the best.

P.S.  The wreath arrived safely--just yesterday.  Love the smell of balsam fir.  Nothing in this country quite so good.

P.P.S.  We enjoyed having Scott and Heather here.  He is a nice kid, and quite a bit spunkier than I thought.  He certainly has a deft way of toning down Heather when she gets a little like her Mom.  And Heather recognizes what he's doing and responds in a very positive way.  Obviously, they've worked out a way to live together that meets their needs and makes them happy.  At any rate, we enjoyed having them here and showing them around our country.  Scott was a little disappointed that I didn't let him ride one of the horses, but we only have one gentle horse (Badger) and it would have been unfogiveable to put Heather on Concho.  I didn't know anything about Scott's riding skills and didn't want to put him Concho either and have Concho make a lawn dart out of him.  I don't have insurance that would have covered him if he'd been injured, and an injury, even a minor one at that point, would have screwed up their vacation.  I hid behind the insurance question, but my primary worry was that Scott wouldn't be able to handle Concho (highly likely) and since we only had two saddlehorses at the time, I wouldn't be around if they rode off someplace and the inevitable "come-to-Jesus" confrontation occurred.  Concho isn't a mean horse, but he's devilishly clever about figuring out a rider's weaknesses and taking advantage of them, and I was afraid Scott wouldn't be up to the challenge.

**★★★★**
# VIEST MOTEL

STRADA PELOSA, 241 - 36100 VICENZA/ITALY
TEL. (0444) 582677 (R.A.) - FAX (0444) 582434 - TELEX 481819 VIEST

APR 1 8 2000

Jim,

Thought you might enjoy these--on a long flight across the Atlantic. The bulkier one is a trifle academic, but nonetheless gives some feel for the situation in Colombia. One of these pieces, obviously, came from a recent edition of the Atlantic Monthly. The other came from a recent visit to Southern Command. When you were living in Colombia the HQ was either in Puerto Rico or Panama, I can't recall. Nowadays the HQ is in west Miami, except for the Army component commander. He's at Fort Buchanan, Puerto Rico. The special ops part of his command is also in PR, but in Roosevelt Roads. At any rate, they're obviously worried about the declining situation in Colombia, and what that may mean for U.S. interests in Latin America.

Everything going well here. I finished my third job for the year two weeks ago. Just in time to come home and do taxes, and get started on the farm work. Including one day spent castrating Bet's pack llamas (don't ask). I think there is something to global warming. Our winters are freakishly mild, and each year we push up the start of the field work by a week or ten days. I don't think anyone will know for sure until we're out of La Nina and the weather can be measured against more nearly normal patterns, but to me it looks like something fundamental is changing. And for those of us on the northern plains, that isn't a good thing.

Heather said your birthday was celebrated in suitably grand fashion, and you laughed immoderately at the "Colonel Duck" anecdote. My interpretation, not hers. Hope so and best wishes for many more. Got to close it down. Bet is cooking something new called "Ginger elk" and there is a freak storm coming in tonight and I have some chores to do.

All for now.

MAY 13 2001

Estimado Senor:

Seems like awhile since last we communicated, and contrary to usual practice it also seems like it's my turn.  Hard to believe, but probably true.  This should put it right.

Everything basically OK.  There are some problems with coalbed methane development in our backyard, of which more later, but basically we're all fine and proceeding, with occasional fits and starts, toward early-onset Alzheimers and adulthood respectively.

In our Xmas ltr I spoke with some pride (and relief) of Travis's planned departure for Montana State University and a career in the Air Force.  It did not happen.  Three days before he left he told us he wasn't going.  He'd been living in town with a couple other guys for several months so we didn't see him every day, but apparently he'd sunk into a serious depression and basically tanked his last semester at Sheridan College.  Didn't leave the house for three weeks, couldn't get motivated to do anything, slept all the time, all the classic symptoms.  Under the circumstances it was pointless to suggest he "soldier on through it", and besides I was very much tempted to believe him.  His grandfather was bipolar his whole adult life, these things are genetically linked, and they usually come on in early adulthood, so we got him a therapist, moved him out to the house, and tried to get him put back together.  I'd say he's about 90-95% now, and he did finish up this semester.  Assuming he passed his finals, and I think he did, he graduated last Saturday.  As to what the future holds, I know he's been thinking about it, but we've made a conscious decision to concentrate on getting him well and out of JC, and have postponed the inevitable "what's next" discussion until he'd graduated.  Given the circumstances I don't think flying for the Air Force is in the cards.  I don't think they're going to want to trust a $50M airplane to someone who has to take mood-altering drugs to stay on an even keel.  I feel so sorry for him because he didn't have a Plan B, but if it hadn't been this it would have been something else and he's going to have to learn to cope sometime.

As for Derek, he's now flunked out of UW twice.  They let him back in on probation, but he was working full-time, the schoolwork interfered with his poker, and the outcome was pretty much predictable.  He's working for an internet company in Laramie called StarTek.  One of the contractors that provides customer assistance for aol.com.  He's apparently good at it, he's certainly knowledgeable enough, and they've promoted him into some sort of firstline supervisory positon and put him on salary.  He makes about $16K a year, plus performance bonuses, which is enough to live on if he's careful.  He's moving out of the fraternity house and in with a couple of older guys, one of them a grad student.  Hopefully, that guy's work habits and attitudes will rub off.  Derek has accepted that he needs a college education, and when he does it he's decided it's to be in business administration, but for right now he's just not mature enough.  And working for StarTek is not the worst possible place to park while he's trying to figure this stuff out.  I think his pride will drive him onward, if nothing else does.  About the time he becomes a training aide for younger college grads, as in "See Ackels in customer service.  He'll get you started out on the right foot," I think he'll look harder at what he's doing and the chances he's already wasted.  Hope so anyway.

Dad still alive and doing OK at 86. His short-term memory is unreliable, but his business skills, long-term memory, and physical health range from frighteningly good to very good, to good enough for his age, respectively. Nan and I are trying to get him to relocate closer to one of us, but he finds it hard to make that decision, and we may have to make it for him when he can no longer manage his affairs. In the meantime he's hired a part-time accountant to handle the bookkeeping, and he motors on. Hard not to admire his tenacity, if nothing else.

Earlier I mentioned a problem with coalbed methane development, and it's impact on our lives on the ranch. In 1999 the Supreme Court handed down a decision in a case called **U.S. v Amoco**, which separated the coalbed methane gas found in association with western coal deposits from the coal itself. A critical distinction for the surface owners. Under the various homestead acts, and there were several, the U.S. Government retained ownership of all underlying coal deposits in the West. All other minerals passed to the homesteaders who met the requirements of the law and proved their claims. It was the Government's position that since coalbed methane was found only in association with government owned coal, the huge deposits of gas laying 400-1000 feet under the Powder River Basin also belonged to the Government. **U.S. v Amoco** clarified that question and set off a boom that over the next 15 years will change the face of the West. I knew I didn't own the minerals on our place and that there were two coalbeds under our ranch, but I also knew that if the Government chose to sell that coal we would be bought out at a fair price and would have both the time and the means to make another move. Under the new rules I find my life changing rather rapidly, with no legal means to protect our interests. Under Wyoming law subsurface rights take precedence over surface rights. The drilling companies can negotiate a surface damage agreement with us if they want to, but if they don't like my terms they can go to court, post a bond equal to the value of the develpment they propose on my land, and take the surface rights away from me.

The unfairness of this procedure has prompted me to become more politcal. I've helped draft legislation for the State Legislature, appeared before various committees and commissions, and in June I'm going to Washington to testify before the U.S. Senate. This isn't how I planned to spend my dotage, and they may still drive me off this place, but in the meantime we've reached some sort of *modus vivendi*. The drillers have stopped about a mile north of me, and have leapfrogged over me about two miles to the south, but for right now we're untouched. My land is still leased, and the drillers have made clear they will exercise their option to drill if they decide they want to, and our wells may still go dry (you have to pump water out of the ground to free the gas from suspension), but for right now we're unharmed. Unfortunately, by the time I know what my future is, it will be too late to get out and recover the value of my investment. Quietly, we're looking for another place, but it may already be too late. Needless to say, a Bush in the White House is not good news for surface owners either. As the Socialists used to say, "La Lute Continue." Motherless fucks. Now I know why the Brits celebrate Guy Fawkes Day.

I know there's little chance you will relocate to Wyoming, but thought it harmless enough to send along stuff about life and property in the undrilled West. Sort of airplane reading for the property-inclined. There's also some other odds and ends in here relating to subjects you once expressed interest in.

My best to Heather, Scott and Chris, and to Tina, if she's still in the picture. You have been a tad vague on that subject, and with uncharacteristic sensitivity I've not pushed the point. Think back and you'll realize how many touchy-feely points I have earned! Now Bet I can't speak for. She may well interrogate you thoroughly, when and if she gets you cornered again. Speaking of Bet, she's in N. Carolina 'til the 15th. Helping her Mom get ready to move into an assisted-living facility and attending a funeral service for her Dad. The Millers have donated $50K to their church for the purpose of building a columbarium on church grounds, and her Dad is to be the first person interred in it. That should have happened today, now that I think upon it.

Enough of this. I've got to get up early to start irrigating, I've got a sick horse, and Bet's garden needs attention. All matters requiring my attention at an unseemly hour tomorrow AM. Hope all is well with you and yours.

*Dale*

P.S. The consulting business continues to go well. I had nine clients/jobs last year and will probably do seven jobs this year. Everything from tracing the ownership of airplanes that crash in Africa to writing Africa-based scenarios for U.S. special ops exercises. I haven't done enough to develop more civilian business but will work on that this summer and see what happens.

The business card is from a seafood restaurant in San Fran. A bit spendy but worth it. I give it 3 stars, 4 egg whisks and about seven smiley faces.

The Sheridan Press published an article titled "North Platte Water Settlement Pleases Attorney General" on Monday, May 15, 2000. The article describes a settlement between Wyoming and Nebraska over division of North Platte River water. The settlement was announced on the same day that the two states would have gone to trial over the dispute. This prolonged legal affair cost Wyoming an estimated $26 million since it began in 1987 (although the conflict dates to the 1930s) and saved the state $8 million that had been allocated for the trial.

They go on to provide some history on the matter, explaining that Nebraska resolved a lawsuit in 1945 that allocated water from Wyoming into Nebraska at 75 percent for Nebraska and 25 percent for Wyoming. According to a 1986 suit, Nebraska claimed that Wyoming was using more than its share agreed upon in the 1945 decree. Since then the lawsuit has remained unsettled. This new settlement is designed to give the issue finality and save the state money.

Dale wrote a letter to the editor in response to the May 15th article, which was published in the Sheridan Press on Friday, May 26, 2000. Here is a copy of what Dale had to say:

## CBM water just as important as Platte River water

Editor:

Ref. your May 15 story about the settlement of the North Platte water dispute with Nebraska.

I confess that matter puzzles me greatly. If I understand the facts correctly, Wyoming spent $26 million in defending our claim to 10,000 acre feet of North Platte water, with another $8 million appropriated for the trial itself. Ten thousand acre feet is assuredly a substantial amount of water, but why isn't the 40,000 acre feet already sent down the draw as the result of coal bed methane operations (through October 1999) equally significant?

If 10,000 acre feet is enough to justify the expenditure of $34 million and a two-year trial, why isn't the loss of 40,000 acre feet of equal or greater concern to the governor and state engineer?

What am I missing here?

Only two possible explanations: either the North Platte flows with milk and honey, or it's "Stump the Electorate Week" in Cheyenne again, and I missed the proclamation.

One's as likely as the next.

A.D Ackels
Sheridan

## James Tiffany

**From:** "A. D. Ackels" <africaresearch@wyoming.com>
**To:**
**Cc:**

**Sent:** Thursday, February 21, 2002 1:46 AM
**Subject:** A Note from Prairie Dog Creek
>Date: Tue, 19 Feb 2002 18:39:18
>To:

Some question whether this went out last night to intended addressees so
I'll retrans. If you did receive the original last night, this is the
product improved version. There was a factual error in the original and
I've altered a phrase here and there. Dale.

Dear Friends: In Xmas cards, phone calls, e-mails and letters each of you
has, at various times, expressed interest in what is going on in Wyoming,
and how Bet and I find ourselves in a situation where we must sell out or
lose everything we've invested in our ranch. Rather than answer each of you
individually, and possibly incompletely, I thought it best to shotgun an
overview; hopefully one that will answer the majority of the questions
you've raised.

This situation has its origins in the late 19th and early 20th Century,
during the period Congress was opening the West for settlement under various
iterations of the Homestead Act. Wyoming was among the last of these lands
to be offered to the public, but with the usual caveat that the Federal
Government retained ownership of all surface and subsurface coal deposits.
At the time this reservation made abundant sense. The nation was literally
powered by coal: railroads, warships, manufacturing, smelting, merchant
shipping, power generation, home heating, virtually all of it depended on
coal, and the USG was exercising ordinary prudence in retaining ownership of
this vital resource in the new lands west of the Mississippi. However, it
was also understood, indeed the grants specifically state, that a
homesteader, once he proved up his claim, owned all other minerals under his
land.

For most of the next 88 years those rules and understandings governed
mineral development in the Mountain West. If you sat on oil, or gold or
deep gas it belonged to you, but if your place sat on coal that belonged to
Uncle Sam. Methane gas, if it figured in anyone's calculations, was simply
a bothersome byproduct of coal mining. A colorless, odorless, tasteless and
potentially explosive toxic gas, always found in association with coal but
of no apparent commercial value. (The mine canary, for example, was an
early means of detecting the presence of methane before it endangered the
lives of miners. If the canary died it was time to evacuate the mine.) In
most cases ownership of the minerals stayed with the family that homesteaded
the land, while surface ownership changed whenever the property was sold.

4/21/2002

In Wyoming this is called a split estate, and is perfectly legal.

The rules changed in June 1999. That month the U.S. Supreme Court handed down a decision (Southern Utes v. Amoco) which seperated ownership of coalbed methane from ownership of the coal deposits where it is found. The USG had argued that since coalbed methane (CBM) was only found in association with coal, it could not be seperated from the restrictions found in the various versions of The Homestead Act. The Supreme Court held for Amoco and against the Government. Overnight every coal deposit in New York, Pennsylvania, Alabama, Colorado, Utah, Montana, North and South Dakota, West Virginia, Kentucky, New Mexico, and Wyoming was in play. As a result of the Nation's insatiable demand for more and cheaper energy the oil and gas companies had figured out a way to extract CBM from underground coal seams at a reasonable cost, and with the technology already available, Southern Utes v. Amoco set off a modern-day version of the Klondike Gold Rush. Landsmen started showing up in courthouses across the Mountain West, figuring out who owned the minerals, and in cases where mineral ownership was cloudy, filing blanket claims on all land not owned by the state or Federal Government. In some instances they began applying for drilling loans, using as collateral the leases they held on these millions of acres of potential CBM lands. As a result some of us found there were now liens on our titles, placed there by the drillers and their creditors as security for drilling loans.

Another unfortunate side-effect of Southern Utes v. Amoco was that it seperated CBM from the strict environmental requirements of the Strip Mining Act. If CBM wasn't coal then it wasn't covered by the Act, and the drillers were free to operate under more relaxed, in some instances virtually non-existent, state rules. In most cases the states were immediately overwhelmed by an anschluss of drillers and "developers." The latter an amorphous sub-classification of humanity found somewhere on the evolutionary chart between professional turkey sexers and Taliban squad leaders, with apologies to any turkey sexers who may receive this. Only Montana, of the states I've studied, has laws that gives the state and concerned citizens an opportunity to look at the whole picture before the drillers begin "developing."

For the drillers the problem was considerably simplified by the fact that in most of the West subsurface ownership rights take precedence over surface rights. These laws were enacted, or embedded in state constitutions, at a time when most of the West was unpopulated and any sort of development was viewed as a positive occurrence. (The 1872 Mining Law is another laughable relic of that era of unrestrained boosterism and Devil-take-the-hindmost exploitation.) Not only am I a restricted owner of my property, under Wyoming case and statute law I have no legal right to compensation for damage done to my property by subsurface owners. As a sop to public opinion, and as a "favor" to us, the drillers will, upon request, offer the surface owner a damage agreement, but as you would expect, the document basically says, "Nothing that goes wrong is our fault." If you protest or refuse to sign an agreement you know to be flawed there is in-place a legal procedure whereby the drillers can take you to court, post a $25,000 bond (supposedly the amount required to repair the damage they will do), and the court will condemn your land. At that point you have no further control of your surface and the driller can come on your place and do anything he wants without your permission. Since every gas well requires a wellpad, an access road, a powerline, a sludge pit, two pipelines, and every half-mile or so (depending on the terrain) a compressor station running 24/7, this court-mandated laissez passe(z) is no small favor for the drillers, and no small imposition on surface owners.

There is also the water problem. CBM is found in billions of tiny bubbles, held on the face of coal seam by water pressure. Indeed water is the other constant factor in this equation. The technology I referred to earlier involves pumping water off the seam to free the gas. According to the just-released Environmental Impact Statement for the Powder River Basin, there will be 51,444 gas wells in the Basin when the development is completed. (I'm told by a source of undetermined reliability there are only 60,000 gas wells in the whole U.S. as I write this.) Since the EIS was written by the gas developers, the actual figure, and the impacts, is virtually certain to be misstated, but for the sake of what follows accept 51,444 as a good number. Each of those wells has a pump capable of lifting 100-125 gallons of water per minute. The drillers say that's too high and the average output over the life of the development will only be 12 gpm. Sounds innocuous but when you do the math, 51,000 wells pumping 12 gpm comes to 881.2 million gallons per day. Multiply that by 365 and you have a decent-sized river drainage headed down the draw every year, lost forever to any sort of beneficial use by agriculture or the general public. Here in Wyoming water is a precious commodity. Within the memory of living Wyomingites people have been shot for stealing water, and it's still not unheard of for irate irrigators to settle some minor point of ditch etiquette with the flat side of a shovel applied vigorously to the offending party's head. In Wyoming if you have water you have possibilities. Without it you have only misplaced optimism. According to the EIS, the drillers are going to dewater the aquifer under me to a depth of 1200 feet. No one knows how long it will take for these aquifers to recharge. The drillers says our water wells will be back to 80% capacity in 30 years, but recent applications for dewatering coal mines suggest the actual figure will be somewhere between 650 and 1500 years. Imagine trying to live on a ranch without water for drinking, washing and livestock for 30 years and you have some idea of one impact CBM will have on us, and 650 years is a little beyond my current horizon. Lowfat diet notwithstanding.

At least one of you will be thinking, "Why didn't he check this out before he bought? Why didn't he know there was coal underneath his surface?" Actually, I did. I did know the coal was under there, but I also knew the coal mine 12 miles north of me has a 200 year reserve under their current lease, and from conversations with local attorneys experienced in coal and gas leases, I also knew that when the Feds leased coal the big mining companies typically offered more than fair market price for the surface. Buying the surface rights is a relatively small part of developing an open pit mine, and for pr reasons the big, experienced companies typically pay well for land. Under the circumstances it seemed like a reasonable gamble.

You must also recall that S. Utes v. Amoco wasn't decided until four years after we bought. What made sense in March 1995 no longer made sense after June 1999. We figured that if the Federal Government ever leased the coal out from underneath us, we, or our heirs, would take our settlement and start over someplace us. The CBM play impacts that assumption in that the drillers want to come on our land and destroy it, but they don't want to pay taxes on it, or pay the real cost of the damage they do to it. In effect, they'd be happy if Bet and I remained on the land as caretakers, but they don't want to assume any responsibility for safety issues, water loss or other damages that occur while we're acting as their uncompensated custodial staff. If I've left you with any remaining doubts about the drillers intentions consider this. There are 89 drillers active in Wyoming at the moment. Virtually all of them are limited liability companies, set up as legal firewalls to shield parent companies from liability if something does go wrong. Included among these titans of American industry is Enron. Their subsidiary, Bearpaw Energy, is working 3-4 miles north of us as I type this screed.

In the preceeding paragraph I also mentioned safety. CBM is a light, volatile gas, and as I mentioned it's colorless, odorless, tasteless and explosive. Once you start dewatering the aquifer there is no guarantee the gas will go up the straw the drillers have thoughtfully provided. It will migrate to any crack in the Earth's surface, or filter through the soil killing every living thing, plant or animal, in its path. On the Southern Ute reservation there's a hogback ridge a mile long and half a mile wide called Dead Mouse Hill. Every biological entity on that ridge is reportedly dead due to surface leakage of CBM. In one case in La Plata County, Colorado, which adjoins the reservation and is seven years ahead of us in this noble experiment, gas came up thru a water well nine miles from the nearest gas wellhead. When the homeowner finally got the drillers to come and look at her problem their comment, as reported in The Denver Post, was, "Better not smoke in the bathroom."

While I hope I've created a certain sympathy and understanding among you, I don't want to leave any of you with the notion you've dodged the bullet. The Senate is on recess at the moment, but when they come back they will be marking up their version of the administration's energy bill. The legislation they will be addressing is the Bush-Cheney energy wish list, (HR 4) which the House of Representatives has already passed. I don't know what they did just before recess, but the two versions of the bill they were working on last week relax Federal clean water standards for CBM developers, permit the Secretary of the Interior to revisit admin decisions designed to protect public lands from oil and gas development and determine if those decisions are still persuasive, and replaces the current public process for making major decisons about national forests by taking decisonmaking authority away from forest supervisors and giving it to political appointees in Wash DC. HR 4 also contains a provison that would require the Federal agencies to explain "on demand" why their stricter environmental standards differ from generally more relaxed state standards. If the Feds can't make the case to industry's satisfaction then the Federal standards are to be dummied down to meet state standards. To give you some idea of how this might work, here in Wyoming the State has no authority to impose any environmental restrictions on oil and gas leases. This provision of HR 4, if adopted by the Senate, would therefore remove any restrictions whatsoever on federal leases. The senior senator from Wyoming has also introduced an amendment that will provide billions of dollars in tax credits to CBM developers. Since most of them reported 60-200% increases in profitability last year it hardly seems necessary to subsidize dirty energy when clean energy is going begging for legislative support, but he hasn't yet accepted that the people who subsidize his campaigns can't enter the voting booth but once. In my own highly personal view this amendment represents nothing less than a wholesale raid on the public treasury, and an administration payoff for support provided by the energy sector in the last election. Forbes magazine, certainly a pro-business house, has characterized CBM subsidies as, "Another Loony Energy Subsidy" and the Wall Street Journal and LA Times have scarcely been more charitable.

Those of you who know us well understand Bet and I are not going quietly. I've become a board member of the Powder River Basin Resource Council, an organization of ranchers and farmers dedicated to responsible development of CBM and coal resources, I've been to Washington lobbying Congress and have participated in informal meetings with both our senators, and I've also testified before the State Legislature on CBM and water issues. Those of us opposed to unregulated development have also been able to place favorable stories in the Philadelphia Inquirer, The NY Times, The Washington Post, The LA Times (twice), The Denver Post (also twice), The High Country News, Time magazine, and The Casper Star-Tribune, plus a host of lesser outlets, and we've done a program with Bill Moyer's documentary unit that aired on PBS last Friday. Basically, we'll go anywhere and talk to anyone to get our story out and explain what's really happening in the Mountain West. Bet and I have lost our fight, but on the larger stage we're holding our own and making the feckless pimps that pass for political leaders in this part of the World justify the unjustifiable.

Bet and I appreciate your sympathy and understanding comments, and we will land someplace, hopefully in Wyoming. We'll let you know. Dale.

Bet & Dale Ackels
305 Lower Prairie Dog Road
Sheridan, WY 82801
April 29, 2002

TO: Alden Ackels
Mary and Buck Brannaman
Viv and Mike Foate
Senator Gerald Geis
Charlie Hart
Rep Jack Landon
Ted Kerasote
Julie and Kyle Koch
Jill Morrison
Patrick Murphy
Maria and Ross Peterson
Mary Ann and Nolan Perry
Jackie and Carleton Perry
Darlene Reiter
H.N.S. (different pkg.)
Senator John Schiffer
Pete Schoomaker
Fay and Ed Symons
Jim Tiffany
Nancy Wagner

SUBJ: CBM and the Legislative Environment

1. At various times I've promised most of you a summary of last summer's lobbying efforts, and the various meetings and interviews I've participated in with lawmakers and opinionmakers on the question of CBM development; how it's being done and what the implications are for those of us living east of Sheridan, along Prairie Dog Creek or in Campbell County. I apologize for my tardiness, but on several occasions I've been on the verge of sending this out and something has come up that substantially altered my conclusions or changed my views. With only 18 days left to comment on the draft Environmental Impact Statement for the Powder River Basin, I don't think it much matters what comes next. It's more important to get this out and let each of you draw your own conclusions, or decide on your own course of action before all this becomes set in administrative concrete and is no longer negotiable.

2. The original stimulus for this letter was a trip I made to Washington DC last summer for the purpose of lobbying those senators and congressmen most involved with energy legislation and policy, and on the last day of the visit to meet our own Congressional delegation and plead for their assistance in "leveling the playing field." By which I meant, insuring the various Federal

agencies charged with oversight of national energy and environmental laws were permitted to do their jobs, in the absence of any meaningful enforcement or policy assistance from our state government or Wyoming's legislature.

3.  I did not go alone, but as a member of a delegation made up of 10-15 citizens from Montana, Wyoming, Colorado and New Mexico. Most were farmers and ranchers (several were active in local Republican organizations), a couple were full-time environmentalists of one affiliation or another, and the remainder were just people from various walks of life drawn together in Washington because of their concern over how this "play" was unfolding and the likely consequences for the West. Among the organizations represented were:

> The Oil and Gas Accountability Project (CO)
> Powder River Basin Resource Council (WY)
> Northern Plains Resource Council (MT)
> San Juan Citizens Alliance (CO/NM)
> Southern Colorado CURE/East of Huajatolla Citizen's Alliance (CO)
> Wyoming Outdoor Council (WY)
> Center for the Wild West (I don't have any idea what it is, say nothing of where)
> The Western Coalbed Methane Project (All)

The week before we reached Washington another, smaller group representing the Colorado Environmental Coalition, the Greater Yellowstone Coalition, the Southern Utah Wilderness Alliance, the New Mexico Wilderness Alliance, and the Wyoming Outdoor Council (again) also came to town for much the same reasons, and somewhere during this time frame I believe a delegation from South Dakota also visited to lobby their members.

4.  Day One we split up into three person groups, each with a series of congressmen and/or senators to visit. We did not in every case see the principal, but where we did not meet with the member we met with the chief of staff, his legislative assistant (one of two principal deputies in a legislator's office), or in one case his legal assistant. I can recall only one instance where we were pawned off on an intern (by the senior senator from Louisiana), but the intern was so sincere and interested in our dilemma it was hard to take offense, and we probably went further in making a convert of her than we did some of the members and experienced staffers who did meet us.

5.  At every office call we argued four points:
- We are **not** opposed to CBM drilling in the West. We recognize its short-term importance, but we want it done responsibly and with due consideration given to the impacts on landowners, agriculture and recreational users.
- We need a landowner's bill of rights (See Inclosure 3) at the very least a Federally guaranteed right to a surface damage agreement, similar to the landowner rights in the Federal legislation governing coal development. (If the states won't give us one why not the USG?)
- In the absence of legislative resolution at the state level, Congress needs to level the playing field. By that we meant, insure that the Environmental Protection Agency, Department of Energy, USGS, Fish and Wildlife Service and the other Federal agencies involved are permitted to do their jobs and meet their legal responsibilities. We acknowledged the major battles will take

place in the state legislatures, but we almost begged our interlocutors for an even hand in administering the Federal programs and laws that impact CBM development. As you will see in later paragraphs, a forlorn hope, but at the time we felt many legislators had not made up their minds, and Senator Jeffords (D-Vermont) defection the week before might have created an openness to compromise among Republican legislators who had never before entertained the slightest doubt about the Bush-Cheney energy package.

- No one is looking at the endgame. What will happen 30 years from now when the drillers are gone and 1/3 of Wyoming is a Superfund site? Who is going to clean up the mess, and pay for it? Minimal bonding requirements in Wyoming ($25K buys you the right to drill as many wells as you want) virtually insures government at some level will wind up with the tab. State and local government won't be able to pay for it, and many (not all) of the drillers are limited liability companies set up to shield the parent company from responsibility for all of this. Who does the state sue in this situation and for what? The LLCs don't own anything but a couple file cabinets and a pickup? That just leaves the Federal government.

6. REACTION TO THE FIRST DAY'S CALLS: Reactions were all over the map. Senator Bob Smith, a sometimes Republican-frequently Independent, senator from New Hampshire greeted our group with, "I don't know why you're here. Don't know why you even bothered to come to town. We struck a deal last Saturday. Florida, the California coastline, and ANWR are off the table, and the Rockies are wide open." Subsequent events indicate either Senator Smith didn't understand parts of the deal, or it fell apart almost immediately. There's been no further agitation for drilling on the California coast and drilling in Florida is taking place some 150 miles off the coast, but the Alaska (ANWR) question wasn't resolved until last week. With reference to Senator Smith's comments about us, somewhere during this day I first heard the Rocky Mountain West identified as the "sacrifice zone," though it's never been clear if this is the Administration's language or it came from one of the Washington groups opposed to unrestricted drilling. What is clear to me is that this "compromise" could not have been reached without our Congressional delegation rolling over and agreeing to it.

As I recall, we visited roughly 30 congressmen and senators and three committees. We got a real hearing from both the Udalls, and from the New Mexico delegation in general (including a follow-on appointment with an Assistant Secretary of the Interior set up by Senator Bingaman), but the Colorado delegates were dismissive, particularly Senator Nighthorse Campbell, the Louisianans were polite but bored (Our state is a mature gas play. Your problems aren't our problems), and as noted earlier, the reaction in the other offices ranged from very interested to noncommittal. One of the most interesting reactions came from a powerful Democratic senator with presidential ambitions who said, "Wyoming may have to become the poster child for bad development to put this on the national agenda. Can you live with that?" At the time it made me squirm, but I fear he's right. Someone is going down the toilet before this gets national attention, and realistically it's probably going to be us. Colorado is seven years ahead of us, and New Mexico is also further along, but we're the biggest gas play, in a poorly regulated state, and I suspect we will in fact become the poster child for whatever is going to happen.

7. DAY TWO. Day Two was set up for visits to our own legislators. I was looking forward to pleading our case with our own crowd, but none of Wyoming's delegation would see us, though

Enzi did stop by briefly to grip and grin before leaving us with his legal aide. The staffers delegated to receive us were civil and took copious notes, and we were given a chance to make our case, but I think all we accomplished with our own delegation was to raise our visibility and identify issues they could expect to hear about again. Not surprisingly given his legal background, Enzi's staffer took a very narrow constitutional approach, somewhat along the lines of, "This is the state's business. Are you suggesting we should usurp the state's authority? Why are you bringing this to us?" which led to another discussion of level playing fields. As our delegation's designated groundskeeper I think I said something along the lines of, "If the state can't meet its responsibilities, and it's already proven it can't, where else can we turn?" I don't think for a moment I convinced him, or had the slightest impact on his views, but he and the other staffers took our names, heard us out, and promised their undying concern. To be fair, some months later, during the last Congressional recess, both Enzi and Thomas did meet with a small group of ranchers and PRBRC members. Thomas seemed to understand and sympathize, Enzi was basically unreadable. A not entirely unpredictable reaction from a seasoned politician (from Campbell County) who must stand for election in November. I cannot say I've formed any opinion on his views, other than a statement made by one of his staffers that he's "for development," whatever that means. Everyone is for development. It's the how, and how fast, that will make the difference in our lives and the lives of our heirs.

8. THE AFTERMATH: Since our visit to Washington their have been several other lobbying efforts. Though the deck was stacked against him, Ed Swartz from Campbell County testified before Cubin's subcommittee, in September as I recall, and last session Kevin Lind from the Powder River Basin Resource Council testified before the state legislature. There have also been numerous meetings with Congressional staffers, senior EPA officials, and anyone else with an interest in CBM development in Wyoming, and we've sent people all over the region to talk about our problems and sensitize voters to the problems we expect to experience as the result of uncontrolled gas development, or "capitalism on crack," as one of my sons characterizes it. Enzi has steered several delegations to Wyoming, but all have been under industry sponsorship and carefully routed away from problems areas and disgruntled ranchers. There is, of course, an alternative tour which we have come to call, "the constituent's tour." In its own way it's as slanted as the industry tour, but an outsider taking both tours could probably arrive at a balanced assessment of what's going on here and where the real problems are. The problem will always be finding that balance. The devil-take-the-hindmost crowd want to see something reassuring, and those with doubts want to see the problem areas.

In that context you all need to look at the Environmental Impact Statement (EIS) for the Powder River Basin. It's 900 plus pages long, **and written by industry**, so the impacts are almost certainly understated, but among other things it says they intend to put in 51,444 wells in the Powder River Basin, and dewater the aquifer under us to a depth of 100-300 feet in Range 84 W, and 600-700 feet on Range 83 W. (Further east they intend to dewater to a depth of 1200 feet.) At full production they will be pumping something like 881.2 million gallons of water per day down the draw, just in the Powder River Basin. Here along Prairie Dog Creek, and at the junction of PDC and the Tongue River, they plan to drill 2589 wells by 2011, but we shouldn't worry, our aquifer will be 80% recharged within 100 years. (Several recent applications for coal mine permits suggest 650-1500 years is a more realistic horizon.) The draft EIS also says we could experience gas seepage in our house wells and thru the ground within a two miles radius of any wellhead, but in La Plata County, Colorado there has been seepage as far as nine miles from the nearest wellhead, so I am inclined to treat industry's 2-mile prediction with skepticism. This matter of seepage is important to all of us since the gas is colorless, odorless, tasteless and explosive. I've talked to several attorneys about seepage and they tell me the causation question has never been resolved in court, and anyone attempting to hold the drillers responsible for seepage damage could be looking at several million dollars in legal fees. Essentially the plaintiff's burden is to prove a particular driller's activities caused the gas seepage that blew up his house or asphyxiated his family. I'm in the process of getting info on methane detectors and will pass it along to those of you in Sheridan County as soon as possible. In the meantime, don't smoke in the bathroom. If you want to see the EIS you can find it on the net at:

www.prb-eis.org/Documents.htm

All of it is troublesome, but several chapters will curl your hair. We have until 15 May to comment on it, if any of you are upset by what you see. Please note the wells to be drilled in the Montana portion of the Powder River Basin are discussed in a separate EIS being staffed by the Montana office of the BLM. They are not part of the 51,000 plus figure. I should also mention that the drillers intend to put in another 10-15,000 wells in the Green River Basin, and perhaps as many as 70,000 in the Red Desert, though this latter figure is purest speculation and I can find no corroboration for it. Last time I checked, there were only 120 test wells licensed for the Jack Morrow Hills. In wrapping up this para I should point out there are allegedly only 60,000 gas wells in the whole country at the present time.

In an earlier para I suggested Senator Thomas seemed sympathetic to our plight and more open to alternative thinking on CBM development. Having said that, in the lead up to the debate on the energy bill, Thomas introduced an amendment that will provide Federal subsidies for the gas drillers. As you can see from Inclosure 4 the major drilling companies are not doing badly now. Their return on investment is reliably estimated at 28-40% per well per year, and all of them posted impressive gains in 2000. My personal opinion is that the drillers would walk on burning gas to drill these fields, without any subsidy, and that this ill-conceived amendment is nothing less than a multi-billion dollar raid on the Federal Treasury. I am at a loss to explain it other than as a payoff to the energy sector for their generous support in the last election. As for Thomas' role in it, I suspect he was chosen because he's sympathetic to industry blandishments, and he doesn't have to stand for election in November. Nothing else makes sense. In future I suggest none of you rely overmuch on my ability to read faces, or predict any politician's behavior inside the Beltway.

At the state level, there has been some limited progress. There is strong sentiment for an increase in bonding requirements, and some sentiment for legislation guaranteeing landowners the right to a surface damage agreement. Two sessions ago John Schiffer introduced a bill that would have given us some negotiating rights. He fought it out of committee, by a 3-2 vote as I recall, but the majority leader, a woman named April Brimmer Kunz representing a senate seat safely outside the Basin in the Cheyenne suburbs, saw that it never reached the floor. Mrs. Kunz's ex-husband is mining lobbyist, and according to the Associated Press she's the largest single recipient of special interest donations in the legislature, so there's little doubt how this happened or where she's coming from. When the bill failed I argued with John that the bill hadn't gone far enough. His position was that it was all that was possible at the time and under those circumstances. In retrospect I think he was right. Geringer would almost certainly have vetoed it anyway. At the time John was the only person in the legislature willing to help us, and it took political and intellectual courage to do it. He took a considerable pounding for his efforts, and I wish I'd been a bit more tolerant and less doctrinaire. You must do what your political instincts dictate, but he's still hooking and jabbing with the riffraff, and I intend to support him strongly next election. I also intend to see that April Kunz gets a little more adult supervision than she's evidently accustomed to. If she's willing to break my rice bowl I'm more than willing to break hers.

That's about everything I would have said if we were sitting around our living room talking about this. Call me if you have questions.

Best regards,

Dale Ackels

4 Enclosures:
1. Fact sheet on CBM production in the PRB
2. Map of coal basins and CBM resources in U.S.
3. Draft landowner's bill of rights.
4. Fact sheet on energy company profitability
5. OGAP message on hydraulic fracturing. Fracing, pronounced fracking, is a process used by industry to break up underground formations and improve the flow of gas laterally within the coal seam. I have a longer e-mail from woman in Alabama who's already seen what this process will do. Call me if you want a copy. It's a particular threat to us because our coal is close to the surface, and so intermingled with our well water.

26 September 2006

United States Senate
Committee on the Judiciary
224 Dirksen Senate Office Building
Washington, DC 20510

The Honorable Arlen Specter, Chairman
The Honorable Patrick J. Leahy, Ranking Democratic Member

Dear Senators:

We write as experienced intelligence and military officers who have served in the frontlines in waging war against communism and Islamic extremism.  We fully support the need for proactive operations to identify and disrupt those individuals and organizations who wish to harm our country or its people.  We also recognize that intelligence operations, unlike law enforcement initiatives, enjoy more flexibility and less scrutiny, but at the same time must continue to be guided by applicable US law.

We are very concerned that the proposals now before the Congress, concerning how to handle detainees suspected of terrorist activities, run the risk of squandering the greatest resource our country enjoys in fighting the dictators and extremists who want to destroy us—our commitment as a nation to the rule of law and the protection of divinely granted human rights.

Apart from the moral considerations, we believe it is important that the Congress send a clear message that torture is not an effective or useful tactic.  As noted recently by the head of Army Intelligence, Lt. Gen. John Kimmons:

> *No good intelligence is going to come from abusive practices.  I think history tells us that.  I think the empirical evidence of the last five years, hard years, tells us that.*

Our nation was created in response to the abuses visited on our ancestors by the King of England, who claimed the right to enter their homes, to levy taxes at whim, and to jail those perceived as a threat without allowing them to be confronted by their accusers.  Now, 230 years later, we find our own President claiming the right to put people in detention centers without legal recourse and to employ interrogation methods that, by any reasonable legal standard, are categorized as torture.

We ask that the Senate lead the way in upholding the principles set forth in the Declaration of Independence and affirmed in the Geneva Conventions regarding the rights of individuals and the obligations of governing authorities towards those in their power. We believe it is important to combat the hatred and vitriol espoused by Islamic extremists, but not at the expense of being viewed as a nation who justifies or excuses torture and incarceration without recourse to a judicial procedure.

The US has been in the forefront of the human rights campaign throughout the 20th century, led by Theodore Roosevelt and Woodrow Wilson. The end of World War II and the horrors of the Holocaust inspired the United States to take the lead in making the case that human rights were universal, not parochial. Until recently the policy of our country was that all people, not just citizens of the United States, were entitled to these protections. It is important that the world understand that we remain committed to these principles. In fighting our enemies we must wage this battle in harmony with the traditional values of our society that were enshrined in the opening clause of the Declaration of Independence, "we hold these truths to be self-evident".
. . .

Respectfully yours,

CIA Officers:
    Milton Bearden, Directorate of Operations
    Ray Close, Directorate of Operations
    Vincent Cannistraro, Directorate of Operations
    Philip Giraldi, Directorate of Operations
    James Marcinkowski, Directorate of Operations
    Melissa Mahle, Directorate of Operations

    Paul Pillar, Directorate of Intelligence
    David MacMichael, Directorate of Intelligence
    Melvin Goodman, Directorate of Intelligence
    Ray McGovern, Directorate of Intelligence
    Mary O. McCarthy, DCI professional staff

U.S. military and Department of Defense:
    W. Patrick Lang, (Colonel, U.S. Army retired, Director Defense Humint Services, retired)

A. D. Ackels, (Colonel, U.S. Army, retired)
Karen Kwiatkowski, (Lt. Colonel, USAF, retired)

U.S. Department of State:
Thomas R. Maertens, Deputy Coordinator, Office of Counter Terrorism, U.S. Department of State
Larry C Johnson, Office of Counter Terrorism, U.S. Department of State

Federal Bureau of Investigation
Christopher Whitcomb, Hostage Rescue Team

**Washington**

# CHAPTER 15

## Newport, Washington

2003-2008

I'm convinced that when Bet and Dale fled Sheridan and methane gas and selected a suburb of Tacoma, Washington ... it was because of the Jesuits. Yes, that religious crowd that conveyed an MA from Georgetown on one Dale Ackels a few years earlier.

Just so there's no misunderstanding, I don't think it was any religious certainty that brought them North to Washington State. It was the Zag's, a basketball team at another Jesuit University ... Gonzaga.

Dale may as well be a Gonzaga grad as well as a University of Minnesota Gopher ... both have a healthy dislike for Wolverines, but his true passion, regard and interest are with the Zag's. Yes, he still follows Minnesota football, as does his sister, both grads, but both realize *Dear Abby* may be more interesting on a Sunday morning than reading Minnesota Saturday game scores!

So why does Dale have an unusual affinity for the *Zags*? In my judgment, it's the three D's ... Discipline, Determination, Dedication ... all Dale's character strengths as well as hallmarks of Gonzaga basketball. Dale never played basketball, except, perhaps pick up, but he lettered in Division 1 competition at Minnesota as a collegiate wrestler. He knows the requirements, similar to the Delta Force or Special Ops, few qualify, most are not up to the task.

Unfortunately, the Zag's weren't enough to keep the Ackels in the Tacoma rural environs. My first alert was Dale's caution when Patti and I visited and were about to take a morning walk ... *"don't go past the tree line on the road to our East, about three quarters of a mile ... when you hear the dog's barking, turn around."*

*"Huh, whatta' ya mean, Dale."*

*"Meth production, Jim."*

I was a happy friend when Winston, Montana became their new home.

## James Tiffany

**From:** "africaresearch" <africaresearch@surf1.ws>
**To:** <jamestiffany@comcast.net>
**Cc:** <bet@surf1.ws>
**Sent:** Monday, February 16, 2004 4:18 PM
**Subject:** Update

Jim: Don't know if this is your current e-mail address (there have been quite a few in the recent past) but if it doesn't go thru I'll just print it and mail it to you.

Been a lot going on over the previous 14 1/2 months. My dad is living in an Alzheimer's residence in Sacramento, suffering from something called Lewy's Body dementia. Similar to Alzheimer's except the patient also has delusions. We tried to get by with other options, but he basically torpedoed our efforts, and we finally had to put him someplace that could deal with him. It's the most elegant facility of its kind I've ever seen, but it's still confinement and with what's left of his reason he knows he's in the "clink." Because of his propensity for escape (2) we finally had to get a conservatorship for his person, giving us the authority to control his living arrangements, but going to court to prove your father is incompetent is not something I recommend on a regular basis. At any rate, he no longer lives in Santa Rosa. He's in Sacto, about ten minutes from Nan's house, in a place called Primrose. He almost died twice in December. If Nan had not investigated the first incident and been sitting with him the second time he would have passed away before Xmas. Hardly a whisper of his old self, but just prior to Thanksgiving someone on the staff asked him if he could spell Primrose. He said he could, "P-R-I-S-O-N". Part of him is still there. It's an elegant prison, but he's right. At the moment Nan and I answer to, "the goddamn bitch and the fucking traitor" but on his good days he seems willing to forgive us our various sins. There just aren't many good days.

Now for the schedule. As I recall you were planning to come see us sometime in March. Here's what I think we're going to be doing.

| | |
|---|---|
| 22-27 Feb | Job in Tampa. |
| 6-20 Mar | I'll be working in Germany |
| 17-27 Mar | Bet will be in Charlotte |
| 29 March(tentative) | Bet has surgery on her hand |
| Late April | Bet has hip replacement surgery |
| 13-21 June | Bet will be at the Wool Market, in CO |
| 11 July | Uninvited house guest, long story |
| Last two weeks in July. | Job in Italy |

Recovery time for the hand surgery forecasted four weeks, for the hip perhaps six weeks. The idea is to get her healthy enough so she can go back to Sheridan to see friends, and launch from there for the Wool Market in Estes Park, CO. Don't know what your schedule looks like for this summer, but early June or early July looks best. Or anytime in August thru early September. Let us know your druthers, but March appears to be a bust. We look forward to seeing you, under circumstances where we can all kick back and enjoy it. Dale.

# LETTERS FROM A FRIEND

**Jim Tiffany**

From:       africaresearch [africaresearch@mail.surf1.ws]
Sent:       Wednesday, September 29, 2004 5:05 PM
To:         James.Tiffany@Navigant.com; jamestiffany@comcast.net

Estimado Senor:  Ivan chased me back home more than a week ago, and at the time I responded to your 13 Sep e-mail, howsomever I suspect my e-mail never reached you.  I'm encouraged in this belief by the fact my ISP sent me a msg saying "Navigant is not a recognized port."  ???   Likely bullshit, but my ISP and another have recently merged and the "seamless integration" of the two systems has been anything but.  To make sure something reaches you I've sent this to all the valid e-mail addresses I have.

First, as for Bet, she seems to be doing fine.  She's lost almost sixty lbs, regained much of her mobility, and is now able to walk almost anywhere she wants to go.  In accomodating the injury to her hip joint some muscles in her upper leg had atrophied, and she's had some difficulty building them up again, but both hand and hip are very much better than they were when summer began.

At the moment she's in S. Carolina attending a family reunion.  Her older brother (56) is dying from a former of mental disease similar to but not identical to Alzheimer's. Classed as a type of frontal lobe dementia.  Very close to what my Dad suffers from but Dad is 33 years older and clearly approaching the end of his life.  Her brother is just now starting to manifest symptoms, but the end game is clear and inevitable, and they wanted to have a family get-together in the Carolinas while he was still in possession of his faculties.  I expect it will not go as planned.  There is significant disagreement within the family over how Jerry's affairs should be managed, and I expect that will all come out over this week.

Dad no longer lives in Santa Rosa.  He lives in an alzheimer's facility in Sacramento, about ten minutes from Nan's house.  He wasn't initially real pleased with us, but he would not accept any of the less invasive alternatives and we could not, by ourselves, deal with all the problems his decline presented.  We tried for six months, but it was clearly beyond both our knowledge and capabilities.  His physical health has improved considerably since we can now insure he takes his meds and eats well, but his mind is gone.  He thinks Nancy is his sister, he can't remember our Mother at all, and when he asks about the family he means his mom and dad.
He remembers Nancy's youngest and his two great-grandchildren please him greatly, but that's only because he's seen them more than the other three.  For example, he thinks Derek is a stray I took in and now I'm stuck with him.  Hmmm.

As far as Xmas goes, Bet is planning a family gathering here for the holidays.  Travis and his girlfriend, and two small children (I know, it's a good story), and Derek is coming in from Colorado
to join us.  Even if there was room I'm afraid the noise and confusion would drive you both mad.  As for early 2005, I'll be taking almost every job offered from Jan-early April, but May would be good.  Winter will be gone, we can travel a bit in the area, if that pleases you, and the snow is off the ground and you can see something of what the area offers.  Let me know your druthers, also how Heather's situation is evolving.  Give everyone my best.  Sorry about the commo lashup.  All that seamless integration got in the way.  Dale

N. Miami

13 Mar 05

Dear Jim:

Been awhile since I did one of these. Internet communications and brief messages couched in internet Mao-speak have pretty much replaced letter writing, but the impulse is still there, and at the moment I have the time so I'll see what can be done.

I got a nice note from Heather at Christmas, and a box of those wonderful Spoon River jellies and salsa. I haven't thanked her yet, but please assure her you've heard from me and I haven't forgotten, and will be sending an appropriate thankee note as soon as I return from this trip.

Miz Bet seems to have recovered from her summer of reconstructive surgery. There is still some discomfort, but her mobility and morale have improved 100% and she's looking forward to riding again this summer. (We brought two of our oatbumers with us from Wyoming and once she's completely healed we plan to see more of the backcountry in the southern Selkirks.)

Since we last talked or exchanged ltrs her family has discovered her older brother has fronto-temporal lobe dementia. Similar to Alzheimer's except it progresses in sudden abrupt stages rather than a long gentle decline. In that sense it's much closer to Lewy's body dementia, the form my Father has. No possibility of a cure. He'll be dead in 3-5 years. Since he's only 54 now this was not anticipated, but the signs have been there for more than a year. They only needed to put a name on it. Jerry's new wife divorced him, full of recriminations because she felt he'd hidden all this from her, and the younger sister is proving to be a problem also, so Bet is hunting for good news anyplace she can find it.

In pursuit of good news we've decided to take a cruise this summer. First to Anchorage, then by train and motorcoach to Denali and Copper River, then down to Valdez, across Prince William Sound by catamaran, and then south thru the Inland Passage to Vancouver on one of the Princess line boats. Nan and John are coming with us. It's not exactly the kind of trip I'd plan for myself, but Nan wasn't interested in anything more sportif and I wanted a trip everyone could be happy with. In planning this I've wished several times Lovejoy-Tiffany was still a going concern. We finally found a Canadian company that specializes in Alaskan touring, but it was painful trying to get to agreement with the local tour companies, or finding someone who knew how to cost out these doodahs. (My spell checker says doodah is not a word. Who knew?) No matter. It's done now. Nothing left to do but enjoy it come late August.

Travis and Derek still out there somewhere. Travis is about a year, maybe a tad more, from graduation from the University of Wyoming. He's working full time at an office supply/furniture store and going to school nights and weekends thru the UW extension service.

As for Derek, he seems content to simply exist. He runs the Colorado in summer and skis in winter, and occasionally takes a lick at an electrician apprenticeship program. He's about a year into a 4-year program, but seems typically vague about what he has to do to become a journeyman. (There are annual work hour and testing requirements that have to be met.) UW wasn't particularly kind to him. In addition to flunking out twice, he got deeply involved in weed and ecstasy, and experimented with other things, and may perhaps have fried a few million gray cells. If you listen to him he is, of course, the master of the universe. Right on top of things and making excellent progress in the dream world he inhabits, but in fact he's barely treading water. On the positive side, he seems to understand what he has to do; he just can't bring himself to do it.

He was also here at Christmas. We listened politely, nodded occasionally, and avoided reiteration of the things we've already told him 2400 times. An Ackels solution rather than a Miller solution, having to do with Bet's desire to have a memorable Christmas with her family, and put, for the moment, they previous year's difficulties behind her--at least for a week. You might not recognize him if you saw him. He looks like Grizzly Adams; about 250 lbs, sunburned, bearded, ponytailed, dresses like a logger but still as full of shit as a Christmas goose.

He does have a funny story about taking Arnold Schwarznegger down the Colorado. Remind me to tell it the next time I see you.

As for me, I continue to do consulting work; mostly defense-related over the last three years. I was diagnosed a Type II diabetic in Sep 2000, apparently Agent Orange induced. I didn't exercise the way I should have and let my weight creep up again, and last month had to go to the VA Hospital to get my blood sugar under control. I should be back under 200 lbs by the end of this week, and my blood sugar is OK again, though for the first time I have to take a pill twice a day. Up until now I've been able to control it with diet and exercise, but when I stopped dieting and exercising that didn't work anymore. What the hell. I had to get in shape for next season anyway.

From time to time you've spoken about coming to visit. We couldn't do it at Christmas, but would love to see you this summer. I've attached a list of current commitments and approximate or actual dates. Please consult with Patti (sp) and let us know when and if you can do it. Once we've got dates we'll lock them in and protect them. I think you'll like the new house. It's certainly more attractive than our little gray rectangle on Prairie Dog Creek, but we both miss Wyoming terribly. There's a character in one of Annie Proulx's short stories that explains it nicely. When asked what he was doing he says, "Still trying to find a way to stay in Wyoming." But for the fact our little farm is now an industrial gas field, and they're now talking 139,000 gas wells in the Powder River Basin (vice 51,444 in 1999) we'd still be there.

Next months marks our 20th Anniversary. You did good work that day in April 1985, for which we remain most sincerely grateful.

*Dave*

P.S. What's Heather's e-mail. She sent it to me, but I lost it.

Projected jobs and trips thru end of 2005

5-22 March           Working in Miami

28-30 March        Working Colorado Springs

1-13 April           Bet in Charlotte

17-26 April         Working in Stuttgart, GE

17-27 May          Scripting and PLANEX @ FBNC

16-19 June         Jake Clark clinic and sale in Ralston, WY

19-25 June         Tentative dates of wagon train in Custer National Forest, MT

24 Aug-7 Sep     Alaska trip and cruise

Late September   Elk hunting on Middle Fork of the Salmon (8 days)

November        Deer season in Washington *(early)*

Early December   Working @ FBNC

## Jim Tiffany

**From:** Dale Ackels [africaresearch@surf1.ws]
**Sent:** Wednesday, September 28, 2005 3:33 PM
**To:** JimT
**Subject:** Update

Estimado Senor:   Seems like awhile since I've heard anything from you.   I can normally rely on Heather to keep me informed but she's shut off the spigot too.   We hope everything is OK, and it's just something in the water.

Not quite sure where we were the last time we exchanged personal e-mails, but I know I mentioned Bet's various operations in my last Xmas ltr.  She's recovered nicely.   Can't go forever, but she's got her life back and has become a strong advocate for hip replacement surgery.   She's been horsebacking with me several times this summer and seems able to do it without discomfort.   Maybe the odd cramp, but her leg stays in it's new joint and she doesn't hurt, and that's a huge improvement.   She's started spinning and making stuff again, and seems adjusted to our new life in Wyo...beg pardon, Washington.

Perhaps the largest change is the death of my dad on May 28th.   He'd been living in an Alzheimer's facility for approx 27 months, and was there when he passed on.   A combination of congestive heart failure, pneumonia, Lewy's Body dementia, and finally a stroke that dropped him in the bathroom, hitting his head on the sink as he went down. Nan and I were with him continuously the last week of his life, and the morning of his death.  I confess I was relieved.   His body was shutting down, but he wouldn't give it up. Something in him refused to let go until the 28th,  and the struggle was most painful to watch.   He always claimed belief, but frankly Nan and I couldn't think of any fitting way to say goodby.   We finally settled on a very brief, family only service at the church where Nan was married, in Sebastopol.   The local snake handler muttered something and I spent perhaps 10 minutes explaining to the four grandsons what their grandfather was really like in his prime.   Not the occasionally grumpy, misanthropic shell of a man they knew, but what he was like and what he stood for when he was at his peak and completely in charge of his life.   Don't know if it helped them any, but oddly enough it made me feel better.  Nan too apparently.   Just the eight of us plus Travis' fiancee.  I should have told you sooner, but I've been stalling.   Don't truly know why.   I just did.

Most of the time since has been taken up with settling his estate and consulting work, but Nan, John, Bet and I decided it was time to see Alaska, and in late August we took a driving tour of the interior, followed by a cruise down the SE coast on the DAWN PRINCESS.   We were looking for a way to accomodate everyone's interests, and a conventional cruise seemed to offer the best combination of fun at sea, and good things to do ashore.   So it proved.   Can't say I'd have done it for myself, but we all had a fine time and enjoyed it.   I hadn't been back to Alaska in 34 years, and the trip certainly rekindled my interest.

That is about it.   Travis is engaged to be married (on 7-7-07) and will graduate from the University of Wyoming sometime next spring.   He will have all his course work done at the end of this semester, and needs only a year of French to finish.   He certainly found a way to make it difficult (he's working full time), but his intended bride has given him direction and purpose and he's smoking now.    What the bleep I guess it doesn't matter how you get there just so you get there.

As for the other one, he doesn't know if he's afoot or on horseback.    He works as a river guide in summer, and until he got fired for mouthing off, he was an electrician in winter. Since they've closed his river, at the moment he's unemployed and mooching off friends in Colorado Springs.   He thinks he can catch on with another contractor in Winter Park, but I'll be surprised  if he does.    He has a certain reputation these days, and in a town that size I don't think anyone will want to fool with him.   At age 25 and an avowed master of the universe he's not my problem anymore.

That's truly about it.   I'm retiring as a regular consultant/subcontractor on 1 Jan 06.   I've told my two principal clients I'll do things having to do with Africa, but don't count on me for regular
contributions after the 1st.   Hope you and your kids are well.   And Patti too, of course. Where does that stand by the way?   I know it isn't any of my business but 'll catch unshirted hell if I don't ask.    KBO, Dale

All,

Quite a cast of characters and great Americans. We have sixteen names. I'm waiting until Wednesday morning before sending the letter. There are three in our group who'd love to sign but, because they are still doing some contracting work, have received clear signals that associating their name with an effort like this could be bad for their financial health.

Accordingly, I want to thank each of you for the courage of your convictions and a willingness to speak truth to power. If this madness is allowed I fear the day will come when a Democrat will try the same nonsense and they'll use the same lame excuses that the hardline Republicans are following.
Best
Larry Johnson

15 November 2005 **DRAFT**

President George W. Bush
Office of the President
1600 Pennsylvania Avenue
Washington, DC 20500

Dear Mr. President,

Most respectfully, we, the undersigned, as former intelligence officers who have served this nation in a variety of capacities, both undercover and in the open, are writing to deplore the breach of trust between this Administration and members of the intelligence community that has resulted from the Valerie Plame case. Moreover, this nation's clandestine intelligence service will be seriously undermined if those culpable of disclosing or discussing her identity are pardoned after being found guilty or allowed to continue holding security clearances.

Mr. President, you entered office with the promise to restore honor to the White House and in the spirit of that pledge later promised to hold accountable anyone on your staff implicated in the leak of Valerie Wilson's classified identity. Mr. President, we are asking you to keep your promises.

As intelligence professionals our allegiance has been first and foremost to protecting the Constitutional government of the United States. This commitment supersedes partisan politics. We have worked undercover, out of the limelight, and employed clandestine methods to gather information about individuals and nations who have sought to harm

# DRAFT

the United States and its citizens. In carrying out these duties we rely on you and the members of your administration to protect our secrets and safeguard our identities.

Inexplicably, this bond of trust was shattered with the exposure in July 2003 of the identity of Valerie Wilson, a CIA case officer working under non-official cover. It is clear that at least two members of your staff—I. Lewis "Scooter" Libby and Karl Rove—were implicated in this act. Most of us are not lawyers and we make no claim as to whether any law was violated. However, the actions of these senior White House officials have compromised and destroyed valuable intelligence assets. It does not matter whether their disclosure of Valerie Wilson's identity as a CIA officer was unwitting or intentional. Their actions destroyed both her career and her intelligence network, which was devoted to protecting this country from the threat of weapons of mass destruction.

Therefore, we are asking that you immediately suspend the clearances of all White House personnel who spoke to reporters about Mrs. Wilson's affiliation with the CIA. They have mishandled classified information and no longer deserve the level of trust required to have access to this nation's secrets.

We also ask that you make it clear that any individual who is convicted of a crime stemming from the leak of the classified identity of Valerie Wilson, will not receive a pardon. The refusal, so far, of I. Lewis Libby to heed your call for full cooperation with the prosecutor raises the specter that he will try to stonewall the investigation in hopes of ultimately being pardoned by you.

We believe that the President, in his role as Commander-in-Chief, has a duty to demonstrate the highest standards when it comes to protecting our nation's secrets. We are reminded that Vice President Cheney, when he was Secretary of Defense, dismissed the Air Force Chief of Staff for inadvertently disclosing classified information to the press. The Vice President recognized correctly that the mishandling of classified information, regardless of intent, must be punished.

If you take these steps you will be sending a clear message that your first priority is the nation's security rather than your aides' well being. You will demonstrate that you will not tolerate people in your Administration who mishandle our nation's secrets and send an unambiguous message to the American people, as well as our enemies, that you are serious about protecting the security and safety of the America.

Respectfully,

The undersigned current and former intelligence professionals— (listed alphabetically):

**A. Dale Ackels**, Col. USA (ret.)
**Robert Baer,** former Case Officer, Directorate of Operations, CIA
**Vincent Cannistraro**, former Case Officer, Directorate of Operations, CIA
**Brent Cavan**, former Analyst, Directorate of Intelligence, CIA
**Philip Giraldi**, former Case Officer, Directorate of Operations, CIA
**Melvin A. Goodman**, former Analyst, Directorate of Intelligence, CIA

# DRAFT

**Mike Grimaldi**, former Analyst, Directorate of Intelligence, CIA
**Karen Kwiatowski**, political military staff analyst, retired Lt Col, USAF, Ph.D.
**Larry C. Johnson**, former Analyst, Directorate of Intelligence, CIA
**W. Patrick Lang**, Col. USA (ret), Chief of DIA Middle East Division, Director Defense Humint Services
**Melissa Boyle Mahle**, former Case Officer, Directorate of Operations, CIA
**Jim Marcinkowski**, former Case Officer, Directorate of Operations, CIA
**John "Jack" McCavitt**, former Case Officer, Directorate of Operations, CIA
**Ray McGovern**, former Analyst, Directorate of Intelligence, CIA
**David Rupp**, former Case Officer, Directorate of Operations, CIA
**Bill Wagner**, former Case Officer, Directorate of Operations, CIA

CC:
The Honorable William Frist,
The Honorable Harry Reid
The Honorable Pat Roberts
The Honorable Jay Rockefeller
The Honorable Denny Hastert
The Honorable Nancy Pelosi
The Honorable Peter Hoekstra
The Honorable Jane Harman

From: "Dale Ackels" <africaresearch@surf1.ws>
To: <jamestiffany@comcast.net>
Subject: 07/07/07
Date: Thursday, March 01, 2007 1:51:33 PM

Jim: I don't recall that we did talk about accomodations but I'm sure Patti's staff had a feel for what was there and the Wingate is the best of an average lot. In a feeble attempt to calm the bride's entourage we are staying at the Holiday Inn. Can't say I'm wild about it, but if Bonnie fills 20 rooms she gets a better rate for her mob. I'll help her where I can. Nan says both her boys are coming, but I'm not sure that will happen. We will see. Derek is the best man so I'm reasonably sure he will show up, with girlfriend. I hope he's thought to replace his front teeth by then. He lost them one season back while taking a religious group down the Colorado. After one particularly exciting set of rapids he let out a manly bellow and spit his teeth into the River. River guiding being the sort of profession it is he hasn't had the money to buy new ones, but his girlfriend and the wedding may spur him to buy some new front uppers.

I've lost some visibility on the Mountain West Conference, but Bet and I have had fun going to Washington State fb/bb games, and we've become passionate Gonzaga fans. John Stockton put them on the map, but with Steve Kerr (I think), Dan Dickau, Richie Frahm, Blake Stepp, Ronny Turiaf, Cory Violette, J.P. Batista, and Adam Morrison (last year's #3 pick in the NBA draft) playing for them they've turned into monsters. They play in the West Coast Conference (should be named the Western Catholic Conference since most of the members are Catholic colleges: Not sure about Pepperdine, but Loyola Marymount, Portland University, Santa Clara, St Mary's, USF, Gonzaga and University of San Diego are.) We were headed for a nice rebuilding season, and an eighth straight WCC championship, when our star center and a redshirt freshman got arrested for possession of weed and psychedelic mushrooms. The mushroom thing is a Class C felony so I would imagine we've seen the last of him. Since then the coach has completely reorganized the team and we're winning again. The Zags won the regular season championship and look good, if not great, for the post-season tournament. When the band breaks into Zombie Nation and the fastbreak is working it's a fun place to be. Odd that I should become a basketball fan at this point in my life. I never played it and barely understand it, but if we leave this place the Zags will be about the only thing we miss. Best to Patti.

Dale

**Subject:** More on the Growth of Islam in Europe
**Date:** Monday, March 12, 2007 1:03:32 PM

This is a continuation of a similar discussion widely circulating several months ago, about the time of the riots in France. It seems to me the weakness in the argument comes from our lack of knowledge of who those Moslems are and why they came. If they are moderates who came to Europe to escape the failed states they live in, and seek only to improve their lives, I suspect they are considerably less dangerous than these pundits imagine. If they don't find what they came for, then I think these people may have reason to worry.

-------Original Message-------

*From:* Jerry
*Date:* 3/12/2007 12:45:17 PM

By Paul Belien

The German author Henryk M. Broder recently told the Dutch newspaper "De Volkskrant" (12 October) that young Europeans who love freedom, better emigrate. Europe as we know it will no longer exist 20 years from now. Whilst sitting on a terrace in Berlin , Broder pointed to the other customers and the passers-by and said melancholically: "We are watching the world of yesterday."

Europe is turning Muslim. As Broder is sixty years old he is not going to emigrate himself. "I am too old," he said. However, he urged young people to get out and "move to Australia or New Zealand . That is the only option they have if they want to avoid the plagues that will turn the old continent uninhabitable."

Many Germans and Dutch, apparently, did not wait for Broder's advice. The number of emigrants leaving the Netherlands and Germany has already surpassed the number of immigrants moving in. One does not have to be prophetic to predict, like Henryk Broder, that Europe is becoming Islamic. Just consider the demographics.

The number of Muslims in contemporary Europe is estimated to be 50 million. It is expected to double in twenty years . By 2025, one third of all European children will be born to Muslim families. Today Mohammed is already the most popular name for new-born boys in Brussels , Amsterdam, Rotterdam , and other major European cities.

Broder is convinced that the Europeans are not willing to oppose islamization. "The dominant ethos ," he told De Volkskrant, "is perfectly voiced by the stupid blonde woman author with whom I recently debated. She said that it is sometimes better to let yourself be raped than to risk serious injuries while resisting . She said it is sometimes better to avoid fighting than run the risk of death."

In a recent op-ed piece in the Brussels newspaper De Standaard (23 October) the Dutch (gay and self-declared "humanist") author Oscar Van den Boogaard refers to Broder's interview. Van den Boogaard says that to him coping with the islamization of Europe ! is like "a process of mourning." He is overwhelmed by a "feeling of sadness." "I am not a warrior," he says, "but who is? I have never learned to fight for my freedom. I was only good at enjoying it."

As Tom Bethell wrote in this month's American Spectator: "Just at the most basic level of demography the secular-humanist option is not working." But there is more to it than the fact that non-religious people tend not to have as many children as religious people, because many of them prefer to "enjoy" freedom rather than renounce it for the sake of children. Secularists, it seems to me, are also less keen on fighting. Since they do not believe in an afterlife, this life is the only thing they have to lose. Hence they will rather accept submission than fight. Like the German feminist Broder referred to, they prefer to be raped than to resist.

"If faith collapses, civilization goes with it," says Bethell. That is the real cause of the closing of civilization in Europe. Islamization is simply the consequence. The very word Islam means "submission" and the secularists have submitted already. Many Europeans have already become Muslims, though they do not realize it or do not want to admit it.

Some of the people I meet in the U.S. are particularly worried about the rise of anti-Semitism in Europe . They are correct when they fear that anti-Semitism is also on the rise among non-immigrant Europeans. The latter hate people with a fighting spirit. Contemporary anti-Semitism in Europe (at least when coming from native Europeans) is related to anti-Americanism. People who are not prepared to resist and are eager to submit, hate others who do not want to submit and are prepared to fight. They hate them because they are afraid that the latter will endanger their lives as well. In their view everyone must submit.

This is why they have come to hate Israel and America so much, and the small band of European "islamophobes" who dare to talk about what they see happening around them. West Europeans have to choose between submission ( Islam) or death. I fear, like Broder, that they have chosen submission - just like in former days when they preferred to be red rather than dead.

------------------------------------------------

Europeans apparently never read John Stuart Mill:

War is an ugly thing, but not the ugliest of things; the decayed and degraded state of moral and patriotic feeling which thinks nothing worth a war, is worse . A man who has nothing which he cares more about than he does about his personal safety is a miserable creature who has no chance at being free, unless made and kept so by the exertions of better men than himself.

**ACKELS
1101 VEIT RD.
NEWPORT, WA 99156**

Estimado Senor:

I was watching a Barrett-Jackson auction the other night; $102,000 Buick Skylarks and similar, when it occurred to me I hadn't sent the promised after action report on the Senegal trip, or any of the other news I'd promised. Your recent string of most welcome and newsy e-mails has goaded me to action and tonight is catch-up night.

When you visited us you said you would watch the San Diego papers for news of unrest in Senegal~possibly attributable to something I might be doing? I doubt your local papers carried it, but there was an American woman killed while I was there. For years there's been a low-level insurgency in the Casamance, which is that part of Senegal below The Gambia. Called the *Movement of Democratic Forces of the Casamance* and led by a Catholic priest named Abbé Augustin Diamacoune Senghor and his younger brother Bertrand, they have been a low-level threat to government control in the south since 1982. These are not Islamists, they are Diolas, the tribe native to the southern part of the country, and by religious persuasion Christians and animists. This, of course, puts them automatically in opposition to the GOS and the northern two thirds of the country which is 90% Sufi Moslem. The deceased woman was an employee of the ICRC working on humanitarian relief when she had the misfortune to drive over an anti-tank mine. She was killed instantly and the other three in her vehicle were badly mangled but survived. Her parents both lived in Dakar and were well known to the French and American embassies, and her death caused quite a stir in the dip community for several days during our stay. A note of conflict (and reality) in an otherwise quiet diplomatic backwater in West Africa, but if it was reported it had nothing to do with me or the reason(s) I was there.

I haven't been in Senegal for 31 years and was eager to see how it had changed. Really not much change at all, just more of everything. Dakar has grown exponentially, and with it more hotels, more tourist related activity, more European banks and businesses, and more people. Hundreds of thousands more, with all that means for a developing nation. People are swarming into Dakar and the other cities hunting for work and a better life, and the economy isn't growing fast enough to provide either. There are signs of modernity everywhere, including tiny little internet kiosks offering internet access, printing, copying and FAX services, but the front of the main post office in the Zone Industrielle has collapsed and fallen into the street, and the little man who sells stamps operates in the shade of a golf umbrella perched in the rubble. Crime has become a serious problem, and the moderate and conservative influence of the Moslem Brotherhoods has declined in inverse proportion to the increase in political unrest and poverty. The coalition between the two dominant parties and the Brotherhoods still exists, and for the moment appears to be holding, but I suspect Senegal's polity is going to feel some strain in the years to come. It's a democratic and pluralistic society, (65 legal political parties) with a competent and well-trained (by African

264

standards) army, navy and gendarmerie, but there just isn't enough of everything to meet everyone's expectations and sooner or later I would expect exasperation with the status quo will find political expression.

You'll recall my primary reason for being there had to do with a organization called the *Salafist Cell for Call and Combat,* or in some translations the *Salafist Group for Preaching and Combat.* The French acronym is the GSPC and that's what I'll use for the remainder of this letter. Either way it's a Salafist group linked to al-Qaeda and Islamic militancy in the Near East, particularly in Algeria where it first surfaced as a lesser and discordant partner of the *Armed Islamic Group.*

In the spring of 2004 the military component of the GSPC drifted into Chad, into an area where 10th Special Forces Group advisors happened to be training Chadian troops. In the resulting brawl the military leader of the movement and most of his troops were killed, and the few who survived were driven back into southern Algeria. From that point on the military threat seemed to be under control, but there was still some concern the organizing and fundraising elements of the GSPC remained intact and might be operating in West Africa.

I had few illusions about our ability to assist the GOS, particularly after I heard the Senegalese Police had been looking for two Mauratanian members of the Dakar cell for six months and hadn't found a trace of them. With their vast local experience and network of HUMINT sources, if they can't find an African somebody he's probably not going to be found, but it was a good training opportunity for us and gave some of our young men got a chance to see how difficult this work can be for white men in a very African setting.

Having said all that, on the 9th of September our police POC asked us to clear out of the Medina, the oldest and most traditionally Moslem *quartier* in the City. When asked why he said something about some unknown somebody threatening to blow up some unknown something. Later that day they flooded the Medina with uniformed police and plainclothesmen, but we were never told what results were achieved or if they caught the guy(s) they were after. I hope so, but for us it was mostly a training opportunity.

 Not long after I returned to CONUS the GSPC announced a formal linkup with al-Qaeda, and some weeks after that they struck again, but in Algeria not in Dakar. Reports are attached just under.

One funny thing among several. We noticed almost immediately we were under surveillance. We assumed host nation police were attempting to pick up on our TTP
(tactics, techniques and procedures), but the group at the embassy had nothing visibly to do with the real work of the team, and we had a bit of fun teaching them something about street surveillance. When we asked Poppa, our police POC, why we were being tailed, he quite readily admitted the French service had paid them to do it. In discussing what the tails had seen he went on to gratuitously add, "The old gray haired one is very focused." Since I was the only gray head on the team not very much doubt who he was talking about. It was wholly unexpected and remarkably candid but I thought it was funny. Also one of the secrets of becoming old and gray-haired.

# LETTERS FROM A FRIEND

I think I've also established a tradition of commenting on local sports?  Perhaps only when something of interest appears?   Hopefully this maintains that tradition.   I believe I mentioned the local high school team is athletically challenged.   I think they lost every football and basketball game this year, but I have been able to satisfy my athletic jones with Gonzaga basketball, Washington State football, and by attending high school games in Spokane.   The Greater Spokane League plays excellent football and their basketball programs have produced Adam Morrison, John Stockton, Sean Mallon, and a host of lesser luminaries.  In fact,  Spokane is a very good basketball town.

If Bet and I don't go down to Pullman for a Washington State home game there is also Whitworth College, a Division III program on the near north side of Spokane.  The campus is quite attractive, and they play their games in a stadium called The Pines.   Seats about 3000 on one side of the field, nestled in a bowl of mature pines with green lawns sloping down to the playing surface and the  Hawaiian Club serving Asian specialties behind the press box; a most pleasant place to watch a good small college team.   They play the run and shoot with appropriate abandon and have been quite successful at it.   They went 11-1 this year and made it to the quarterfinals of the Division III playoffs before perennial powerhouse St Johns knocked them off here in Spokane.

Though unlikely to make it to the NFL, their qb was quite capable, they have a junior safety and wideout  named Jay Tully who likely will make it to the NFL, and they featured a monstrous young tight end named Michael Allan who's getting a lot of NFL attention.   NFL scouts were around all season and he was invited to play in the Hula Bowl and Shrine East-West Game.   And he went to the NFL combine,  so I guess he's got a chance.   He's 6-7 and 267 but I thought he might be too slow to play in the pros.   We'll see what the scouts think of him when  the draft rolls around.   I've included some of his press in the packet.

I've also included some stuff about Stefan Humphries.  I don't know if you remember him but he played offensive guard for Bo while majoring in microbiology and pre-med, and later won a Super Bowl ring playing for the 1985 Bears.  Turns out he practices medicine in Spokane and I thought you might enjoy reading about him, and what has become of him.   Still sounds like a useful citizen.

And finally something about our favorite innkeeper.   He's finished his new tower, just  across the street from the Davenport Hotel.   I don't know why he thought Spokane needed a 21 story safari-themed hotel, but now we have one and it's done with the same contempt for cost he showed in rebuilding the original.   I haven't been in it yet, but plan to this weekend.   Just walk around and oogle while I'm downtown getting a shotgun repaired and hunting up some sushi.

I know you sometimes keep my letters if you find them of interest, but this one should probably never see the light of day.   At least not until I'm dead, and maybe not then.  I was a little indiscreet, but it's almost certainly my swan song and if I can't trust you there isn't anyone on the planet I can trust.

266

All for now.

*Dave*

My best to Patti. Enclosed n3 stuff is designed to prime the pump. Also, hope your recovery is going well.

*Nancy and Dale, sister and brother, July, 2007*

Nancy _____
David _____

I have no idea why this article appeared this Xmas, but it brought back many memories of my year at Cal Poly. I was there in 1959-60, the academic year before this happened, and practically everyone involved in this crash was known to me. Three of the freshmen ballplayers were very good friends, perhaps the best I had in the freshmen dorms, though they were sophmores by the time of the crash: Roy Sciallaba, Brent Jobe and a big lineman named Bill Dunphy or something very much like that from Downey, California. All three of them survived, though two of them were convalescent until the next season and may not have played again. Random thoughts in tick and bullet format.

~ Ted Tollner. I forgot he played there. Later went on to be head coach at one of the San Diego schools (I think it was SDSU) and still later head coach at USC. He might have been the guy just ahead of the incumbent, though I think there was someone between him and Pete Carroll.

~ This game had been booked two years earlier, when Cal Poly and Bowling Green were considered the two best small college teams in the nation. There was no Division IAA, II, III and NAIA then. Just large schools and small ones. By the time the game rolled around Bowling Green was still good, but we were somewhere in the middle. Not bad, but no longer great.

~ Our team was built around older players, many of them former Service ballplayers, which had important implications in the aftermath. A number were married and had kids. One in particular sticks in my mind, a backup fullback named Ray Porras. To supplement his scholarship he worked in the school cafeteria bussing dishes. He left behind a wife (rumored to be functionally illerate) and four children. Most of the upperclassmen were sitting up front and most of them died. The underclassmen were in the back and most of them lived.

~ I didn't know Curtis Hill but I certainly knew who he was and had watched him practice many times. He may have been as good as Bernie Casey; he certainly had a chance to catch on in pro football. He was a big, fast wideout before big, fast wideouts became fashionable.

~ Cal Poly had used this carrier and airplane before, with somewhat indifferent results. My freshman year this same plane had pancaked in the Nevada desert while carrying our wrestling team to a meet with Weber State. They were cheap and they'd fly anywhere, pilot rest meant nothing to them, and no one saw the pattern until after the fact. Maybe pancaked is too strong. I remember they made an emergency landing someplace in Nevada, but after thinking it over I can't really recall if they were on an airstrip or swanning about in the great beyond when they did it. At any rate no one got killed-that time.

~ Until I saw this piece I didn't realize John Madden had played for Cal Poly. He's usually associated with one of the Oregon schools, and I think that's where he graduated. In high school he played for Jefferson, in the North Peninsula Athletic League. The same league we were in, though he was two years ahead of me and I'm certain I never played against him. (I did play

269

against Dick Vermeil in high school.   He was the qback at Hillsdale their first year.)

~ I tried out for the wrestling team as a walk-on and the coach subsequently offered me a scholarship for the 1960-61 season, but the long pole in the tent was I was also going to have to play cornerback on the football team.   I thought I was a step too slow and several lbs too light to play at this level, but I was excited about the wrestling aspect of it. Cal Poly had proven to be a good fit socially and academically and I had every intention of coming back, but, that was also the year Mom and Dad moved to Minnesota and while they'd been pleased with my <u>unexpected</u> academic success, they were reluctant to leave me on the Left Coast while they were so far away. I think Dad was OK with it, but Mom felt the whole thing would unravel without her benevolent presence 300 miles north.  It became a bit heated, but the compromise we worked out was that I would come to Minnesota for one quarter and if I didn't like it I could return to Cal Poly and claim my scholarship.  That was the Fall of the crash, and all the scholarship money for all intercollegiate sports was subsequently used to help the widows and orphans of dead ballplayers. It was no longer a question of whether I liked the U of M.   There was nothing to come back to. Every time I got selfish about it I thought of Ray Porras and his widow and, of course, realized the State Board of Education had made the right decision.   And that was also the origin of the Mercy Bowl.

~ Playing the what-if game, if I'd come back to Cal Poly in the fall of 1960 chances are pretty good I'd have been on that plane.   Sitting in back with friends, and probably surviving, but there's no way of knowing.   Odd the turns fortune and fate take.

I don't know if Dave would be interested in this but since he's a Mustang I thought he might. If yes please pass it along to him.

# Mercy Bowl all but forgotten

**BY BEN WALKER**

Associated Press

Exactly how high the plane got off the ground is hard to say. No one could really be sure that foggy night in Ohio nearly a half-century ago. Some folks swear the old C-46, a leftover from World War II, never lifted off at all.

Ted Tollner, a quarterback at Cal Poly, was sitting over the left wing, on the side where the

See **MERCY BOWL, C6**

*Spokane Spokesman – Review, 25 Dec 08*

FILE Associated Press

**Students and faculty at Cal Poly bow their heads during a memorial service at the school gym.**

## MERCY BOWL
### Continued from C1

engine gave out. "After we hit, it was all a blur," he said.

The Arctic-Pacific charter split in two and caught on fire at Toledo Express Airport on Oct. 29, 1960. It was the first airline crash involving a U.S. sports team. Of the 22 people killed, there were 16 Cal Poly players, a manager and a booster.

The next year, with support from Bob Hope and a blessing from President Kennedy, a game was held at the Los Angeles Coliseum to offset burial costs, pay medical expenses and set up an educational fund for the victims' families and survivors.

They called it the Mercy Bowl.

Almost 50 years since that game, the college postseason is filled with 34 bowls that make millions of dollars for the schools and conferences that participate. None is held to solely benefit a greater cause.

Today, most fans don't even recall the Mercy Bowl or why it was played.

"It did get lost," said NFL Hall of Fame coach John Madden, who anchored Cal Poly's lines in the late 1950s. "It's like it just went away."

A crowd of more than 33,000 turned out to see Fresno State beat Bowling Green 36-6 that Thanksgiving Day in 1961. Check eBay and it's easy to find ticket stubs – stamped with "Benefit Cal Poly Plane Crash Fund" – and souvenir programs for sale.

Tollner was there as a spectator, still nursing the right ankle smashed in the accident. He went to a life of coaching in the NFL and college, always wondering why he was allowed to survive.

Shortly before the flight, Curtis Hill asked Tollner to switch seats. The gifted receiver became ill on the trip to play at Bowling Green, and figured he'd do better near the front of the plane going back home to San Luis Obispo.

Tollner traded, moving back a few rows. Minutes later the pilot, flying with a license that had been revoked by the Federal Aviation Administration, tried to take off.

"I was pretty much the cutoff," said Tollner, now the quarterbacks coach for the San Francisco 49ers. "About 100 percent of the people sitting in front of me were killed. Curtis was one of them. The people in my row and back mostly survived."

"A lot of things go through your mind when you get an extra bonus of 48 years to live. Why me? Why not them? You don't know why. You think about those things when you've been spared," he said.

Those tied to that day find it puzzling how the details faded so quickly.

Many fans are well aware of air disasters that impacted sports. Knute Rockne, Roberto Clemente and Thurman Munson were killed in plane crashes, the U.S. figure skating team was lost in 1961, as was the Marshall football team in 1970, inspiring the movie "We are Marshall."

But during this blitz of almost three dozen bowls, chances are the old Astro-Bluebonnet will get mentioned more than a game that raised over a quarter-million dollars for a tragedy.

"You hear 'Mercy Bowl' and it sounds dreadful," said Bernie Casey, a former Bowling Green star who became a Pro Bowl receiver in the NFL. "You think of bowls of being a celebration. We're going to the Whoopee Bowl or Good Times Bowl.

"I don't have a clue why it didn't get more attention. It should have."

An accomplished athlete, actor and artist, Casey was among the nation's best collegiate receivers in 1960. His Falcons were unbeaten going into the game against overmatched Cal Poly that October.

Bowling Green romped 50-6. With several hours to spare before their bus to the airport, some Cal Poly players went to Halloween parties at campus sororities. Others hung around the student union. That's where Casey ran into Curtis Hill.

"We were talking about California. It had such a mystique for me, being raised in Ohio," Casey said. "We were talking about the East-West Shrine game. I told him that maybe I'd see him out there."

Already it had been a busy day for the C-46 plane, a military transport. Earlier it carried the Youngstown University team back from a game in Connecticut, then flew to Toledo.

"It was real foggy, real hard to see," Tollner said. "I've heard that some of the guys said, 'Let's give it the ol' college try.' They might've, but I didn't hear that."

There was zero visibility, in fact, the Civil Aeronautics Board later concluded.

The pilot got to make the final call on whether to take off, and Donald Chesher decided to roll with 48 people on board shortly before midnight. According to an FAA timeline, his license had been revoked for several violations. He kept flying, pending an appeal.

This turned out to be his last flight.

The twin-engine plane slammed into the ground on its left side, broke apart and wound up in an orchard. Several passengers were thrown from the crash, strapped to their seats.

"Some of the people on the plane could walk, some couldn't.

I couldn't," Tollner said. "The ones that could tried to go back in to help. Finally, some people started shouting that you couldn't go back in, the plane's on fire and is about to blow. It did, soon after that."

Back at Bowling Green, Casey was hanging out with teammates when someone burst in with the horrific news. They ran to their cars and drove to the airport.

To this day, Casey is struck by one image.

"At the terminal, the people that couldn't be saved, their bodies were wrapped in blankets and stacked up. Not disrespectful, but they had nowhere to put them," Casey said. "And they were right under a sign that said 'Get Your Insurance Here.' I'm not sure why I remember that, but I do."

Out West, the initial report said there were no survivors. Tollner's wife heard that while she was playing cards with the wives of other Cal Poly players.

The next day, Madden returned to the Cal Poly campus to console friends and families. He played there in 1957-58 before going to coach at Hancock Junior College. Over time, stories spread that he was on the plane, and that the crash triggered his aversion to flying.

"Neither one is true," he said. "I didn't like getting on planes before that. I got claustrophobic, and it got worse over the years."

Cal Poly canceled its final three games of the season. Shaken by the crash, Bowling Green decided to avoid air travel and instead took a train to its next road game – a 2½-day ride to play Texas Western in El Paso.

After the crash, the Arctic-Pacific company lost its certificate and the FAA reviewed its procedure on takeoffs under certain conditions of poor visibility.

Five wives in the Cal Poly family lost their husbands and nine children lost their fathers. Many of the survivors spent months in Toledo hospitals and left with burns and crippling injuries.

By the following spring, a game was in the works. Pulitzer Prize winner Jim Murray of the Los Angeles Times endorsed it in his column:

"On Thanksgiving morning this year in the Coliseum, a 'Mercy Bowl' benefit game will be played to help San Luis Obispo write off its obligations to the tragedy victims, the children they left behind them, and the survivors.

"My feeling is, it is not only their obligation. It is the obligation of all of us interested in athletics. I can think of no better way to give thanks on that day that we are here and healthy, than to contribute to those who are alone with only memories on that day."

Bowling Green was picked to play because of its association with the crash. Fresno State College earned its spot by winning the California Collegiate Athletic Association – among the teams the Bulldogs beat was Cal Poly, which decided to continue its program in 1961 with 10 crash survivors on its team and went 5-3.

A day before the Nov. 23 game, JFK wired a telegram to the president of the Fresno State student body.

"Your efforts to aid survivors and families of victims are most commendable and merit support. Heartiest congratulations to the Mercy Bowl game and best wishes to the participating schools," it said.

While a 26-station radio network broadcast the game and asked for donations, Beau Carter threw two touchdown passes and ran for two scores. Fresno State won with a unique strategy, sending in 11 new players midway through each quarter – substitution rules, at the time stated that once a player exited, he couldn't return until the next quarter.

Years afterward, Tollner visited a Fresno State team reunion.

"He told us how much it meant to them," Carter said. "I think it really hit us later, when it was all over. I still live here in the Fresno area, a lot of us do. I still run into people who tell me they were at the game and how much it meant."

Tollner was there, too. At halftime, he helped unveil a memorial plaque to the 1960 Cal Poly team that remains at the Coliseum. He often passed it when he coached at Southern California.

"There are so many bowls now, I have trouble keeping track of all of them, and I'm in the business. I've been lucky and gotten to coach at a lot of bowl games. Head coach at a Rose Bowl win," he said. "But I don't think any of them were any more meaningful than the Mercy Bowl."

All the proceeds went to the memorial fund, providing $278,000 to those affected. In 2006, Tollner spoke at the dedication of Mustang Memorial Plaza on the Cal Poly campus, honoring those killed.

In 1971, there was a hastily arranged Mercy Bowl II, with Cal State Fullerton beating Fresno State 17-14 in Anaheim. The game was a benefit for the children of three Cal State Fullerton assistant coaches and a pilot killed in a plane crash a month earlier.

"You know, it wouldn't be a bad idea to play a game like that again," Madden said. "Hold a bowl game for a cause. There are a lot of good ones. I'd like to see that."

*Sorry this took so long. It wasn't much help to you.*

MAY 0 7 2009

*ACKELS*
*1101 VEIT RD.*
*NEWPORT, WA 99156*

TO: Nan and John
     Patti and Jim ✓
     Pat and Jerry

Approximately 24 months ago, give or take a month, Bet and I went to New Zealand on a holiday. Several of you asked for an after action report, but for one reason or another I never got around to it. Now I've waited so long Patti and Jim have already gone. Not much left to surprise them with, but I thought I'd send the final product anyway. If for no other reason than to compare notes and see what we missed in 2007.

This trip was to participate in a crafter's tour of New Zealand. Bet had seen it advertised somewhere, and on a whim I gave her the trip for her 2007 birthday. These tours had been put on by the Interweave Press, a publishing house specializing in books on spinning, weaving and combat knitting, and I believe they also publish a magazine called Spin-Off. At any rate it's a tour for people with very special interests. Sometime in 2006 or early 2007 they decided not to do it anymore, and two of their guides took it over as their project. Nola and Jane Fournier, a mother-daughter team; Nola still living on South Island, NZ and the daughter Jane in Helena. They'd written a very technical and well-respected book on sheep fleeces and their properties, and when Interweave gave it up they stepped in. They had the know-how and contacts, and they wanted to do it so it was a logical, and I hope profitable, progression for them.

My ltr is somewhat scattershot. In addition to the tourist stuff, my info addees are involved in stock raising and they expressed an interest in that aspect of what we saw and did. One is developing a commercial alpaca herd in central Missouri, another runs sheep and cattle on his place in south-central Missouri, and the third is in the process of converting part of the family ranch in Wyoming from beef cattle to black Dorpers (a meat breed). The middle individual has also hunted in NZ, and shares my interest in hunting, fishing and the field sports in general. As a result, you will find scattered throughout the letter references to sheep breeds, carding machines, alpaca farms, and various other things you might not have expected to find in a letter on tourism in NZ. Please bear with me. I'm trying to hit a lick for everyone.

I'd been to New Zealand once before, in 1968. I flew down from Tokyo for a red deer and chamois hunt in the Southern Alps, but the focus of that trip was hunting and fishing, and I saw little or nothing of the cities and people, and nothing at all of North Island. This was to be different in that I was along as supernumerary and baggage handler, and the primary purpose was to learn about NZ crafts people. If I managed to sneak into a gun store or talk to some outfitters

273

that was a plus, but this was, by design, Miz Bet's trip.

You can get there by direct flight from either San Francisco or Los Angeles on Air New Zealand. We chose LA. It's 10,850 km, 12 hrs 20 minutes flying time, with arrival just before sunrise. Nice airline, nice clean plane and a nice crew. Plus nearly 12 hours of watching the All Blacks pound Australia, France, South Africa, the UK and assorted Polynesians in rugby football.

Day 1 was acclimation day. We were staying at the Sky City Hotel. Industrial innkeeping carried to its logical conclusion, but a good location in the center of Auckland. All I remember about it was a concessionaire on the front terrace selling a chance to jump off the hotel roof. It's not really bungee jumping, or BASE jumping either. The jumper comes down on a cable affair, strung between two guidewires. One hundred ninety two meters for NZ$195. Not only do they kick you off the roof, they dress you up in a jump suit and you get a free photograph of yourself a couple dozen feet off the ground, wondering if the cable brake is going to work.

Not what we had in mind. We took a bus tour of the tourist sites, at one point standing on top of Mt Eden, one of the 40 plus volcanos and cinder cones the city is built on. Somewhere in there we also stopped at the Auckland Museum, which in retrospect was much the best museum in the country, particularly for Maori culture and artifacts. That one I'd go back to see, though preferably with a night's sleep behind me. By mid-afternoon we were cruising in Waitemata Harbor. Somewhere in my traps there's a picture of me and the recently retired Chief Justice of the Navajo Supreme Court piloting a 50' ocean-going sailboat through the harbor. Sun burned, salt encrusted, late middle-aged mariners, squinty-eyed, watching the horizon for the Exxon Valdez, Somali pirates or whatever else threatens passengers and crew. Actually the squinty-eyed part was just jet lag but I liked the imagery and kept the other stuff in. What you can't see is the two experienced yachtsman standing close by to take control if it looked like we're going to ram the North Auckland Bridge. Amazingly responsive boats, and fast. One of NZ's candidates for the Americas Cup was practicing in the outer harbor and I suggested we drag him for pink slips, but wiser heads prevailed. Even tacking, which I thought would be a major undertaking, was ridiculously easy.

One of the founders of Netscape (James Clark) had his yacht the *ATHENA* tied up at the Hilton Hotel pier. Three masted, 290' long, with a crew of 19, built at a cost of $100M. Obviously, when Microsoft crushed him he escaped with a few pennies. The crew actually sails the boat wherever Clark wants to vacation, then he flies to their location and lives on the boat. Clearly not a sunburned, squinty-eyed, salt encrusted sailor like some I met that day.

New Zealand's population has doubled since my last trip; from 2M to 4M, but 3M of those live in and around Auckland. For its size it's a surprisingly liveable city, and on Day 2 we took off to see it on the LINK bus, which circles the City on a regular route. All the way around for NZ$1.60, clockwise or counterclockwise. Your choice. You can get off and on anywhere on the same ticket. We stopped in Newmarket, ate lunch (regrettably missed the Dog's Bollix Pub), walked around, shopped a bit, and were back at the hotel in time to watch two more dummies jump off the roof, eat dinner at the Harborside Restaurant and get caught up on sleep.

Day 3 we're headed south on the Southern Motorway, thru Manakau, Papakura, Bombay Hills, Mangatarata, Matamata, then by x-country roads to Hwy 5 and into Rotorua on the west side. A word about Matamata. It's where much of the filming of **LORD OF THE RINGS** took place and a major tourist stop for Japanese and mainland Chinese bus tours. The town is small to start with and literally crawling with rice-burning hobbits. We grabbed a sandwich and got out of there as fast as possible.

Enroute we stopped at the Agrodome, which I thought from reading the promotional material was going to be a stock show. It's more of an exhibition, and for our tour the beginning of the "real stuff" our group came for. A brief introduction, with the actual animals, of all 19 sheep breeds found in NZ, followed by a demonstration shearing, some dog work and a demonstration of a century old industrial carding machine. A massive, multi-ton piece of post-industrial ironwork, all gears and rollers and strapping, brought to NZ in 1906-07 and in continuous use since. The proprietess uses it for demos, but she also does commercial work for local sheep and alpaca farmers.

During the dog trial part of it we were introduced to a new breed (for us). Called the Huntaway, it's a mixture of black lab, German shepherd, bloodhound and something else. Perhaps Border collie? Later the bus driver, herself married to a dairy farmer, told us the Huntaway was a good dog, but, "Always has to have the last word. Too loud for me." They are loud, and big.

The local Border collies are a bit different too. One of the farmers told me he crosses his Border collies on whippets to get more speed and agility. In the outdoor demo he established to everyone's satisfaction his dogs could get around.

We stayed in the Sudima Hotel for two nights. My first time in Rotorua (or anywhere else on North Island for that matter), though I've read about it all my life. But for the stench from the sulphur pots, a volcanic feature on the south side of town, another tidy and comfortable town. Good restaurants, a jade factory, good markets and a laudable respect for their architectural heritage. Every noteworthy public and private building in town has been rehabbed and put to use. There's no particular pattern to it, but the overall effect is interesting and pleasing. And the lake fishing for big rainbows is still said to be good.

Our second day schedule (in Rotorua) called for a visit to Te Puia, advertised as a Maori cultural center. I assumed it would be something like Bomas of Kenya, but it was very well done and the Maori docents were knowledgeable and helpful. It begins with a traditional welcoming ceremony, which looks suspiciously like an invitation to single combat, a live performance in a restored *mawae* (clan meeting house), Maori weaving and carving demos, a discussion of Maori boatbuilding and canoes, and a better than average summary of Maori religious beliefs. Twelve heavens with twelve gods to guard them; each representing the most important virtues and elements of the Maori cosmology. And all of it reflecting a decidedly singular and unusual religious agenda.

Miscellaneous Maori facts: (1) All Polynesian languages are mutually intelligible. Regional differences have evolved over time, but a Maori can understand a Cook Islander, a Tongan, a

Samoan, a Fijian or a Hawaiian. (2) Though they are mutually intelligible, the Maori dialect is said to be the most direct and "aggressive." (3) The culture, particularly costumes and singing, is evolving continuously. The message remains constant but the details are always changing. (4) The faces shown on the 12 god carvings are deliberately warlike but it's an artistic convention, not the normal way of depicting them. (5) Each god carving contains a male and female component, and the cloak contains clues showing you who you're looking at. In a sense traditional carvings are memory aides.

We also stopped briefly at the Waiparu and Te Werenga geysers on the way out of town, but probably wouldn't do it again. If you've seen Yellowstone Waiparu won't be of much interest.

Other apparently upscale hotels in Rotorua of possible interest: the Regal Palms, Prince's Gate (it might have been Princess Gate), the Koura Lodge and Pukeko Landing. Didn't see the last one but heard good things.

We left Rotorua via Lake Taupo (another famous fishing destination), and past an unremembered thermal feature, Huka Falls and Te Kuiti. Of the four Huka Falls is probably most interesting, but under other circumstances I could have happily spent a full day on Lake Taupo. Our route took us over the main spine of the North Island ranges, past perhaps a dozen parks and forest reserves and several more promising trout streams. In crossing east to west the drive takes you past miles of commercial evergreen forests. As you would expect it's a monoculture with little to recommend it, other than the problem of figuring out what it was. It looked like a pine, but not like one I remembered, and I asked the driver what it was. She said it was an American variety, *pinus radiata*, which didn't help me much, but when I got home I looked it up and it's the Monterey pine. It's a protected species in Monterey County and the North Coast; just a view scattered groves left. It may be rare in California but the Kiwis are down to their last couple hundred thousand acres and I don't think it's going extinct anytime soon.

Our destination was New Plymouth, on the west coast. New Plymouth is NZ's energy capital, but in spite of offshore oil wells, geothermal energy plants, one or more methanol plants, and a proposed wind farm in the vicinity, like most New Zealand towns, it's pleasant, clean and liveable. The Kiwis seem to have a knack for integrating necessary industrialization and urban environments without finding it necessary to destroy their quality of life, and New Plymouth was no exception.

Our real purpose in visiting New Plymouth was to attend the Creative Fibre Festival, called Taranaki 2007, held at the local rugby field. A trade show and sale on the ground floor; fibre, looms, spinning wheels, weaving and spinning accessories on the second deck; and a fibre crafts exhibition on the third floor. I have to admit the exhibition was eye-opening.
All of it done by local crafts people, but all of the highest quality and showing considerable imagination and craftsmanship.

We had a second, free day in New Plymouth so with another couple we rented a Nissan Bluebird from an agent in Spotswood and took off to "Ride the Big Circle" around Mt Taranaki, the dominant terrain feature in the immediate area. Think of Mt Shasta or Fujiyama and you have the basic idea. We made several stops but nothing of particular interest and I don't think it's necessary to rehash it. Just a pleasant day in the country.

From New Plymouth we flew, via Wellington, to Nelson, our first stop on South Island. This is Nola's home town, and she had several things she wanted us to see. Beginning with the Museum of Wearable Art and Classic Cars in nearby Richmond. Which proved to be a collection of truly bizarre women's clothing~and, as advertised, classic cars. I was particularly taken with one mannikin sporting what looked like two chromed tire irons protruding from the front of her Merry Widow, and another made up with bicycle parts to look like a samurai in full body armor. As for the cars, there was a gull-wing 1983 Lola, a right hand drive 1937 Cord, mid-century Fords and Studebakers, a nice Jag sedan, a raft of Fleetwoods and El Dorados, even a 40's era Packard. All of them nicely restored and displayed.

Lunch at the Seifried Winery, which is also in Richmond on the road to Rabbit Island. Kiwi winemakers are about where Washington State was 30 years ago and California was after Prohibition. Still trying to figure out what grows best in their climate and what they can make from it. So far there's general agreement on their sauvignon blancs, but you can buy almost any varietal you can buy in California and it will be drinkable. Different perhaps, but drinkable. Lunch outdoors at the winery was relaxing. Had a nice glass of their new gewurztraminer with dessert and sampled everything else. This area of 15-20 square miles is mostly wineries, and you will be able to duplicate our experience at any one of a dozen or more vineyards and restaurants. In some ways the area reminded me of the Paarl wine growing region in South Africa. Just a little newer and not as well-established, but with a bright future.

Nelson is a very pleasant, small city on the edge of the water but constrained in its growth by high ridges on three sides. Across the Bay, around Motueka, there is plenty of good farm ground and an equally pleasant climate. In addition to the wine grapes already mentioned, they grow table grapes, apples, oranges (including mandarins), pears, tomatoes, cut flowers, berries, kiwis, hops, truck crops and cherries. Also, some kind of small melon I couldn't identify.

There was an intermediate stop at a lace museum near Upper Moutere, but I stayed out in the yard and watched birds. From the lace museum north thru Lower Moutere, Motueka and Riwaka to the beach community of Kaiteriteri, a favorite of South Islanders and the jumping off place for boat and kayak trips to Abel Tasman NP. Worth a second visit for adventure travel in sea kayaks.

Late in the day Nola took us to the Fibre Spectrum, a handweaver's coop she belongs to in downtown Nelson, but we had time for a slow walk back to the Rutherford Heritage Hotel and dinner at Oceana. Supposedly one of the ten best restaurants in NZ, and based on our experience it probably is.

April 17th was a travel day, from Nelson cross island to Christchurch, with stops at Murchison for coffee, Hope River for lunch, and Black Hills Farm to look at a nice herd of (naturally) colored sheep and watch local women model clothing they'd made for an upcoming show. One lady was covered from head to toe in a knitted brown wool sleeping bag. It looked like a vanload of

Norwegians had run over an IED and when the debris settled this poor woman was left standing, covered head to toe in parts of 15 sweaters. Bet heard her say God told her to do it, but I'm sure the message must have been garbled in transmission. Most likely God told her never to do that again, or he'd bust her spinning wheel.

We stayed at the Rydges on the square in Christchurch. There are over 400,000 people in Christchurch now and almost nothing looks the same except the Cathedral that gives the city its name and the parks along the Avon River. Bet went to hear a traditional story teller and I spent the first full day in Christchurch prowling sporting goods stores and booksellers. Some nice stuff but nothing worth busting my baggage allowance for. I came away with one book and a lot of exercise.

The following day we drove to Lyttelton, to see the harbor and take a brief cruise out to the ocean. Lyttelton sits at the head of a long, very narrow and circumscribed bay, almost like a fiord. It's significant because it's the place the first settlers landed in 1830 (?), and because it's one of the few places you can see Hector's dolphin, supposed to be the smallest member of the dolphin family, (though I've since discovered there's an even smaller species living at the head of the Gulf of California). No matter, we saw a Hector's dolphin and had a pleasant cruise. At various times Lyttleton has been a whaling station, an immigrant quarantine station, a military port and a fishing port, but at this point in its evolution it's a container port, and a shipping point for coal and lumber. Two large container ships arrived and one departed in the four hours we were in the harbor. Hard to imagine they can turn them around that fast in those narrow and confined waters, but clearly they do it.

Enroute to Lyttleton we stopped in West Mellon, at a business called Southern Alpacas. As the name suggests, it's an alpaca farm. They run 200 females and 27 studs on a relatively small acreage, and they appear quite successful. Apparently because they've vertically integrated their business to insure they derive income from every stage in the process. From breeding and showing, marketing, processing fiber and selling roving and finished products. I was surprised at how many had bad feet, but that's not what they're breeding for and I guess you can't argue with success. They do a land-office business, with tours coming and going all day. The owner told me they got about $1.96 an ounce for raw fleece, but Bet bought 300 grams for NZ$18 and seemed quite satisfied.

The 20th of April was ANZAC Day, commemorating the joint Aussie~NZ effort at Gallipolli in WWI. Bet and I bought our red poppies and checked out of the Rydges about 0900, bound for Central Otago by way of the Ashford Factory in Ashburton, The Tin Shed (another wool and fleece outlet), and the villages of Geraldine and Fairlie, where we would join up with a farm family and spend the night. NOTE: Other hotels in Christchurch: the Sequoia on Old North Main, Warners on Cathedral Square, and the Millenium and Heritage, also on Cathedral Square. Warner's will doubtless prove a bit spendy, but it looked the most interesting.

Ashford is the largest manufacturer of spinning wheels in the World. There are all sorts and types of craftsmen-built wheels available, but Ashford seems to stand alone at the head of a (very) short list of high quality factory makers. Over 500,000 wheels made since they went into business. They make several models, plus carding machines and winders; all of it made almost entirely of silver birch grown for them in Southland. Nola used her connections to get us a factory tour, followed by another nice lunch on the factory grounds. I seem to be getting good at lunches. I never was a slouch in this area, but this week in NZ has given me much needed practice, and added a touch of alcoholic indolence that wasn't there before.

Geraldine proved to be a museum stop and another grip and grin with more of Nola's friends. Some nice planes and old cars, but all in need of funding and a general cleanup. Not Nola's friends, the cars. Speaking of which, and before we leave the Canterbury Plain, the Royal New Zealand Air Force Museum is just outside Christchurch. I didn't visit it but I'm told it's well done and a must stop for airplane guys.

Our surrogate families were waiting in front of the pub in Fairlie when we rolled in. Everyone paired off and we drew a very nice young couple, Sarah and Simon Cowan. As soon as we got the bags unloaded we jumped in the jeep and Simon gave us a tour. They run about 900 Romneys on 200+ hectares, using the NZ grazing system (not too surprising). They also raise their own feed, do some apples and pears for home use and fatten a few market calves. Simon runs the place by himself, with the help of a couple stock dogs, and seasonal help with the shearing. (One of his dogs was a Huntaway). Their lifestyle isn't opulent, but they're certainly very comfortable, and we enjoyed the chance to slow down and talk to people whose primary focus was not on tourism or selling us something. The next morning everyone on the tour seemed to have had an equally positive experience.

The bus is starting to feel like home and I was glad to get back on it and head for "my" Queenstown. The city we used as a jumping off place for my hunt in 1968, and still one of my favorite places. From Fairlie we went by way of Timaru, Waimate, Omarama (for tea), Lindis Pass, Tarras, Cromwell and then into Queenstown and another iteration of the Rydges Hotel chain.

Our principal enroute stop was at Albrey (sp) Farms, outside Waimate. Another sheepman, but his special niche is internet sales of naturally colored fleeces~ for handspinners. He runs about 500 head on 100 hectares, all of them Romneys, Merinos or Polworths (1 part Lincoln or Leicester and 3 parts Merino), and all of them naturally colored in shades of gray, brown, tan, roan or blue-gray. Some are mottled in several shades and some are also a dark chocolate color. Obviously, in his breeding program he's selected for natural color and quality of fleece, and it must be working. In addition to his global internet sales, he's also opened an outlet in Alaska. I know a lot of money and raw wool changed hands during our visit.

He showed me how to skirt a fleece (trim and prepare for processing), and later served us yet another lunch. This time in their garden with a nice view of the mountainside. I'm starting to expect it at every mid-day stop. "What no lunch! Get back on the bus."

The 22d was spent in Arrowtown, a very attractive small town a few miles NE of Queenstown. The town is only 7-8 miles from the Shotover River, where gold was first discovered on South Island, and Arrowtown itself was also the scene of a significant strike. Nan, in many ways it will remind you of Sierra City. Substitute the Arrow River for the North Fork of the Yuba, and add a very nice museum, (the Lake District Museum) and you have it.

One of my must-do things was a trip up Lake Wakatipu on the TSS Earnslaw, a 340-ton coal-powered steam packet that's been on Lake since very early in the 20th Century. In 1968 it was already carrying some backpackers and vacationers, but its primary mission was to haul freight to 11 sheep stations on the Lake; outposts inaccessible by land. Only two stations left now and the *raison d'etre* has become tourism. The cargo handling gear is still there, but the hatch covers have been taken off and replaced with seats, and at night it looks like a floating nightclub. The Lake is 83 km long and we didn't go all the way to the north end, but we did go as far as Walter Peak to pick up a load of daytrippers at one of the lakeside resorts and carry them back to Queenstown.

A few random thoughts and potentially helpful facts:
~ Tourism has become a big thing. The year of my first trip only 38,000 visitors came to NZ but the year before my second trip there were approximately 2,000,000. Most of it driven by the Ring movies and outdoor adventure travel.
~ Gasoline was the equivalent of US$4.28 when we were there. Don't know what it's done since but gas for a rental car won't be cheap. Rental cars, on the other hand, are cheap, or at least reasonable.
~ The ferry between North and South Island is also very expensive. NZ$1500 for a bus and NZ$190 for a car, and it's not that far across the Straits. Best, I think, to fly between islands.
~ There's an airport departure tax of NZ$25.
~ ATMs are available nearly everywhere and your card will work.
~ Don't know what kind of touristy things you might be interested in, but plant material and seeds are a waste of money. I brought back several seed packets, an acorn (?), and a rose hip from a plant Bet particularly admired. I declared them all and Dept of Agriculture took them all away. The rose hip and the acorn were almost expected, but they even took prepared seeds in packets.
~ One item almost everyone buys is greenstone. I told a friend here in Pend Oreille County that it was *jadeite*, the true jade found in Burma and southern China, but it isn't. Under magnification it has the same pebbly surface as true jade, but it's actually *nephrite*, the same material we call Wyoming or Alaska jade. Like true jade it's primarily found in shades of green, but there's some that's almost black, a little bit of white, and even some gold colored pieces. In 1968 Billy Hayward, a hunting friend from Wanaka, and I climbed up into the headwaters of Greenstone Creek with day packs and a claw hammer. The stuff was everywhere, in boulders the size of stoves, in stream-washed rocks and slivers, and in pieces lying about where earlier prospectors had broken up larger chunks. I just knocked off several pieces with Billy's hammer. Can't do that now. Between my two trips the Government reached a settlement with the Maoris over longstanding land disputes. Several hundreds of millions of dollars involved, the Maoris were able to reclaim some of their most important sites and were given right of first refusal when other significant sites appeared on the market, and they were given Greenstone Creek. In its entirety. As a result, if I did that same thing today I'd apparently be arrested and fined, if not jailed. The odd thing is most of the Maoris and most of the carvers are on North Island, but the greenstone is found only at that one place on South Island and South Island prices are better. One of the travel guides Bet and I read before the trip said the little town of Hokitika in Westland has the best

prices of all. Can't say, I've never been there, but will let you know 'cause Bet and I are leaving next week for another visit. I'm leaving the 13th for a weeks hunting in the Southern Alps and Bet is following along on the 19th. We'll meet in Christchurch on the 22d and go south and west from there.

Hope this has been some help to all of you, and I hope you all make the trip. Again, if you've already been, and once for sure if you haven't. Whatever your interests are, you won't be sorry. If you've got questions let me know and I'll do my best to answer, within the limits of my experience.

cf: Phil Glenn, Jerry Fry, Eric Barlow

1 Incl: List of hotels

## New Zealand Hotels

| | |
|---|---|
| Auckland | Sky City Hotel |
| Rotorua | Sudima Lake Rotorua |
| New Plymouth | Copthorne Hotel Grand Central |
| Nelson | The Ruthorford Hotel |
| Christchurch | Rydges Hotel Christchurch |
| Queenstown | Rydges Hotel Queenstown |

# CHAPTER 16

## Winston, Montana

2009-Present Day

# LETTERS FROM A FRIEND

AUG 2 6 2009

Box 135
Winston, MT
59647

Nan and John
Patti and Jim
Pat and Jerry

Watching the All Blacks play Australia in rugby last night reminded me I still owed an after-action
report on the most recent visit to New Zealand.   I'm trying to do better than my two year delay
between trip and follow-up report on Kiwi II.   Kiwi II was the ltr discussing our 2007 trip, and
this will be Kiwi III.   Don't know if there'll ever be a Kiwi IV, but I do know it won't be anytime
soon.

I reached NZ a week before Bet.   Long story but I was hunting on South Island for tahr, arapawa
rams, red deer and ducks.   Winter came a month early this year and I couldn't stay in the high
country long enough to find a tahr, but the rest of it went well and I was pleasantly sore and tired
and ready for a bit of general tourism when she arrived.

**Christchurch to Queenstown~498 km**

First day took us from Christchurch to Queenstown, over Lindis Pass and Burk's Pass.   It was
snowing when we started to climb but only 3-4 inches accumulated and we pushed thru without
having to chain up.   A pleasant night at the Tanoa Aspen Hotel, a brief look around the town,
then on to Te Anau.   Rain, mist and overcast most of the way but we got great looks at Lake
Wakatipu and Lake Te Anau enroute.

**Queenstown to Te Anau ~180 km**

Te Anau has always been a priority on my list, if for no other reason than because it's the capital
of Fiordland and I'd never been in Fiordland.  First stop was a night cruise to the glowworm
caves on the west side of the big lake.   About 45 minutes by boat from Te Anau.   The whole
complex is called the Aurora Caves, some 7 km long.   It takes four days of steady slogging
around underground to see it all, but the glowworms are found only in the first 250 meters, easily
reached by trail and boat.   The glowworms are a species of larval fly, but only the larval stage is
bioluminescent.   The glow is to attract moths and other prey to the sticky fishing lines lowered
from the ceiling.    They're also a bit cannibalistic.   Every worm has his personal space and he'll

eat any other worm that encroaches. Floating around underneath them they look like clusters of faint blue stars in a distant galaxy. Interesting but not reason enough by themselves to come to New Zealand.

Next day was Milford Sound. Almost every tourist pamphlet contains one or more pictures of the Sound, and of Mitre Peak. There are 14 major fiords on the SE side of the Island. Milford is the most northerly, the shortest, and the best known, but all of them are magnificent. Rather than drive from Te Anau to Milford to catch a boat, we bought a package in Te Anau. Roughly 45 miles each way with intermediate stops at Mirror Lake, The Chasm and another place whose name escapes me. Most all of this part of the country is part of Fiordland National Park. The largest park in NZ. Roughly 3.2 million acres, most of it untouched by man. Blanketed by forests of silver, red and mountain beach, cabbage trees, manuka, tea trees, tree ferns and a variety of other species I can't even begin to identify. We rode the MILFORD MARINER out to the Tasman Sea and back, took photos of the various waterfalls enroute, and generally enjoyed ourselves. I somehow thought Milford Sound would be isolated and that we'd have it all to ourselves, but there were three other tour boats coming out of the dock. Outward bound we looked like a WW II convoy coming out of Murmansk. Still, another good day.

Dinner at the Redcliff Restaurant on Mokunui Street in Te Anau. Bet had wild venison, portobello mushrooms, stuffed kumara (a species of native tuber), and house salad. I had Redcliff paté with crushed berries, smoked salmon with citrus aioli on honey-glazed kumara, and we both had lemon-passion fruit brulé for desert. I tell you all this because it was our one splurge and the best restaurant meal I've had in years. Damn it was good. Forget the glowworms, instead head for the Redcliff and talk about worms.

A word about the pronunciation of Te Anau. I've been wondering for years, but figured I'd find out on this trip. Particularly since the bus driver who took us to Milford was a Maori and he would surely know. Everyone agrees the first word is pronounced *tay*, but there are two competing theories on *anau*. Some say an-noo and others say a-now. Unfortunately, the bus driver said it both ways so I'm no closer than when I started. I'd go with *tay an-noo*, but it's six to five and pick 'em.

**Te Anau to Haast~427 km**

The 26th took us back thru the Gibbotstown Valley wine-making region, thru Queenstown, then to Wanaka and over the mountains to Haast on Hwy 6. 427 kilometers, some of it slow going thru the mountains. We're in Westland now, another first, and staying at the Haast World Heritage Hotel. (If I had to do it over again I'd try the Heritage Park Lodge.) As the name of the hotel suggests, Haast is a designated World Heritage Site. No one reason. It's the isolation, the Haast River, forests, rare birds, and the sea mammals. Sea lions inshore, orcas just off the coast and the great whales out to sea.

Haast wasn't settled 'til the 1920s, and wasn't connected to the rest of South Island until Nov 65 when a road was completed from Otago. Before then they were resupplied by boat once every three months, and their mail was brought 90 miles by horseback from Hokitika. If my memory is right I think the round trip took a week. Once called *"Far Downers"* because of their isolation, there are still only a few hundred people living in this corner of Westland.

## Haast to Greymouth~Approx 331 km

Next leg was Haast to Greymouth, with an intermediate stop at the greenstone factories in Hokitika. Enroute we stopped just north of Lake Mapourika. At that one place there's a notch in the mountains and on a clear day you can look back to the southeast and see Mt Cook, the highest peak in NZ. First time I've seen it in 41 years.

Can't say I was much impressed with Greymouth. It's a seaport, and the home of Monteith's ale (which speaks well for it) but it's scrunched up against the side of a mountain, and in the winter there's a dense pall of grey coal smoke hanging over the city. So thick it's kind of hard to breath. But Hokitika proved interesting and informative.

I've never been any place in Westland before this trip, but both of us wanted to see Hoki because it's the location of most of the greenstone factories and dealers in NZ. First stop was The Jade Factory. Four carvers working on the premises, and a most interesting display of slabbed, backlit greenstone (nephrite) variations in an adjoining hallway. The most expensive piece I saw was a ceremonial weapon; sort of a traditional symbol of office, for NZ$15,900, which was on that date $9699 US. But, you could also buy a greenstone putter for N$155 ($195 shafted), or a black nephrite putter for NZ$1500, if the urge to own a jade putter becomes compelling.

For Pat Weeks: In Kiwi II I said something like," Greenstone Creek is the only source of NZ jade," but I discovered on this trip there are six other smaller deposits scattered about the NW quadrant of South Island. Greenstone Creek is certainly the largest and best developed source, but I now know there are others. A similar mineral called *bowenite* is also found on the beach at the mouth of Milford Sound. One of the carvers explained the difference. *Bowenite* comes in the same range of colors, but it's softer and more easily carved, and differs chemically from *nephrite*. Though it looks like *nephrite* he said it's actually closer to *serpentine*. The little piece I brought back came from the beach at the mouth of Milford Sound, and I suspect it will prove to be *bowenite*. Don't know, just guessing.

Several other jade outlets in Hoki but they were closed by the time we left the The Jade Factory and we didn't get to see them. Before leaving Greymouth we stopped at another jade factory, this one called The Jade Boulder. Perhaps cheaper than the Factory for smaller pieces but even pricier for major sculptural pieces . Two items in the shop were N$50,000 each, which at today's prices is US$31,280.

## Greymouth to Nelson~Counting diversions, 360 km

Next stop was to be Nelson where we were to meet a friend from Kiwi II. We stopped enroute at Punakaiki and Cape Foulwind to see the unusual rock formations and look for sea lions. The Pancake Rocks at Punakaiki were formed when layers of limestone were laid down over some kind of softer material. As the softer rock gradually eroded the limestone sort of pancaked~ like layers of mineralized frosting. It looks volcanic but according to the signs it's all erosion. An unusual place and I think worth the hour we gave it.

Cape Foulwind is off the most direct route to Nelson but the name intrigued me. Its origin becomes clear as soon as you see it. This is the Roaring 40s and the prevailing winds blow onshore. Any traditional sailing ship trying to weather the Cape therefore stands in considerable danger of being blown ashore and wrecked. (Notice the familiar use of nautical terms, none of which I fully understand, but they give this paragraph credibility it might not otherwise command.) There was a sailing yacht several miles off the coast and he did not look like he was having fun. Probably reminding himself the next time he does this to do it on one of the Princess line ships. The wind blows like hell and there were sea lions. Dinner at the Oceano Restaurant in the Rutherford Heritage Hotel on the Square. Supposed to be one of the ten best restaurants in NZ, and it is good, but after the Redcliff the grub tastes like White Castle.

Next day we did some shopping for the grandkids and met our friend Nola Fournier for lunch at the Anchor Bar and Grill, which is someplace down in the dockyards but I couldn't find it again if my life depended on it. Good place. We got caught up on Nola's life, made arrangements to process fleece from the arapawa ram I shot, (one less problem in passing thru customs), and talked at some length about national politics, ours and hers. We didn't exactly beat the sun out of town. More like we eased out of town in mid-afternoon, headed for the wine country around Blenheim and our overnight stop at Kaikoura.

### Nelson to Kaikoura~252 km

Blenheim is clearly the center of the NZ wine industry, particularly the cultivation of sauvignon blanc grapes and the production of wines made from them. Miles and miles of vineyards east and west of the City, and between Blenheim and the sea. Most of them seem to be young plantings, which is predictable given the relative age of NZ's wine industry.

We're staying at The White Morph out on the peninsula in Kaikoura. The name derived from a local seabird which occasionally produces a solid white variant. Looks like an albatross to me, but I think they said it was some kind of petrel. Good restaurant, by the same name, next door. Also recommend the Café Encounter for breakfast, just down the street, which also acts as a booking agent for whale and albatross watching.

Kaikoura is a wonderful little town on the NE coast of South Island. Before leaving we drove up onto the headland. We couldn't see the mountains clearly, a storm coming, but could see for miles up and down the beach, and we could also see the remains of a Maori pa, a fortified camp, on a nearby hilltop. In Maori legend the Kaikoura Peninsula is the place where Maui (yes, that Maui) braced his foot when he hauled up the giant fish that became South Island. It would look more like a fish but his older brothers didn't follow instructions and nibbled on the edges, which is why the coastline now looks the way it does. Can't say with perfect confidence that's what happened, but Kaikoura is most interesting and worth a stop.

### Kaikoura to Christchurch~190-194 kms

Last day on the road. Even with a little inspired dithering it didn't take all day. We stopped in Rangiora to hunt for a friend from the 60s, and in the little farming town of Cheviot in North Canterbury for lunch. And that proved to be an inspired stop. I hate to go all Emeril on you, but the Two Rivers Gallery in Cheviot serves the best mussel chowder in the World. Made from local green-lipped mussels, curry and I don't know what else. That stuff is life-altering. It will raise your IQ on average ten points, and restore your hearing in that always difficult high range. If there are teenagers in the home it won't make them any smarter but it will make them better behaved, though after eating this stuff they may decide to drop their AP classes and become cooks. I forgot to ask for the recipe, and I don't know if they'd give it to me anyway, but I still have their address and intend to write. Their chowder is almost worth a trip to NZ.

**Wine and Related Matters**

When Grandad was still alive and we still had the farm in Sonoma County I cared a lot about wine and went to a lot of trouble to find out about the wines made in Northern California. I'm 30 plus years out-of-date now, but still curious and we spent a bit more time this trip finding out about NZ's wine industry. I think we've visited five of NZ's wine making areas now, certainly all the big ones and one of the newest.

First one we tried was Peregrine pinot gris. Made in the Gibbotstown Valley, one of the newest wine-making areas, it's conceptually similar to and fills the same niche as rosé, rosetta, white Zin and beaujolais. Good plonk but there's nothing in those bottles that will offend anyone.

In Kiwi II I mentioned that sauvignon blanc is the best known of the kiwi wines. I've tried four or five of them and they are all very much different. You'd really have to know the wineries and vintages to decide what you liked best, but I think they'd all go best with fish and seafood. Some of them have an earthy after-taste I didn't much care for, but anything strongly flavored should work with any of them. You are going to have favorites though, and it won't take long to figure out which ones they are. And the price is right.

The best wine we had was the chardonnay. I think the California winemakers have kind of lost the bubble on chardonnay. Somehow they've decided that it must be bone dry to be good. They've conditioned the buying public to believe if it won't take the paint off a tugboat it's somehow inferior. NZ really opened my eyes to the possibilities. Particularly Shingle Peak and Neudorf. It's hard for me to describe these two without lurching into cliche, but let's just say these are big wines with complex flavors and I liked them very much. If the Kiwis can make chardonnay like this I don't know why they're screwing around with sauvignon blanc. (Actually I do know why. The sauvignon blanc was the first commercially successful wine they produced and their largest properties are planted in it.)

**Wrap-up**

We turned in our car on 31 May. 2339 km in nine days. We've now been in every region of New Zealand, but still haven't seen Dunedin and Invercargill in Southland, Stewart Island, or the northernmost tip of Northland. I guess we'll just have to go back. I hope your trips work out well and you have as much fun as we've had.   Let us know what happens.

Best, as always.

Bet & Dale

14 Sep 09

Jim & Patti —

As you can see from the return address, we're in Winston. House is full of boxes, but we're working our way thru them — at a moderate pace. And as the neighbors say, we have all winter to deal with the final touches. We may even set up the computer next week. Nah! Devil made me say that. By Xmas anyway.

Best, as always,

Dale's letter to my daughter on the occasion of my 60th birthday. I guess it's allowable to exaggerate to a good friend's daughter.

2000

Dear Heather,

Got your "green" note and the request for a humorous anecdote. Hard to pick from so many possibilities, but perhaps this one, from many years before you were born will do the trick.

At the time I first met your Dad he was a first lieutenant in the Army, just back from a tour as a general's aide-de-camp in Korea, and as full of himself as any young man I'd ever met. I'd never (then or later) met anyone quite so aggressive or self-confident, or quite so charming, and I started following him around just to see what would happen next. In those days I tended to regard senior officers as adversaries, dangerous when provoked, and unworthy of either my confidence or trust. Sort of like grizzlies on a garbage dump. Instructive and interesting to watch, but not something you wanted to take liberties with. Your Dad saw them in an entirely different light. Jim would seek out their company, study them intently for several weeks, figure out where the hot buttons were, then play to their weaknesses and personalities with a view toward manipulating them to his own purposes and ends. In general he was spectacularly successful, the single exception being a rather crusty lieutenant colonel named Wenceslas Konopka. Konopka recognized your Dad's manifest talents, but he knew he was being stroked and also saw quite clearly that Jim didn't know enough about the Army to avoid all the potential minefields. Jim was normally careful in talking about his seniors to use their correct name and title, and unless he liked the individual, to mask his actual feelings behind an impenetrable veneer of civility and charm, but in frustrating some of Jim's more exuberant schemes Konopka sometimes sometimes frustrated Jim too, and in doing so he earned the *nom de guerre* "The Good King", or "The Stud Duck." Konopka was inordinately fond of the latter phrase and would use it in all sorts of situations, frequently proceeded by some reference to your Dad. As in, "I know The Illustrious Tiffany is behind this. Find the stud duck in the Student Officer's Company, and tell him I want it changed back the way I told him to do it the first God-damned time we talked about it."

For a man of 23 or 24 years, perhaps 25 at the most, your Dad was unusually polished and socially adept. There wasn't much competition among the lieutenants of that era, but Jim stood out, and his sangfroid and ability to think on his feet in social situations seldom deserted him. Well almost never. Because Aberdeen was the home of one of the Army's schools there were frequent social events; greeting new classes, graduations, welcoming new commandants, all that sort of thing. These were mandatory turnouts for staff and faculty. Dress blues with bow ties, high and tight haircuts, and in those pre-Vietnam days, our two ribbons and a date. On one of those occasions Jim was proceeding thru the receiving line with his date when he reached Lieutenant Colonel and Mrs Wenceslas F. Konopka. He got by Mrs Konopka, a charming, warm-hearted Frenchwoman, with his customary style and flash, but in introducing his date to The Good King he let down his guard for a second and said, "Colonel Duck I'd like you to meet Irene McCabe." He knew instantly his future hung by a thread, but he also knew if he so much as hiccuped, say nothing of laughed, he was dead meat. Konopka had a ferocious temper and was a stickler for military courtesy, and he would have assumed, on good grounds, that Jim meant to be disrespectful. The only thing standing between Jim and a very important mid-20th Century ass-chewing was Konopka's uncertainty. He couldn't quite believe he'd heard what he thought he'd heard, and he couldn't tell from Jim's frozen smile if he had reasonable grounds for suspicion. It seemed unlikely his most cunning lieutenant would do something like that, and in the absence of corroborating evidence he shook Jim's hand and passed him along to the next *functionaire* with a sort of thoughtful stare. By the time he got to the general's end of the receiving line Jim was considerably unnerved, but several stiff scotches and our smirking laughter soon got him going, and by the end of the evening he was laughing as hard as the rest of us. The Illustrious Tiffany had dodged a potentially fatal encounter again, with nothing in his hand but a lot of cheek, a healthy dose of charm and motherwit, and a strong will to survive.

I doubt this yarn will actually embarrass him; at the most it'll make him laugh, and perhaps remember some of what those years before the war and real adulthood were like. In actuality, I would never do anything to embarrass him. He's my oldest, most valued and most loyal friend; the one man I could always count on for a sympathetic ear, and one of three or four men I've met in my life I think I could count on for anything. We have nothing in common except 35 years of respect, irreverent laughter and friendship, but I can't think of anything else except my family I value as much. I hope he lives another sixty, or multiples thereof. Wish him Happy Birthday for us, but remind him that one e-mail does not make him a correspondent. Dale.

NOV 2 2 2010

Dear Patti and Jim:

No special reason for this. It's just a collection of good ideas and semi-interesting articles; stuff that's been accumulating on my desk since a bit before your last visit. Particularly the things about China. Chris has chosen an unusual time to be living there, though I suspect most of this is not visible to him.

I was deer hunting in Cochise County, Arizona a week ago and on my way home I stopped in Sedona to see if it had changed. Without putting too fine a gloss on it, it has. There's a 4-lane highway from Oak Creek Village to Sedona now (that's the southern approach), but Oak Creek Canyon is still pretty much untouched. Here and there a cabin or a small B & B has been squeezed in, but whoever is in charge of preserving that unique piece of ground has done a pretty good job.

Sedona, on the other hand, has become Carmel-in-the-Canyon. Some beautiful homes, certainly more than existed when we passed thru, but also some that looked like upended Easter eggs, painted appropriately in mutant shades of yellow and raspberry. It's also become a major New Age center for the investigation of whatever phenomena those people investigate. As I understand the drill it involves a certain amount of sitting on exposed ledges, contemplating the infinite and soaking some of it up (through their bums?). Sedona supposedly sits on a vortex, which facilitates this kind of knowledge accumulation. I regretfully did not sign up for a New Age sun tan, but there are regular tours to places of particular interest to that crowd. ( I apologize for the poor quality of the photographs, but I was using one of those fixed focus fire-and-forget cameras, and as a result most things are slightly out of focus.)

I also retraced a portion of our route thru the Navajo reservation. The trading post at Gray Mountain, (where a young Navajo man asked you to carry his sister to Phoenix), is apparently closed, and there's a motel across Hwy 89 from the trading post now, but that place basically looks much as it did. However, the trading post at Cameron's has become Bloomingdale's in the desert. Busloads of French and Japanese tourists stopped there to ogle the genuine Indian handicrafts and watch a "real" Indian weaving. I wonder what they're going to do with all those dream catchers and bits of dyed turquoise when they get back to Plessy or Lyon, or wherever they came from. The Navajo have also gone into pottery in a big way. About 2000 years after their neighbors. Nasty derivative stuff painted with Indians and sunsets. I'd almost hope TSA confiscates it.

"Madam, our screening shows you're carrying a five inch Navajo pot. I'll have to ask you to throw it in the barrel before we can let you on this airplane."

Since it's so close if we get cabin fever we may drive down there and do a preliminary recon before April. Much as we did for Chico Hot Springs, and for the same reasons. Scientific inquiry, in its most basic and easily justified form.

Wind chill of fourteen below yesterday, and probably 20 below (actual temp) tonight or tomorrow, but the horses are blanketed, Carroll College won again, the basement is sealed, we've got propane (enough for two months), and we're settling down to take care of our winter chores. All is right in our world. Hope it is in yours. Happy Thanksgiving from your Montana correspondents. .

*Bet &*

P.S. We saw SDSU handle the Zags the other night. To my untrained eye it didn't look like a fluke. Hope you have a great season and maybe we'll see you again in the Round of 16??
*(and we forgive your boys for beating our boys!)*

# LETTERS FROM A FRIEND

FEB 2 3 2011

The Ackels
P.O. Box 135
Winston, MT 59647

Dear Jim:

Stuff is building up and I owe you a book report on *The Fourth Star* here we go.  First, the book.  I liked it very much; so much that I read parts of it twice.  I think it is an excellent summary of where the Army was at that point in time, and of the four personalities Cloud and Jaffe chose to profile.  As for my thoughts on the individuals:

**Chiarelli:**  Frankly I'd never heard of him 'til he showed up in Iraq.  Not too surprising since he's from the heavy community and after 1980 I was either in the special operations fraternity or doing FAO things.  He sounds like an excellent man and I'm sorry I don't know him.  Last I knew he was Vice Chief of Staff of the Army.  In essence the guy who runs the Army Staff.

**Casey:** One of the pleasant surprises of this book.  He has the reputation of being a bit of a plodder.  Well liked and very well respected, but not considered a point man for anything.  This book revised my thinking, in that he comes across as a man of substance, conviction and character.  Clearly all of us who *don't* know him underestimated him.  I never knew he'd gone thru Delta selection until I read this, and that alone is a considerable test of character~and will.  I think I would have enjoyed serving under him.  He just turned over as Chief of Staff of the Army.  I imagine he's retired now.

**Abizaid:** Again, I didn't become aware of him until OIF.  I would say he's the highest ranking FAO in or out of the Army.  We've had two who made major general but never one to make four.  I've never met him.  I'm told he was a company commander in 2d Ranger Battalion, and that he was in the assault element when they helicoptered into Grenada to rescue the students at the second campus, but I was either at Point Saline or up on the ridge above St George and I know I didn't see him or meet him that day.  Too bad.  A uniquely qualified individual for what he was asked to do.

**Petraeus:** Clearly the most controversial of those profiled.  I think the authors have caught him well enough.  All ambition and energy, with more than a touch of arrogance.  Several years ago there was media speculation that he intended to run for President.  He didn't deny it, but he certainly didn't confirm it either.  If he does there will be some health issues  (he passed out cold at a Congressional hearing last year), but in rewriting our doctrine for counterinsurgency and then applying it successfully in Iraq he has done the country and Army an immense amount of good, and I think he deserves the recognition he's received.  But this one ain't over yet, particularly if he is successful in Afghanistan.

Many thanx for giving me the chance to read the book.  I think it will be footnoted for years to come~in every study subsequently done about this era.

Bet and I were in Colorado last week, setting up the rehearsal dinner for Derek and Hannah's wedding. The rehearsal party will be on the 17th of June at the Whitewater Bar and Grill, a local hangout for rafters and guides in the area. Very, very casual, in that some guests will be wearing cut off jeans and T-shirts. Ceremony will be the next day at the parent's house outside Guffey. To be performed by an Indian shaman, feather not dot. I can hardly wait to see the expression on the Eastern rels faces. Oh, and Derek has negotiated a special rate for a zipline ride across Royal Gorge, for those who want a bit more tingle in their rehearsal dinner. Or an excuse to drink.

I've enclosed some brochures covering things to do in the area. We've looked at the Hampton Inn in Canon City as a place for out-of-town guests to stay. The rooms are quite nice, clean and new, and the bus service for the rehearsal dinner and wedding will leave from there. Various rafting companies will provide the buses. Hopefully the seats will be dry, but I make no promises. If you'd prefer something a little more comfortable and scenic I'm sure you can find a nice B and B somewhere in the surrounding countryside, but if you decide to use the Hampton Inn tell them you're associated with the Schechter-Ackels wedding and they should give you the special rate we negotiated. As I recall it was $112 a night, but it might have been $102. I'll ask Bet when she comes back and let you know if the figure is wrong.

Now for serious matters. Bet and I visited Guffey while we were there. It's basically a ghost town that has by some means found a way to hang on. Even has a post office and library. As for the election of a mayor, tradition dictates that the pet of the man who owns the general store is automatically the mayor, however, politically ambitious pets have moved into the area in the recent past and the rotation has become thoroughly screwed up. Film at eleven.

Patti: Please don't worry about the chickens jumping out of mailboxes. Chickens that are allowed to run loose will naturally roost in trees to escape predators. Young acrobatic ones up high and matronly layers down lower. I've seen them as much as 15-20 feet above ground. When the sun comes up they naturally fly down, sometimes as much as 40 feet from the tree. If you dropped a 3 ½ lb layer from ten feet she might hurt herself, but to win the contest you need those acrobatic biddies that can almost fly and they do fine.

All for now. Thanx again for the chance to read the book.

*[signature]*

*Hope your team does well this weekend against BYU. Zags knocked off St mary's last night to clinch WCC co-championship.*

## 15 March Ltr

**From :** Dale Ackels <nyati41@gmail.com>
Wed Mar 23 2011 2:49:35 PM

**Subject :** 15 March Ltr

**To :** Jim Tiffany <jamestiffany@comcast.net>

Dear Jim: Got your good ltr of 15 March and will attempt to answer all in order presented.

~ Bet did have a steroid shot (one) in her hip joint when it was bothering her the most. It was supposed to last somewhere between several weeks and perhaps six months, but it only lasted a couple weeks and provided little or no long-term relief. She's been told or heard somewhere that these injections tend to work better on knees. I have been told by people who've had 'em that knee replacement tends to be troublesome for about a week, but improvement (in pain and function) comes very rapidly after that. I have a friend who just had both of his replaced. I'll write him and ask for his experience.

Glad to see the Aztecs have passed thru to the round of 16, but they have some heavy going ahead of them. Nothing easy from here on. I was surprised to see BYU handle the Zags so easily, but that seems to be our recent pattern. We win our conference (12 times-I think) and during the season we knock off several high-ranking majors (most recently UNC, Baylor (9th at the time), St Mary's, Wash St (when they were still good), Okla State, Washington, and Memphis come to mind. But then we get in the tournament and fold in the round of 32. This was far from the best team we've ever sent, but they'd come together in the last half of the season and I thought they might make it to the Sweet Sixteen. Anyway. Tell Patty we'll be watching SDSU and hoping for the best.

As for the Glacier trip, I think your notion of postponing it is best. You've certainly got more important things on your plate this summer, and we have done nothing to improve our knowledge of Glacier NP since you visited last. We don't know anything more about lodgings, locations, or routes than we did last year and it would probably be best if we did a little pre-mission scouting this summer and built up our target folders. We haven't made any reservations or spent any money so postponing isn't a problem in that regard either. And Bet's brother and his wife are planning on visiting just after the wedding.

One other thing I told you in connection with the wedding has proven to be wrong also. If you decide to stay at the Hampton Inn in Canon City you should ask for the special rate for Derek and Hannah's wedding. Vice the Schechter-Ackels wedding. Don't know why they chose to enter it in their computers that way, but other guests ran into a problem with it and told us. And it's $110 per night, plus tax.

I saw the same article in The Atlantic. I would guess we're both subscribers? I'll reread it and send it along to another friend who has retired more recently than I have and will doubtless have more current information. We went thru something very similar to this after Vietnam and somehow that came right. Hope this will too. One thing I said in my comments on The Fourth Star has subsequently proven to be wrong. Casey is still Chief of Staff. His successor has been identified but hasn't gone thru Senate confirmation yet. The handover is supposed to take place later this spring. Best to Patti and good luck with your remodel. Glad it's not us, and I'll let you know what the friend with new knees has to say about the process. Dale.

APR 0 7 2011

The Ackels
P.O. Box 135
Winston, MT 59647

Dear Jim and Patti:

Just a moment for a brief trip report on the Gallatin River Lodge.   We were there early in the week, taking advantage of the gift certificate you gave us last year, and our need to get out of the house and see some new country.   Sort of helping winter along, I guess you'd call it.

The Lodge is not a wilderness destination.   The town of Belgrade and the city of Bozeman are just a few dozen miles away.  But it's pleasantly rural and as you must have suspected it's very much a flyfishing destination.   There's a casting pool in the front meadow, and the interior is decorated in a trout fishing *motif.*   Rooms are large and comfortable.   The food is <u>very</u> good indeed (breakfast and dinner only), and the staff is very accommodating.  We moved in and settled down like we'd been coming there for years.

I'd never fished the Gallatin River before (it's one of the three constituent rivers that form the Missouri at Three Forks), but it's a lovely stream, easy to fish, and the Lodge has access to two miles of the lower river for it's guests.   That's more than anyone could conceivably make use of in two weeks.  Spring runoff hasn't started yet, but the snowpack is at 125% of normal and when it comes, in about six weeks, it will be memorable.   Right now the River is low and clear and fishable.  The weather didn't cooperate but I had a wonderful time on it and very much appreciate the chance to see it and determine it's potential for summer and early fall.

Many thanx for the gift certificate, and for thinking of us.  It was most pleasant experience, and just what we should have done for ourselves.

Best wishes, as always, and thanx again.

*Best & Dave*

# LETTERS FROM A FRIEND

NOV 1 0 2011

The Ackels
P.O. Box 135
Winston, MT 59647

Dear Jim:

I was going to hold out for Xmas but the sheer weight of it mandates an earlier mailing. First, many thanx for the political article from *The New Yorker*. Always like to see that stuff. I'll send it along to Nan and John, along with a copy of the enclosed piece from *The Washington Monthly*.

Watching the Paterno/Penn State debacle unfold this morning reminded me of some football stuff. I understand Boise State is coming to your house next week? It will be a busy afternoon for your club. They're starting a kid named Matt Miller, from Helena's Capital High School. He's a medical redshirt so this is his first year actually playing, but he's having a breakout year and unless something breaks he's a handful. I saw him play his last two years in high school and next to John Ritchie I thought he was the most dominating high school player I'd ever seen. Capital won the state AA championship every year he played,* and he was first team all state or state champion seven times in three different sports while I watched him, or was aware of him. Also the equivalent of player of the year in football. #2 on your program.  *but one*

I think I've also mentioned that Carroll College, our local Catholic college has an exceptional program. They play in the NAIA, which is the division/conference/whatever for very small colleges. Smaller than Division III. In the last nine years only Georgetown (of Kentucky), and University of Sioux Falls have managed to get beyond Carroll and win a national title. The other six belong to Carroll. They have good players but so far only two, both tight ends, have managed to catch on in the pros. Casey FitzSimmons played for the Detroit Lions for about ten years, and last year's marquee receiver, a lad named Bubba Bartlett, is with the Texans. Signed as a free agent. On pg 7G of the program there's a reference to a running back named Chance Demaris. He's big and fast and elusive, and I think he may have a chance if someone will look down into small college football deep enough. If Carroll makes it to the NAIA championship game in December that will be shown on national TV and may give him an opportunity to showcase his talent.

Also included the wine article from *Sunset*. We haven't had a chance to try any of these yet, but since Patti likes chardonnays, and there's several on the list, I guessed you might want to see it. The vocabulary of wine analysis still leaves me hiccuping with laughter. "Brambly black currants and berries with a dusting of," dirty saddle blanket and Brylcream, "on a long finish." Dear God. At least they're drawing their samples and winners from other wine-producing areas. I suppose that's a good thing.

Recovery going well. I've been in cardio rehab well over a month now and so far haven't run into any unusual challenges. Also, may not have to have the kidney operation I spoke of earlier. The local chancre mechanic says he believes my problem can be treated with meds. To be looked at again in late December.   May still have to have it if the meds don't work, but there's a glimmer of hope anyway.

Hope the house is coming along nicely, and you got into the Tarheel-Spartan game.   We'll be watching on TV.

Best,

MAY 0 1 2013

Estimado Senor:

Back from Afrika a bit more than a week, and thought I'd let you know what happened. The inclosures are things I thought you might find useful. Some airplane reading and a relatively new map of the Southern Cone. Perhaps the principal utility of the South African portion is that it reflects adjusted political reality. Sometime in the last decade we've gone from five provinces to 13-14. I thought they would be based on tribal geography but with three exceptions they don't seem to be. Eastern Cape Province is largely made up of the now defunct homelands of the Transkei and Ciskei, and is therefore largely populated by Xhosa, Limpopo Province seems to be mostly Shangaan, and Kwa Zulu remains the Zulu heartland. For the rest, who knows.

The hunt went very well indeed. I killed six animals on Woodlands. Nice Eastern Cape kudu and Cape bushbuck, a nice representative black wildebeest, good red hartebeest and blesbok, and a very ordinary impala. I was very pleased with the performance of my "new" 7mm Rem Mag, at least on the first two animals. It flattened the wildebeest and kudu decisively, but on the third day my scope gave out and I finished the hunt with Kevin's very useful 7x57 Mauser. Don't know if you remember it but it's built on an Oberndorf Mauser action. He calls it a sporterized Afrika model, but I can't find that in my limited reference library. I suspect it's a carbine or mountain rifle. His son Keith stocked it in a plain but very straight piece of walnut, blued it and mounted an older Leupold variable. It's got a wonderful trigger, and I used it with great satisfaction for the remaining four antelopes. Incidentally, Keith has moved from Westley Richards to Purdey.

As for the animals, there are still good populations of kudu, black wildebeest, pigs, zebras, steinbuck, duiker, waterbuck, springbok, bushbuck, giraffe (9), eland, Chacma baboons and mountain reedbuck. Also a few blue wildebeest and one leopard; a transient who wanders thru on a regular basis in pursuit of the odd baboon or impala cutlet.

The impala have been knocked back by mange, and the red hartebeest have been similarly affected by mange and red heartwater disease (don't ask-I don't know what it is either), and the gemsbok are completely gone. Kevin still hunts gemsbok in this province but on a different property. He's got access to a farm called Wood Vale; about 15,000 acres an hour and a quarter SE of Woodlands.

Woodlands also has five Cape buffalo now. Sort of a complex tale of local intrigue and unauthorized animal trading. Keith had bought or traded for a nice nyala bull, with the long-term intention of building a huntable population of nyala on Woodlands. Somehow a hole appeared in his fence and the nyala wandered across the road and onto the despised Price Brother's ranch. Keith asked for his return but the Price Brothers refused to do it, whereupon a hole appeared in their fence and five of their numerous buffalo were persuaded to cross back into Woodlands. When asked to return the buff Keith invoked the same rule the infamous Price Bros used in justifying their retention of the nyala, and that's pretty much where we stand.

Speaking of Keith and Fran, their situation has become a bit precarious.  As you know they sold Woodlands several years ago to a minister or junior minister in one of the recent Norwegian governments.  Unfortunately, he proved to be an embezzler and as a result he's now doing time in one of those very comfortable white collar Norwegian prisons.  The Government of Norway (GON) seized his assets, which means they now own Woodlands and are attempting to sell it to recover some of their money.  Two possibilities currently under discussion.  One, turn it into a rhino sanctuary, and two, sell it to the South African Government, at a ridiculously low price (set by the GoSA),  who intend to break it up into small farms and redistribute it to the local Xhosa.  In the second instance Keith is finished.  In the first case he and Fran will be permitted to stay on as managers.   His situation has been made somewhat worse by the fact his staff has been unionized.   Under a mandate from the ANC his domestic help, cooks, skinners, drivers, everybody now belongs to the union and his head tracker is his union rep. I think he's looking forward to retirement.

After a most pleasant stay in the eastern Cape we drifted north to Kruger Park.   More accurately into the Greater Kruger Reserve.   Many thousands of acres south and west of KNP have been converted to privately owned reserves and the fences between them and KNP have been dropped to facilitate the movement of surplus animals into and out of the park.  Some of the reserves are hunting concessions, but most are game viewing/birdwatching operations. Hard to get an accurate count but I think there may be something like 13-14 reserves of various kinds along the south and west boundaries.    We stayed at Umlani, in the reserve called Timbavati.   Very rustic place, six Shangaan huts, built the usual way but on poured concrete slabs, with the basic amenities.  No electricity, no wifi, no e-mail,  no i-anything, and no contact with the outside world.  For the digitally enslaved it's Hell on earth, but it exactly suited us and we spent a very pleasant three days driving around, looking at the lions, leopards, elephants, buffalo, and lesser beasties, and sleeping.

From Umlani on to Zambia and Zimbabwe.  Our primary purpose was to see Victoria Falls, from both sides of the Zambezi,  and we did that.  It's in full flood now.  Five hundred fifty million liters per minute going over the drop, along a width of 1.7 kilometers.   The baTonka called it the "Smoke that thunders," and it does.  At the various overlooks the primary sound is the roar of immense amounts of water going over the Falls and landing in the rocks.  Sort of a watery tearing sound, but underneath that is a base line; a deep subterranean booming.  Something ominous and from the very center of the Earth and perhaps the most memorable feature of a very memorable place.

Finally, many thanx for introducing me to Kevin.  As you predicted we got along famously and became very good friends in the nine days we stayed at Woodlands and at their place in Bathurst.  His back story was of great interest, and his terrific sense of humor added greatly to our overall experience.   I owe you a great deal for introducing me to him.  Though we may have screwed up Bet forever.  This was her first hunting camp, in Africa or anyplace else, and she may think they're all that much fun. At several points she was laughing so hard I thought she might injure herself.  Particularly the story about Dolph and his "minor ammunition problem."  That's already become a household phrase, as in "What we have here my dear is a minor ammunition problem.''  Followed by a half  minute of snickering.

On two occasions, while discussing his new magazine, he mentioned how much he owed you for helping him as a writer.  He's very grateful for your advice and assistance and considers you a mentor in this new phase of an already  interesting and adventurous life.            •

That's about it.   Best to Eileen and all who dwell therein.   Further deponent sayeth not.

Cast of Characters:

Keith Gradwell ~ Fifth generation South African.  Former owner of Woodlands.   Our host.

Kevin Thomas ~ Our professional hunter.  Former Rhodesian soldier and game scout.

Keith Thomas ~ Kevin's son.  Gunsmith at Purdey's in London.

*3d variant*

AUG 2 5 2013

Jim,

More recreational reading - at least
I hope it is.  Detroit, Bugatti
automobiles, cruise ships, Chinese
banking, and an exhaustive article
about the FARC's domination of
tungsten mining in Colombia.
From what I've seen in the recent
past it seems likely China is heading
for some kind of recession.  First,
the real estate bubble and now this.
And I'm resonably certain this isn't
all of it.  If there are problems
in banking, real estate and employment there are bound to other problems lurking just ahead.

I didn't write a day by day account
of the recent trip to Africa, but
I did write a summary ltr to a
well known writer and editor in the
hook and bullet trade and I've
included a copy of that also.

RMEF

SEP 2 2 2013

Dear Patti and Jim:

Home safely, but with happy memories of our swing thru southern and central California.

The Nixon Museum was more interesting than I expected. His docs are not yet catalogued and on file, but the display parts of the Museum are finished and they were interesting. A pretty straight forward treatment of Watergate and its aftermath, and a useful summary of the things he did accomplish. The Paris Peace Accord, the opening to China, seven landmark environmental laws, even the first substantive proposal to provide universal healthcare. But for the character issues, not a bad legacy.

We also went to the Gene Autry Museum. I thought it was in Palm Springs or somewhere in San Bernadino County, but it's actually in downtown LA, just underneath Griffith Park. A very impressive physical plant with excellent displays of saddles, presentation Colts and a massive collection of Hopi artifacts. The best of it donated by individual collectors who wanted to see their collections maintained intact. But, it's not really about the West, or cowboys, or ranching. It's overarching theme is Hollywood's perception of the West, and the different eras in western moviemaking. To learn more about the West the Cody Musuem, the Charlie Russell Museum (in Great Falls) and the big museum in Oklahoma City are probably better choices. The Cody is still my favorite.

I would guess you've already seen San Simeon. While stationed at Monterey, at the Defense Language Institute, I drove down to San Simeon one weekend, but I was too late to take a tour. All I got to do was walk up to the fence and look at the Neptune Pool, but this time we spent the whole day and I must say it is unusual. William Randolph Hearst put it together in the years just after WW I, when most of Europe was for sale. His agents bought parts of castles and several monasteries and his long-suffering architect, a lady named Julia Morgan, found a way to incorporate some of his purchases into the nearly finished building. But talk about change orders. She was on the job somewhere between 20 and 30 years! And when he died there were still 220,000 artifacts in his various warehouses. American Pickers gone mad.

From there to Moro Rock, Monterey and the Monterey Aquarium. Monterey and Carmel have been favorites since I lived there, and I always enjoy the Aquarium. As I described it in a recent postcard to you, it's the San Diego Zoo of aquariums.

Several months ago I sent you an article about the Denver Botanic Garden and their bonsai collection. Just before we flew to San Diego Bet and I stopped at the Garden to see what they had. If my count is correct they had 23 major bonsai in pots, and several more nicely shaped plants in the ground. At least one was 250 years old. Plus several insignificant small plants. Starter kits. Just next door they had a very nice Japanese garden largely planted with Ponderosa pines. In designing it they'd taken 150 weather stunted ponderosas out of Roosevelt NP/National Forest, and those trees have become the basis of the garden. It's not the National Arboretum, but it's very nicely done and worth the stop. Should your travels ever take you back to Denver, the Botanic Garden is on York Rd, between 11$^{th}$ and 12$^{th}$, in the southeastern quadrant of the City. All the photos in this packet came from that place. (The viewing rock is actually a composite of three different rocks cleverly inletted by a talented stone mason to look like a mountain range at a distance.)

Some bad news while we were in Monterey.   I think one of us mentioned that Derek and Hannah are expecting another baby in February??  A boy, but in routine testing for various genetic problems they found that it's likely going to be a Downs baby.   The test they use yields 5-15% false positives, but they are having a more accurate test done and should know for sure within the next ten days.   Don't know what they'll do but they've got some figuring to do in the next few weeks.

All for now.

Bet & Dave

MAR 1 7 2014

Tim—

A frequently reliable source tells me I missed it again— by eight days this time. I don't know if that's an improvement over last year or business as usual, but I am sorry. Hope you and Patti did something fun and/or interesting. Preferably both.

We're off on Thursday (friday actually) for a grandson viewing. Blizzard(s) permitting we'll be back on Thursday the 27th— likely with another 1200 pix of a little towhead, and a miniature brunette boy blowing milk bubbles and squinting at the flash. First time we've seen the new one so expectations are high.

Hope all is well, and Happy (belated) Birthday!

Bel & Dale

Jim:

MAR 1 8 2014

This was beginning when I
lived there, some 45 years
ago.  I confess I didn't
particularly care for the
scotch being made in Japan
at that time, but it sounds
like the biggest, and/or
the best makers have since
made a virtue of necessity
and worked to perfect what
they do make.  Let me
know what it's like if
you find a bottle before
I do.  I've checked the store
in Winston and there's
none there.

*Jim and Dale*
*Glacier National Park, September 2014*

OCT 0 6 2014

Dear Patti and Jim:

You'd think I'd have passed on all the (hopefully) worthwhile clippings during your last visit, but apparently not. What set this packet in motion was *Sunset's* most recent wine testing. Once I cut that out the rest of it just sort of fell into place. Lucky you.

Our brief stay in the Lakes Basin country of northern California was hampered by smoke from the Yosemite and Pollock Pines fires, mostly the latter, but while there we did have a chance to visit the village of Graeagle in Plumas County. Nancy had recommended a yarn shop in the village and I thought an afternoon away from the smoke and ash would be a welcome break for Bet so off we went. The yarn shop proved to be a great success, but while we were there we also found a tasting room belonging to Indian Peak Vineyards and that proved an even greater success.

They had a 2009 merlot that was one of the best wines I've ever tasted. Not the regular merlot, but the one marked "Reserve". It was delicious. Full bodied, with wonderfully rounded and complex flavors, no scald or harshness; just an all round great table wine. The parent winery is in Tehama County, further north and west, near the town of Redding, but we're going to play hell getting our hands on more. They only make 240 cases a year and most of that is gone by the end of the summer. If we don't buy it at the vineyard or Graeagle I'm afraid we won't be able to buy it at all.

They also make a sauvignon blanc and a chardonnay, but the sauvignon blanc is even more restricted, only 57 cases a year, and they start selling the new wine in February and by summer it's unavailable, even at their tasting rooms. Don't know a thing about their chardonnay but they don't use their own grapes for that and it may or may not measure up to their other varietals.

When I asked the co-owner why in the world they put their only tasting room in a remote mountain village like Graeagle, he said, "My family visited Graeagle in the summertime and we always liked it so when we bought the winery we decided we might as well sell our wine someplace we liked and wanted to be. Hell, we're all just a bunch of Tehama County winos anyway. We didn't know anything when we began so we thought 'why not.'" Why not indeed. If all else fails I'll buy you some next summer, while we're back at Sardine.

About all for now. About a day after you left it suddenly occurred to me that I'd substantially erred in telling the story about my early days as a consultant and possible appointee to the Pentagon as a civilian. It was the Department of Army Staff, not DoD. Under the Assistant Secretary of the Army for Installations, Logistics, and something else. ( International logistics would have been a subset of that worthy's responsibilities. ) Didn't have anything to do with DoD, other than the fact DoD has overall responsibility for international sales and IMET training, under the day-to-day supervision of the Defense Security Assistance Agency, but I would have been a creature of the Army Secretariat. You'd think after 30 odd years I'd know the difference, but it's been 19 years since those events took place, and frankly I seldom think about it. That's my excuse anyway. Could also be creeping senility.

About all for now.

# LETTERS FROM A FRIEND

DEC 1 7 2015

Dear Patti and Jim:

Hope this arrives in time.   The shipping clerk at the local pack and ship assures me it will, but there is a cosmic backup someplace in the pipeline and I has me doubts.

First, the wine.   You may recall I wrote you a ltr in October 2014 in which I carried on immoderately about a small winery in Tehama County, near Mt Shasta.   They made a *merlot* that impressed me greatly and they also make a small bottling of *sauvignon blanc* each year.   At that time I hadn't tried their sb but I promised to in 2015 and if it had merit, to ship you a bottle.   Well, I went back to Graeagle again this year, where their tasting room and sales outlet is (roughly 100 miles NW of Tahoe), and gave it a try.   I don't think I like it as well as I liked that wonderful bottle you served us, but I was able to get a bottle because this year they put up 97 cases and there was still a bit left in September.   I think it will go well with food, but you will, of course, make up your own minds.

The Indian Peak Winery and vineyard was almost destroyed by fire this past year.   Saved at the last minute by a fireline established along the entrance driveway.   In an effort to save something the owners put up what pinot noir he had left  and labeled it *Driveway Pinot*.   He also brought in a machine that chemically removed the smoke flavor from the finished wine.   Didn't know such a thing existed but after trying it I'm not sure it made that much difference.

I also tried the 2012 *Merlot Reserve*, but it's a very different wine and I didn't like it nearly as much as the 2009 I carried on about last year.   Perhaps a bit more age or a bit less smoke will help.   We shall see.

In the aftermath of the Ponderosa Fire, and in an attempt to salvage something from the wreckage, he also blended  his remaining reds into a new wine that he's marketing as *Theoretical Red*.   If memory serves it's cabernet sauvignon (purchased from someone else), merlot and pinot noir, but I've forgotten or misplaced the percentages.  I bought a bottle and will try it at Christmas.   He's a tough bugger and I wish him every success, but he's not going to remember 2015 with any particular fondness.

Most of the articles speak for themselves.   The wine articles come from our local paper, but I like them because they convey practical info about the wines they describe, and they're written in layman's language.   Always a sore point for me.  If the producers and middlemen ever want their product to appeal to ordinary buyers they're going to have to write about it in such a manner that the *dinamatero* at the Sunlight Mine knows what the bleep they're talking about.

I sent along the piece about *chablis* because I enjoyed it and thought you might.   What I know about the district could be stuffed in a thimble, with room left over for the Magna Carta.  I didn't even know where it was, and I'm not at all certain about the safety factor in inviting yourself to dinner at a  Frenchman's home.   "Mon dieu, what was the ignorant savage thinking?"   Perhaps after he's known you for 30 years, certainly no sooner, but the article itself was unusually satisfying and I thought  Jim and Patti might like this. Again, you're going to get a chance to decide for yourselves

The book is about a Frank Lloyd Wright building we visited last summer.   Based on a 1927 design for a project in Wisconsin, the current owners bought the plans from the Taliesin Foundation and used them for their golf course and lodge.   Unmistakably one of his buildings, but perhaps not as satisfying as the earlier projects.   In a couple places he got a little precious.   He calls the fire pit the campfire and the central spire the teepee or wickiup, or something along those lines.   They have about as much to do with a campfire and a traditional Plains Indian shelter as Westminster Abbey does, but that's Frank for you.   It's in the tiny little mountain village of Clio, not far from Graeagle and the Indian Peak tasting room.   Come to think of it, that's a good day trip.   Get 'em both and drive back to Tahoe substantially illuminated in every sense of the word.

Many, many months ago you asked me for copies of the second printing of the anthology I contributed too.   I think it was 20 copies?   Whatever the number is I immediately added it to the group's next order, but our problem is the member who was supposed to make all the author's changes and send in the order hasn't yet done it.   She say's she's done the editorial stuff, but hasn't had the time to finish.   Whatever the problem is it will be sometime between January and Christmas 2016 before we see the second printing.   If you'd like to decrease your order there's still time and I certainly won't be offended.

I'm also writing a book.  My own collection of short stories about Vietnam.   Conventional wisdom in the publishing game is a collection of short stories should have a minimum of 12 stories and be 180 pages long.   I'm just a scrunch over halfway, but am rapidly running out of stories.   I can see my way to eight stories, but after that it really is going to be a work of fiction.   I'll let you know when I'm done, and what's happened to the book.

Several reliable sources tell me Patti didn't think much of my sending donations to charities last Christmas, in your names.  After hearing the reasons I have to say I agree with her.   This began several years ago with Bet's side of the family.   The children were almost all gone and virtually all of our material needs had long since been met.  We were looking for ways to do something positive and we seized on this.   There were no real tax implications because though each of us benefitted from the donations we made, the other donors also benefitted from the donations they made.   In many cases it was educational institutions:  Salem College,  Oglala Lakota College,  Berea College,  Red Cloud Indian School.  St Joseph's Indian School,  St Labre's Indian School, but there were also several churches or church supported charities, plus things like the Heifer Foundation, including that Marxist prick running their seed saver project in Peru (and doing a very good job of it), the Mercy Ships (one of our favorites), OXFAM, Medicines san Frontieres (before they won the Nobel Prize), and a couple local charities in the Greater Charlotte area that Margot felt strongly about.   At various times there have been eight families and individuals involved,  and each Christmas we probably distributed about $3200 to various worthy causes.  Including one year to your zoo.  Still, I agree with you.  I should have asked where you wanted the money to go.  It would have made sense to send it one of the charities you work on,  but at the time it never crossed my mind.  I went for imagination rather than practicality, but in this case practicality should have been my ruling principle. Sorry, if for no other reason because I never explained what we were doing or how you fit into the larger picture.

Your present arrived while I was finishing this.   Much appreciated.  It made us both smile.

All for now, best wishes and Merry Christmas to you both.   Annual Christmas letter to follow.

Bet and Dale

Nan
Jim

Just a brief, or maybe not, note to update you on my adventures with the medical community. I know Bet sent you detailed reports as events unfolded, but my perspective is bit different, and there have been some changes, and besides I promised to keep you updated and I haven't done that.

As you now know I was basically saved by the efforts of a Russian-trained cardiologist named Lyudmila Toole. Don't know what her maiden name was, or how she got to Montana, but she's married into a prominent Missoula family, and she's known everywhere in Missoula's medical community as "Mila." She never passed the cardiology boards due to language difficulties and unfamiliarity with some advanced procedures, but she was too competent and far too resourceful to relegate to physician's assistant. I suppose the modern equivalent would be interventional cardiologist. Whatever she is she's shown on the International Heart Institute's wire diagram on the same line with the department chairmen, and that seemingly minor fact pretty much tells the story. She does the pre-op workups and research, coordinates surgeries and participates in some, and coordinates the post-op care. And she also maintains her own cardio practice and patient list, of which I am an admiring member. As you will come to understand, she can also prescribe meds and do virtually anything else she thinks is necessary. She enjoys the complete confidence of the senior staff and all other members of that community, and is known universally as Mila. As in, "Who asked for this test? It's not on the form. Mila did." "Oh well why didn't you say so. If Mila wants it it must be alright." Not Doctor Mila, just Mila.

By early spring Bet could see that I was losing ground and as soon as I came back from an Alberta bear hunt she took me to see Mila. We both felt my symptoms indicated some kind of cardio problem and we both had unlimited confidence in her, so she was a natural place to begin the process. For two days she bled me and probed and tested and sometime on the second day she said, "This is not cardio. It's something else. You must see an endocrinologist. I vill set it up." She also decided I needed an MRI image of my brain and set that up.

She also energized the radiology staff and somewhere in that time frame the IHI (International Heart Institute) radiologist compared the new scan with an older one done in October 2016 by the VA and discovered I had a cyst or a tumor growing at the lower edge of my brain, in close proximity to my pituitary gland. About the size of a regular lima bean, it was laying on my pituitary and in close proximity to my optic nerve for who knows how long. There's even a possibility I'd had it since birth, but the part of these findings that set me off was the fact that the cyst was clearly visible on my October (VA) scan, and no one at the VA had told me about it. These little truffles growing on the brain are usually benign, but roughly 3 to maybe 5% are malignant and must be removed. Fortunately, the comparison showed the cyst hadn't grown since October and therefore was probably not malignant.

Mila was now fully commited. It wasn't cardio but it was something, and she meant to move heaven and earth until she found the problem. Or at least defined it. A check of VA records and several of Mila's blood tests established that my pituitary was as dead as a canned salmon, and wasn't producing four critical hormones the body needs to regulate its normal functions. At this point Bet and I disagree a bit on how she did it. However she did it she was homing in on it, but there was some question if she would find it in time.

By the morning of the 15th (of June) I was dying and I knew I was dying. I was not in pain, and I didn't see a descending column of pure white light, nor did I see my soul fluttering over the bed, but the reality

315

of my life was slipping away from me.   My normal instinct was to fight this someway, but the morning of the 15th we still didn't know what was wrong and how do you fight something you and your doctors don't yet understand?   In the absence of something concrete to hang this on I decided it was simply my time.   After all, I was nearly 76 and had led a somewhat adventurous life (guffaw), and maybe I wasn't meant to understand it and this was just the end.   A little too soon for my tastes but painless, and understandable as simply the normal process of aging.

About 7 PM Mila called and said something like, "I've found it."   Speaking to Bet she went on to ask if Bet had a car and could she get to the WalMart Pharmacy in Helena immediately.   There was a prescription waiting for her but she needed to pick it up soonest.   I was vaguely aware of Bet flying out the door and sometime later of taking a pill, but I didn't see or do anything else until the following morning when I woke to find somehow during the night I'd been partially cured.   I wasn't yet Batman, but I was fairly close to Robin, and I felt wonderful.   Over the next several days my dosage was adjusted and a second hormone preparation was added, but my "cure" progresses rapidly and at least for the near term I have my life back.

Looking back this has been building for several years.   Over time I've lost body mass and grip strength, endurance, my appetite (imagine that), most of my hair,   and a significant chunk of my memory.   And a small amount of exercise typically left me breathless.   At Hazel's memorial ceremony I was having trouble walking and the family assigned one of Bet's cousins-in-law to follow me around and make sure I didn't pitch over or fall down the stairs.    I was also sleeping 14-16 hours a day and letting family business slide until I felt better.   Some of this had started over two years ago, but I'd convinced myself, particularly the memory part,  that it was normal aging and paid little attention to it.   Bet noticed but didn't know what was happening and didn't harass me about it until it was painfully evident I was crashing.    Then she was everywhere and did everything.   Next to Mila she did more to save my life than anyone.

I didn't get thru this without burning several switches.   The effects have been felt particularly strongly in my memory, my ability to do simple subtraction and my typing ability.

I used to have a better than serviceable memory but parts of the dictionary are missing.   Over the past four weeks I've needed help to recall the names of the two hormones I take, and words and phrases like abate, income, curate, truffle, boarding stable,  malignant (I substituted malevolent, which conveys the idea), and several dozen more, but of course I've forgotten them all.

I was somewhat startled to discover I'd also lost my ability to do simple subtraction.   The endocrinologist asked me if I had children.   I said, "Two boys, grown and gone."   "How old are they?" I started with Travis but after several seconds of scribbling and ineffectual pawing at the paper I blurted out 81.   Some other part of my brain said how can he be five years older than you are?   When Derek's turn came I just asked Bet and that solved that problem.   Since then I've been teaching myself to do subtraction and it's going well. Within a few weeks I should be able to tell anyone how old TJ is.

Typing has been a real problem.  I was an accomplished typist and had been for 60 years but the first time I sat down to do a ltr I got something that looked like it had been done by a fifth grader.

It's gotten better, but this example illustrates what's left to be done:  " Note:  practice uses email, text, and/or calls to notify patkeints of information available regarding your, care, test resultsappointments and financial statements.  Sign in to manage our contact preferences online.  Pleswe do not reply to tis email.  It was ssencd from an unmonitored inbox."

Actually, that is getting better.  In my mind this para was all done correctly, but somewhere bwtween brain and  keyboard bad things happen.   I may be the first person in years to actually wear out a spell checker and  grammar checker.  *caps*

That's about it.  I have several more appointments remaining in August.  Another with Mila to have my blood checked to make sure levels are correct and to provide results to my endocrinologist. Immediately thereafter an appointment with the endocrinologist to tinker with dosages, and the third with a neurologist to review the bidding and I suppose make the go-no go decision.  If the replacement hormone therapy continues to work we'll stay with that, unless the tumor starts to grow or it interferes with my vision.   In which case I'll have an operation called a transsphenoidal hypophysectomy to remove the tumor.  The operation is a bit baroque but I think it's an important option, and overall I like mychances.  Two good, viable options and I know where to go for help.  As I said a sentence earlier, I like my chances.

Hope all is well and Jim's operation is healing properly.   Yo' friend and brother. *Uav's*

Let me know how the leg is going. Best to Patti.

*Dale*

The Brewster guy mentioned in the article was (briefly) the head coach at the U. of M. He got fired rather promptly.

# LETTERS FROM A FRIEND

SEP 2 9 2018

Jim and Patti:

Don't think there's much point in speeding this to you, or carrying it to Ireland, but it will be in SD when you return. I may have waited a bit too long to send some of these, but it's been a complicated year and several of our best friends have been shorted in the correspondence department. With this letter and parcel I'm nearly caught up.

As I mentioned in our FONCON, on a recent visit to Albuquerque we visited a museum called the Indian Pueblo Cultural Center. Lots of interesting culture and exhibits, but the thing that caught my eye was a grouping of satirical cartoon paintings by a man named Dan Coté. Most of them built around First Contact, from a decidedly Indian viewpoint. I believe he lives in San Domingo Pueblo, and if you decide to do your political cartoonist gathering again he might be an unusual and well received addition. P.S. Nan tells me the guy in Sacramento (Orman or Ohrman, something like that) is doing his own display and exhibition this year. He liked what he saw in San Diego and decided to do his own show, apparently drawing on the assets of the Sacramento Bee to support his undertaking. Don't know where he stands is preparing his copy of your exhibition but I will urge Nan to send along anything the Bee prints on this subject.

A word about the Silver State Classic. As the article makes clear, it's a bodacious car race across the Nevada desert outside of Ely. We blundered into it last year enroute to Sierra County and our annual layabout at Sardine Lake. Same this year. It's headquartered in a motel on the near north side of Ely. Every kind of fast car you can think of: All those mentioned in the article, plus custom built street rods, dragsters, trucks, rat rigs, everything the fertile minds of America's car guys can conceive of. And they do go fast. If my algebra is still reliable it takes a driver going 195 mph 27 ½ minutes go 90 miles. I don't think my eyes go that fast anymore, but I mean to find out one of these Septembers. If you're interested in next year's doodah contact the White Pine County Chamber of Commerce for info. As a car show it's vastly entertaining. Add on the speed factor and it must be something.

I'd never heard of the gallowglass clans before but they must have been formidable. This article came from a recent issue of **Military History,** which does a decent, if short, job on a variety of military issues, current and past.

**Doonesbury** seemed particularly appropriate that week. I hope Patti laughs. In any event tell her to send me your cable bill. <☺). Don't know where that emoticon came from but it seems appropriate.

See you soon.

Dan

# CHAPTER 17

## Christmas Missives

# CHRISTMAS MISSIVES

Nobody really saves Christmas letters, unless written by Dale Ackels.

I've selected some of the more memorable ones.

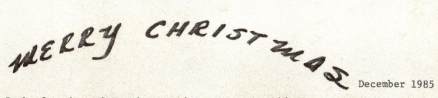

**December 1985**

Both of us have from time to time sworn we would never do a Christmas letter, but after getting married, moving, changing jobs, starting college (civilian and military), and sorting out two households worth of furniture we've decided this isn't much of a compromise at all.

For those of you wondering who this is from, or who recognize one or more people in the photograph but none of the others, we should explain that Elizabeth Miller Colenda and A. D. Ackels got married last spring. Reactions to that have ranged from ill-concealed amusement to wild-eyed astonishment, but be assured it's true. If the first eight months are a reliable barometer, we both have much to be thankful for.

Not only did we get married, but Dale acquired a family. Two boys, Travis, age nine, and Derek, age five. We were a little worried about how they would handle the change, but they've adapted very well indeed. Dale is now Double Daddy, which is not a rude comment on his growing girth, only an acknowledgment that there are two of them to be accounted for.

Travis has also made the adjustment to his new school with considerable aplomb. The northern Virginia school system is notoriously rigorous, but his first report card indicates he can handle anything they give him. He's also been playing soccer in the 3-4th grade league, and is about to start his first season of competitive basketball. He's also doing a bit of hunting with the previously mentioned DD, and starting to show an interest in music. Some recent compositions include I'M THINKING ABOUT GOOD MUNCHIES and I WAS BORN IN A MILKY WAY (with apologies to the Beach Boys and Bruce Springsteen). The latter composition was orchestrated for tabletop, tape recorder, and Converse sneakers.

Derek began kindergarten this fall. At the moment his relationship with America's educational system is somewhat guarded, but we remain basically optimistic. He seems destined for a career as a game show moderator. "Let's make a deal. If I eat a piece of corn, three greeny beanies, and one piece of carrot I get a pint of ice cream, a liter of Magic Shell, 12 pounds of sprinkles, and I get to stay up to 9:30, huh?" At their request we are in the process of changing the boys last name. Travis has suggested we change both Derek's first and last names. If we change his first name to Yancey he becomes Yancey Miller Colenda Ackels, or YMCA. Film at eleven.

Bet has started back to school at George Mason University; studying public administration, and somehow finding time to swim, garden, do a little jazzercise, and a bit of hunting. Both of us are looking forward to a trip to Charleston at Christmas.

Finally, Dale left Fort Bragg in late May heading for the Pentagon and the Army Staff. At the moment he works in the Security Assistance Division of the Office of the Deputy Chief of Staff for Operations. He'll probably spend two years in that job then move on.

on the East Coast. And, as you can see, we're also meeting interesting people.

We hope this finds you all well and looking forward to a happy and prosperous 1986. Please write or call when you're in town.

Best regards.

*Dale* and *Bex*

*Derek* & *Travis*
Travis

*Many thanks for all you did for me last year.*

*Dale & Bex*

1993

Fellow Collin Street Bakery Addressees:

Hard to know where to begin this year.  Lots of
changes, if not in physical location, in every other
aspect of our lives.  Perhaps the most
significant change involves our source of family revenue.  Dale
retired this fall, after 27 1/2 years of rather varied service.  The
Army is getting smaller, and a decision has apparently been made to
drastically curtail or do away with the regional specialist's program.
In that environment we really didn't have much choice.  We could have
stayed at the War College for 10 more months, but at that point
retirement would have been inevitable, so we checked out.  Can't
really say we've been sorry.  The Army was the center of our lives for
so long, but the divorce has been amicable and the withdrawal pains
almost non-existent.  As for the future, we're looking at teaching
positions in the Rocky Mountain west, or jobs that exploit some aspect
of Dale's military background.  Jobs in education are tough, but we've
still got paper working at two schools in Oregon, one in southeastern
Washington State, and one in Maricopa County, Arizona.  There's also a
remote chance we'll catch on with a government parastatal in New
Mexico, but at this point those prospects don't look particularly
good.

Travis is a sophomore now at Boiling Springs High School.  For all the
usual and readily understandable reasons, he does not particularly
want to move.  He's doing well in sports.  He was co-captain of the JV
soccer team 'till mid-season, then moved up to the varsity lineup and
played an important part in taking his team to a league championship
and the district/state playoffs.  He's made a commitment to his coach
and this program, and asks nothing more of life than to stay here and
play for Ol' BSHS his junior and senior year.  Not that sports are his
only reason for staying.  He has a social life Madonna would envy, and
this part of the country is well-situated to take advantage of many
other things that interest him.  He spends a week on the Outer Banks
every summer with some of his cousins and Bet's family, he visited the
historic village at Chatauqua, NY earlier this year, and he'll be
going to the oceanographic research facility at Woods Hole this spring
to find out if he really wants to be an oceanographer.  We should also
mention that he started working this summer.  Picking strawberries,
raspberries and lowbush blueberries on a local Mennonite's farm to pay
for a car.  The transformation from **homo recreationalibis**, or
Skateboard Man, to **homo economicus** (Berrypicking Man), was a
horrifying thing to watch.  The sudden loss of illusions, the equally
sudden realization that stuff costs money, and the appalling certainty
the future will include more of this.  Definitely not the kind of
thing impressionable children should see.

Derek remains the same happy-go-lucky kid he's always been.  He's
still an honor student, or rather his parents are honor students, and
he plays every sport ever devised for the diversion of half-grown

boys.  Soccer, baseball, basketball, street hockey, touch football,
and something called night tag, which I gather is the misdemeanor
pursuit of similarly inclined twelve-year-olds thru neighboring
cornfields and gardens in the middle of the night.  It's all sort of a
blur; large seasonally specific piles of athletic clothing all over
the back porch and a practice schedule that consumes most of the
memory of an IBM System 400.  This is the first year Derek can legally
hunt.  Last Saturday he shot his first deer in Franklin County.  Later
this year we're all going down to the Eastern Shore of Maryland to
exercise the geese.  Somewhere in here we also plan to work in a
couple of pheasant hunts.  If nothing else, there'll be enough protein
in his diet!

As usual, Bet is the busiest of us.  She's finishing up her
pre-nursing program this spring, with the second half of anatomy and
physiology and microbiology.  So far she's still a straight A student.
She plans on applying to nursing school at Harrisburg, and several
western schools, though we're not sure how those schools will receive
an application from "abroad".  We're discovering that slots in nursing
school are very closely controlled, and at least in the western
states, there's a strong desire to insure nursing training is given to
those people likely to stay in the state and benefit its citizens
directly.  A sensible attitude, but a bit irritating when you're
trying to coordinate three or four people's lives and plans at the
same time.  She'll be in nursing school somewhere next fall.

Hard to say what the next two years will bring.  If Bet's accepted at
Harrisburg we may just stay here until she and Travis graduate.
Whatever we do we don't want to lose track of you.  Best wishes for
the holiday season, and let us know what your future(s) hold.

Jim-
   Many thanks for the balsam
wreath. It arrived yesterday-in
great shape. Nothing particularly
exciting in our lives at the moment,
other than deer season and getting
ready for Christmas. Kind of fun
to have the time to enjoy them
both. When you see Chris tell him
I know I owe him a ltr, but responding
to his last magnum opus will probably
require a major research effort, extensive
footnoting, and access to the Vatican
Library. Look for it somewhere between
the Sugar Bowl and the Super Bowl.
                    Dale
P.S. I heard from SGSM. Not interested in me,
but I do appreciate your help.

We seem to have established something of a tradition with this thing. People have come to expect it, and we confess to getting a certain amount of fun out of sitting around and figuring out what the high spots of the previous year, if any, might have been.

First, as usual, there's Derek. Number 81 on your program and number one in your hearts. The lad groweth apace. At the request of the Bureau of Weights and Measures and the NFL Scouting Combine, we have decided to provide current statistics. Shortly after his 14th birthday, and with the benefit of a substantial Thanksgiving repast under his belt, he was 5 feet 11 inches tall and weighed 217 pounds. Though he did not play football this fall, due to several unfortunate personal decisions he made last spring, he has asked me as his acting agent, to inform all members of the Combine that if drafted by the Cincinnati Bengals out of high school he will not sign. Rather than join a club with no playoff potential, he intends to hold out a year and sign with the 49ers as a free agent. Young Mr. Ackels has recently expressed some interest in playing for the Carolina Panthers, but only if they are willing to let him wear a 49er uniform. For most of the last year Derek's relationship with the academic community has remained guarded (He will not be the American Federation of Teacher's poster boy again this year), but he's done some really good things in school recently, and as a result will be playing basketball this winter. Both his mother and father are looking forward to the first game with ill-concealed sniggering and some suppressed apprehension. Watching Derek go to the hoop is kind of a lesson in high school physics...mass x velocity = lots of little dweebers laying around on the floor. There is little doubt **THAT** rebound is in friendly hands! It's a gruesome sight for parents not accustomed to mayhem and slaughter in the schoolhouse. Those of you with children in urban schools will, however, understand perfectly.

Travis finishes high school this year. Don't know for sure where he will go to school, but he's applying to Shippensburg University, the Mt. Alto campus of Penn State University, and the University of Wyoming, with York College also a possibility. If he had to leave tomorrow, there's little doubt Shippensburg would be his first choice, but he's working the angles, and wants to have options available when it comes time for Dad to start writing checks. This will probably be his last year of soccer, but he's had quite a run with it (no pun intended), and given all the other members of the family a lot of pleasure. His team won or tied for the league championship two of the last three years, and went to the district/state playoffs all three years. I can't say Bet or I were passionate about the game when he started, but his involvement has gradually brought us around, and I'd estimate we now understand at least 49% of the rules. We do know that when the blond kid rips across the field and legwhips some 27 year old Croatian exchange student, we should cheer, and we've done Hell's own amount of that over the last three seasons.

As for Bet and Dale, we continue to chug along in our various pursuits. After some considerable soul-searching, Bet has decided to drop out of nursing school. It wasn't an academic problem, she had a 3.65 average and was somewhere in the top 3-4 in her class when she withdrew. It was the emotional strain. As she got more intensively

into clinicals she found it more and more difficult to separate the
patients lives and problems from her own life.  Put another way, she
found it difficult to leave the patients in the hospital.  To do the
kind of nursing she was interested in doing she would have had to work
in hospitals for several more years after graduation, and she just
didn't think it was worth the wear and tear it was causing.  There's
little doubt she was miserable, and no residual doubt she did the
right thing.  I asked her the other day if she regretted her change of
heart, and she seemed well content with the choice she made.

As for me, I've become a consultant, which one knowledgeable
friend describes as an "expert from out of town".  I didn't really
mean to do this, but my first feeble attempts at filling in the time,
and earning some walking around money, have gotten completely out of
hand, and I'm spending more time away from home than I am in Boiling
Springs.  This wasn't supposed to happen, and I intend to cut back
significantly after the New Year.  Well, after March 31st.

We're still planning on moving to Wyoming this summer.  Can't say
where for sure, but Cody looks like a frontrunner.  Many of you have
been following this "plan" for several years, and will probably be as
glad to hear the end of it as we will be.  While you're waiting for
the denouement, please accept our thanks for your cards and letters,
and our wish for a happy and prosperous New Year.  Give us one year to
replace the woodstove, take off the sod roof, and put in indoor
plumbing, and come see us in our new digs.  Just don't do it during
elk season.  There will be a deafening silence roundabout Schloss
Ackels in October and November of next year.

Jim-

I saw Chris again in mid-November.  He's fine; getting ready for finals
now I would imagine.  He invited Travis to come down to Wash DC and hang
out with him for a day.  Chris did a great job of squiring him around
and showing him the campus.  Travis' grades are not good enough to get
him into Georgetown as a freshmen;  being the adopted son of the antichrist
might prove a barrier also, though the Jesuits are fairly flexible in
these matters and might take on the challenge just for the intellectual
exercise.  Anyway, Chris bent over backwards to help sell GU and
the idea of a high-viz campus.

As for losing Ritchie--19 carries a season.  I send you the best high
school football player in the Class of '92 and Moeller gives him the
ball twice a year!  Zut alors.  Too bad Walsh resigned at Stanford.
My boy Ritchie would have flowered in the Bill Walsh offensive scheme.

All best wishes.

*Dale*

P.S. This job ends on the 30th. I've just signed
a contract to do a 3-month project in Germany and
Carlisle, Jan-Mar of '95. Not looking forward to the
travel, but the money is right, so —

*1995*

Dear Tim & Chris —

At this age some folks go on holiday to Europe or Hawaii, some settle down to write the great American novel, and some make major changes in their lifestyles and domestic arrangements. We haven't done any of those things, but we did move to Wyoming, and therein lies the makings of our Christmas letter.

The idea for the move has been simmering for years. Dale had wanted to come back to the northern Rockies when his military career ended, but we didn't do anything about finding a place until 1990. Over several summers, and five or six trips, we'd looked at rural property from southern New Mexico to the Canadian line, and from the Willamette Valley to the Black Hills. Lots of places appealed, but the West has changed a bit since Dale first began prospecting for a retirement home, and it took many months, and more than a bit of reflection to eliminate Durango, Jackson, Silver City, Afton, Sand Point, the Paradise Valley, and some of the other, well known mountain retreats from consideration. For a number of reasons the final choice came down to Sheridan or the Cody-Meteetse areas, both in Wyoming. Unfortunately, through the end of February we hadn't been able to find a place that met our needs. However, in March, while Dale was working in Germany, our realtor called to tell us about a small "ranch" outside Sheridan. It sounded so good Bet flew to Sheridan, made the man an offer and we became the owners. We hesitate to call it a ranch, but it's a violation of the state criminal code to call a rural property a farm in Wyoming, and rather than do hard time, we've chosen to go along with customary practice and characterize it as a ranch. It's bigger than a "place in the country" and smaller than the Ponderosa. Anywhere else in North America it would be a small farm.

It came with a dilapidated house, a wonderful old barn, a large machine shop, an architecturally challenged machinery shed/cowshed, and an assortment of corrals, horse traps, and other paraphrenalia needed to work cattle and keep saddle stock. None of it in exemplary condition, but we liked the location and the view of the Big Horn Mountains, and at that point I don't think either of us particularly cared how much work we needed to put into it. Our first priority was the house. The original homesteader's house had burned in the 50's. The owner replaced it with two salvaged mine buildings, sort of welded together at the waist. The resulting composite was uglier than Levittown, but since it was framed with "borrowed" mine timbers it was unlikely to collapse anytime soon. We gutted everything but the kitchen, added several new rooms, painted or put siding on everything else, and moved in August 30th. The yard still looks like a Superfund cleanup site, but we've got a roof over our heads, a garden started and high hopes for the future. Though we can't shake the feeling that somewhere within a 100 mile radius there's a Union Pacific trestle leaning dangerously to port for lack of several key framing timbers.

We still don't have a name for the place. The Fairly Little House on the Prairie, and the WalMart Ranch both have their adherents, but a final decision has not yet been made.

Our oldest son, Travis, stayed behind in Pennsylvania to start his first year of college--at Shippensburg University. Not much doubt we'd rather have him closer, but going to Ship was important to him, and he seems to be working hard and taking advantage of the opportunity. He'll be home for Christmas, and working in Wyoming next summer, so we'll soon have a chance to get caught up.

Derek, our youngest, has adjusted rather well to the move. The prospect of all that hunting, fishing and skiing, practically in his front yard, has been some consolation, and there's always FOOTBALL. The day he turned 15 he was a whisker under six feet tall and weighed 226. It didn't take long for the 9th grade football staff to notice him. Even making allowances for parental bias, the kid can play. Next year it'll be for Sheridan High School. They've won the state AAAA championship 22 times since 1921, most recently in '82, '86, '90, '91, '92, '93, and 1995. Derek's never been part of anything like this before, but he got a taste of it watching this year's championship team, and we're all looking forward to next season.

Should any of you decide to come visit, maps are available upon request. If you get lost enroute we've prepared a series of guidelines to help establish if you're in the right state. With apologies to Jeff Foxworthy, you know you're in Wyoming:

- When local TV carries National Finals Rodeo updates.

- When the proper noun used by local media to describe residents of Wyoming (Wyomingite) sounds like the 113th element on the periodic table.

- When local stores have a back-to-school cowboy boot sale.

- When four cars arrive at a 4-way intersection simultaneously, and none of us can recall who has the right-of-way.

- When the elevation on the city limit sign is several times larger than the population. And finally,

- You know you're in Wyoming when the Mary Kay cosmetics lady drives a candy apple red pickup.

On that note, best wishes for the holiday season.

*This hasn't been the easiest move we've ever made. We were 2 months late getting into the house, and the van carrying our HHG turned over on the interstate, but things have calmed down now and we're enjoying Wyoming. Proper letter to follow. Dale*

1998

Dear Jean

I fear we've established something of a tradition with these things. They're not all that wonderful, in concept or execution, but for those marooned on the Coasts it's about the only way we have of keeping you informed of our approximate whereabouts, and what we're doing here in Heartland America. Since we do enjoy catching up on your lives, it seems the least we can do to scribble a few lines about ours.

First, but by no means least, Master Derek. As in years past, most of the year's high points involved sports. Track and field in the spring, football in the fall, and now wrestling in the winter months. He skipped a year of track, but came back last spring to throw the shot and discus, with some success. Following a couple weeks of football camps, he left for Ecuador in July; to spend his summer with an Ecuadorian family under the auspices of the Experiment in International Living. He spent three weeks in Quito, a week in the Amazon and a week cruising in the Galapagos Islands. Not surprisingly, his Spanish improved rather markedly, as did his appreciation for all things Hispanic. His football coaches were worried he'd miss too much training time in South America, but he came back 26 pounds lighter and quite a bit faster, and ready for another season of Bronc football. Unfortunately, this season wasn't as successful as some we've experienced. When the Broncs were on they were devastating, but they were inconsistent and were eliminated in the semifinals of the State playoffs. Only the second time this decade we didn't make it to the championship game. Though the team didn't meet everyone's expectations, Derek had a fine year and received some post-season recognition as a center. His coaches seem to think he can play in college, and we have started receiving inquiries from NAIA and NCAA Division III schools. Hard to say what will happen. If he doesn't accept an athletic scholarship we expect him to be in school at Sheridan College or the University of Wyoming next year. In the meantime there's wrestling (as a heavyweight, of course) and spring track, and all the other stuff that goes with being 18 years old, a senior in high school, and about to graduate. Is the World ready? Is Derek ready? Doubtless the answer is no in both cases, but there doesn't appear to be anything we can do to slow the *anschluss*. The World will have to look out for itself.

Our oldest son, Travis Jeffrey by name, came back to Wyoming in August to start school at Sheridan College. He's been living and working in Pennsylvania since September of 1996, but after a couple years of scrambling and toughing it out, he's decided college is something he wants. His academic skills are a bit rusty, but his age and maturity have made a tremendous difference, and he's doing very well in Information Systems Management. He's not certain that will be his major, but on the theory that you need advanced math and computer skills in just about every profession, he thought this was a logical beginning. Seems so to us, and we're most pleased to have him close-by again. TJ is our hunting and fishing son, and having him back has given Dale yet another excuse to ignore what he's supposed to be doing and go wander in the mountains. So far the pair of them have been rather successful. Late season trout, a couple deer, an elk, and by

the time you read this, a couple of turkeys and some of our resident pheasants. Not much chance any of the common protein deficiency disorders will crop up along our part of Prairie Dog Creek this winter. Travis plans to stay at Sheridan College for at least a year (possibly two), then transfer to UW, Montana, Montana State, or one of the other regional four year universities.

As for Bet and I, we keep uncommonly busy doing the little things that ranch life requires. From time to time Dale does some consulting work, this year perhaps a bit busier than last year, but most of our time, energy and thought goes into fixing up the house, patching fences, propping up sheds, putting in trees, ditches and new irrigation systems, fixing tractors, tending horses and gardens, planting and selling alfalfa; all the myriad things the life we've chosen requires of us. To some who've visited us, it seems a tedious, even uninteresting existence, but it suits the two of us, and with a little more time for camping and horsebacking, probably will for the rest of our lives.

All best wishes for the coming holiday season and the New Year.

Dear Jim —

We enjoyed seeing you and really enjoyed Heather & Scott's wedding. Know they had a wonderful trip to Hawaii. As you've noticed I've enclosed some info on tracing family tree. This is the stuff I e-mailed you about — Sorry it's taken me so long to get it to you. I really enjoyed getting to meet your Dad and visit with him a little. Hope you can find out more about your grandfather. If I can help, let me know. We've received our beautiful candy cane for our door — Christmas is here! Thank you so much.

Glad to hear you're thinking of coming for a branding. One of our neighbors usually brands around the 8-9 of May. Charlie Hart usually does his Friday of Memorial Weekend. Derek graduates Sun., May 30th. Mama & Margot may or may not be here and Dale might be leaving early on the 31st for a jib in Asia. Can live with the idea of you staying at the Holiday Inn and would love for you to come for branding and D's graduation —regardless of who's here (or who's not here!)

Hope to see you in May and hope you, your dad and other family have a wonderful Christmas and New Year

Love,
Bet, Dale, Travis & Derek

2003

Dear ~~Friends~~ *Jim*

Sorry no pictures this year, for reasons I hope will become clear as we proceed. Basically, we've moved, about seven weeks ago, to the southern end of the Selkirk Mtns. After 4 ½ years of fighting with the State of Wyoming and the Federal Government over methane development, we accepted defeat and (reluctantly) left Sheridan. We live about 3 miles south of the unincorporated village of Diamond Lake, in Pend Oreille County, Washington. On a small flat spot on top of a granite ridge, with miles of pine, fir, spruce, tamarack and hemlock in every direction, and a nice stand of old-growth quakies at the bottom of the ridge, where our dirt meets the county road. Pend Oreille County is the most northeasterly county in Washington. We're roughly 65 miles from British Columbia and perhaps ten miles as the crow flies from Idaho. Those who saw the old place on Lower Prairie Dog will find it hard to understand why, given the greater visual appeal of our new place, we are homesick, but we are. In time I know this place will come to mean as much to us as the old one did, but for now, we're expat Wyomingites living in Washington. Next Christmas we'll be proper Washingtonians (?), and there will be pictures.

Both boys still alive and doing OK. Travis is still in Wyoming and has gone back to the University of Wyoming to finish his degree. He and his pretty-damn-significant other, a young lady named Tiffany Oswald, are both psychology majors. She's majoring in child psychology and TJ is working on counseling and adult problems. After graduation they plan to open a joint practice; sort of a one-stop, cradle-to-grave approach to retail psychology. "From that first inappropriate thought to the final *denouement*, see Ackels and Ackels for all your mental health needs. Family discounts available on request."

Derek is sort of a snowbird. In summer he guides rafting trips on the upper Colorado and Arkansas rivers, and in winter he works as an apprentice electrician in Bay County, Florida. Can't say what his future holds, but I know he'll be back on the river come May. Bet and I took a short trip with him on the Colorado this summer, and he's pretty good at it. Predictably (if you know Derek) he's got a nice patter, he makes the raft go where he wants it, the clients like him, and he seems to love the work. D is sort of our 21st Century mountain man. If it can be done in the mountains, from skiing to floating, he's there. Can't say where it will all end, but know his search for a fun, fulfilling, and financially rewarding lifestyle, free of responsibility, will provide fodder for Christmas letters for the next quarter century.

Bet and I are mostly occupied with moving in. We're at that ugly stage where you've got enough stuff unpacked to live, but all the easy decisions have been made and there are still boxes without homes scattered in all the rooms. And one extra china cabinet standing like a hall monitor at the entrance to the kitchen. She's spinning and knitting (mostly llama and wool, but there's a full envelope of mountain goat fleece on the kitchen counter). As I write this she is painting the craft room-- expressing her inner raspberry (after 18 years of married life-who knew?)--but she smiles every time she looks out the windows and contemplates her new surroundings, and after four-plus years of uncertainty and fighting government(s) that counts for a great deal.

As for me, except for the spinning and knitting, I'm basically doing what Bet is doing. I did quite a bit of consulting work before the move, including working on the U.S. part of the humanitarian relief mission in Liberia in July-August, and I've started writing magazine articles again, but my focus for the near term is on the new place and finding out more about northeast Washington. Spokane is only 40-odd miles away, with all the attractions a large city offers, and there are four universities in-town or in the immediate vicinity, so I'll also have a chance to see some Gonzaga basketball and PAC-10 football. Come spring we need to build a run-in shed for the horses and Bet's pack llamas, and there's several miles of fencing to build. I won't be bored. We hope the same can be said for all of you. New address is on the envelope. Phone number is (509) 447-2576 and e-mail is africaresearch@surf1.ws or bet@surf1.ws . All best wishes in all things for the coming year.

*Bet & Dale*

December 2005

Dear Friends: *Jim*

Saturday's mail brought Christmas cards from a motel chain in Fayetteville, NC, and a stockbroker in Deer Park, both vitally concerned with our Christmas plans and overall level of holiday well-being. That generally means it's time to take station behind this infernal machine and process a couple hundred words summarizing the previous year.

Our oldest boy, Travis, remains in Sheridan, Wyoming, still working full-time and going to school full-time, and hoping to finish at UW in two more semesters. Kind of a hard way to do it, but he's usually on the Dean's List, and he seems extraordinarily happy with his life and the direction he's taken, and if he's happy we're pretty close to ecstatic. One reason for his cheerfulness is that he and Tiffany have announced their engagement. The wedding to take place when they've both graduated from college, in the summer of 2007. Tiffany has two sweet and interesting children by a previous marriage, but Travis has adapted to surrogate parenthood without visible effort, and Miz Bet has made a similarly quick and enthusiastic adjustment to grandmother-hood. In this quadrant everything seems to be tracking toward graduation and matrimony in 12-18 months.

As for the Master of the Universe, he's involved in the "leisure industry". He still runs raft trips down the Colorado in summertime, and works as an apprentice electrician or in something having to do with skiing in the winter. At the moment he's working in a ski shop in Winter Park, Colorado while waiting for the Federal Government to turn on his river again. No telling what his future holds, but he's talking about going to Alaska in the springtime. We shall see.

Bet and I remain tied to our ridge top in Pend Oreille County. Building barns and corrals, doing some stonework and fencing, putting in a yard and a vegetable garden, and in Bet's case teaching a class in combat knitting at CREATE, a local craft guild/coop in Newport. Bet has become adept at every aspect of spinning, dying, blending, and knitting fiber ~ both the fleece from her own llamas and fibers from local specialty flocks. As a result, winter is not the challenge for our family it is for some. We haven't had a case of frostbite in who knows how long. As time permits we do a little horsebacking and regional travel, and this past summer we took a trip to Alaska with my sister and her husband. I hadn't been back in 34 years, and Bet had never been, so we combined some of our outdoor interests with a cruise down the ~~Inland~~ *Inside* Passage to Vancouver. Great fun and we're planning on going back next summer to see more of interior Alaska.

As for me, I lost my Dad in late May to the accumulated wear and tear of 89 years, and I'm semi-retired (again). Not truly retired but I'll be doing less Defense work and focusing more on Africa, and projects that interest me at this stage in my life. My second career has been a nice run, but it went off in an unanticipated direction, and I plan to spend the coming months getting Africa Research Associates back on track.

The address is on the envelope, but you can also reach us at **africaresearch@surf1.ws** or **backels@hotmail.com**. If you're overcome by an uncontrollable urge to communicate we urge you to indulge it. Our very best to you all, in all things.

*Hope to see you and Patty somewhere in 2006*

*Bet & Dale*

Dear Jim:

About that time of year again--when you try to remember the age, gender and sequencing of the children your friends are talking about--and assume, based on no evidence whatsoever, they've still got a firm grasp on yours. I think that's why we went to an illustrated Xmas letter some years back, but can't really remember that either.

Derek, our youngest, now 20, is as I type, working in Laramie. He took an involuntary sabbatical from the University of Wyoming last summer, then went to Texas to sell books and make his fortune. The details are a little fuzzy, but he did **not** come home in a BMW. From this we have surmised there are no fortunes to be made in book sales in and around Waco. He's now working for an internet company as a technician and customer service rep, and planning to go back to UW for the spring semester. Don't know what he'll major in but business administration and sports medicine have been mentioned, perhaps with twin minors in Spanish and Tantric philosophy??? We're a little uncertain where this will take him, but somewhere down the line New Mexico may get a broadly educated PE teacher, who sells Amway on the side.

Our oldest is Travis, now 24. He graduates from Sheridan College this month and leaves almost immediately for Montana State University (in Bozeman), where he intends to get a degree in psychology and counseling and earn a commission in the Air Force. I've searched my conscience from end to end (it didn't take long) and still can't figure out where I've failed the boy. Or even where he found out we had an Air Force. But, he's determined to do this--to fly four engine jets--and he's more than earned his shot. The last two years have been terrific. His mother and I spend a fairish amount of time laughing and high-fiving when his name and future plans come up. With a bit of luck he should graduate at the end of fall semester in 2002. There will be pictures.

As for Bet and I, we continue to play around with hay farming and livestock raising, we work when we get tired of moving irrigation pipe, and the rest of the time we do Wyoming/Northern Rockies stuff. A bit of fishing in the spring, a bit more hunting in the fall, and the rest of it is hobbies, reading, upgrading the house and fixing things the wind blows down. Bet spent a week in September riding 50 miles with the wagon train celebrating the tenth anniversary of the Bozeman Trail Centennial. This one wasn't as big as the original; as I recall she said there were ten wagons and less than 100 people involved, but she had a fine time running the sutler's wagon and learning how all this stuff was done. And before you ask, the wagonmaster really does give them a direction-of-travel and shout, "Wagons, Ho," when they break camp.

As for the pack llamas, there are three now. We had two, but we were at a sale last May and they led one into the ring with soulful, wounded bunny eyes, and in a color we didn't have. The outcome could have been anticipated by anyone with even a shred of imagination.    Unless they come in fuschia or turquoise, or with stripes, I think this will be it.

In my last Xmas missive I spoke about acceptance, and the fact there are people here now who came after we did and think we're old-timers.    There are, of course,  tests available to separate *wannabe* Wyomingites from the genuine article.    After months of exhaustive research we've come up with the following:

You really are from Wyoming if:

- Your kid's Halloween costumes are sewn to fit over a snowsuit.

- You have more miles on your snow machine than you do on your car.

- You think sexy lingerie is tube socks and a flannel nightie with less than eight buttons.

- Your snowblower has been stuck on the roof at least once.

- The mayor greets you on the street by your first name.

- The parish fund-raiser isn't bingo; it's sausage making.

- You find minus 40 degrees Celsius a bit chilly.

Now if we could figure out what the Military Order of the Cooty, Cloud Peak Pup Tent #7 actually is, we're certain we'd be fully acculturated, and accepted as such.    While we're puzzling through this most recent, and wholly unexpected, litmus test of citizenship, we hope you and yours have a most happy holiday season and a wonderful 2001.

Bell & Dale

*Hope all is well.*

December 2007

*Dear Patti & Tom*

I've noticed this year's Christmas notes have the flavor of letters between friends. There's less of that "Mort's cousin Lud (you haven't met him) was fishing crab in the Bering Sea in March and fell off the boat again," so endearing to connoisseurs of Christmas correspondence. I sometimes waver in my commitment to and interest in Lud's life choices, but a letter from a friend talking about people we actually know and care about is a much more pressing matter, and in that spirit I'd better go into full Norman Mailer-Virginia Woolf lockdown. A week earlier than last year, for those who keep track of such things and assign virtue based on on-time performance. You know who you are.

Last year's Christmas letter mentioned a wedding in July, and we did do that. Travis and Tiffany got married in Sheridan, Wyoming on the 7th of July. It was a big, pretty much traditional sort of affair, held on the grounds of the Kendrick Mansion on the bluffs above Sheridan. The celebration brought out the best in everyone. Travis and Tiffany were obviously very happy, the proud parents were happy for them but perhaps a little wistful, and everyone else (rapidly) got into the spirit of the thing and had a good time. For us it was a Blue Light Special in that, in addition to an admirable and well-loved daughter-in-law, we acquired kinship with two potty-trained grandchildren. All in less than an hour. I have it on good authority this is not the traditional path to grandparent-hood, but at my age speed matters and under the circumstances we figure we've fallen into another pot of jam. Photo evidence underneath.

After a star turn as best man at Travis' wedding Master Derek is now in Sandpoint, Idaho, working for a company that hauls skiers into the back country~somewhere behind Schweitzer Mountain. We don't know much about the job, but he presumably leaves them someplace they can ski out of before February. He'll be guiding again somewhere in the Rockies come spring, but I suspect his long-term direction will be influenced by girlfriend Hannah's job prospects. She's in the thesis writing stage of an MS in resource management at the University of Idaho, and will probably move on to a wildlife or recreation management job upon graduation. With luck somewhere in the Rockies, but possibly in New Zealand.

Speaking of New Zealand, Bet and I went this April. I hadn't been since 1968, and had never seen North Island, and Bet had never been. We don't own fleece animals anymore, but Bet has become a demon spinner and knitter so the emphasis was on visiting stock shows, farms, fibre co-ops and retail outlets involved in fibre production and manufacturing. Bet satisfied her fibre jones, and came home with bags and sacks of patterns and fleeces. If there had been a fleece sniffing dog in the airport he would have been catatonic after the first suitcase. We also squeezed in some ordinary tourism and wildlife watching, and had a most satisfactory time. I got to see things I'd never seen before, and as result of watching the All Blacks play for 22 hours on Air New Zealand, Miz Bet has become a rugby fan. Obviously, total immersion does work ~ in special circumstances. Who'd a thunk it?

Don't know what our near-term future holds, but we're giving serious consideration to moving back to Wyoming or perhaps Montana next year. Nothing firm, but we're looking. Hope the coming year is kind to you and all those you care about. Our very best wishes ~ in all things.

*Bet & Dale*

*(over)*

Patti and Jim-

I haven't checked my e-mail in a week, but Bet tells me Patti
has sold her company.  I trust you got all you wanted from the
buyers and are content with the deal.  Very much hope so anyway.
What role will you retain the in management of the new company?
I assume they'll want you to stay close and show them the ropes
until they're comfortable with it.  Congratulations, in any event.

As for the piece of rock with felt pads on the bottom.  Never occurred
to me to ask Jim if he still has bonsai, but I was putting stone
steps this spring and noticed the local slate pavers split
horizontally.  Unfortunately, they split in straight lines, but
if you prefer a more rounded, less angular look I think you can do
it with a Dremel tool and a grinding wheel.  At any rate, that's
a bonsai stand.

Hope everything else is in good order.  Yo' friends in the snowy
Selkirks.

I know you were at the wedding and saw all this, and I understand
I'm dangerously close to the kind of "Lud fell off the boat" ltr
I spoofed in para 1 of the Xmas ltr, but I plead special extenuating
circumstances.  And throw myself on the mercy of the court.

2012

Dear Friends and family ~ *Jim*

In a probably futile attempt to get ahead of ourselves in Christmas preparation we decided to essay a Christmas letter early this year. At least it was early when we wrote it. No telling when it will be mailed, or what form it will take at mailing time, but let the official record show, in our own minds we were early, or very nearly so.

As she explains it, Miz Bet has taken this year to "get back under warranty." She's had a spare bone removed from her hand and wrist, ligaments cut to relieve carpal tunnel syndrome, and a hip removed and replaced with something Buck Rogerish that looks like a medieval Iraqi mace, is made with the stuff they build fighter planes with, and is guaranteed to put TSA on huckleberry alert if she drives past a departure terminal. Can't say she enjoyed the process, but so far everything seems to be working as designed, and she's very pleased with the improvement in hip and hand function and her overall quality of life. She's been able to return to her spinning and knitting, and next spring she'll be able to ride again.

When we left Sheridan and moved to the Inland Empire, Travis stayed behind to finish an undergraduate degree at the University of Wyoming. He's somewhere at the beginning of his senior year and if all goes according to plan will graduate next year at Christmas. He's doing quite well indeed and plans to keep going and get a masters in counseling. His significant other, Ms. Tiffany, and her two children are still very much a (happy) part of his life. I think I see a trend developing here, but what do I know?

Derek is also in the Rockies. He spends his summers guiding raft trips on the Colorado and Arkansas Rivers, and his winters chasing electrons in Winter Park, Colorado. Unconfirmed reports suggest access to big mountain skiing may have played a minor role in his choice of winter domicile, but he's ostensibly an apprentice electrician. We're happy enough that he has a plan, can feed and clothe himself, and with a spot of luck will pop out of the system as a journeyman electrician in 4 plus years. Whatever he's doing, he seems happy enough with it, and that works for us.

For the rest of us, we spent most of our summer leveling a site and building a barn and pens on top of *The Rockpile*, as our neighbors uncharitably describe our Selkirk mountaintop. It's not exactly farm ground, which means Tying Down Woman has tarped her last haystack, but it's home now and we've come to appreciate its virtues and started modifying it to meet our own desires and expectations. Many of you, of an urban bent, would probably find it astonishing to discover what it costs (in time, money and patience) to create ½ an acre of flat ground on top of a granite ridge, and build something on it, but we "Got 'er done," and our two remaining saddle horses and Bet's two llamas, are living up here with us. For now everything that's supposed to be corralled is, but we'll see what happens this winter when a moose or elk wanders down the ridge in the middle of the night and jumps into the corrals. I hope I sleep through it, but suspect no one within half a mile will. Come to think upon the matter, there is no one within half a mile.

We hope this finds you all well and happy. Please accept our very best wishes for the coming year and let us hear from you, as time permits. *Your Xmas trip sounds like fun. We look forward to seeing you and Patti come spring.*
*Bet & Dale*

*Dear Patti* *of*

Greetings from the *Tine*
Inland Empire:

Christmas '08

Though this will, in all                                                                likelihood, be the last time we
send them from here. We're                                                    moving to Broadwater County,
Montana in the spring. Pend Oreille County hasn't been a particularly good fit for us, and we decided to make
a change. We bought the new place in September, but at the moment we seem to be a bit over-housed.
There's some problem getting rid of the house we're currently in. Apparently there's a lot of that going
around. Winters here tend to be a bit more rigorous than they are in Montana so we decided to stay here over
the winter, (to protect the buildings) but if we haven't sold it by June we'll move anyway. New address will
be: POB 135, Winston, MT 59647. Look for new phone # and e-mail tag sometime in late June.

On the off chance you haven't heard of Winston, it's a x-roads about 19 miles south of Helena. There'll be 17
people in town when we get there, though I don't think they plan to repaint the city limits sign on our account.
Canyon Ferry Lake is a couple miles east of us, there are wonderful rivers and other lakes close by. We'll be
roughly equidistant from Bozeman and Missoula should somebody throw a culture craving on us, and as
mentioned previously, Helena, a very nice small city and the state capital, is only 19 miles north. Winston is
probably not a candidate for a lead article in NATIONAL GEOGRAPHIC's travel mag, but Lewis and Clark
spoke well of the area, and about a mile north of the post office there's a little oasis in a couple hundred acres
of quakies and our new domicile sits in the middle of that. It's not all ours, in fact there's quite a bit less land
than we had in Wyoming and Washington, but there's a live creek running thru it, there's stuff for the horses
and a nice view of the Big Belt Mountains to the east, and Miz Bet is wild about the house. And, it's 5 ½
hours closer to Travis and Tiffany. Those last two points weigh heavily. In fairness I suppose I should
mention that Carroll College, the best small college football team in the nation, is in Helena, and Helena's two
5A high schools also play at a very high level. In case I get weathered out during elk season I'll have
someplace to go.

Our boys are just about where we left them last year. Travis and Tiffany and their two children are settled in
Sheridan. Tiffany has found professional employment with the State Department of Family Services, and likes
her job. The company TJ works for has undergone some turbulence but he has, so far, survived the various
buyouts and upheavals, and they're planning to buy a house next year. They're increasingly looking like long-
term Sheridanites.

Derek and Hannah remain in Sandpoint, Idaho for the near term. Hannah is in the final throes of a master's
thesis, and has caught on with the Forest Service in Kremmling, Colorado, for next year. They plan to head
south in April. Derek is talking about training as an EMT, either at the National Outdoor Leadership School
in Lander, Wyoming, or an equivalent institution in central Colorado. While he's waiting for a vision he's
working as an office manager in Sandpoint ~ for Selkirk Powder Company, a back country ski outfit, naturally.

That's about it for us. Hope you're all well and prosperous and looking forward to a better year in 2009.
And if you're looking for a lovely mountain retreat on 38 acres in the Emerald Empire, give us a call. I'll
make you good deal and throw in a tractor. If you decide not to do that then just come see us in Winston
someday.

*Bet & Dave*

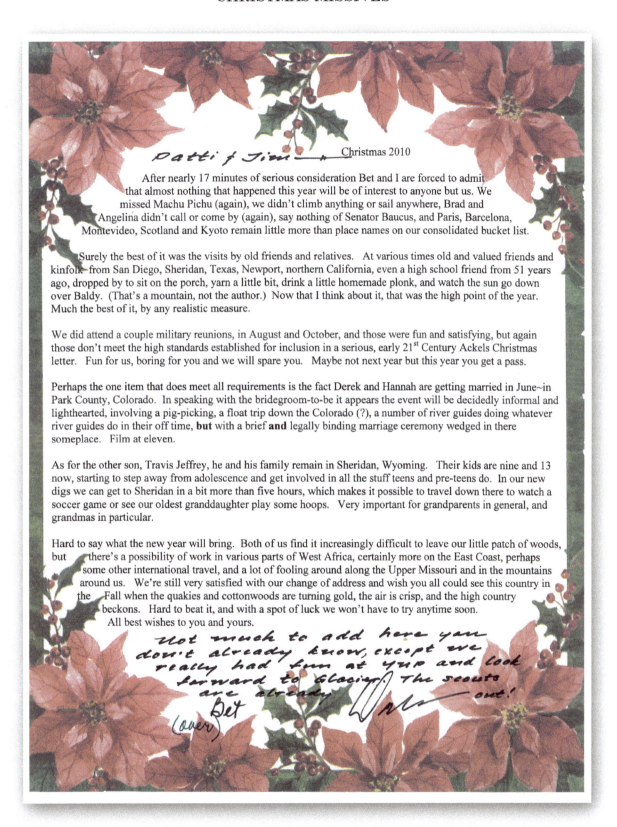

*Patti & Jim* → Christmas 2010

After nearly 17 minutes of serious consideration Bet and I are forced to admit that almost nothing that happened this year will be of interest to anyone but us. We missed Machu Pichu (again), we didn't climb anything or sail anywhere, Brad and Angelina didn't call or come by (again), say nothing of Senator Baucus, and Paris, Barcelona, Montevideo, Scotland and Kyoto remain little more than place names on our consolidated bucket list.

Surely the best of it was the visits by old friends and relatives. At various times old and valued friends and kinfolk from San Diego, Sheridan, Texas, Newport, northern California, even a high school friend from 51 years ago, dropped by to sit on the porch, yarn a little bit, drink a little homemade plonk, and watch the sun go down over Baldy. (That's a mountain, not the author.) Now that I think about it, that was the high point of the year. Much the best of it, by any realistic measure.

We did attend a couple military reunions, in August and October, and those were fun and satisfying, but again those don't meet the high standards established for inclusion in a serious, early 21st Century Ackels Christmas letter. Fun for us, boring for you and we will spare you. Maybe not next year but this year you get a pass.

Perhaps the one item that does meet all requirements is the fact Derek and Hannah are getting married in June~in Park County, Colorado. In speaking with the bridegroom-to-be it appears the event will be decidedly informal and lighthearted, involving a pig-picking, a float trip down the Colorado (?), a number of river guides doing whatever river guides do in their off time, **but** with a brief **and** legally binding marriage ceremony wedged in there someplace. Film at eleven.

As for the other son, Travis Jeffrey, he and his family remain in Sheridan, Wyoming. Their kids are nine and 13 now, starting to step away from adolescence and get involved in all the stuff teens and pre-teens do. In our new digs we can get to Sheridan in a bit more than five hours, which makes it possible to travel down there to watch a soccer game or see our oldest granddaughter play some hoops. Very important for grandparents in general, and grandmas in particular.

Hard to say what the new year will bring. Both of us find it increasingly difficult to leave our little patch of woods, but there's a possibility of work in various parts of West Africa, certainly more on the East Coast, perhaps some other international travel, and a lot of fooling around along the Upper Missouri and in the mountains around us. We're still very satisfied with our change of address and wish you all could see this country in the Fall when the quakies and cottonwoods are turning gold, the air is crisp, and the high country beckons. Hard to beat it, and with a spot of luck we won't have to try anytime soon.

All best wishes to you and yours.

*Not much to add here you don't already know, except we really had fun at yur and look forward to Glacier. The scouts are already _____ out!*

*Bet*

*(over)*

Right now it looks as if Derek & Hannah will tie the knot on June 18. We hope you'll be able to come... and you could just fly back to Mt with us— I'm sure Dale & I will be ready for a little vacation with good friends by then ☺

DEC 1 5 2010

Patti and Jim:

Heifer Int'l provides working
livestock (and small stock) to
the rural poor in the developing
world.  I've donated a hive
of honey bees and a flock of
chickens in your names.  Don't
know where they will go but
most of their animals go to
Africa, SE Asia, and Central
America.  With here and there
animals for Central Asia and
India.

Your wreath has arrived and has
p/ride of place on the front door.
Many thanx.  Xmas card to follow.

Bex

RMEF

(over)

Susan Sarandon
just fronts the
organization. I
don't think she's
mucked out any
stalls lately.

2011

**Dear Friends and Correspondents:**

Four years and change now in the Northern Rockies. We've been here long enough most of our neighbors have forgotten we're not real people. Neighbors stop by to tell us who's getting a divorce, and how we shouldn't hold it against her even if she is in the wrong, how much they like the new roof (replacing the one the wind blew off), whose black bull knocked down how much fence, and whether it was done in pursuit of female companionship or out of sheer bovine contrariness, or how they caught some sumbuck sneaking into our north pasture the other day and run him off. Said he was pheasant hunting--with a rifle! Heaven forfend. It was probably another damned Coloradan, or a gas driller, and who knows what mischief they could be up to. Who indeed. At any rate, we're settled in.

Those who last saw our boys when they were little dweebers will perhaps find it difficult to visualize them as they are now, but Derek has graduated from high school and gone off to the University of Wyoming, and Travis is 23 now, finishing his second year at Sheridan College and looking around for a four year college and a painless way to decide on a major. Several smaller colleges in Montana and the Dakotas showed interest in D as a football player, but he decided he'd had enough and believed he'd watch for a change. Hard to say what he will major in, other than the female fandango and the UW social ramble, but he's got time to puzzle it through, and in the meantime he's involved with a fraternity, and with learning how to be dead cool on the miserable stipend his parents send him each month. There's circumstantial evidence he may even be attending classes, though final confirmation waits on his first semester grades.

Since his Mother finished up at Harrisburg, Travis has become our designated student. Several years living below the poverty line convinced him there's a future in scholarship and since reaching that delayed conclusion he's flat torn it up! The small college atmosphere at Sheridan apparently agreed with him, and now he can just about go anywhere he wants. I'm not quite sure what we'll do if he says it's to be Harvard or Yale; I guess just gulp and try to make it happen. We're hoping for UW, Montana, Montana State, Colorado College, or someplace we can see him as much as we have these past 16 months. He hasn't made a final decision on a major yet, but marine biology, forensic psychology, some branch of biotechnology with a business minor, and flying for the Air Force appear to be front-runners. Whatever he decides is fine with us. We just stand around and smile a lot, and pretend we knew all along this was going to happen.

As for Bet, she continues to thrive in Wyoming. She helps with the hay crop, does her share with the saddle steck, puts in a big farm garden each spring, and has embarked on a second career as a llama husbandress. We're basically grass farmers, but within the next 12-18 months we're going to start raising alpacas, and to prepare for that we've bought a couple pack llamas for Bet to practice on. (An alpaca is another fleece-bearing camelid--from a better neighborhood--with a better sweater). The fleece isn't as fine, but the physiology and care requirements are the same, and llamas are bigger so we can pack these two for short summer trips in the Bighorns. When she's not involved with something at the ranch, she works as a volunteer with the HEELS DOWN RIDING PROGRAM, a charitable foundation that helps children with severe neurological disorders through horseback riding. It doesn't sound like the most promising approach for a child with cerebral palsy or Downs Syndrome, but it works surprisingly well in building confidence and coordination and it makes Bet very happy indeed.

As for me, I raise and sell horse hay from late May to September, flyfish in the spring and hunt in the Fall, and spend the rest of the year explaining Africa to people who are generally astonished to find they're paying real money to hear this stuff. I won't pretend it's a growth industry, but there's enough out there to keep 2 or 3 of us busy, and it meshes nicely with the rest of our lives. Between major events and seasonal changes Bet and I go to horse auctions, help our neighbors with spring branding, attend the summer rodeos and horse shows, ride a bit when horses and riders are both sound, and work on the countless projects required to bring the ranch back into production and make it a comfortable, decent place to live. Oh, and last spring I sent myself off to packer's school at Ninemile Remount Depot to relearn how to pack horses and mules. You may tell your friends you correspond regularly with a *diplomate* of the Forest Service Packer's School. Or Mule Tech, as some of the less reverent members of my family have chosen to describe my alma mater.

All best wishes for the Holiday Season and coming year.

Haven't received your arrival date and flight info — look forward to hearing from you soon and ringing in the New Year with you!

Dale & Bet

# Christmas 2012

*Patti & Jim*

'Tis the season to be ~ informative,                    if not exactly literary.   In any event, the field of strictly literary endeavors                    has already been plowed this year. And they don't award a Pulitzer for Christmas letters anyway ~ or the specialty would be more crowded than it presently is.  Nothing to do but lay it out, chapter and verse, and hope our efforts will find modest favor among an increasingly demanding reading public.

There is a form to this.  Certain questions must be addressed and expectations must be met to qualify as a Christmas letter.  In an attempt to facilitate texting we have decided to put the usual comments in bullet format.

1. I/we got married. ( Did that ~ 27 years ago.)
2. We had a baby.  (Physiologically unlikely.)
3. I/we got the job.  (Unless it's kinfolk, neither of us cares who got the job.)
4. One of us got a grant to study something in a semi-interesting place.  (Didn't apply.)
5. We went someplace.  (No we didn't.)
6. We're both feeling better.  (Bingo!  I'm well on the road to recovery from last summer's cardio repairs and Bet had another hip replaced, and both of us are back under partial warranty.)
7. We had a grandchild.  (Aha!)

Hannah and Derek had a baby boy on the 7th of September.  One Gavin Anthony Ackels, by name.  A stout little fellow; just lays there and waves his little arms and feet, and smiles at the world.   As long as the groceries arrive on time and someone sees to his skivvies he's a happy little dude.  As are his parents and grandparents.  I think Bet and I had more or less accepted that we might be out of the grandparent business, but Gavin's arrival has energized the whole family and there is the possibility of another from the same source in the future.  Pix available on request but you'll need a dedicated IBM Silverlake to store that many images.

Tiffany and Travis remain in Sheridan with the two senior (in date of rank and time of service) grandchildren.   Travis finished his work at the University of Wyoming last spring and is looking around for new opportunities in north-central Wyoming.  So far nothing of interest but he'll find it.  Miz Tiffany still works for the Wyoming Department of Family Services as a case officer. She's not been well these past several months but a combination of new meds and new doctors seems to have helped and she continues to chug along.

Their daughter, Dani, is 15 now.   She's at that interesting time of life somewhere between a happy-go-lucky young woman and the Empress of China.  She's a very good student and at various times she's played volleyball, basketball and track, but track is probably her primary diversion at the moment.  That youngster can *fly.*  She ran on the varsity team as a freshman and I'm sure will again this spring.  Fun to watch and Bet and I try to find plausible excuses to be in Sheridan when we know she's running.  Though at our ages we have to lead her a little to keep her centered in our trifocals.

Their son, Tristin, is also a sports demon.   Football, baseball, and soccer so far, but his Dad thinks baseball will prove to be his favorite.   His teams have won several state championships in youth soccer but it probably is too soon to tell.  He seems determined to sample everything and that can't be all bad. Except perhaps academics. That's still a work in progress. Those few, those proud survivors who knew me in the sixth grade will be tempted to see similarities. His grandmother describes the effect as genetics by osmosis, though she may have been referring to some other personal trait when she said it.

Bet and I are going back to Africa in four months. In this case to the Eastern Cape of South Africa. Some hunting, some touring, and who knows what else, but I haven't seen it since 1977 and Bet has never seen it so it will be fun. Hope your 2013 is all you want it to be and let us know what you're doing. Best wishes....

*Bet & Dan*

**CHRISTMAS**                    **2013**

*Pat & Tim*

This year we (finally) have wandered a bit. First to Dallas in early January for a convention and trade show, then to southern Africa, and from there to northern California with my sister and most of her family -- and our oldest son and his wife and children -- to visit a mountain retreat that's been a summer destination for members of our extended family since 1951. A couple months later we came back to the Coast to visit old friends, and revisit northern California, again with Dale's sister and brother-in-law. We stayed home 'til late September then off to Saskatchewan for early waterfowl, back to Wyoming for antelope and elk, both the latter excursions substantially limited by early season blizzards, and then home to Montana for late season elk and deer. While Dale was accumulating protein in various places, Bet made two trips to North Carolina to see her family, another to Kremmling to see the newest grandson, and we both went back to Colorado for young Gavin's first birthday. In between we worked on the garden, planted trees, did some logging, and pursued pocket gophers with unswerving determination (In the sense that it involved doctrinal differences, improvised explosive devices, toxic chemicals, and booby traps, *jihad* may be the appropriate way to describe it). In general we did the things rural folks do when winter is always only one to five months away.

The South African jaunt probably requires some explanation. I'd been in the Eastern Cape in the mid-70s on guvmint business, but Bet had never seen it and I thought she would find it interesting. We'd do some hunting, maybe some saltwater fishing, see the elephant reserve at Addo, then fly up into Limpopo Province and spend time in the Greater Kruger Reserve. Looking at elephants, lions, rhino, buffalo, leopards and whatever else spilled out of the Park along the southern boundary. From there on to Zambia to see Victoria Falls and cruise the Zambezi River, with a brief one-day diversion into Zimbabwe to see the Falls and the afternoon rainbow from the Zim side. Everything went well and we had a most excellent time. Bet got an appreciation for a part of Africa she'd never seen before, and we made several new friends at various points along our route. If I was a betting man I'd wager we're going back to the Southern Cone in 2015.

Good times notwithstanding there **have** been several minor medical setbacks. Some original parts appear to be out of warranty and in early in 2013 I went back in the hospital for more depot maintenance. Everything appears to be working again, but Bet will have reconstructive shoulder surgery in mid-March, and that will slow us down until she's able to travel. Once she's able to reach the overhead bin in a 777 we're going back to New Zealand. This will be my fourth trip and her third, but we haven't seen the southernmost part of South Island, nor the northern tip of North Island and that needs doing before we can check NZ off our bucket list, or think of another excuse for going back.

Our kids and grandkids are all well. The oldest son and his family are still in Wyoming and the youngest and his wife and child remain in Colorado. And we're expecting another grandchild in February. Derek, and more importantly Hannah, are expecting another son about the middle of the month. Hannah's mom is medically unable to help out so Bet will be going down to Kremmling for a couple weeks to assist. ☺ One of the reasons she's chosen not to have her shoulder repaired before March.

In large swaths that's about it for 2013. Thank you all for staying in touch, and let us know what you're doing. All our best wishes for a happy and healthy new year -

*Bet & Dale*

**Christmas**                                                                    **2014**

*Patti & Jim*

This is inevitably going to be a bit late.  For reasons that I hope will become clear as you progress through the letter.  Looking back on 2014 I think we will remember it as a series of pilot episodes for ***Marcus Welby, MD.***  We tried, with some success, to break or maim nearly every unbroken bone in our collective bodies.  In January I fell and broke my elbow, requiring surgical repair and eight weeks of therapy, and in June Bet had her right shoulder rebuilt, which earned us another 12 weeks in the gym/clinic.  As the summer progressed both our daughters-in-law faced very serious medical challenges, and Bet became a travelling nurse practitioner slash babysitter while the two couples wrestled with the life-altering difficulties they were facing.  We attempted to reconstruct it and we think she was gone approximately six-seven weeks in three different bursts of activity.  I do know she came home last Tuesday; I recognized her smile immediately.  Just to make her feel welcome I was able to report a horse rolled on me in the Scapegoat Wilderness and wrenched my knee, but since that one healed without surgical intervention I don't think I'm going to get even partial credit for it.  With a spot of luck we'll both be home 'til sometime in the spring.

In spite of the medical mayhem there were some positive highlights too.  Derek and Hannah had a second son in February.  They've named him Logan Riley Ackels, and he's proving to be an amiable little fellow.  Cheerful, outgoing, friendly, curious, and as his paternal grandmother describes him, "Handsome, and the smartest little baby ever born."  I realize there are other candidates for these latter two distinctions, but until we're challenged directly we're sticking with our preliminary negotiating position.

In between elbows, triceps and shoulders we also got a chance to go back to New Zealand.  We'd seen most of the main islands in three previous trips but we'd never seen the southernmost part and the northernmost headland so needed to take care of that—and did.  Not quite sure what we're going to do now. The country is just going to have to get bigger.

In rereading this I noted a certain air of self-pity in the opening paragraph.  Almost as though we were the only ones experiencing these difficulties, 'til it suddenly occurred to me that everyone who wrote this Season has gone through similar problems and mostly triumphed.  Clear evidence Ackels Unnumbered Law #4 applies.  Sometime in your late 60s or early 70s you're going to be faced with medical challenges.  If you fight through them maybe you get another 10-15 years.  If you don't go after them aggressively there's no telling, but you're probably not going to like the outcome.  That's been our recent experience and we hope very much it proves to be yours.  While we're all waiting for statistically meaningful results please accept our best wishes in all things.

*Bet & Jim*

*Hope Patti is better and you're both resting comfortably someplace warm and quiet.*

*Patti & Jim*    Christmas 2016 ————————————

When we start these things I'm never quite sure how they will evolve, but they always seem to wind up the same way and I'm tempted to believe there is an immutable outline to all of them. Sort of an iron-bound *schema* that must be obeyed if one is to call himself a fully qualified Christmas scribe. Macro-family events, micro-family events, recent grandchildren's adventures, grandchildren's future plans, and anything that doesn't fit into any of the above categories. Some minor variations are acceptable but not encouraged if one is to maintain board certification.

Under macro: Dale and his younger sister, and a similarly inclined nephew, packed into the Ansel Adams Wilderness in late July, in pursuit of the always elusive golden trout. Been awhile since any branch of the Family did something like that, other than elk hunting, but as children the High Sierras were our natural habitat, and it was fun to see some of it again and catch a few goldens and golden-rainbow hybrids.

Fast as we got home from the Sierras Bet and I launched for Ireland. It's been on our bucket list for several years and so many friends and family have gone before that we felt compelled to see it thru our own eyes. We didn't visit all of it by any means but we did make a brief reconnaissance into the West Country and the south, then more or less straight north from Cork and Cobh to Dublin. Rolling hills, gorgeous farms, castles and keeps, great pubs, interesting cities and towns, virtually every crossroad and village has some historical importance. All good stuff, highly recommended; we liked it so much we're going back in 2018 to see more of what we enjoyed on the first pass. Probably 3-4 additional days in Dublin, the same in Connemara, and another partial week in Killkenny, or around Galway. We'll see.

Home long enough to do laundry then off for the Sierras again for our annual visit with family and friends in the Lakes Basin country of Sierra County, including a return visit to Great Basin National Park. Never seen or heard anything about that, but it's a very worthwhile stop and we will plan our route next year to take us by again.

Under Micro Events: Travis and family remain in Sheridan, Wyoming. Granddaughter Dani is attending Sheridan College and working several jobs. She is engaged now and planning a July wedding. Tristin is playing football for the State Champion Sheridan Broncs, working on cars, and doing all the stuff teenage boys are involved in. He's got two more years 'til graduation, but no clue what his future holds.

Derek and Hannah are still in South Korea, in Daegu, with their two preschoolers, Gavin and Logan. What with industrial pollution, Kim Jong Un's increasingly bizarre behavior, and a recent rash of earthquakes, they may occasionally wonder about setting up housekeeping on the Korean Peninsula, but they've only got 1 ½ years left on this tour and perhaps the next job will be more compatible with family life and outdoor activities. We're going to see them sometime in March-April. I don't remember Taegu/Daegu with any particular fondness, but when your kids are there you find yourself revisiting places you thought you'd never see again.

In addition to the South Korea trip, Bet and I are planning to go to Australia at mid-year in 2017. I'm going for the hunting in Arnhem Land and we're both going for the tourism. Should be fun. Hope all is well in your lives, and if you decide to send us a formulaic Christmas letter, it will be read with great pleasure. And it will lead us to respond appropriately next year, if not sooner. *Great card. We hadn't seen photos of two oldest grand- daughters since they were infants.*

not much doubt they are Tiffany progeny. Best to both.

Bob & Dale

*Patti & Jim*

NEW YEAR 2019-2020

Some of you will recall we were more than a bit remiss with our Christmas greetings last year. For medical reasons it was a bad year for both us, and at the end of the year it was simply too much to get out our usual holiday missive. Very sorry, and thank you all very much for keeping us in your loop and sending your usual, and most welcome, updates. This year has been a year of recovery. My brain tumor proved to be benign, and after a prolonged period of healing Bet has regained much of the use of her leg. She's still not 100%, but she can get around and do many of the things she once enjoyed. This year my sister and I, more or less independently, decided to skip the Christmas letters and send New Year's greetings instead. It's not as lengthy, and certainly not as frivolous, but we both hope we hit the high spots and the half-pagers will be acceptable to close friends and family.

We had a houseful of close relatives at Christmas; our sons Travis and Derek and their wives and very significant others, plus three of our five grandchildren, even a German exchange student. That doesn't happen every year, but by-and-large it worked out well. Two of our grandsons decorated the tree, Hannah and Monica helped prepare a very considerable quantity of traditional Christmas specialties, and our young German guest made us Christmas cookies to help us through the difficult times between bowl games. Oh, and we have a great grandchild. Our granddaughter Danielle Martinez and her husband Lucas have a little boy, William David, born about a year ago. I know that's not terribly important to most of you, but its a big deal in these parts, and we're in the process of learning how to fit him into our lives. Or perhaps it's the other way around. We shall see.

Hope the Holidays went well and our very best wishes for the New Year.

*Bet & Dave*

# CHAPTER 18

## Remembering Shirley Temple Black

I made a point of devoting a chapter to one of Dale's letters, because it is vintage Dale Ackels, recognizing and remembering a person whose service to our country was, to an extent, unheralded and possibly underappreciated by the public at large.

Shirley Temple, child film star of the 1930's was only known to Dale as the consummate diplomat: Ambassador Shirley Temple Black in the mid-1970's. His letter suggests that and more.

Her assent into government service came as a result of her involvement in the political process, running for public office, activity within the Republican Party, and being active in a California public affairs forum. Henry Kissinger heard her speak about West Africa at a dinner party and was surprised at her acuity. That helped launch her diplomatic career.

She served under three Presidents: President Nixon as a delegate to the UN General Assembly; President Ford selected her as Ambassador to Ghana; President George H.W. Bush appointed her Ambassador to Czechoslovakia.

After Dale wrote this letter and we talked, he mentioned he had written feelings about her in an Obit, which he sent to the Los Angeles Times. They never printed it. This letter speaks volumes.

2014

It is with regret, and a certain sense of nostalgia, that I read of the passing of Shirley Temple Black on __ February 2014. The press reported her death in more than usual detail, but the emphasis in the post mortems was on her early years as a child star, and not necessarily on her later career as a diplomat , and that to my way of thinking is a mistake.

I cannot claim I was a friend, or even a long term acquaintance, but for a couple weeks in the mid-70s I was posted to the embassy in Accra while she was our ambassador, and the experience shaped my memories of her and caused me to track her career for many years afterward.

My travelling partner, Captain Jack Weber, and I were Army Foreign Area Specialists in training. We were living in Ethiopia, but our one year of "directed travel and study" included a swing through West Africa and we were roughly a month into our orientation tour when we arrived in Ghana. I knew Shirley Temple Black (STB) was our ambassador, but our focus was on military matters, political affairs, and the economy, and we saw our appointment with STB as little more than a courtesy call. A chance to grip and grin, explain the purpose of our visit and get any guidance she might have on our travels in "her" country.

Our appointment with her was in the afternoon, but we had interviews with several embassy officials in the morning and it quickly became apparent that STB was not an ordinary political appointee. There were a couple detractors, but most of the senior staffers were passionate, hardcore supporters and very much wanted us to understand that before we met her. Most embassies are run through a country team, a group of office and section chiefs who between them represent every functional area in the embassy, but Embassy Accra was run by the ambassador and a kitchen cabinet. A small, select group of proven staffers she had come to know and trust. In this case the deputy chief of mission, (the number two man in the embassy hierarchy), the food and agriculture advisor and the defense attaché. Because of her trust and respect for their abilities these three men acted as her de facto staff and with her support and blessing frequently involved themselves in matters outside their normal areas of responsibility.

After listening to the pros and cons all morning I went into my appointment with her determined not to be impressed. I'm not quite sure to this day what happened to me, but I'd just been reoriented by an expert. It is not a significant exaggeration to say I came out of my initial meeting prepared to commit a triple hatchet murder if she asked me to. My first impression was reinforced considerably when her secretary later informed me they'd had a bit of a disturbance immediately prior to my arrival. Somebody had gotten into the office and threatened her with a knife and the Marine Security Guards had disarmed him and forcibly ejected him 15 minutes before we arrived. During our interview she was gracious and perfectly relaxed and gave no indication that anything unusual had happened at any point during the day.

As we were leaving she asked us what we were doing that night. We said we didn't have plans, to which she replied, "There's an exhibition of Russian tractor art opening down on the waterfront tonight. If you want to go I'll get you passes. You'll need them to get in but I'm sure I can get them for you." We immediately agreed and shortly after dark Jack and I and the defense attaché showed up at the exhibit.

At the appointed time we took our seats and the Soviet ambassador began his welcoming address. There was a television camera and a single high intensity light illuminating the ambassador as he spoke, but no STB in sight. I knew she was planning on coming and was wondering what happened to her when there was suddenly a buzz along the side of the hall and STB walked in. The TV camera swung toward her, followed immediately by the light, leaving the Soviet ambassador completely in the dark and unable to read his prepared remarks. She walked slowly to her seat, smiled sweetly toward the camera, quickly greeted several members of the diplomatic community and sat down facing the podium. Once she was seated the camera and light swung back to the Soviet ambassador whose face by now was the color of ripe tomatoes. For this to make sense you must understand that by this time in her tour STB was the most popular person in the country. An art show is just an art show but an STB appearance was always news, and she took advantage of her popularity to take over what the Soviets clearly saw as a major propaganda event and turn it to our advantage. As I expected, the evening news was dominated by coverage of STB at the art show. The Russian got a few seconds but STB was the story and got most of the coverage.

When I laughingly accused her of doing it on purpose she smiled and with a twinkle in her eye said, "I was just a little late, that's all, and besides I can't control who or what the local TV station covers."

She just had a gift for this stuff. I'm quite sure she understood the real issues in our relationship and could discuss them with anyone, but it was the people-to-people part of the job where she absolutely excelled. She could make people like her and want to befriend her, and she could use that ability in furtherance of US interests and policies. And she could do it with such subtlety that the intended target often wasn't aware he was the victim until it was much too late to consider the alternatives. Or ask himself what he should have done or said.

An excellent example occurred several months before Jack and I reached Accra. STB had gone up-country to attend the enstoolment of a chief; a newly appointed ruler in one of the tribes that owes allegiance to the Asantehene of the Ashanti, the most powerful ruler in the region and still a force in Ghanaian politics. An enstoolment of a new ruler is a very important, traditional ceremony which involves, among many things, picking up the chief and passing him over a sacred stool, usually made of gold, which is the symbol of political power and legitimacy in the Akan tribes in west central Africa. He is not the chief until this event and the day-long ceremonies attending it take place. STB had taken her daughter with her, probably in her late teens or early 20's at the time and from all accounts an attractive and accomplished young woman, and at some point in the ceremony the newly appointed chief expressed a desire to take Shirley's daughter as one of his wives. This had the potential to be embarrassing, but without missing a beat STB said she was already promised to another and since he'd already paid the bride price she could not in good conscience entertain such a flattering and generous offer. Crisis averted. The response was culturally correct, and the chief understood perfectly why the matter could be dropped without further discussion.

Somewhere in the photo archives of the mid-70s there's a photo of her taken that day being carried through the streets of the city on the shoulders of a throng of Africans. Perfectly calm and relaxed, completely at ease and not at all put off by being carried on the shoulders of a soccer stadium full of adoring Ghanaians. Regardless of how she really felt, or how she got up there in the first place, she was in her element and complete master of her situation.

Just two of countless stories about STB in her prime. Everyone who ever served with her has several good stories and knows half a dozen more. All of them revolving around that special gift she had for reaching across cultures and making people warm to her, and through her to the United States. Perhaps her film experience and her very early popularity gave her the personality and skill set, and had something to do with it, but **Bright Eyes** and **The Good Ship Lollipop** was the least of it. The very least of it, and it's not how she wanted to be or should be remembered. She was exceptional and her early success in films is hardly more than a footnote to a long and very productive life.

# CHAPTER 19

## Dwight

# LETTERS FROM A FRIEND

# DWIGHT

This is a fitting closing chapter to Dale's remarkable career. I never knew about this assignment until March, 2021, fifty years after it occurred.

Duty. Honor. Country

## DWIGHT

When I returned from Vietnam I asked my assignment officer to send me anyplace in the 11 states west of the Mississippi. Vietnam returnees were supposed to get preferential assignments, but it won't come as a surprise to anyone familiar with the Army they sent me to the Tank Arsenal in Detroit, Michigan. I checked my preference list several times but couldn't find Detroit on the list. "Needs of the Army," don't you know. OK, maybe next time. I didn't know much about tank design or maintenance (the only tanks I'd ever driven were an old M-48 and later a Russian T-55) but ignorance and lack of training has never stopped me before and I thought, "It can't be as bad as where I've been. I'll figure it out."

And I did. Most importantly the procedures that made the whole supply system function at the national level. But, making the system work for the soldiers and front line deployed units was only part of the job. The most important part certainly, but not all of it. Because we were the only installation in the immediate area with a large number of junior officers assigned we also drew various kinds of support and notification duties. I had three POW families assigned to me, and I'd also done death notifications on several occasions. In a city the size of Detroit and its suburbs there were quite a few death and wounding notifications, and those seldom go seamlessly. One of my peers had been backed off a porch at gun point and several were recipients of screaming tirades by stricken parents. The notification officer was the physical manifestation of the Army, and the Army had killed their son, so the whole load of pain and anguish typically got dumped in his lap.

Some parents realized you couldn't possibly be responsible, and invited you and the chaplain into their homes. Those families wanted to talk about what you did in Vietnam, and where their son had served, and most importantly when would his body be returned. If anything those notifications were the worst because you wanted so much to do something for them, and you couldn't. Everything you could or did say rang false. One of my notifications was a young lieutenant who had been killed by friendly fire. There was a note with the casket that said his corpse had been mangled and the people who'd prepped the body recommended the casket stay closed, but the mother wouldn't have it. She wouldn't believe her son was in there until she saw him with her own eyes. I finally convinced her to let an uncle who knew the boy well do the verification and that seemed to satisfy everyone. Mercifully.

All this by way of explaining my interaction with Dwight Hal Johnson. I was up on my notifications and it wasn't my turn to do a family assistance call, but I got called into the ops center and told they had a new service-related death and the general wanted me to handle it. A Congressional Medal of Honor winner named Dwight Johnson (from Detroit) had been shot to death holding up a grocery store, and his family wanted him buried in Arlington with full military honors.

My job would be to take charge of the body after the local funeral and convey it to Washington, D.C., where I was to turn it over to a another funeral director for internment at Arlington. They had arranged my travel and the movement of the coffin, and all I had to do was stay with it wherever it went until it was delivered. This was a custodial job. When they said stay with it that's exactly what they meant. I would ride in the hearse to the airport, watch the coffin being loaded before boarding myself, and after landing reverse the process. Watch the coffin come off the plane, insure it's loaded in the gaining undertaker's vehicle, see that the custodial documents are signed by the funeral director, and the next day make sure the remains are brought to Arlington for the ceremony.

Everything went as planned until the coffin was unloaded. The funeral director wasn't there and when I called the funeral parlor they'd closed for the night. I was standing on the parking apron at DC National (now Reagan Airport) with an embalmed hero's body and no place to take it until tomorrow.

The freight manager took pity on me and offered me a Northwest hanger for the night and for want of any other option, that's where we went. An entire empty hanger, big enough for a 707, with Dwight's coffin in the center and a chair for me beside it. One light shining down on the two of us. We were settled in by 10:30 and there we stayed until eight thirty the next morning. With water but no food and no phone until the hanger dudes arrived the next morning.

The next ten hours gave me ample time to consider the complex tragedy of Dwight's life, and perhaps a little of my own future. Dwight was a big, gentle young man, gone to Vietnam as a draftee in early 1967. His tour had been unexceptional until January 14th, 1968 when a column of four tanks from his company were trapped on a hillside enroute to Dak To, in the Central Highlands. As was their usual practice the Vietcong took out the lead tank in the column, probably with a rocket propelled grenade, and set it afire. Normally, Dwight would have been in the lead tank, but this time he was the tank commander of the second tank, safe for the moment but able to see what was happening to his friends and crewmates in the lead vehicle. When it caught fire at least one of his friends tumbled out of the first vehicle, his clothing and skin on fire, several more struggled to get out and couldn't before that lead tank exploded in flames. Most likely the ammunition in the main gun storage racks detonated; whatever it was there was no question the rest of the crew had been incinerated.

At this point Dwight went stark, staring crazy. He climbed out of the second tank and ran helplessly toward his burning friends but it was, of course, too late. Standing alongside the flaming M-48 he was suddenly confronted by a Viet Cong rifleman who tried to shoot him, but his rifle misfired or was empty and Dwight either had a rifle with him or recovered one from the second tank and killed him. At that point he gathered more guns and ammo from his tank and set off up the hill on a one-man crusade, trying to kill every Viet Cong on the hillside in retribution for the death of his friends. Every time he ran out of ammunition he sprinted back down to the column and reloaded. I don't know how many times he did it, or how many VC he killed. Accounts vary between 20 and a hundred but when the relief column arrived he was reportedly still running across the hillside above the ambush site, trying to find more Vietnamese to kill. Accounts vary but they either had to give him morphine to calm him or restrain him in a straightjacket, but they had, by some means, to run him down and physically prevent him from trying to find and kill more Viet Cong. Chances are it was morphine. I can't imagine why anyone would be carrying a straightjacket in a tank.   At that point I think he would have killed any Asian he encountered.   Innocent or guilty.

He was already out of the Army when he got his Medal of Honor.   He'd married a local girl and they'd had a baby,  but he was having trouble finding work and his wife had gone to work waitressing at a local club owned by a Detroit Tigers baseball player to make ends meet.

The announcement of Dwight's MOH changed everything.   He was suddenly the darling of the local media, and a number of black American celebrities and business figures put together a banquet for him at the Joe Louis Arena.   He was presented with gifts,  numerous speeches were delivered, and job promises were made.   Several of these very important and otherwise inaccessible people told him if he needed a job to come see them, which must have been music to his ears, and so he did.     But when he stopped by for an interview nobody had anything for him.  The PR guy at the Arsenal had helped him deal with the media and knew him fairly well,  . and he told me the response was some variation on, "Jeez Dwight I'd like to help you, but I just don't have anything right now.  I'll let you know as soon as I get something; I know you'll find a job somewhere." If he'd gone to the big auto plants he could have caught on right away, but he was relying on his newfound friends in the black community, and they clearly didn't expect him to take them up on their offers of employment.

In desperation he reenlisted in the Army, at his old grade of Sergeant, E-5.  That gave him some income , supplemented by the extra $100 a month paid to MOH winners.  He was assigned to recruiting duty in Detroit so he could theoretically take care of his family, but that ship had already sailed and his marriage was breaking up.  His wife had  seen a different lifestyle at the club and more and more he was being left at home to take care of the baby.  And the life of a recruiter didn't fit him either.  He just wasn't a hail-fellow-well-met kind of guy.  It wasn't in his nature to sit down and schmooze with some 18 year old about his future in the Army.  He simply couldn't get past his natural shyness, or present himself as any kind of authority figure

And there were the dreams.  I'm told he was bothered by recurrent dreams of the burning tank and the VC he'd shot, and he couldn't seem to put them behind him either.  In an attempt to help him sort through all the baggage he was sent to Valley Forge Army Hospital for evaluation and psychiatric treatment, but he didn't stay long and sometime in mid-April he went AWOL.

Everyone expected him to turn up in the Detroit metro area, but for several days no one knew where he was, until on the night of 30 April 1971 when he walked into a mom and pop grocery in Detroit with a gun in his hand and shot the owner.  The storekeeper fell behind the counter but he also had a gun on a shelf under the cash register, and when Dwight leaned over the counter to finish him the owner put four rounds into his head and chest.

Two days later I was assigned to assist the family and one day after that Dwight and I were ' temporarily living in a Northwest Airlines hanger, awaiting the final act in the complex tragedy that that had been his life.  After I heard the story I certainly didn't feel Dwight was an inherently bad person.   He'd simply been pushed further than his limited education and abilities would take him.  He was well known in the black community in Detroit, but he couldn't get a job and he couldn't provide for his wife and baby the way his spouse expected him to.  He certainly was not the murderous psychopath he'd been on that mountainside in the Highlands, nor was he the hero that most people expected him to be.  He didn't act or think like a public figure.  It was not his nature.  He was a kind and generous young man who acting under extreme duress exploded in a paroxysm of violence and murderous retribution one afternoon in January, and in doing so joined the pantheon of heroes who have received this singular decoration.  Frankly, no one cared who he really was.  It was his actions that day that cemented his place in the history of the Vietnam Conflict.  And that he is how he will undoubtedly be remembered.

A little after eight AM someone opened the door and the hanger office and gave me access to a telephone, and I called the undertaker.  He came down to National and picked up the body, and I called a taxi and drove up on Columbia Pike to the Cherry Blossom Motel (how is that for ironic) for a couple hours sleep.  The undertaker had agreed to have the body at Arlington about 1 P.M. for the beginning of the funeral, and those four hours between delivering the body and the beginning of the funeral were mine to rest and reflect.  Mostly rest.

A nice breakfast, a snooze, a shower and  shave,  and a fresh shirt and freshly pressed uniform put me back in good order and I took a taxi to Arlington in a somewhat improved state of mind, in plenty of time to greet Dwight's family and make sure the coffin was on hand.

Not long after my arrival the media found me.  In this case Dan Rather and Sam Donaldson.  They were both assigned to their network's Washington Bureaus, and had not yet achieved the national recognition that was to come later, but they were a formidable pair and I was a little leery about facing them on national TV.  The interview was not complicated.  They had only one line of inquiry, the assumption that because of the manner of his death the Army intended to deprive his family of some of the benefits they normally would have received.  I answered quite truthfully that some of the veteran's organizations in Detroit had wanted to deny Dwight burial at Arlington, but no one in a position of authority or in my chain of command had *suggested such a thing,*  and he *would* receive a normal burial for MOH winner.  By that time the relationship between the media and the Armed Forces was so poisonous they clearly didn't believe me and Donaldson began to press harder.  I was starting to get a little defensive and friends who saw the interview on the national news that evening later told me I probably didn't have much of a future in broadcast journalism..

 At that point a smarmy little public affairs major from the Pentagon appeared, apparently sent over to Arlington to handle situations like this.  Hair down to his shoulders, uniform dirty and ill-fitting and his shoes hadn't been shined since Christ was the Chief of Chaplains.  He looked like something that had washed up on a beach in Puget Sound.  I stayed and listened to a little of his patter, but the last truthful word they got out of the Army that day was lost somewhere in my last sentence.

# DWIGHT

Was that night in the hanger and Dwight's burial the end of my personal war? Perhaps, but not completely. I still think about it and I still read *Vietnam* magazine, and I can't begin to list how many books I've read on various aspects of the Vietnam Conflict and the wars in Laos and Cambodia. And many of my closest friends are Southeast Asia vets or men I soldiered with someplace else whose professional lives have been shaped by the lessons we learned and the tactics we developed in Southeast Asia.

Dwight's funeral was not quite the end of it. Several years later his story became an off-Broadway play entitled *Strike Heaven on the Face,* written by Richard Wesley, and still later *The Medal of Honor Rag* by Tom Cole, and a poetry collection entitled *Debridement* by Michael Harper, also purported to tell Dwight's story   I saw the first of these on PBS. I can't say I enjoyed it, but it was well done and they got most of the story right. It came across as both a tribute and a tragedy, and I do think that's about right.

The *Detroit Free Press* did a credible job of covering the story, but the reporter from the *New York Times* did a magnificent job. His piece was a wonderfully accurate, yet restrained summary of the major parts of the story, and it also struck just the right note for the family. I have not then or later seen a better job of covering a regional story by a reporter who did not have firsthand knowledge of it. Both articles would have appeared sometime in the first week of May 1971.

From receiving the MOH from the president to overnighting in an airplane hanger with a man he never met and wouldn't have trusted if had known me.

Sic transit gloria (Thus passes all earthly glory.)

# DWIGHT HAL JOHNSON
## TANK DRIVER BRAVED ENEMY FIRE TO SAVE HIS FRIENDS

**By Doug Sterner**

Dwight Hal Johnson had no dreams of being a hero. In his youth, the large, strapping boy had a fighter's body but a peaceful spirit. Johnson grew up in the deteriorating Corktown neighborhood of Detroit with his single mother and younger brother. Bullies often chased him home. "Don't you fight, honey," his mother told him, "and don't let them catch you." He didn't.

Drafted at age 19, Johnson arrived in Vietnam in February 1967. He was a tank driver in Company B, 1st Battalion, 69th Armor Regiment, 4th Infantry Division. By January, Johnson, a specialist 5, had orders to return home in two weeks. He had never seen combat and was content with that. Johnson's destiny changed on Jan. 14, 1968, when he was transferred from his usual tank to one whose driver was sick.

**HALL OF VALOR**

The next day, four M48 Patton tanks of Johnson's company raced down a road toward Dak To in the Central Highlands. Suddenly enemy rockets slammed into two tanks. Johnson raised himself from the hatch of his M48 to return fire with its .50-caliber machine gun as waves of enemy infantry swarmed the remaining tanks.

He saw his former tank about 60 feet away—and his buddies for the past 11 months trapped inside the burning hulk. Leaping from his tank, Johnson ran through gunfire to save their lives, ignoring the pleas of Stan Enders, a gunner in his new crew, who shouted, "Don't go!" Johnson pulled out one man, who was burning but still alive, and dragged him to safety before the tank exploded, killing the rest of the crew.

When Johnson saw the burning bodies, something inside snapped.

Rushing back to his tank, he seized a submachine gun and charged into the ambush, attacking first with automatic fire, then with his pistol. Coming face to face with an enemy soldier wielding an AK-47 rifle, Johnson pulled the trigger only to find his pistol empty, so he killed the man with the stock of his empty submachine gun. Returning to his tank, Johnson manned the externally mounted .50-caliber machine gun and remained there until his adversaries withdrew. Johnson had fought ferociously for about 30 minutes, and his comrades estimated he had taken out as many as 20 enemy soldiers.

Although the battle ended, an enraged Johnson had to be restrained to prevent him from attacking captured troops. Three doses of morphine were needed to calm him. Placed under restraint, he was evacuated to the hospital in Pleiku.

After the soldier returned home, his friends assumed Johnson had never seen combat. He did not correct them. Johnson's day of heroism was a dark, haunting experience he wished he could forget. Constant nightmares were filled with the burned bodies of his dead friends and the face of the enemy soldier he killed at close range.

One bright spot in Johnson's life was his marriage to his sweetheart and the birth of their son. But he couldn't find work to help them.

One day, a colonel called from Washington to tell Johnson that he and his family should come to the capital. On Nov. 19, 1968, President Lyndon B. Johnson presented Dwight Hal Johnson with the Medal of Honor.

Johnson became a local celebrity and received job offers. Eventually, he returned to the Army and worked as a recruiter in Detroit. Constant nightmares and cold sweats still tormented him, however, and he suffered from severe survivor's guilt—his tank transfer had saved him from the explosion that killed his former crew members.

Back in Detroit, on the night of April 30, 1971, Johnson walked into a store with a pistol and demanded cash from the register. He fired a round that struck the arm of the store owner, who shot the 23-year-old Medal of Honor recipient four times. Johnson died at the hospital.

Later his mother told a *New York Times* reporter that she wondered if her son was having suicidal thoughts. The hero of Dak To, who struggled in his battle with post-traumatic stress disorder, was buried with full honors at Arlington National Cemetery. **V**

*Doug Sterner, an Army veteran who served two tours in Vietnam, is curator of the Military Times Hall of Valor database of U.S. valor awards.*

Reprinted with permission of Vietnam magazine. Doug Sterner, Dwight Hal Johnson: Tank Driver Braved Enemy Fire to Save His Friends. *Vietnam, October*(2020), 64.

# EPILOGUE

# EPILOGUE

This book would not have happened if the other author, my near life-long friend Jim Tiffany and my sister, Nancy Wagner, had not seen some value in my correspondence and saved dozens (close to a half century) of my letters and emails. I meant them to be factual and entertaining, occasionally even whimsical, but I did not expect them to become a book, or that others would find merit in my lifetime field reports. Some of these topics deserve more attention than I gave them, and indeed in many cases there are credible books and articles covering these matters. The only virtue of my writings on these topics is that I was on the inside looking out, and in many instances my views were considerably different than the hardbound, academic versions that have become revealed doctrine in so many cases. If Jim had not decided that these letters had merit none of them would ever have been seen by my family or the public. For this I am forever grateful. I don't know if he's my Boswell or I'm his, but without his 56 years of friendship, curiosity, and profound good humor, none of this would have happened, and I find it hard to find the words needed to express my gratitude. I'm afraid a simple thank you for everything will have to suffice. But, it doesn't seem enough.

— Dale Ackels

CPSIA information can be obtained
at www.ICGtesting.com
Printed in the USA
LVHW070412100721
692328LV00001B/1